BEYER ON SPEED

New Strategies
for Racetrack Betting

Andrew Beyer

HOUGHTON MIFFLIN COMPANY

BOSTON · NEW YORK

Preface copyright © 2007 by Andrew Beyer
Copyright © 1993 by Andrew Beyer

For information about permission to reproduce selections from
this book, write to Permissions, Houghton Mifflin Company,
215 Park Avenue South, New York, New York 10003.

Visit our Web site: www.houghtonmifflinbooks.com.

Library of Congress Cataloging-in-Publication Data

Beyer, Andrew.
   Beyer on speed : new strategies for racetrack betting / Andrew Beyer.
      p. cm.
   Originally published: 1993. With new pref.
   Includes bibliographical references.
 ISBN-13: 978-0-618-87172-8
 ISBN-10: 0-618-87172-1
   1. Horse racing—Betting. 2. Horse racing—Betting. I. Title.
      SF331.B445 2007
      798.401—dc22   2006100900

Printed in the United States of America

MP 10 9 8 7 6 5 4 3 2 1

Past performance charts are reprinted with permission from the
copyright owner, Daily Racing Form, Inc. and Equibase Company.
Copyright © 2006.

BEYER
ON SPEED

BOOKS BY ANDREW BEYER

Picking Winners

My $50,000 Year at the Races

The Winning Horseplayer

Beyer on Speed

TO SUSAN

CONTENTS

Preface   *xi*

ONE   *The Value of Speed Figures   1*

TWO   *Probabilities and Patterns   30*

THREE   *How Was the Figure Earned?   50*

FOUR   *How Will He Run Today?   93*

FIVE   *The Mathematics of Pace   126*

SIX   *Turf Racing: Lessons from Two Continents   148*

SEVEN   *Exotic Betting Strategy   172*

EIGHT   *A Week in Las Vegas   202*

Acknowledgments   *231*
Appendix   *233*
Bibliography   *238*

Preface

Horseplayers often express nostalgia for what they remember as the good old days, when American racetracks were filled with unsophisticated, ill-informed customers and studious handicappers had an edge that enabled them to make consistent profits. I felt such sentiments when *Beyer on Speed* was first published in 1993.

My impetus for writing the book had been the inclusion of Beyer Speed Figures in the *Daily Racing Form*'s past performances. In my previous books I had painstakingly explained the methodology that would enable handicappers to calculate their own numbers. The process was sufficiently difficult and time-consuming that only the most serious bettors were armed with speed figures. But after those figures started appearing in print, every reader of the *Daily Racing Form* had access to the same valuable tool. Speed handicappers had lost a crucial advantage. With that edge gone, how could we now beat the game? I attempted to answer that question in *Beyer on Speed*, but I knew that playing the horses would be tougher than ever and yearned for the good old days.

I could not have imagined that horse racing was just about to enter a golden era. Horseplayers today have more betting opportunities than their counterparts in the past could ever have conceived. And contemporary players have an arsenal of handicapping tools that would be the envy of bettors in any other era.

The most profound change in American racing has been the advent of full-card simulcasting and online betting, enabling handicappers to follow tracks from coast to coast and bet dozens of races a day. In *Beyer on Speed* I chronicle a week I spent in Las Vegas, where I was mesmerized by the chance to watch and wager on ninety races a day from a casino's race book. At the time it was a novelty to indulge in so much action. But since then full-card simulcasting has become a fixture at almost every American track; bettors typically spend their day in front of a bank of television monitors instead of looking at live animals.

The benefit of simulcasting has been to give horseplayers many more options; they can choose where they want to concentrate their attention instead of being locked into nine races a day at their home track. Some of the worst periods of my gambling life occurred in the pre-simulcasting era, when I was stuck at a track where the racing was unproductive. In 1994 I rented an apartment in Saratoga for a season that was marred with rain and filled with dismal four- and five-horse fields that offered little promise. Because I had no alternatives I was betting anyway, and I suffered through a financially disastrous season. If simulcasting had been available then, I could have shunned Saratoga and turned my attention elsewhere. Now players can seek out the most promising opportunities. In *Beyer on Speed,* as in my earlier books, I stress the importance of identifying track biases and exploiting them. Some of the biggest scores of my gambling life have come from spotting horses who ran poorly because they were compromised by a bias (for example, a tendency to favor speed horses on the rail) and then betting them in their subsequent starts. In the age of simulcasting, handicappers don't have to wait for a bias to appear at their home track; they can study result charts online and seek out tracks where a bias might exist.

In this book, too, I maintain that horseplayers have a better chance of beating the game by making occasional big scores in exotic bets instead of trying to grind out slow, steady profits. Opportunities for those big scores used to be limited. Now they abound, as simulcast bettors get to play pick-six carryover jackpots in California, New York, Kentucky, and other locations.

The availability of so much action at so many tracks demands discipline from horseplayers. Too many bettors try to play dozens of races a day on the basis of a quickie study of the *Daily Racing Form*. They are doomed to fail without the knowledge that gives them an edge in the parimutuel competition.

But horseplayers willing to study can obtain the necessary edge. Along with the simulcasting revolution there has been another profound change in the racing game: an information revolution, made possible by computer technology and the Internet. For most of my life as a horseplayer, obtaining information was a large part of the handicapping battle. Much of *Beyer on Speed* is devoted to the proposition that a horse's figures must be viewed in the context of the way he ran his race: whether he lost ground on the turn; whether he encountered traffic or other trouble during the race; whether he was affected by a track bias. To make the most of these judgments, a handicapper has to watch films of races—and they have not always been accessible. In the mid-1990s, only a few tracks had replay centers that enabled handicappers to summon films of past races. A limited number of them sponsored televised replay shows on a local channel. Many did not make available the vital head-on shots of their races.

When horseraces first appeared on the Internet, the quality of the video was laughably bad, but by 2006 improvements in software and the speed of broadband connections made it possible to see races clearly on a computer screen. Horseplayers could wager and watch live races at a variety of Web sites. They could have access to an extensive library of past races at sites such as Youbet.com and RaceReplays.com. Serious horseplayers who want to assess how a horse ran a recent race no longer have to depend on the often sketchy information in the published past performances. Now a handicapper can watch almost any past race with the click of a mouse.

Handicapping has been revolutionized, too, by the *Daily Rac-*

ing Form's software known as Formulator. It enables the user to download the past performances for a day's card to his computer screen and then click on various segments of the past performances to obtain a wealth of important data. Click on the name of a trainer and find the record of every horse he has saddled in the past five years. Specify different criteria and find the trainer's success rate under those conditions—for example, with horses laid off for six months or more and dropping in class. Click on the date of a horse's last race and see the records of all his rivals in that field.

Formulator streamlines the analysis of many handicapping factors emphasized in this book. It is extremely important to judge a horse's prior performances in the context of the pace of the races. A horse who earns a moderate speed figure after a hard duel for the lead may be much better than the number suggests. But what constitutes a hard duel? With Formulator, a handicapper can look at the fractional times of other races on the card to judge if the pace of a race was relatively fast or relatively slow. He can look at the past performances of the other horses involved in the duel to see if they are fast, habitual front-runners. Obtaining such information used to require a library of back issues of the *Daily Racing Form;* now it is available with a couple of clicks of the mouse.

Formulator can also aid handicappers who rely on the Beyer Speed Figures. Almost all fans occasionally question the numbers, suspecting that the figure for a particular race may be too high or too low. Our eight-man team of figure makers sometimes has doubts, too; there are many situations in which a day's data can be confusing or ambiguous. In those cases, we may wait to make a final judgment until we see how horses in a questionable race perform the next time they run. With Formulator, any handicapper can do the same. He can look at the subsequent performances of all the horses in a field and see the figures they have earned. If the winner of a race has run an implausibly large number, but the runner-up has come back to run well and to confirm the number, the winner's figure is probably trustworthy.

The availability of Formulator, online replays, and simulcasts have altered the way I play the horses, but my basic ideas about handicapping haven't changed much since the original publication of *Beyer on Speed*. There is, however, one significant difference in the nature of the game since I wrote this book, and it is one that every horseplayer must take into account. The identity and effectiveness of the trainer has become a supremely important factor in modern racing. In many cases, the skill of the trainers seems more important than the ability of the horse.

Of course, trainers have always been a key part of the handicapping equation. I devoted a chapter to trainers in *Picking Winners*, written in 1975, and I have always tried to learn the strengths, weaknesses, and techniques of the principal trainers at any track I follow. But American racing in recent years has seen the rise of supertrainers who achieve rates of success and accomplish feats that are unprecedented in the history of the sport.

There was a time when it was exceptional for a trainer to win with 25 percent of his starters. Charlie Whittingham, one of the most acclaimed horsemen in history, never achieved a success rate of more than 20 percent during the years when he was the country's top trainer. Now it is commonplace to see the leading trainers at a race meeting with win percentages of 30 percent and higher. Accordingly, the betting public automatically plays horses saddled by men such as Todd Pletcher, Bobby Frankel, Steve Asmussen, Scott Lake, and Dick Dutrow—almost regardless of the past performances of their horses.

The supertrainers are particularly dangerous when they acquire a horse by claim or private purchase. Over a three-year period, California-based Jeff Mullins won with an astonishing 34 percent of the horses he had claimed in their previous starts. In 2004 he claimed a horse named Kid Royal, who in his four career starts had recorded Beyer Speed Figures of 62, 11, 67, and 8. After entering Mullins's barn, Kid Royal promptly won with a figure of 98, and recorded six consecutive figures between 82 and 102. Many horseplayers suspect that the use of illegal medications must account for the contemporary supertrainers' powers, because the best horsemen of the past were never able to transform horses in such a dramatic fashion. Whatever the explanation, bettors must deal with the fact that certain trainers' horses may defy logic. I always pay extra attention to any horse who gets a new trainer, particularly if he is someone, like Mullins, who has a demonstrated record of improving new acquisitions. But because the supertrainers' horses are regularly overbet, I try not to fear taking a position against them—particularly when their horses have established form and inferior speed figures.

The emergence of the supertrainers underscores the fact that horse racing never remains static. Bettors must always be observant of changes and be ready to adapt to them. But even amid such changes, speed figures remain the central handicapping factor and give players a framework with which to understand the entire game.

BEYER
ON SPEED

ONE

The Value of Speed Figures

When I started calculating speed figures and using them to bet the horses, I saw quickly that they were the most powerful tool in the game. By taking into account the difference in surfaces over which horses run and the different distances of thoroughbred races, they translated every horse's performance into a single number that neatly defined his ability. They addressed the central question of handicapping: Who can run faster than whom? But there was a time and place where speed figures were more than a tool. They were magic.

Winter racing in Florida has traditionally attracted stables from all parts of the country, and in the 1970s, before speed handicapping became fashionable, the nature of this competition bewildered most horseplayers. Could a $15,000 horse from New York beat a $25,000 horse from Chicago? Was an allowance-class horse from Canada better than a high-priced claimer from Kentucky? Conventional handicappers could only guess, because there were no direct lines of comparison between those horses. I didn't have to guess. I knew.

Before each Florida season, I spent weeks at a desk stacked high with regional editions of the *Daily Racing Form*. I analyzed each day's results at the tracks that would be sending horses to Hialeah and Gulfstream Park, calculated my speed figures, and transcribed them with a red Flair pen into plastic-covered notebooks. Before the computer era this was a laborious task, but for me it was a labor of love, and I knew that the work would pay off handsomely. When the $15,000 New York horse met the $25,000 Chicagoan, the speed figures told me who was faster. It was as if I were interpreting the data in the *Daily Racing Form* with a code that nobody else possessed. I would collect payoffs at memorably high odds on horses I knew were standouts, and I would expect my profits during the winter in Florida to equal or exceed my annual salary as a journalist.

The basis of this success was not only the accuracy of my speed figures but the simple fact that I had them while other people didn't. Parimutuel wagering is a competition among bettors, and I had the critical edge. But it couldn't last forever. When my book *Picking Winners* was published in 1975, many handicappers began to recognize the possible value of speed figures. When I wrote *The Winning Horseplayer* in 1983, I acknowledged that the increasing sophistication of American bettors was making the use of figures less and less profitable; it was becoming tougher to stay ahead of the crowd.

At Gulfstream Park in 1990, all of my worst fears about the nature of the parimutuel competition materialized. My speed figures — which had now advanced into the computer age — had never been so refined. I was watching races, assessing individual horses' efforts, and detecting track biases more astutely than ever before. I was handling my money and my emotions with skill and maturity — a great step forward from the time I punched a hole through the wall of Gulfstream's press box in a rage over an unjust disqualification. I felt that I was at the very top of my game as a gambler. And still I couldn't win. My lack of success was due not to bad luck or photo finishes or any of the other traumas that plague all horseplayers. My frustration was best demonstrated by some of the winners I picked — by horses like Memorable Skater.

In his nine-race career, Memorable Skater had finished out of the money nine times against maiden competition. Now he was running against winners, and any traditional handicapper would have dismissed him on those grounds alone. But his speed figures were competitive with those of his rivals, and, in his last start, he had been forced to race wide on a track with a strong rail-favoring bias. Now he was running again on a day when the rail was an advantage, and he had drawn post position 5, with four slow-breaking horses inside him. I concluded that the maiden would be able to drop to the rail and lead all the way. When I went to the track that day, prepared to make a killing, I thought Memorable Skater embodied all of the handicapping skills I had spent a life-time learning.

The race went just as I expected. Memorable Skater popped out of the gate, angled to the rail, led all the way to win by six lengths — and paid $6.20. A pitiful $6.20. Even at a track heavily popu-lated by tourists and retirees, the betting public had become smart and well informed. Virtually all of the high-rolling gamblers at Gulfstream used speed figures, which were now available from many commercial sources. In addition, racegoers had been edu-cated by a new wave of serious and sophisticated handicapping literature. A decade earlier, few people noticed or mentioned the biases that were commonplace at the Florida tracks; now even casual fans were talking knowledgeably about the rail-favoring tendency of the Gulfstream strip.

But perhaps the greatest change in the makeup of the racetrack population had occurred among the least sophisticated horseplay-ers, the numbers players and the hunch bettors. They weren't there anymore. Most American racetrack executives had been moaning for years about the impact of state lotteries on the horse business, but the lotteries certainly weren't attracting any serious students of the game. They had taken away those hunch players whose money in the betting pools gave an extra edge to the good handicappers. In their absence, the game had become a battle of sharks against sharks, and it seemed to be unwinnable. By the end of the Gulfstream meeting, I had already abandoned any thoughts of returning to my beloved Florida in 1991, and I was making plans to spend the next winter in Sydney, Australia. Perhaps a studious horseplayer could still find some opportunities and edges in the Southern Hemisphere, even if they had disappeared north of the equator.

I was so dispirited when I got back home to Washington that I didn't plan to spend much time at Pimlico's spring meeting. I couldn't have imagined that I was about to experience the most electrifying days in my life as a gambler. The Maryland tracks offer an exotic wager called the double triple, which requires bettors to pick the 1-2-3 finishers in both the third and fifth races. Those who hit the third race share half the money wagered that day (less the track's cut, of course), and they get to exchange each winning combination for one on the fifth race. If nobody hits the fifth-race triple — which is usually the case — the other half of the betting pool goes into a jackpot that keeps growing, day after day, until somebody hits both halves of the wager.

Nobody won the double triple in the first week of the Pimlico meeting, and the jackpot rose to $100,000. As the big bettors and the syndicates got interested, the pot grew faster, to $200,000, then $300,000. By now those big bettors and syndicates were chasing their own money, and the formidable size of the jackpot started attracting attention beyond the racing community; you might hear a double-triple conversation at any sports-oriented bar in the Washington-Baltimore area. Because of the widespread interest, I started writing my columns in the *Washington Post* almost exclusively about aspects of the wager. About its mathematics: "Even if a bold syndicate was prepared to invest $50,000, it could cover only 1 percent of the possible combinations. With 12 horses in each race, there are 1,742,400 possible combinations in the double triple." About racetrack etiquette: "If anybody asks me 'Who do you like?' before today's third race, I am apt to snap, 'I wouldn't tell my mother whom I like here.'" About strategy: "The secret of the double triple is to wait for the track to offer a worthy betting opportunity rather than to pursue a big jackpot just because it's there." With some difficulty, I was trying to follow my own counsel.

On a Thursday that was the twenty-first day of the Pimlico meeting, the jackpot had reached $820,855, and somebody finally picked the 1-2-3 finishers in the third and fifth races. But the red INQUIRY sign was illuminated on the tote board, stewards disqualified the third-place horse in the fifth race, and the wager was alive for another day. Horseplayers are not a softhearted breed, but even the most hardened gambler had to feel a pang of sympathy for the poor soul who had missed the score of a lifetime. What was he thinking and feeling?

By pure chance, I found out the next day. I was at the track's video-replay center, studying films of the horses in that day's double triple, when I saw the previous day's fifth race on the screen next to mine. I turned to the stranger watching it and said, "There wasn't much doubt about that disqualification."

"That cost me the double triple," the man said with almost no trace of emotion in his voice. When I looked at him with disbelief, he reached into his wallet and produced the ticket with the ill-fated 7-9-1 combination. The man introduced himself as Bill Graham, vice president of a Manassas, Virginia, company and a twice-a-month racegoer. He said he had invested about $400 in the double triple, hit three winning combinations on the third race, exchanged them — and left the track. He knew that his chances of winning the wide-open fifth race were remote, and, besides, he had to get back to Virginia for an afternoon business meeting. "I planned to watch the races on the replay show at eleven o'clock," he said, "but I fell asleep and I didn't know what happened until I opened the paper this morning and saw the headline. I'm glad I didn't see the race till now. But after watching the race you can't feel too bad about the disqualification. I've had 'em taken down before. That's horse racing."

I could only admire Bill Graham's stoicism. I couldn't have stayed so calm. Indeed, I couldn't stay calm after my initial look at Saturday's third and fifth races. In contrast to the indecipherable offerings on previous days, this double triple looked analyzable and eminently bettable. I prayed that nobody would hit the wager on Friday. When nobody did and the jackpot had reached $1 million, I proceeded to scrutinize the past performances and the films of every horse. But it was the numbers that made the third race look so clear-cut. These were the speed figures for the last race of each horse in the $5,000 claiming event:

Barong	75
Departing Dream	72
Cretaceous	71
Balloon Meet	60
Follow Me Please	60
Choix	58
Runaway Investment	57
Ognir Rats	54
Too Outrageous	53
Spring Wise	52
Milord D'Accord	31
Chops in Bed	17

The three top horses regularly ran figures in the 70s, and they appeared likely to dominate the field. Excitedly, I phoned my wife, Susan, and told her to cancel our plans for the evening; I was going to need those hours to plot my betting strategy. After I was finished that night, I called a few friends who like to buy a small piece of my double-triple plays and told them, "We're going to hit it tomorrow! Be there!"

I slept fitfully, waking up every hour or two to declare, "We're going to hit it!" And my wife, instead of telling me to shut up, answered, "If you're to take a shot to hit it, then bet what you've got to bet. You don't want to miss this because you cut corners to save a few hundred dollars. Don't wimp out!"

(Having written in *Picking Winners* that "women and gambling don't mix," I had obviously found the perfect wife after forty-two years of bachelorhood. Susan Vallon, an interior designer, had the right genes for marriage to a gambler. While her parents are paragons of rectitude, her grandfather had run dice and poker games in Boston, had operated as an illegal bookmaker at dog tracks, and had spent every winter at Hialeah. When he died peacefully in his sleep at the age of 92, he had not done a day of conventional work in his life. Susan understood the gambling life.)

We went on Saturday to Laurel Race Course's Sports Palace, a Las Vegas–style room that simulcasts the Pimlico races and where the atmosphere is even more intense than at the track. Both Laurel and Pimlico had imported busloads of mutuel clerks from West Virginia as the tracks braced for the biggest non-Preakness day in the history of Maryland racing. The double triple preoccupied everybody. As I walked into the Sports Palace, parking lot attendant Bob Vogelsang greeted me with a cheery, "Good luck, Andy! I hope you hit it!" I told him, "Bob, I *am* going to hit it; give me a twenty." He didn't hesitate to reach into his pocket for a small investment. Entering the Sports Palace, I bumped into trainer Bud Delp, who surveyed the bustling scene and said, "There's just nothing like this!" — a considerable statement from a man who had won the Kentucky Derby and the Preakness with Spectacular Bid. When they played the national anthem at 11 A.M., my friend Carlos Meyer, one of my minority investors, remarked, "It feels like the World Series is about to start." Indeed, I've never been as excited before a World Series or a Kentucky Derby as I was before these cheap claiming races.

I was investing $4,578 — the second-largest wager of my life — and I had plotted every combination meticulously. I was going to box the three standout figure horses in the third race in order to have sixty live tickets if they finished 1-2-3. But I wanted to give myself a reasonable margin of error, especially because one of the three, Cretaceous, was being ridden by a little-known jockey from a minor league track. I would play the figure horses in the top two positions while using all the other marginal contenders in the third-place spot. If I had one of these tickets, I'd have twenty-six live tickets.

The third race developed almost exactly as I had expected. Barong and Departing Dream, the top two figure horses, fought for the lead, dominated the race, and finished 1-2. Cretaceous never got into contention, but one of the marginal contenders, Too Outrageous — who was getting Lasix for the first time — finished

third, and I was alive. If the Sports Palace had been electric before
the third race, it was now as frenetic as the floor of the New York
Stock Exchange. I caught a glimpse of Bill Graham leaving the
Sports Palace quietly, but virtually every syndicate that had made
a good-size investment had a few live tickets, and everybody in the
room seemed to be asking everybody else, "Do you want to do
business?" By joining forces, bettors with a few tickets would be
able to make a cohesive play and greatly increase their chances of
winning. I spurned all such offers. I had come to the track with a
sheet of paper listing the twenty-six combinations I would play in
this situation, and I didn't waver. I was again concentrating on the
horses with the top speed figures. The core of my play was to use
numbers 1, 10, and 11 first and second, with 2 and 12 added in
the third spot.

I never even had to root. My horses controlled the race from
start to finish. At the top of the stretch they were running 11-1-
12-2-10, and if they had stayed that way I might have won the
entire $1.3 million pool. But when they finished 11-1-2 I was not
complaining. I was one of ten winners collecting a $134,161 payoff
— the first six-digit win of my life. After parceling out stacks of
$100 bills to my partners and drinking a champagne toast, I left
the track emotionally drained and headed to the parking lot,
where Bob Vogelsang gave me an expectant look. When I said,
"We hit it," he leaped into the air and almost clicked his heels
together. Even for someone with two-fifths of 1 percent of the
winning ticket, this was an unforgettable day.

As Susan and I celebrated that night over a grilled duck *foie gras*
and a 1983 Château Pomard, I reflected that this double triple had
been, in many ways, a defining moment in my life as a gambler.
Certainly, it reinforced my conviction that I am playing the greatest game in the world. There may be a million easier ways to make
money, and there will always be a lot of frustration involved in
serious gambling, but how many people get to experience the
sense of anticipation, the dreams of glory, the pulsating excitement, and the ultimate feeling of triumph as a horseplayer will on
a day like this one?

These events had bolstered my belief, too, that exotic wagers offer bettors their best chance to make significant profits. (My conviction would grow even stronger five months later, when I hit another double triple at Laurel for $195,000.) While most books on handicapping urge a conservative approach to betting and rarely endorse anything as risky as an exacta, their advice contradicts the experience of the most successful professionals I know. Most would agree that their good years are the ones in which they have made a blockbuster score or two; they know they can't depend on grinding out a slow, steady profit because the parimutuel competition nowadays has become so tough. Fortunately, the racing industry has finally given players regular chances to shoot for windfalls. Most tracks offer a pick six, pick nine, or double triple; virtually all offer trifectas and pick threes. And the trend toward exotica is gaining momentum with the creation of innovative wagers like the National Best Seven and the Breeders' Cup Pick Seven. While it is vastly tougher to beat the races today than it was in the 1970s and earlier, when bettors weren't so sophisticated, modern horseplayers have this one advantage over their predecessors: They can beat the races by cashing a single ticket.

The experience of collecting $134,161 on a wager based solely on standout speed figures also allayed my worries that figures have become too popular to be the source of parimutuel profits. Exotic betting has altered the way horseplayers should look at the usefulness of handicapping methods. The traditional way to evaluate any method or system is to look at its performance over a large sample of races and calculate the net return from a $2 win bet on each selection. Successful methods are the ones that produce some long-priced winners and a positive return on the total investment. But if there should be a $500,000 pick six carryover at Hollywood Park, what does a gambler want: a 10-to-1 shot of a type that, over the long run, would produce a positive return on investment, or a 5-to-2 shot who looks like a mortal lock? Anybody who plays the pick six seriously knows that the 5-to-2 shot is infinitely more desirable because that horse can be the focal point of the whole investment. (If the 10-to-1 shot is in a wide-open race, big bettors are going to stumble onto him anyway because they use so many horses on their tickets.) Speed figures are the most reliable handicapping tool, and they will produce the plays in which a horse-player can have the greatest confidence. If the horseplayer is contemplating a substantial investment, that confidence is critical.

There are countless situations, too, when speed figures will point the way to solid and lucrative betting situations, even though one horse may not have a conspicuous, standout number. If, for example, three horses in a field seem evenly matched, but two of them earned their figures with soft front-running victories while the other had to overcome some adversity, that third horse may be an excellent wager without being an obvious one. The increased popularity of speed handicapping usually means that its practitio-ners must look beyond the obvious to find the best bets. Instead of wagering blindly on the horse who earned the top figure in his last start (as I did, profitably, in the 1970s), a horseplayer must learn to interpret and use the numbers with some sophistication.

The value of speed figures goes far beyond their picking a certain percentage of winners or generating a certain return on investment: They offer a framework for understanding the whole sport. Faster horses will beat slower horses most of the time; but when the slower horse prevails, the reason will often be a source of enlightenment. When my friends who called themselves trip handicappers would airily dismiss the chances of my top-figure horse and would often prove to be right, I came to recognize the merits of their approach and to appreciate how the dynamics of a race can affect horses' performances. When I made my first foray to California and saw how often top-figure horses were beaten by rivals with superior front-running speed, I began to understand more about the effects of pace on the outcome of a race. When I contemplated some of the subtle flaws of speed figures in turf races, I had a revelation about the distinctive nature of competi-tion on the grass. To me it is partly irrelevant that the changing fashions in handicapping will continuously make certain methods more or less profitable. A student of horse racing must begin with the basics, and understanding the significance of horses' times brings a handicapper close to the core truths of the game.

Younger horseplayers might be amazed that anyone ever doubted the importance of time as a factor in handicapping. In any type of race, the speed of the competitors is of central importance. Anyone who watches television coverage of races in the Olympics will note that the athletes are principally defined not by the honors they have won or by their competitive spirit but by the speed of their past performances: Who is the world record-holder? Who has the fastest qualifying times? And, in most cases, the race is to the swift. If parimutuel wagering were permitted on the Olympics, there would be a lot of $2.80 payoffs.

Yet thoroughbred racing developed a mythology which held that an intangible quality called class is more important than speed. In contrast to the commentators on the Olympic telecasts, Howard Cosell would tell the audience watching the Kentucky Derby that it was irrelevant if a 3-year-old had been running slowly in his prep races. "Time," he liked to say, "is important only when you're in jail."

Why did so many people question the importance of time? They did so because the final times of races, taken at face value, can often be confusing and misleading. Unlike, say, Olympic 100-meter runners who may do virtually all of their racing at precisely 100 meters, horses compete at many different distances, making it difficult to compare their times. And unlike human athletes, who compete under relatively standardized conditions, thoroughbreds race over tracks that can differ greatly. Spectacular Bid came into the 1979 Kentucky Derby after winning three 1⅛-mile prep races, on three different tracks labeled "fast," in times of 1:50, 1:48⅖, and 1:48⅘. The California colt Flying Paster had won his two prep races at the same distance in 1:47⅗ and 1:48. When Spectacular Bid won the Derby with Flying Paster ten lengths behind him, many people looked at the evidence and concluded that Spectacular Bid's class had prevailed over Flying Paster's speed. In truth, Spectacular Bid had been running superior races before the Derby; his times had looked slow only because he was competing over relatively slow racing surfaces.

Speed handicappers developed methods to measure the inherent speed of any racing surface so that the times of horses can be interpreted properly. They also learned to compare times at different distances with precision. Their techniques were so effective that the popularity of speed handicapping boomed through the 1980s. Its practitioners were the most serious horseplayers — the ones who had the time to calculate their own figures or the money to buy them from others. But speed handicapping entered the mainstream of American racing on April 25, 1992, when the *Daily Racing Form* began to include Beyer Speed Figures in its past performances. The numbers that I had once guarded jealously became part of the record of every horse at every recognized track in the United States and Canada. They were now the product of a team effort — a team that had been years in the making.

When I was producing my figures with the red Flair pen, the plastic-covered binders, and the stack of *Racing Forms*, the process was wearisome and time-consuming, as I warned prospective speed handicappers in *Picking Winners*. One of the early readers of that book was an Albany businessman named Mark Hopkins. We met at Saratoga, and I saw that Mark was as meticulous and obsessive about his numbers as I. So we decided to divide the work on the northeastern tracks for which we wanted speed figures. Soon I met two colleagues in the press corps, Randy Moss of Dallas and Dick Jerardi of Philadelphia, who were also doing Beyer-style figures for the tracks in their region. We also started swapping information, albeit in a decidedly low-tech fashion. If a horse from Oaklawn Park had shipped to Pimlico, I would phone the Oaklawn press box and say, "Randy, I need a figure."

We already had this informal network in place in 1987 when a Lexington, Kentucky, operation, the Handicappers' Data Base, expressed an interest in marketing these figures to its subscribers via computer. Out went the old plastic-covered binders and in came the computers. Instead of making our numbers by poring over *Racing Forms*, we began downloading the necessary data, making our calculations in the old-fashioned way, and then entering our figures into the computer. Our operation had become fairly sophisticated by the time Robert Maxwell, the British publishing tycoon, decided that he wanted to launch a new racing newspaper in the United States, challenging the monopoly of the

Daily Racing Form. Maxwell hired as his editor-in-chief the *New York Times'* Steve Crist, who was not only a top-class journalist but an expert handicapper who appreciated the value of speed figures and believed that they should be part of the newspaper's past performances. The new *Racing Times* signed us up and promoted the Beyer Speed Figures heavily. But the venture lasted less than a year. When Maxwell fell off the side of his yacht and drowned, his financial empire unraveled quickly and the *Racing Times* died. I went out to buy a new supply of red Flair pens and plastic binders.

To my surprise, however, the conservative *Daily Racing Form* wanted our figures — and wanted them for every track in the United States and Canada, including some I had never heard of. Kin Park? Metrapark? Kamloops? Mark and I had already formally turned our activities into a partnership, Beyer Associates, and added three astute figure-makers to our staff: Joe Cardello of Baltimore, Paul Matties of Hudson, New York, and Dennis Harp of Foster City, California. I had mixed feelings about these developments. I had always cherished the self-image of a renegade professional gambler; I never wanted to be too respectable. And I had always preferred to make a dollar gambling than two dollars with honest toil. But I also chafed at the way nongamblers in racing failed to recognize the value of speed figures, the time-is-only-important-when-you're-in-jail nonsense. The *Daily Racing Form* was putting the imprimatur of the American turf Establishment on my cherished figures.

Large numbers of readers were seeing serious speed figures for the first time, and many were skeptical. Often, their only previous exposure to speed handicapping had come from the old-style speed rating and track variant, which have been part of the *Racing Form's* past performances for decades, despite their obvious deficiencies. When a filly named Tipsy Toes won a $4,000 claiming race at Thistledown on December 4, 1992, she earned a speed rating and track variant of 105-08. When Paseana won the Breeders' Cup Distaff a few weeks earlier, her numbers were 97-03. Since bettors commonly add the two numbers together and then equate one point with one length, Tipsy Toes appeared thirteen lengths better than America's champion racemare. The wariness of the public was understandable.

People who have been newly introduced to Beyer Speed Figures don't need to learn the whole step-by-step process behind their construction but ought to understand enough to appreciate how solidly grounded they are in mathematics and logic. Conversely, horseplayers who get hooked on figures may benefit from the demystification that comes from understanding them better. Every single number is calculated by a handicapper who uses his judgment to analyze a day's results and who may sometimes be confused by the data he confronts. There is no all-powerful magic formula behind our figures.

Indeed, there is nothing even slightly exotic about their basic ingredients. They have two components, just like the old-style *Daily Racing Form* calculations: a speed rating, which translates the time of every race into a number; and a track variant, which measures the inherent fastness or slowness of the racing surface on any given day. The *Form*'s speed rating and variant are listed separately — i.e., 100-08 — and readers commonly add them together. Our figures, which bear no relationship to these, have already combined the rating and the variant. (If a horse earns a Beyer Speed Figure of 100, it doesn't matter if he had a speed rating of 80 on a track with a variant of +20, or a rating of 120 on a track with a variant of −20. A 100 is a 100 is a 100.)

Computing a finely tuned track variant is important because the inherent speed of a racing surface will change from day to day, influenced by weather as well as the way the maintenance crew works on the strip. Tracks in the Northeast can change so drastically during inclement winter weather that a horse who runs six furlongs in 1:09 one day might run in 1:13 the next. Yet even at Del Mar, where the weather is consistent, no rain falls, and the track is labeled "fast" every day, the speed of the surface will often change by two-fifths or three-fifths of a second from one day to the next.

Speed handicapping would be much more understandable if we

could always talk in terms of actual time: "The track was two-fifths of a second fast." Harness handicappers do just this, calculating a variant in fifths of a second and using it to adjust the final time of a race. When a standardbred paces a mile in 1:57 on a track three-fifths of a second slower than the norm, he has an adjusted final time of 1:56⅖. Harness racing is simple because virtually all races are run at the standard distance of one mile. In thorough-bred racing, though, saying that one horse ran an adjusted six-fur-long time of 1:10 while another ran an adjusted seven-furlong time of 1:23⅕ doesn't enlighten us very much. To facilitate comparisons at different distances, it is necessary to translate times into figures — for example, to say that one horse ran a 106 and the other a 101. Unfortunately, moving into the realm of abstract-looking numbers gives speed handicapping an aura of mystery that it shouldn't have. Many users think the figures are a witches' brew of ingredients that tell everything about a horse's past, present, and future. They do not. They simply combine a speed rating and track variant and express how fast a horse ran in past races. Period.

Comparing horses' times at different distances is not monumen-tally difficult, but old-time handicappers made a mess of the job. They would start, properly, by looking for times at different dis-tances which could be equated. The old *Racing Form* ratings used the track record as the starting point, but the problem was that a single exceptional performance (Secretariat's Belmont Stakes vic-tory, for example) would throw every horse's rating at that distance out of whack. It is sounder to look at the performances of a large sample of horses for a particular class. Let us say that we calculate — or, rather, ask a computer to calculate — the average winning time for all the bottom-level $6,500 claiming races at Calder dur-ing 1992. The computer spits out these numbers:

6 furlongs	1:12⅗
7 furlongs	1:25⅘

We now know these performances are equal, in some sense. Speed handicappers of the past would assign an arbitrary number to these times — call it a 70 — and then add or subtract a point for each fifth of a second faster or slower that a horse ran. They would call their product a parallel-time chart, and part of it would look like this:

1:12	73	1:25⅕	73
1:12⅕	72	1:25⅖	72
1:12⅖	71	1:25⅗	71
1:12⅗	70	1:25⅘	70
1:12⅘	69	1:26	69
1:13	68	1:26⅕	68

There is a fallacy in every parallel-time chart equating one point with one fifth of a second, and it should have been glaringly obvious. The ordinary claiming horse running times in the 1:12– 1:13 range would require 13⅕ seconds to travel an additional furlong. But when we move to the upper reaches of the chart, it shows that a six-furlong time of 1:08 would equal seven furlongs in 1:21⅕, and a champion running so fast would also need 13⅕ seconds to go an extra furlong. That clearly defied common sense.

A Harvard classmate, Sheldon Kovitz, showed me how to surmount this difficulty; when I described the method in *Picking Winners,* the logic of it was suddenly crystal-clear to many readers. A fifth of a second is proportionally more significant at a shorter distance than at a longer one. (A horse who misses Belmont's six-furlong track record by one second may be no better than an allowance-class runner; a horse who misses Secretariat's 1½-mile track record by a second is a superstar.) So a fifth of a second should be weighted differently at each distance. How much differently? A six-furlong time of 1:12⅗ seconds equals 363 fifths of a second, and one fifth of a second is ⅟₃₆₃, or .28 percent, of the entire race. A fifth of a second is .23 percent of the comparable seven-furlong race. Moving the decimal place for easier use, we assign 2.8 points to each fifth of a second at six furlongs, 2.3 points at seven furlongs, and our new comparative chart looks like this:

1:12	78.4	1:25⅕	76.9
1:12⅕	75.6	1:25⅖	74.6
1:12⅖	72.8	1:25⅗	72.3
1:12⅗	70	1:25⅘	70
1:12⅘	67.2	1:26	67.7
1:13	64.4	1:26⅕	65.4

We round off the decimals and construct an entire speed chart in this fashion. At its lower portions, it would show that six furlongs in 1:16 equals seven furlongs in 1:29⅘ — those plodders would plod an extra furlong in :13⅘. Up the chart, a six-furlong time of 1:10⅕ equals seven furlongs in 1:23 — with those horses traveling the last eighth in :12⅘. All of this looked logical and sounded logical in theory. But, then, so did trickle-down economics. What has proved remarkable about the chart is the way experience has verified the theory. In 1991–92, for example, the average winning time at Hollywood Park for all the $10,000–$14,000 claiming races for older males at six furlongs was 1:10⅕. At seven furlongs it was 1:23 — exactly as the theory suggested it should be.

The speed-rating charts that are the basis of our figures, and that appear in the Appendix, have changed very little since I started computing figures. The chart for races around one turn is virtually universal, though there are a few tracks (Churchill Downs and Keeneland, among them) that differ from the norm. The chart for route races around two turns is similarly standard. What is not universal is the relationship between the one- and two-turn races at any given track. At Santa Anita, for example, we add 5 points to the two-turn races to bring them in line with the sprints; at Hollywood, we add 2 points; at Del Mar, no adjustment to the two-turn chart is necessary. For every time at every distance at every track in America, we have a numerical rating to compare with every other time and distance.

Once a handicapper has a speed-rating chart, he can proceed to gauge the condition of a track — to calculate a daily track variant. We do this by comparing how fast a race ought to have been run with its actual time. We know that the average winning time of a six-furlong $14,000 claiming race at Hollywood Park is 1:10⅕; speed handicappers call this the par for the class. If such a race is actually run in 1:09⅖, it would suggest that the track is four-fifths of a second fast. Or, looking at the values on our speed chart, we can express this another way: The average winning figure, or par figure, for the class is 103. The speed rating for 1:09⅖ is 115, so the evidence suggests the track was 12 points faster than par. After making similar comparisons for every race on the card, we average the results. If, for example, the average race turns out to be 10 points faster than it should have been, the track variant for the day is −10. We would therefore subtract 10 points from the rating for every race to take into account the fastness of the racing surface.

Most speed handicappers use par times or par figures as the basis of their calculations; it's easy to program a computer to make figures this way. But it is much more accurate to create a track variant by comparing today's time with the way the actual horses in that race should have run. This is called the projection method, and we use it to calculate every Beyer Speed Figure which appears in the *Daily Racing Form.* Consider, for example, the night of October 18, 1991, at the Meadowlands, when Twilight Agenda ran 1⅛ miles in 1:46⅖ to nip Scan in the rich Meadowlands Cup. Twilight Agenda had run figures of 109, 115, 116, 115, and 116 in his last five starts. Scan had just won his last start at the Meadowlands, the Pegasus Handicap, with a figure of 116. It seems logical to assume that Twilight Agenda had duplicated his best recent figure to score that photo-finish victory and that Scan had equaled his last effort. So we project 116 as the probable figure for the Meadowlands Cup. The time of the race translated to a rating of 135, suggesting that the track was 19 points fast. Mark Hopkins evaluated every race on the program in this fashion; his worksheet looked like this:

MEADOWLANDS 10/18/91

Race	Projection	Speed Rating	Difference
1	88	104	−16
2	74	98	−24
3	—	86	—
4	80	98	−18
5	86	110	−24
6	102	115	−13
7	85	104	−19
8	91	112	−21
9	90	106	−16
10	116	135	−19
11	55	75	−20

Average difference (Track variant) −19

The tenth race was the Meadowlands Cup. The third race wasn't included in the calculations, because the data wasn't reliable enough to support a meaningful projection. The average race at the Meadowlands on this evening was 19 points faster than it should have been; the track variant is −19, which is applied to the speed rating of each race to produce the winner's figure. In the Meadowlands Cup, the rating of 135 minus 19 produces a figure of 116 for the winner — exactly what we thought it should be.

After we have entered the winning figures into the *Daily Racing Form*'s computer, the figures for the losers are calculated mechanically, according to a formula. (A chart in the Appendix shows how beaten lengths are translated into points.) Handicappers using our speed figures should remember that the quest for accuracy has required us to junk the convenient equation of one length, one point, and one-fifth of a second. In our system, the value of a length changes according to the distance, as follows:

5 furlongs	1 length = 2.9 points
6 furlongs	1 length = 2.4 points
6½ furlongs	1 length = 2.2 points
7 furlongs	1 length = 2.0 points
1 mile	1 length = 1.8 points
1$\frac{1}{16}$ miles	1 length = 1.7 points
1⅛ miles	1 length = 1.7 points

If every racing date was as logical and tidy as October 18, 1991, at the Meadowlands, a staff of speed handicappers would not be needed to produce reasonably decent figures. A computer could be programmed to do it. Reality, however, can be messy, as on this day at Churchill Downs:

CHURCHILL DOWNS 11/08/92

Race	Projection	Speed Rating	Difference
1	74	85	−11
2	76	85	−9
3	59	72	−13
4	52	67	−15
5	68	74	−6
6	71	75	−4
7	Turf		
8	88	93	−5
9	91	92	−1

Here the average race is 8 points fast and the track variant is −8. Or is it? The Churchill Downs track may have been faster early in the day and slower after the fourth race. I concluded that it would be better to make the variant −12 for the first four races and −4 for five through nine. And there are many other situations when a day's races won't produce a single variant. Sometimes sprints may be faster than routes, or vice versa, and it will be necessary to make a separate variant for different distances.

But the most ambiguous, troublesome situations arise when the normal calculations produce a figure that makes no sense. Mark and I fretted about this one for days:

AQUEDUCT 4/22/89

Race	Projection	Speed Rating	Difference
1	92	60	+32
2	78	53	+25
3	79	48	+31
4	Turf		
5	—	75	—
6	Turf		
7	96	72	+24
8	110	99	+11
9	75	47	+28

The track was officially designated "fast," but on this day the Aqueduct strip was very slow, with a variant that averaged out to +25. Applying this number, the winning figure for the eighth race would be a blockbuster 124, which would have significance for the whole national racing scene. This was the Wood Memorial Stakes, Easy Goer's final prep for the Kentucky Derby and his much-awaited confrontation with Sunday Silence. Could he possibly be this good?

Mark was responsible for the Aqueduct numbers, but I had to chime in with an opinion: "Easy Goer may be the best horse we've seen since Spectacular Bid. He ran a 118 in the Gotham Stakes two weeks ago, and he can certainly improve on that. He can run a 124!"

"No way," Mark countered. "He was only three lengths in front of Rock Point and Triple Buck. If we give Easy Goer a figure of 124, that means the other two got a 119 each, and that makes them the second- and third-best 3-year-olds in the country. Neither one of them has ever run a number better than 100 before."

"Well," I said, "3-year-olds do sometimes improve a lot at this time of the year. I could barely believe the big figure that Pleasant Colony got in the Wood Memorial in '81 — but it turned out to be legit and he won the Derby."

"I just can't buy the idea that three horses all happened to run sensational races all at the same time," Mark said. "That's too much of a coincidence. The track superintendent probably just souped up the track for the Wood Memorial. I can't see how the figure for this race could be more than a 110." Mark decided to assign the Wood Memorial a figure of 110, which he thought was consistent with the capabilities of all the horses. We call this projecting the number; some people might call it arbitrary and unscientific.

Anybody who has ever calculated figures knows that such aberrations do occasionally arise from a sudden (if invisible) change in the condition of the track or perhaps from a malfunction in the electric timer. When this happens, we would rather be arbitrary than assign a figure that defies common sense — especially if the figure was so big that bettors might want to mortgage their houses to wager on horses coming out of the race. In this case, Mark's decision was vindicated. Easy Goer went into the Kentucky Derby with the second-best speed figure and finished second to Sunday Silence. The horses who had been three lengths behind him at Aqueduct proved not to be budding superstars. Triple Buck finished ninth in the Derby; Rock Point never won a race for the rest of his career.

There are other situations in which we may not be able to calculate a normal figure with a normal variant; the most common of these will involve grass races. On the many days when a racetrack will card a single turf race, we won't have enough evidence about the speed of the course to make a variant. In such circumstances we'll project a figure — and pray.

When we assign these occasional arbitrary numbers, our computer system allows us to second-guess our own decisions. We can summon a report on any race which shows what figure each horse earned in his next start after that race. After reviewing a troublesome race, we may conclude that subsequent events have contradicted our original judgment. When that happens, we'll go back and change the number. Sometimes the only way to produce a trustworthy figure is through hindsight.

Computers have permitted us to make other refinements that were impossible in the red-Flair-pen era. The greatest of these has been the exactitude with which we can now compare horses at different racing circuits. In the past, this was a problem for anybody who made speed figures. A handicapper might have a good set of numbers for Santa Anita and a good set for Kamloops, but how can the two be related? How can he know that a 90 in one place means the same thing as a 90 in the other? The traditional method was to assume that low- to mid-level claiming horses were the same everywhere and that the average $10,000 claiming race would be won with the same average figure on virtually any circuit. This assumption was convenient, even if it wasn't necessarily accurate.

But now I am able to instruct the computer: Show me every horse who shipped between Track A and Track B in the last year and the figure he ran in each place. I analyzed southern and northern California and saw that the average shipper was running two points higher in the north; I subtracted two points from all of my northern California numbers to get the two circuits in line. I proceeded to compare northern California with Washington, then Washington with Oregon, then the Northwest with western Canada, making the necessary adjustments to equate the figures on each circuit, fitting everything together like pieces of an enormous jigsaw puzzle. When this weeks-long exercise was over and the figures at every racing circuit in the United States and Canada were aligned, I asked the computer to show me the average winning figure for different classes at any track in the country. These are the average winning figures for older male claiming horses in the $10,000–$14,000 bracket at a variety of tracks:

Santa Anita	85
Laurel	83
Arlington	82
Suffolk	80
Turf Paradise	80
Garden State	78
Detroit	76
Albuquerque	73

These differences from track to track are much greater than I ever imagined; like many handicappers, I had once erred in basing figures on the premise that all $10,000 claimers are pretty much the same. This difference in ability among horses with the same claiming price has philosophical as well as practical implications, going to the heart of the ancient debate over the merits of speed versus class. Defining a horse as a $10,000 claimer (or an allowance-class runner or a Grade III stakes winner or any other class designation) is woefully imprecise. But if we know that a 4-year-old male regularly runs a figure of 85, we know exactly what he is; we know the level of competition where he belongs at any racing circuit in the country.

Most racing fans find it hard to accept the fact that class is a superfluous handicapping factor. After the Beyer Speed Figures made their debut in the *Daily Racing Form,* the question I was most often asked about the numbers was, "How do you take into account the class levels where horses earned the figures?" Those who asked were usually appalled by my answer: "I don't. When you have good speed figures, class is irrelevant."

To this absolutist philosophy I hasten to add one qualifier. Much of this book will be devoted to the proposition that the speed figure a horse earns in a race will be influenced by the way that race develops. If, for example, a front-runner gets an unchallenged early advantage, he is apt to run better than if he is subjected to a gut-wrenching duel for the lead. A horse may well encounter easier circumstances in a $10,000 claiming race than in a $20,000 claiming race, and in such a case he may find it easier to earn a big number in a cheaper race. But if the races are run in a similar fashion, the class of the races is indeed irrelevant.

Horseplayers initially resist this notion because they tend to think that speed and class are totally different attributes; they expect to encounter horses with superior figures who are obviously overmatched — Tipsy Toes vs. Paseana, for example. But figure-oriented handicappers know that speed and class are two different ways of expressing the same thing — a horse's level of ability — and that speed figures measure that ability more precisely. The close relationship of the two is evident whenever a horseplayer calculates the average winning figures for the different classes at a particular track. If the sample is large enough, the par figure for any class will be greater than that of the class below it. The $6,500 claimers run faster than $5,000 claimers, who in turn run faster than $4,000 claimers. The following table shows the maximum par figures in claiming races for older horses:

$2,500	65
$3,000	69
$4,000	72
$5,000	76
$6,000–$7,400	80
$7,500–$9,000	82
$10,000–$14,000	85
$15,000–$20,000	90
$21,000–$34,000	93
$35,000–$49,000	96
$50,000–$75,000	98
$75,000+	102

(For races limited to fillies and mares, subtract 8 points.)

Obviously, there is a close relationship between speed and class, but the figures provide a universal language with which to talk about horses' ability. If a claimer has run an 85, if a 2-year-old has broken his maiden with a figure of 88, if a highly acclaimed Kentucky Derby candidate has a top figure of 103, those numbers resonate with meaning to anyone who has become familiar with our system.

These numbers don't have any neat starting point, as, say, does the system of figures developed by author Bill Quirin, who defines 100 as the average winning number for $10,000 claiming horses. Inflation and changes in the racing economy affect the value of horses; the ability of $10,000 claimers in 1993 isn't exactly the same as $10,000 claimers in 1985, and we want our numbers to be useful from a historical as well as a handicapping perspective — to measure, say, how the current Kentucky Derby winner stacks up against Derby winners of the past.

What a number means in terms of a horse's class level depends, as we have seen, on where he is racing. The figures in the above chart represent the pars for claiming races at the strongest racing circuits around the country; a 90, for example, would be good enough to win a $20,000 claiming race in New York, California, or anywhere. At tracks of lesser quality, the quality of the claiming races will be somewhat lower, and the disparities in maiden-special-weight and allowance races can be extreme. In southern California, for example, the par for the bottom-level allowance condition — "nonwinners of one race other than maiden or claiming" — is 98. At Thistledown, the par for the same category is 66. A table showing the pars for different classes at many American tracks appears in the Appendix.

This table lists the pars of races for older horses only. Races for 2- and 3-year-olds are confusing because horses improve steadily as they age. A $20,000 claiming race for 3-year-olds in January would differ from such a race in May. As a rough rule of thumb, horses improve at the rate of about 1 to 1½ points per month until they reach their peak early in their 4-year-old season. Alysheba's development was typical. He ran a figure of 95 when he finished third in the Breeders' Cup Juvenile as a 2-year-old; he earned a 113 when he won the Preakness as a 3-year-old; he improved to 122 when he won the Breeders' Cup Classic at 4.

What constitutes a stakes horse will, of course, vary from track to track, but a horse who runs 110 will be a solid stakes performer anywhere. A horse who runs 120 is a potential champion; a horse who reaches the mid-120s is in the superstar class. From 1986 through 1992, seven horses earned figures of 123 or better: Sunday Silence, Easy Goer, Precisionist, Turkoman, Best Pal, and the sprinters Phone Trick and Groovy. Of course, good horses can demonstrate greatness in ways besides running fast final times. When Alysheba was almost knocked down at the head of the stretch but recovered to beat Bet Twice in the Kentucky Derby, even an ardent speed handicapper was not going to denounce him because he failed to earn a big number. Eventually, though, Alysheba satisfied speed handicappers by running exceptional figures

— the great ones always do. Speed figures define a horse and often paint a vivid picture of his whole career, as they did in the case of Scan.

Scan — **B. h. 5, by Mr Prospector—Video, by Nijinsky II**
Br.—Claiborne Farm & Gamely Corp (Ky)
Own.—Perry William Haggin — **Tr.—Schulhofer Flint S (—)**

Lifetime		1991	11	2	4	2	$522,480
16 5 6 2		1990	5	3	2	0	$205,200
$727,680		Turf	1	0	0	0	
		Wet	1	1	0	0	$106,560

2Nov91- 5CD	fm	1	Ⓣ:48	1:12^2	1:37^2	3↑Br Cp Mile	**100**	6	11	11^{4¼}	14^{8¼}	11^5	8^{5¼}	Santos J A	B	123	15.00	92-06	OpnngVrs126^{1¼}VldsBos-Fr126^{no}StrofCzzn123	No factor 14
2Nov91-Grade I																				
18Oct91-10Med	fst	1⅛	:46^3	1:10^1	1:46^3	3↑Med Cup H	**116**	7	4	3^{1½}	3^{1½}	2^{hd}	2^{nk}	Santos J A		116	*1.70	102-06	Twilight Agenda121^{nk} Scan116^{1½}SeaCadet115	Game try 9
18Oct91-Grade I																				
20Sep91- 9Med	fst	1⅛	:46	1:09^3	1:46^2	Pegasus H	**116**	7	1	2^{hd}	1^{hd}	1^{1½}	1^{1¾}	Santos J A		119	*1.50	103-07	Scan119^{1¾} Sea Cadet119^4 Sultry Song114	Sharp score 8
20Sep91-Grade I																				
2Sep91- 8Bel	fst	1	:45^1	1:09^2	1:34	Jerome H	**112**	4	6	5^{1¾}	5^{¾}	1^{1½}	1^4	Santos J A		117	2.40	100-12	Scn117^{4}ExcellentTipper113^{1½}KingMuts113	Going away 8
2Sep91-Grade I																				
8Aug91- 7Sar	fst	7f	:22^4	:45^4	1:21^3	3↑Alw 30000	**103**	3	4	7^{4½}	6^{3¼}	3^3	2^{1¾}	Bailey J D		112	*.40	95-09	Nymphist117^{1¾} Scan112^{½} King Mutesa112	Fin. well 8
8Jun91- 8Bel	fst	1½	:46^3	2:02	2:28	Belmont	**102**	2	4	4^3	3^{2½}	5^{5½}	5^{7¾}	McCarron C J		126	10.30	82-08	Hnsl126^{hd}StrikThGold126^{3}MnMinistr126	Bid, gave way 11
8Jun91-Grade I																				
26May91- 8Bel	fst	1⅛	:46^1	1:10^2	1:49^2	Peter Pan	**102**	1	2	1^{½}	1^{hd}	1^{hd}	3^{1½}	Bailey J D		126	*1.50	80-31	LostMountain114^{hd}ManAlright114^{1½}Scan126	Weakened 6
26May91-Grade II																				
8May91- 8Bel	fst	1	:45^4	1:09^3	1:34	Withers	**101**	2	6	4^1	1^{hd}	1^{½}	2^{¾}	Bailey J D		126	*1.10	99-13	Subordinated Debt126^{¾} Scan126^8 Kyle's Our Man126	9
8May91-Grade II; Broke slow, hit rail, bmpd trn																				
6Apr91- 5SA	fst	1⅛	:46^2	1:10^1	1:48	Sta Anta Dy	**89**	7	8	7^{6¼}	7^{5¼}	5^{7½}	5^{11¼}	Bailey J D	LB	122	7.50	79-11	Dinard122^{½} Best Pal122^{1¾} Sea Cadet122	Broke slowly 9
6Apr91-Grade I																				
17Mar91- 8SA	fst	1 1/16	:46	1:09^4	1:41^4	San Felipe	**97**	6	7	6^{5¼}	4^{3½}	2^3	2^3	Bailey J D	LB	119	4.30	91-10	SeCdet119^{3}Scn119^{1¼}CompellingSound116	Broke slowly 8
17Mar91-Grade II																				
10Feb91- 4SA	fst	7f	:22	:44^1	1:21^2	Sn Vcnte B C	**85**	4	3	3^1	3^{½}	3^3	3^9	Bailey J D	LB	123	5.60	87-10	Olympio120^{no} Dinard118^9 Scan123	Lugged in late 6
10Nov90- 8Aqu	sly	1⅛	:48	1:12^3	1:52^2	Remsen	**98**	7	4	4^{1½}	2^{hd}	1^{hd}	1no	Bailey J D		119	*.90	74-33	Scan119^{no}SubordintedDebt115^{¾}Kyle'sOurMn113	Driving 8
10Nov90-Grade II																				
28Oct90- 7Bel	fst	7f	:22^2	:45^4	1:23^2	Cowdin	**108**	1	8	5^3	3^1	1^{hd}	1^{3½}	Bailey J D		122	*.80	87-17	Scan122^{3½} Formal Dinner122^{13} Mineral Ice122	Driving 8
28Oct90-Grade II																				
30Sep90- 6Bel	fst	7f	:22^1	:45^2	1:22^4	Md Sp Wt	**95**	6	3	3^2	1^{hd}	1^6	1^{10½}	Santos J A		118	*.40	90-10	Scn118^{10½}ZroForConduct118^{10¼}YongDnl118	Ridden out 6
31Aug90- 5Bel	fst	6f	:22^1	:45^1	1:10^4	Md Sp Wt	**79**	7	10	6^5	4^7	3^{2½}	2^{nk}	Bailey J D		118	2.10	85-16	SbrdntdDbt118^{nk}Scn118^{5¼}SldrtyChf118	Stumbled early 11
3Jun90- 5Bel	fst	5f	:22^1	:46^2	:59^1	Md Sp Wt	**73**	5	7	4^{4½}	3^3	2^2	2^{3½}	Bailey J D		118	2.10	88-18	Vermont118^{3½} Scan118^{14¼} Iceberg Ahead118	Slw st. 7

The column of numbers in boldface show Scan's Beyer Speed Figures for each of his races. In the Cowdin Stakes of 1990, Scan earned a figure of 108, the best by any 2-year-old that season. He went to Santa Anita for the winter to prepare for the Kentucky Derby, but there he was an absolute flop. Californians may have thought this was just another overhyped eastern colt; trainer Scotty Schulhofer insisted, "He just didn't acclimatize." The numbers indicated that Schulhofer was probably right. While 3-year-olds almost always improve as they mature, Scan regressed, never running a figure better than 97 at Santa Anita. When he went back to New York, he ran respectably in stakes company during the spring and summer, but the figures (in the 101–103 range) suggested that he hadn't lived up to his early potential. Finally, in the fall, Scan found himself. His back-to-back 116s at the Meadowlands were better than Strike the Gold or Hansel had run in the

Triple Crown series, better than Festin had run in the Jockey Club Gold Cup, equal to In Excess's figure in the Woodward Stakes that fall. Scan's poor number in his career finale, the Breeders' Cup Mile, demonstrated that he wasn't as good on turf as on dirt, but he nevertheless may have been the best colt of his generation. Maybe the Japanese had a speed-figure consultant when they bought him for stud duty.

If Scan didn't get the recognition that he deserved, it was because he was overshadowed (in Schulhofer's view, especially) by his contemporary and stablemate, Fly So Free. As a 2-year-old, Fly So Free had won both the Champagne Stakes and the Breeders' Cup Juvenile. Speed handicappers may not have been impressed — his figures in those races were 96 and 101 — but Fly So Free was a professional racehorse, and those prestigious victories earned him the Eclipse Award as the champion of his generation. He was the future-book favorite for the Kentucky Derby, and he provoked a lot of excitement when he won his first important 3-year-old prep race, the Fountain of Youth Stakes, by six lengths. But the numbers kept saying that he was overrated. Fly So Free's Fountain of Youth figure was a 103 — hardly the kind of performance that will earn a colt the blanket of roses at Churchill Downs.

Running figures in the 103–106 range, Fly So Free disappointed in the Blue Grass Stakes as the 1-to-5 favorite, disappointed in the Kentucky Derby, and disappointed in the Travers Stakes. Schulhofer kept looking for a problem that he could correct, but Fly So Free's only problem was his own level of ability: He wasn't going to beat Grade I stakes competition with figures in the low to mid-100s.

With the Breeders' Cup approaching, I phoned Schulhofer to interview him for a newspaper column, but I had a pecuniary motive: Scan was 35 to 1 in Las Vegas's future-book wagering for the Classic, and he had the credentials to win it. Would he run? Schulhofer said no. He might give Scan a chance on the turf, but Fly So Free was his horse for the world's richest race.

I tried to explain that Scan's speed figures indicated that he was one of the top horses in the country; Fly So Free had never run a single number to make him competitive with the likes of Twilight Agenda, Festin — or Scan. My entreaties were in vain. "I know you all believe in your figures," Schulhofer said, "but don't you think that class has something to do with it?" A generational and philosophical chasm lay between us, and I knew it was useless to say: Scotty, class has *nothing* to do with it.

Fly So Free finished fourth in the Classic, while Scan was relegated to a turf race where he didn't belong. I will always believe that he might have won the Classic. The validity of his figures was verified when his rival from the Meadowlands, Twilight Agenda, finished second in the Classic. Speed figures had defined both Scan and Fly So Free perfectly — as they do with most horses. But what do we do with the vital information they convey? In Schulhofer's case, the answer should have been obvious: Give a superior horse the chance to win a $3 million race. For the rest of us, the answers are not so easy.

How do we use speed figures in conjunction with other important aspects of handicapping, especially in cases where other factors may seem to contradict the figures?

If we assume that the early fractions of a race can influence a horse's final time, how do we relate the crucial factor of pace to speed figures?

In what situations are figures most and least reliable?

Are there patterns and trends and configurations of numbers which will predict that a horse is about to improve or deteriorate?

In an era when virtually all bettors have access to figures, these are the questions that modern speed handicappers must answer in order to maintain an edge in the parimutuel competition.

TWO

Probabilities and Patterns

Handicappers who calculate their own speed figures are often so preoccupied by the mechanics of the task that they don't think much about how to use the numbers. The very creation of the figures is an end in itself. For much of my life as a horseplayer, my strategy for using speed figures was so rudimentary that it could be summed up in a paragraph.

A horse's most recent start is by far the most important indication of his current condition, so I begin my study of any race by looking at the last figure of each entrant. The one with the highest number in his most recent start is designated the "top figure" and becomes the frame of reference for the entire race. I try to judge if that figure honestly reflects the horse's ability — whether, for example, he earned it at a distance and under track conditions similar to today's. Then I scrutinize the competition. Horses who have never earned a number close to the top figure can usually be eliminated. But if a horse has previously delivered a performance better than the top figure, I examine him more closely. Is there a reason to ignore his most recent figure or figures? Was he compromised by a muddy track? Was the distance unsuitable? Such a horse might be a standout on the basis of an earlier figure. However, any wager based on a single good figure entails a significant risk that the horse won't repeat it. A superior betting situation arises when a horse's last two figures are both larger than everybody else's last two. Such a horse — a double figure or, simply, a "double fig" — has a built-in safeguard against the possibility that a single big race might have been a fluke. A triple fig is better still. The rarest and most exciting discovery for a speed handicapper — comparable, say, to a bird-watcher's sighting of an ivory-billed woodpecker — is an omnifig, a horse whose every figure is superior to every figure of every other horse in the field.

As speed figures have entered the public domain, more and more handicappers are studying them and trying to find the best ways to use them. Many computer buffs have undertaken statistical analyses that may yield a lode of valuable information about speed figures — but that also threaten to lead the analysts into an old, familiar trap.

For as long as the game has existed, bettors have searched for simple, straightforward ways to win at the track. Just as archaeologists solved the riddles of Egyptian hieroglyphics with a single discovery, the Rosetta Stone, so bettors have sought a Rosetta Stone of handicapping. This is why horseplayers of the past were often seduced by peddlers of systems, mechanical sets of rules for picking winners. These systems were always accompanied by data showing that they produced a hypothetical profit when applied to a series of past races, but buyers invariably found that systems didn't predict the future when real money was at stake.

Now, in the computer age, more sophisticated handicappers can apply countless sets of parameters to past races and look for those that produce a profitable return on investment, or ROI — the average return for a $2 bet. The computer analyzes the performance of trainers, jockeys, or rules of handicapping, and when it finds a situation that yields, say, an ROI of 2.60 — *voilà!* A winning method has been discovered. Now the computers are humming and analyzing speed figures. One computer whiz in Nevada told me that the best results with the Beyer Speed Figures come from looking at the last ten starts of each horse and betting the one with the highest second-best figure. Other analysts have tinkered with the averages of horses' recent figures, even if the idea of averaging the numbers makes no sense. (If a horse's last two figures are a 90 followed by a 60, it is possible that the 60 reflects his current form or that the bad figure was excusable and the 90 represents his capability, but in no way does the average of 75 correspond to reality.)

If a computer scans enough parameters, even senseless ones, it will inevitably unearth some that have produced a profit in a series of past races. But even if a premise is fairly logical, no simple, mechanical way of playing the horses can succeed in the long run. The nature of the sport ensures that it cannot have a Rosetta Stone. Horse racing is a dynamic game, not a static code waiting to be deciphered, and ideas that were valid in the past may be irrelevant today. Even if a method of playing the horses is both logical and enduring, bettors will eventually recognize its value and drive down the odds in the winning situation until the value has diminished. A startling example of this phenomenon is the history of the late Oscar Barrera, who in the early 1980s performed the most amazing feats in the history of thoroughbred training. New Yorkers assumed that Barrera possessed some magical (and highly illegal) elixir, because he would claim horses and immediately improve their speed figures by 30 or 40 points. Smart handicappers made a profit on Barrera's claims for a while, but soon the public jumped on the bandwagon. Barrera might claim a horse who had lost a race by twenty lengths, step him up in class sharply, and run him four days later — and the horse would be an overwhelming favorite despite his horrible-looking credentials. Barrera remained a formidable force in the game — he could never be ignored — but bettors could no longer count on him as a source of easy profits.

This, of course, is what has happened to speed figures. In the past I have collected odds as high as 50 to 1 on horses with the top figure. I would guess that as recently as 1990 a bet on every top figure would have yielded a profitable ROI. But the inclusion of speed figures in the *Daily Racing Form* has inevitably depressed the odds on horses with good numbers. In view of this reality, how should handicappers use speed figures today?

To find the answer, I asked the *Racing Form*'s computer experts to examine the performance of speed figures in a large sample of races. I was not looking for gimmicks — for example, filly sprinters who have an advantage of 6 to 10 points in the figures and made their last start in the last 15 to 24 days will produce a positive ROI. I wanted facts about the strengths and weaknesses of speed handicapping today. These were the ground rules of the study: Only races on dirt were considered, because turf events are confused too often by the presence of horses who haven't raced on grass before. Only races on fast tracks were used. Races were not considered unless every horse had at least two career starts, so that first-time starters wouldn't confuse the study. If the horse with the top figure had not run within the last 45 days, the whole race was disregarded.

After looking at the most recent figure of each horse in more than 10,000 qualifying races, the *Racing Form*'s computer produced a surprisingly unambiguous answer to one question: What constitutes a meaningful advantage in the figures? The answer is: A top figure is significant when it is at least three points higher than the second-best figure in the field. In sprint races, three points translates into a margin of a length or more. But in just about every category the computer examined, an edge of only one or two points proved to be relatively inconsequential.

This was the overall performance of top-figure horses with an advantage of three points or more over the competition:

Number of horses	Win percentage	ROI
3,710	29	1.85

It might seem logical that wagers based on the speed of horses would be more productive in shorter races than in longer ones, and, indeed, this was the case:

Distance	Number of horses	Win percentage	ROI
Routes	1,972	28	1.80
Sprints	1,738	30	1.90

There was also a difference in the predictability of the sexes:

Sex	Number of horses	Win percentage	ROI
Females	685	26	1.64
Males	3,025	30	1.90

Although betting blindly on every horse with a top figure can no longer produce a net profit, these results underscore the enduring power of speed handicapping. An ROI of 1.90 in sprints and races for males, or 1.85 overall, is a loss of only 5 to 7½ percent — overcoming much of the 17 percent tax bite to which bettors are typically subjected. And this study did not attempt to weed out weak horses by applying any handicapping logic (except the exclusion of horses laid off 45 days). If a plodder had earned his top figure running at two miles and was now going five furlongs, he still counted in the sample. If the rivals of the top horse seemed certain to improve because they had an excuse for a poor recent figure, the computer didn't recognize that fact, either. Nor did these statistics take into account the most important consideration in gambling: value. A horse who is a good bet at 3 to 1 might properly be shunned at 6 to 5. And, of course, the ROI statistics generated by the *Racing Form*'s analysis are based only on win bets, which are not necessarily relevant to exactas, trifectas, and other exotics and which can offer much more attractive opportunities — as subsequent chapters of this book will demonstrate. Yet without the application of any skill, judgment, or intelligent betting strategy, speed figures can take a horseplayer to the brink of profitability.

Moreover, the broad *Racing Form* study looked at a sample that included plenty of marginally superior top figures. If it was possible to achieve an ROI of 1.90 with this large group, surely a bettor could make a healthy profit by waiting for powerhouse double-fig and triple-fig situations — races like the third at Laurel on November 15, 1992. These were the figures for the last three starts of each horse:

Latchburn	87	79	82
Dr. Tom	72	65	67
Groom's Reckoning	65	61	58
Jay Pee	64	47	41
August Bum	63	42	48
Gee Jamie	61	34	17
Paya	60	53	67
Lulu's Boy	58	30	65
Exclusive Envoy	56	63	32
Dancing Elite	55	55	64

Latchburn wasn't quite as rare as an ivory-billed woodpecker, but he was close — a triple fig. The worst of his last three races was seven points superior to the best of his rivals. Yet, because he was a shipper from Thistledown, the Maryland bettors were a bit wary of him and let him go to the post at 3 to 1. Latchburn won by nearly four lengths, earning another figure of 87, and paid $8.20. Wouldn't it be profitable to wait for such standouts? I asked the computer this question, and the computer responded: Not really.

Here was the performance of one category of standouts, double-figure horses who had an edge of ten points over the field in both of their last two starts:

	Number of horses	Win percentage	ROI
All	188	39	1.96
Sprints	82	41	2.15
Males	160	39	1.98

One might think that a purely mechanical handicapping system that picked around 40 percent winners would be stunningly profitable. But when the public identifies a simple, obvious winning situation — as it did with Oscar Barrera claims — it will bet en-

thusiastically enough to destroy the odds. Other types of overwhelming speed-figure standouts had similarly impressive winning
percentages and unimpressive ROIs. The only such horses who
may occasionally produce decent value are those who have arrived
from a lesser racing circuit (as Latchburn did) and those who are
stepping up sharply in class.

There is an important lesson to be learned from these statistics.
The quest for the most profitable uses of figures is not going to be
answered by looking for obvious standouts. Bettors need to interpret and apply speed figures with a bit more subtlety — to find
horses who have strong speed-handicapping virtues but who aren't
the obvious no-brainers that anybody can spot. But how? One
man, Len Ragozin, has spent much of his life pondering that
question, and his imaginative answers have influenced a generation of horseplayers.

Ragozin's father, Harry, was always a gambler of sorts. He lost
heavily in speculation on commodity futures, and he was driven to
the brink of bankruptcy when the price of stock in the family's
textile business plummeted. As an escape from his worries, Harry
started going to the racetrack, where he perceived that he might
find excellent opportunities for profit. He assumed that the best
way to judge horses' ability was to understand how fast they could
run, and he recognized the flaws in the *Daily Racing Form*'s speed
ratings and track variants. So Harry hired a statistician to study
hundreds of races, and with this data he developed a set of speed
figures based on pars for various claiming classes — a visionary
idea in the 1950s. Eventually he was plotting the figures on a
graph so that he would have a vivid picture of every horse's race-
by-race development.

Len Ragozin had always taken an interest in his father's racing
activities, but he intended to pursue a career in journalism, and he
went to work at *Newsweek* after his graduation from Harvard. It
was the height of the McCarthy era, and Ragozin's politics were
inconveniently left wing. When the FBI began to make inquiries
about his political associations in college, Ragozin was passed over

for a promotion, and he decided that he didn't have much of a future in journalism after all. He joined his father in working on the speed figures, raising them to an even higher plane of sophistication. In addition to the basic speed rating and track variant, Ragozin incorporated calculations that took into account the effects of weight, wind velocity, and the ground that horses lost by running wide on turns. In his system, the fastest horses get the lowest numbers. Champions earn a zero on their best days, while ordinary claimers run in the 20s and 30s.

Ragozin gambled successfully with these figures in the 1950s and during this period he made an observation that would eventually become the central part of his approach to the game. "It became clear to me," he said, "that horses run in patterns. They have peaks and valleys. As I was betting for a living in Florida, I started marking the letter 'A' on horses who seemed to be in improving condition. And the A's were all winning over the horses who had the better numbers. Instead of saying, 'Let's see who has the best numbers,' I started saying, 'Let's see who has the best patterns.'"

This perception eventually influenced the thinking of horseplayers across America. Even while he was using his figures successfully at the betting windows, Ragozin felt he didn't have the ideal temperament to be a gambler. For a few years he operated his own racing stable. Then he began to sell his figures to a small number of gamblers, owners, and trainers. Each horse's numbers appeared on an individual 5½-by-8½-inch sheet of paper, and Ragozin's coterie of customers became fanatical devotees of the "Sheets." At the New York tracks, many of the most conspicuous high-rollers became Ragozin clients, and when they collectively liked the same horse, they could cut his odds in half. Owners and trainers started using the Sheets as the basis for buying, selling, and managing horses; Ragozin clients such as Glenn Lane and Tresvant Stable ranked among the country's top race-winning owners.

For many years, however, Ragozin's operation seemed as much a cult as a business. Perhaps his left-wing proclivities made him uncomfortable with ardent capitalism. But a former employee and client, Jerry Brown, had no such compunctions. After a falling-out with Ragozin, Brown started a rival business, Thoro-Graph, in 1982, using essentially the same system of numbers, promoting it with advertisements, television appearances, endorsements by trainers, and instructional videos. Ragozin responded with a more aggressive sales and marketing strategy for his own product, now officially named "The Sheets" (although the term is popularly used for both his and Brown's numbers). And both gurus preached a gospel based on Ragozin's original insight from the 1950s: The form cycle of every horse has peaks and valleys. Those who use the Sheets should not simply look for good figures, but for patterns of figures. The crucial pattern, the foundation of the entire theory, is one that has become solidly established in the lexicon of modern handicapping: the bounce.

According to the theory, a horse who improves sharply, earning an exceptional or career-best figure, is likely to give an inferior performance the next time he runs. He will "bounce" to a poor effort because he needs time to recover from the physical stress of an unusually good race. In a profile of Ragozin for the *New Yorker,* Jeff Coplon wrote, "It was a remarkable theory, both obvious and radical, and only a Marxist might have embraced it so readily. Ragozin considered the bounce a case study in dialectics. 'You're dealing with complicated ebbs and flows, the two-sidedness of every development,' he says. 'When a horse runs a good race, it's both good and bad. . . . Did that race hurt him, or was it a springboard for further good efforts?'"

In the 1989 Laurel Futurity, the 2-year-olds Go and Go and Robyn Dancer produced a pair of extraordinary performances. Go and Go was an unheralded arrival from Ireland who had never raced on dirt before, and Robyn Dancer was a Maryland-based colt who had never run notably fast, but they battled to the wire to earn speed figures of 109 each. The Sheet numbers were similarly impressive, and a Ragozin client, trainer Darrell Vienna, bought Robyn Dancer after the Laurel race. Both colts ran two weeks later in the Breeders' Cup Juvenile at Gulfstream Park, where their figures towered over their rivals', but they finished eighth and ninth, earning figures below 90. I wondered if the fast time of the Laurel Futurity had somehow been an aberration, but subsequent events proved that neither horse's exceptional effort had been a fluke. Go and Go returned to the United States the next June and won the Belmont Stakes; Robyn Dancer ran a figure of 118 as a 4-year-old. In the view of Sheet readers, both colts ran poorly in the Breeders' Cup because they bounced.

The concept of the bounce has been accepted by many horseplayers who aren't customers of the Sheets or who aren't speed handicappers at all. Californians, in particular, recognize that the stress of a tough, fast-paced race over their hard tracks will take a toll on a horse if he isn't given enough time to recover. In *Figure Handicapping,* James Quinn wrote that a bounce is most likely to occur after a horse has a hard race, winning or finishing within a length of the leader, in his first start after a layoff of five months or more. If he returns to competition within six weeks of that hard race, Quinn says, a bounce is likely.

After a horse suffers a bounce, he is likely to make a recovery of some sort, and this is the point where the study of patterns becomes an arcane art. In an instructional video aimed at new customers of Thoro-Graph, Brown discusses what he calls some typical patterns and cites the colt Deposit Ticket, who ran numbers of 9¼, 14¼, 9, and 14½. This, says Brown, is the OXOX pattern, where O represents a top and X represents a bounce: "The OXOX pattern is most often seen in 3-year-olds." The filly Wilderness Song ran numbers of 11, 11½, 14¼, 9. Sheet readers consider a pair of similar good numbers to be especially significant, as in the case of the 11 and the 11½. "If one top didn't make a horse bounce, two will," Brown says. Wilderness Song declined, modestly, to a 14½, but this was what Brown describes as "the pause that refreshes." Now, with this bounce out of her system, she was ready to move forward — and she improved to a 9.

The possibility of predicting the future according to patterns of numbers is fascinating and seductive, which is one reason the Sheets have developed such a rabid following. They bear a resemblance to the technical school of stock market analysis, which attempts to predict the future according to patterns on charts of previous price movements, despite the insistence of many experts that the whole premise is hokum. The quest to use numbers to foretell the future also evokes the image of roulette players who earnestly chart the patterns of the numbers that come up on a particular wheel — even though such study is an exercise in futility if the wheel is honest. People who stare hard enough at any sequence of numbers, no matter how random, can always find what they think are patterns and trends. Can past patterns of speed figures really predict the future?

I used to snicker at the idea, telling readers of the Sheets that they might as well study tea leaves. When the *Racing Form* undertook its study of the Beyer Speed Figures, I had the chance to examine some patterns and determine if they had any bearing on a horse's future performance. I asked the computer what happens after a horse has run a sequence of three improving figures or three declining figures on the dirt during a four-month period. If, for example, he earns figures of 70, 65, and 60, is he likely to continue his decline? I expected that such trends would have little or no value as predictors of the future, but I was dead wrong. Of 3,592 horses who had run three declining figures,

1,173 (32 percent) continued their decline.

134 (4 percent) ran the same figure as in the previous start.

2,285 (64 percent) ran an improved figure.

These statistics may be slightly misleading. Although the majority of horses improved their figures following the three-race decline, they nevertheless did not make good bets. Only 10 percent won, and the ROI for the whole group of 3,592 horses was 1.61. (While some went from bad to worse, many of the ones who earned better numbers didn't improve enough to do themselves much good.) But trends in the opposite direction seemed to be significant. Of 4,518 horses who had a sequence of three improving figures (such as 60, 65, 70),

1,125 (25 percent) improved again in their next race.

192 (4 percent) ran the same figure as their previous start.

3,201 (71 percent) declined in the next race.

2,368 (52 percent) declined by 6 points or more.

When I first saw the results of this study, I could not believe that 71 percent of all horses run worse after three ascending figures, and I suspected that the statistics were an aberration or the result of a programming error. So I took a stack of *Racing Forms*, tallied the performances of horses with three improving figures — and got virtually the same results. In the 1992 Breeders' Cup, for example, eight horses came into dirt races with three ascending figures:

Horse	Last 3 figures	Breeders' Cup Figure and Result
Rubiano	108 110 111	102 3rd in Sprint at 2-1
Arrowtown	91 93 103	97 6th in Sprint at 31-1
Eliza	80 84 99	92 Won Juvenile Fillies at 6-5
Supah Gem	69 77 81	80 4th in Juvenile Fillies at 75-1
Fowda	95 98 101	89 9th in Distaff at 8-1
Shared Interest	94 96 109	86 11th in Distaff at 44-1
Saratoga Dew	99 101 106	82 12th in Distaff at 2-1
It'sali'lknownfact	53 77 85	86 2nd in Juvenile Fillies at 47-1

Of these eight, only It'sali'lknownfact ran an improved figure in the Breeders' Cup — and he did so by a single point. The other seven declined, although one of them, Eliza, won anyway, having gone into the Juvenile Fillies with a 14-length edge over her nearest rival. Rubiano and Saratoga Dew both failed as favorites, declining by 9 and 24 points respectively.

If Ragozin had his "bounce" and Brown had his X's and O's, I obviously needed a name for this phenomenon, which I christened the three-and-out pattern. But what is its significance as a handicapping tool? A bettor cannot automatically throw out horses whose figures have been improving: 14 percent of the sample won their next starts, with a respectable ROI. Certainly, young and lightly raced horses shouldn't be viewed negatively if they display the pattern; they are eligible to improve steadily as they mature. However, a bettor should be somewhat wary of older horses with the three-and-out pattern.

For me, the most important lessons to be drawn from the existence of the three-and-out pattern are conceptual ones. It verifies Ragozin's premise — which I had always doubted and often derided — that patterns of past figures may indeed be meaningful. It suggests that many other such patterns may exist. And it confirms Ragozin's central tenet that a peak performance is apt to be followed by a decline.

A similar analysis also supported Quinn's theory about the specific conditions most likely to produce a bounce. The computer looked for horses fitting Quinn's guidelines — those who won or finished within a length of the leader in their first start after a layoff of 150 days or more. The figure that each horse earned in this good race was compared with the figure in his subsequent start. Of the 331 horses,

87 (26 percent) ran an improved figure in the subsequent start.

22 (7 percent) ran exactly the same figure.

222 (67 percent) ran a worse figure.

158 (48 percent) ran a figure that was worse by ten points or more.

This data points to a larger truth. An exceptionally stressful race of any sort — not just a good race after a layoff — may take a toll on a horse and affect what he does afterward. This fact is supported not only by statistics but also by specific poignant cases. My friend Paul Cornman owned a turf specialist named Lucky Mathieu, who had run well in stakes in 1991 but had been dogged by various minor ailments before launching his 1992 campaign. Cornman and trainer John Hertler wanted to give the horse a tuneup to get him ready for the Saratoga season and entered him in a six-furlong race in which they didn't expect him to do much. But Lucky Mathieu was such a competitor that he engaged in a tough battle all the way around the track and won in a photo finish. Afterward, however, he started running a fever, then developed an infection that spread through his body until he couldn't stand up in his stall anymore. He had to be humanely destroyed. "I believe the stress of that race was responsible," Cornman said. "You could say that Lucky Mathieu bounced to his death."

One of the worst humiliations of my journalistic life occurred because of a similar bounce. After the Kentucky Derby of 1986, there was no doubt who had been the best horse in the field: Badger Land had been bumped hard at the start of the race and was dead last after a sixteenth of a mile. Then he rushed into contention, moved six-wide around the final turn, and delivered a heroic effort to finish fifth. Two weeks later I told readers of the *Washington Post:* "Mortgage the house. Hock the family jewels. Crack open the kids' piggy bank. Badger Land is a mortal lock to win the Preakness." But a bedraggled Badger Land, suffering from the effects of that stressful race in Louisville, barely picked up his feet in Baltimore, and, indeed, he was never the same again. Nor, I suppose, were some readers of the *Post.*

In neither of these cases, however, would students of speed figures have necessarily predicted a bounce. Badger Land and Lucky Mathieu had not run exceptional speed figures, which, according to Ragozin's theories, would have foretold a decline. There's nothing wrong with this, of course; patterns of figures can't predict everything. Yet Ragozin and his disciples seem to think they can, and their single-minded focus on numbers alone is what led me to dismiss them as a bunch of kooks and to doubt the validity of their basic ideas. Many of Ragozin's insights into the nature of horse racing are indeed brilliant, but, like his hero Karl Marx, he turned his view of the world into a rigid, almost suffocating dogma. If the concept of bounces and patterns of figures is valid, it is because the numbers reflect realities about the horse's changing physical condition. Yet, to Ragozin, the numbers themselves are the reality. He says adamantly that he barely thinks of horses as flesh-and-blood creatures; a horse is a slim piece of paper with numbers written on it. He tells trainers whether a horse's condition is improving or declining, based on the numbers, and listens condescendingly when the trainers express a firsthand opinion about that animal's health and fitness. Ragozin's narrow view has been adopted by many of the Sheets' clients, who become so mesmerized by the numbers that they ignore the real world. I have never heard a Ragozin disciple say anything like this: "This horse's patterns say he's supposed to bounce, but he looks so good on the track today, so full of energy, that the horse is telling me he's going to run a good race anyway." There are innumerable situations when sound handicapping judgment should properly override an interpretation of speed-figure patterns, as in the case of Polish Numbers.

Polish Numbers — **B. h. 6, by Danzig—Numbered Account, by Buckpasser**

Own.—Phipps O — **Br.—Phipps O (Ky)** — **Tr.—McGaughey Claude III (—)**

Lifetime								
10	4	2	1	1991	2	2	0	0	$36,600
$80,493				1990	6	1	1	1	$16,715
				Turf	2	0	0	1	$2,145
				Wet	2	2	0	0	$36,600

23Sep91- 6Bel fst	6½f	:23	$:45^2$	$1:14^3$	3↑Alw 33000	**104**	2	3	$3^{3½}$	3^2	$3^{2½}$	$1^{¾}$	Perret C		119	1.80	104–10 PolshNumbrs119¾TrckRbl115^{nk}JoyThStudnt113	Driving	5
14Sep91- 5Bel my	6f	:22	$:45^1$	$1:09^3$	3↑Alw 28000	**105**	5	5	$3^{2½}$	1^{hd}	$1^{2½}$	$1^{2½}$	Perret C		117	3.30	92–13 PolshNmbrs117^{2½}ShwnhollrHr109^{5½}Crr'sPlsr115	Driving	7
21Sep90- 9Med fst	1⅛	$:46^2$	$1:09^3$	$1:47^1$	Pegasus H	**80**	4	4	$5^{5½}$	$7^{8½}$	11^{13}	$11^{14¾}$	Perret C	L	113	14.50	84–01 SlvrEndng119^{2}MscPrspctr116½RnwyStrm113	Thru early	12
21Sep90-Grade I																			
1Sep90- 9Mth fm	1 1/16	(T)$:50^1$	$1:13^1$	$1:43^3$	Choice H	**80**	2	4	5^2	4^1	$7^{3¼}$	$7^{6¼}$	Saumell L	L	114	8.10	82–13 Groscar120^{nk} Go Dutch114^{1½} Dawn Quixote117	Tired	10
1Sep90-Grade III																			
15Aug90- 9Mth gd	1	(T)$:46^2$	$1:11^1$	$1:37^3$	3↑Alw 19500	**90**	5	4	$4^{4½}$	2^2	2½	3^{nk}	Saumell L	L	113	3.10	86–14 RylNnj116^{hd}PntBttrOnt116^{nk}PlshNmbrs113	Outfinished	7
16Jly90- 8Mth fst	6f	$:22^1$	$:45^3$	1:11	3↑Alw 17000	**81**	4	4	5^2	3^2	1^1	$1^{2¾}$	Saumell L	L	113	*.70	86–15 PlshNmbrs113^{2¾}SlntPlgrm111^{nk}ChplRvr112	Drew clear	7
17Mar90- 3GP fst	7f	$:22^2$	$:45^2$	$1:25^1$	Alw 19000	**68**	7	5	$5^{2¾}$	$6^{2¾}$	$4^{4¼}$	$4^{7¼}$	Perret C		119	*.40	73–15 Cordob117^{1½}Izvst117^{1¼}BgAl'sCntry122	Lacked response	7
2Feb90- 8GP fst	6f	$:21^4$	:45	$1:11^2$	Alw 19000	**82**	1	7	1^{hd}	2½	2^{hd}	2^{nk}	Perret C		119	*.30	88–17 NiceRuler122^{nk}PolishNumbers119½Mnhwkin122	Gamely	10
29Nov89- 8Aqu fst	7f	$:22^4$	$:45^4$	$1:24^3$	J O Tobin	**86**	6	3	4^1	$5^{1¾}$	$2^{3½}$	2^2	Perret C		117	*.60	77–23 RichrdR.119^{2}PolishNumbers117^{3}SixthSens119	2nd best	9
5Nov89- 7Aqu fst	6f	:22	$:45^1$	$1:10^4$	Md Sp Wt	**92**	7	7	$4^{2½}$	3^2	1½	1^4	Perret C		118	*.80	86–19 PolshNmbrs118^{4}BmboSht118^{nk}FrstndOnly118	Drew off	13

Polish Numbers had been idle for almost a full year before he made his 4-year-old debut at Belmont Park. He vied for the lead and drew away to score a victory in which he earned a Beyer Speed Figure of 105. Then he returned to action only nine days later. He met the Sheets' criteria that he ought to bounce, having just run a career-best figure. He met all of James Quinn's standards for a bounce — a layoff of more than five months, a hard race, a return to competition in less than six weeks. But there was a hole in the bounce theory here: Shug McGaughey. Polish Numbers' trainer, is an Eclipse Award winner, one of the most astute and judicious members of his profession. He always takes time with his horses, and he would certainly not rush a horse into a $33,000 allowance race if he thought the animal wasn't in perfect shape. He knew Polish Numbers better than any theorist of form cycles: The colt ran another good race, earning a figure of 104. If Polish Numbers had been in the hands of an ordinary trainer, a handicapper might reasonably have expected a sub-par performance. But I hesitate to throw out a sharp horse from a good stable on the assumption that I know more about that horse's form cycle than the trainer does.

Here is a horse whom students of form cycles would correctly diagnose as a candidate to bounce:

Big Sur — **B. c. 3(Mar), by Alydar—Laday, by Lyphard** — **Br.—Mabee Mr-Mrs J C (Ky)** — **Tr.—Lukas D Wayne** — **119**

Own.—Lukas-OvrbrkFm-SugrMpleFm

Lifetime 10 3 1 1 $210,930 — 1992 2 1 0 0 $60,000 — 1991 8 2 1 1 $150,930

7Mar92-10OP	fst	1	:46^{3}	1:11	1:36^{3}	Southwest	**111**	1	1	1^{hd}	1^{hd}	1^{1½}	1^{2½}	Guillory D		119	17.40	94-17	Big Sur119^{2½} Pine Bluff122^{hd} Lil E. Tee115	Driving	6
4Jan92-10BM	gd	1	:47^{1}	1:11	1:37^{1}	Cal Juvnle	**47**	3	5	8^{5¼}	10^{13}	10^{17}	10^{21}	Chapman T M	B	118	2.10e	63-18	BigPl114^{1¾}RunRetsinRun118^{1}HmmrMn115	Tough early	10
4Jan92-Grade III																					
2Nov91- 6CD	fst	1$\frac{1}{16}$	:46^{3}	1:12	1:44^{3}	Br Cp Juv	**57**	10	8	7^{5¼}	7^{6¾}	10^{21}	11^{25¾}	McCarron C J	LBb	122	69.00	66-09	Arazi122^{5}Bertrando122^{3½}SnappyLanding122	Tired badly	14
2Nov91-Grade I																					
13Oct91- 8SA	fst	1$\frac{1}{16}$	:45^{4}	1:10^{2}	1:42^{4}	Norfolk	**68**	6	8	9^{13}	9^{8¼}	7^{9}	6^{15¼}	Nakatani C S	B	118	3.00e	74-16	Bertrando118^{9} Zurich118^{¾} Bag118	Jostled start	9
13Oct91-Grade I																					
20Oct91- 8SA	fst	7f	:22^{4}	:45^{3}	1:23^{1}	Sunny Slope	**79**	5	2	3^{½}	4^{2}	3^{1½}	3^{1½}	Nakatani C S	B	122	1.60e	85-13	RichrdOfEnglnd115^{1}Ebonir116^{½}BigSur122	Always close	6
11Sep91- 8Dmr	fst	1	:45	1:10^{2}	1:36^{2}	Del Mar Fut	**61**	10	4	4^{2}	3^{1}	4^{7}	7^{12¼}	McCarron C J	B	120	5.60	72-18	Bertrando114^{3½} Zurich114^{4½} Star Recruit115		10
11Sep91-Grade II; Lugged in badly final 3/8																					
24Aug91- 8Sar	fst	6½f	:21^{3}	:44^{2}	1:17^{3}	Hopeful	**46**	5	5	4^{5½}	4^{8½}	6^{8}	7^{21¼}	Antley C W		122	1.50e	66-14	Salt Lake122^{9} Slew's Ghost122^{hd} CallerI.D.122	Bmpd st	9
24Aug91-Grade I																					
10Aug91- 9Mth	fst	6f	:22	:45^{1}	1:10^{4}	Sapling	**90**	2	6	2^{1½}	2^{hd}	1^{hd}	1^{2}	Migliore R		122	3.20	87-18	BigSur122^{2}NeverWvering122^{3}Dr.Fountinstin122	Driving	8
10Aug91-Grade II																					
28Jly91- 4Sar	fst	6f	:22	:45^{1}	1:11	Md Sp Wt	**80**	8	1	1^{½}	1^{½}	1^{2}	1^{2¼}	Bailey J D		118	2.30	89-13	Big Sur118^{2¼} Tri to Watch118^{hd} Devil OnIce118	Driving	12
14Jly91- 4Bel	gd	5½f	:22^{1}	:45^{2}	1:03^{3}	Md Sp Wt	**77**	1	2	1^{1}	1^{½}	2^{½}	2^{4}	Bailey J D		118	2.80	97-06	West by West118^{4}BigSur118^{3½}SeaBaba118	Second best	8

Erratic as a 2-year-old, dismal in his 3-year-old debut, Big Sur exploded to win Oaklawn Park's Southwest Stakes with a figure of 111 — a sensational number that was 21 points higher than his lifetime best and would have been good enough to win the Kentucky Derby later in the year. When he was favored in his next start, the Jim Beam Stakes at Turfway, students of form cycles might have predicted that he'd "bounce to the moon." And they would have been right. Big Sur finished tenth in the Jim Beam and never came close to a 111 for the rest of the year. But look at the horses who were behind him in the Southwest Stakes:

Lil E. Tee — B. c. 4, by At the Threshold—Eileen's Moment, by For The Moment
Br.—Littman Lawrence I (Pa)
Own.—Partee W Cal — Tr.—Whiting Lynn S (—)

Lifetime 6 3 2 1 $52,306 — 1992 2 1 0 1 $23,200 — 1991 4 2 2 0 $29,106 — Wet 1 0 1 0 $3,912

7Mar92-10OP	fst	1	:46^{3}	1:11	1:36^{3}	Southwest	**106**	4	5	4$1\frac{1}{2}$	4$3\frac{1}{2}$	34	3$2\frac{1}{2}$	Day P		115	2.10	91-17 Big Sur119$2\frac{1}{2}$ Pine Bluff122^{hd} Lil E. Tee115	Steadied 6
9Feb92- 8OP	fst	6f	:21^{4}	:45^{4}	1:10^{1}	Alw 22000	**92**	6	5	5$4\frac{1}{2}$	5$1\frac{1}{2}$	11	1$4\frac{1}{2}$	Day P		116	*.70	88-19 Lil E. Tee116$4\frac{1}{2}$ Rockford114$2\frac{1}{2}$ Mr. Shocker116	Handily 8
12Nov91- 4CD	fst	1	:46	1:12^{2}	1:39	Alw 27660	**86**	7	4	1^{hd}	12	1$1\frac{1}{2}$	13	Day P	LB.	115	*.60	82-22 LilE.T115^{3}Corrntino118^{3}InMyFootstps121	Steady drive 8
1Nov91- 4CD	sly	$1\frac{1}{16}$	:49	1:15	1:48^{4}	Alw 27660	**86**	2	1	12	1$1\frac{1}{2}$	2^{hd}	2^{nk}	Day P	LB	112	*.70	71-29 ChoctwRdg118^{nk}LIE.T112^{7}SsdDncr121	2nd best, gamely 6
6Oct91- 4Crc	fst	7f	:22^{4}	:46	1:24^{2}	Md Sp Wt	**92**	7	3	2^{hd}	2^{hd}	15	11$1\frac{1}{2}$	St Leon G		118	*.70	93-12 LilE.T118$11\frac{1}{2}$KindrgrdnChmp118^{3}LtItBsunny118	Handily 9
28Sep91- 4Crc	fst	6f	:21^{3}	:45^{1}	1:11^{2}	Md Sp Wt	**80**	2	5	43	44	2$3\frac{1}{2}$	2$4\frac{1}{2}$	St Leon G		117	3.70	88-14 ImBigLgur117$4\frac{1}{2}$LilE.T117$3\frac{1}{2}$Bruc'sFolly117	Second best 10

LATEST WORKOUTS ●Feb 10 FG 6f fst 1:13 H — Feb 3 FG 4f fst :49 H — Jan 28 FG 6f fst 1:14^{2} H — Jan 20 FG 5f sly 1:03 B

Pine Bluff — B. c. 4, by Danzig—Rowdy Angel, by Halo
Br.—Loblolly Stable (Ky)
Own.—Loblolly Stable — Tr.—Bohannan Thomas (—)

Lifetime 8 3 1 2 $304,988 — 1992 1 0 1 0 $20,000 — 1991 7 3 0 2 $284,988

7Mar92-10OP	fst	1	:46^{3}	1:11	1:36^{3}	Southwest	**106**	3	3	3$\frac{1}{2}$	2^{hd}	2$1\frac{1}{2}$	2$2\frac{1}{2}$	Perret C		122	*1.00	91-17 Big Sur119$2\frac{1}{2}$ PineBluff122^{hd}LilE.Tee115	Bid, weakened 6
7Dec91- 8Aqu 7Dec91-Grade III	fst	$1\frac{1}{16}$ ⊡	:47^{1}	1:12	1:46	Nashua	**98**	6	3	21	21	1$\frac{1}{2}$	1$2\frac{1}{2}$	Perret C		124	*1.10	78-26 PineBluff124$2\frac{1}{2}$Spekerphone114^{2}BestDcortd114	Driving 11
16Nov91- 8Aqu 16Nov91-Grade II	fst	$1\frac{1}{8}$	:47^{2}	1:12^{1}	1:50^{4}	Remsen	**93**	1	2	2$1\frac{1}{2}$	2$\frac{1}{2}$	12	1$4\frac{3}{4}$	Perret C		113	5.20	82-23 Pine Bluff113$4\frac{3}{4}$ Offbeat113$1\frac{1}{4}$ Cheap Shades122	Driving 8
2Nov91- 6CD 2Nov91-Grade I	fst	$1\frac{1}{16}$	:46^{3}	1:12	1:44^{3}	Br Cp Juv	**78**	3	7	33	44	6^{12}	71$3\frac{1}{2}$	Perret C	B	122	27.50	78-09 Arazi122^{5}Bertrndo122$3\frac{1}{2}$SnppyLnding122	Tight 1st turn 14
12Oct91- 8Bel 12Oct91-Grade I	fst	1	:45	1:10^{2}	1:36^{3}	Champagne	**74**	4	7	7$3\frac{1}{4}$	32	5$7\frac{3}{4}$	3^{11}	Perret C		122	9.10	76-16 TrtWtch122$7\frac{1}{2}$SnppyLndng122$3\frac{1}{2}$PnBlff122	Bobbled brk 15
15Sep91- 8Bel 15Sep91-Grade I	fst	7f	:21^{4}	:44	1:23^{4}	Futurity	**78**	1	7	7$6\frac{3}{4}$	54	31	31	Perret C		122	5.40	84-13 Agincourt122^{1} Tri toWatch122^{no}PineBluff122	Bid, hung 7

Anyone using the Beyer Speed Figures as a point of reference would have concluded that Lil E. Tee was a prime candidate for a bounce, too. After earning figures in a fairly narrow range up to that point, he had improved by 14 points. Yet Lil E. Tee won the Jim Beam Stakes in his next start, trouncing Big Sur, and went on to capture the Kentucky Derby. Pine Bluff might have been seen as a potential bounce candidate, too. He had had a hard race in the Southwest after a three-month layoff, and he had earned a career-best figure. But he proceeded to run a 105 in his next start, the Rebel Stakes, and a 106 in the Arkansas Derby. Why did Big Sur bounce while the others didn't? The answer explains a large number of supposed bounces.

On the day of the Southwest Stakes, the Oaklawn racing strip gave an apparent advantage to horses on the rail. Big Sur not only broke from post position 1 and stayed inside all the way, but he found himself in a field without much front-running speed. He was able to get the lead in a very slow pace — a quarter mile in 23 seconds, a half mile in :46⅗. (Earlier in the day, a $25,000 claiming race for 3-year-olds went in fractions of :22⅗ and :46⅕.) Big Sur had everything in his favor and was therefore able to run a big race. When he subsequently raced under conditions that were normal or adverse, he ran worse — not unexpectedly. Conversely, Pine Bluff and Lil E. Tee had earned their figures in the Southwest Stakes honestly, and they proceeded to repeat those good performances, undeterred by any bouncing.

These horses suggest a danger in relying solely on figures alone as an indicator of form cycles — a danger to which Sheet readers seem especially susceptible because they are looking at numbers out of the context of a horse's past performances. Neither the Beyer Speed Figures nor the Sheets take into account pace, biases, or any of the countless other factors that might cause a horse to run well or poorly, and ignoring such vital information will distort any effort to understand a horse's form. Brown's instructional video, *Introduction to Thoro-Graph Handicapping*, demonstrates both the seductiveness and the pitfalls of trying to assess form cycles strictly by the numbers.

Having recognized the existence of the three-and-out pattern, I assume that there may be many other patterns that are similarly potent, and students of the Sheets are decades ahead of me in the search for such form cycles. Any patterns relevant to their figures would presumably be just as relevant to the Beyer Speed Figures, so I watched Brown's presentation in an effort to learn more. I thought his discussion of horses' patterns was very persuasive — until I looked at those horses' records in the *Daily Racing Form*.

Deposit Ticket
Thoro-Graph figures: 9, 14$\frac{1}{4}$, 9, 14$\frac{1}{2}$.
Beyer figures: 107, 90, 100, 81.

This was the pattern that Brown described as "OXOX," a succession of peak efforts followed by bounces. But when the speedy sprinter suffered his first bounce, he was entered at a mile — a distance at which he had failed dismally in his only previous attempt. Did he really bounce because his previous performance was too fast or was he simply entered at the wrong distance?

Wilderness Song
Thoro-Graph: 14$\frac{1}{4}$, 11, 11$\frac{1}{2}$, 14$\frac{1}{4}$, 9.
Beyer: 86, 95, 96, 84, 96.

According to Brown, the filly had bounced mildly after a pair of tops, but the bounce enabled her to move forward to a new peak performance. But in the races where she had paired those good figures, Wilderness Song had taken a clear lead and set a moderate pace. In her poor performance, she was head-and-head for the lead, going a half mile in $45\frac{4}{5}$ seconds in a duel with a fast male rival, possibly serving as a sacrificial lamb for her stablemate, Dance Smartly, who was shooting for the second leg of the Canadian Triple Crown. Was this a pattern or were all of Wilderness Song's figures dictated by circumstances?

Take Me Out
Thoro-Graph: $9\frac{3}{4}$, $9\frac{3}{4}$, 12, $6\frac{3}{4}$.
Beyer: 98, 103, 90, 107.

This, said Brown, is another case of a paired top followed by a bounce, followed by a new high. However, Take Me Out ran his poor race on a day when the inside part of the track at Belmont Park was highly disadvantageous, and he was trapped on the rail in a head-and-head duel for the lead. Was he living out his foreordained pattern or was he accidentally affected by conditions on that day?

Most bettors — not only students of the Sheets — will sometimes assume that they can easily predict a horse's performance because his figures are steadily getting better or worse. But even seemingly obvious evidence can be clouded by circumstances affecting the running of his past races.

No Dispute — Gr. c. 2(Mar), by Known Fact—Grey Doreen, by Grey Dawn II

$11,500 Br.—Izaacs Harry Z (Ky)

Own.—Lancaster Carlyle J — Tr.—Capuano Dale (55 10 8 8 .18) — **114**

Lifetime 8 1 0 1 $10,410 — 1992 8 1 0 1 $10,410 — Turf 1 0 0 0 — Wet 2 0 0 0 $930

20Oct92- 4Lrl	fst	6½f	:22^3	:46^4	1:18^2	Clm 25000	46	4	5	5$^{4\frac{1}{2}}$	5^5	5^7	5$^{7\frac{1}{4}}$	Luzzi M J	Lb 114	4.80	78–14	HolmForGlry109^{no}JstcTrmphs114$^{5\frac{1}{2}}$ALghngDvl114	Wide	7
9Oct92- 4Lrl	my	6f	:22^4	:47	1:12	Clm 25000	48	8	8	6$^{6\frac{1}{2}}$	6^8	7$^{9\frac{1}{4}}$	5$^{11\frac{1}{4}}$	Castillo F^5	Lb 109	5.70	70–22	Stelios Art114$^{6\frac{1}{2}}$ Silver Key114$^{2\frac{1}{4}}$ Granlund114	Outrun	8
27Sep92- 8Pim	sly	6f	:22^4	:46	1:12^3	Alw 17100	56	3	8	8$^{9\frac{3}{4}}$	6^{13}	6^{15}	5^8	Ladner C J III	Lb 114	10.00	74–18	DpprDoc114$^{2\frac{3}{4}}$DownHmDctr114^{nk}JrgfMxc114	No factor	8
15Sep92- 6Pim	fst	6f	:23	:46^2	1:12	Alw 16800	58	2	7	7$^{9\frac{1}{2}}$	6^{11}	6^9	5^5	Castillo F^5	Lb 109	13.90	80–15	DprtngCld114^{1}DwnHmDctr114$^{1\frac{1}{2}}$DpprDc114	Broke in air	7
5Sep92- 8Atl	gd	5½f ⓣ	:22^2	:47^3	1:07	World's Play	–0	3	9	10^{14}	10^{18}	10^{24}	10^{33}	Prado E S	Lb 115	3.80	41–32	Ingroove117^{1}AssetImprssion114^{5}HitMnHrry117	Trailed	10
7Aug92- 6Lrl	fst	6f	:22^2	:46^3	1:12^2	Alw 16800	60	1	4	2$^{\frac{1}{2}}$	3$^{2\frac{1}{2}}$	4$^{3\frac{1}{2}}$	3$^{5\frac{1}{4}}$	Rocco J	b 114	10.10	74–22	StormFlight114^{nk}VeiledVin114^{5}NoDisput114	Weakened	7
3Jly92- 2Lrl	fst	5½f	:22^2	:46^1	1:05^2	Md 25000	52	4	6	3^2	3^2	2^2	1no	Prado E S	b 120	11.70	92–12	No Dispute120^{no} Stelios Art120$^{1\frac{1}{2}}$ Cullen120	Driving	9
25Jun92- 5Pim	fst	5f	:22^2	:46^1	:58^2	Md Sp Wt	11	2	11	11^{13}	11^{16}	11^{23}	12^{19}	Prado E S	120	16.20	77–13	GlRoyle120$^{\frac{1}{2}}$DownHomeDoctor120$^{6\frac{1}{2}}$Cchumb120	Outrun	12

LATEST WORKOUTS Nov 23 Lrl 4f gd :50 B — Nov 17 Lrl 5f fst 1:02 B — Nov 3 Lrl 3f my :38 B

Here is the most elementary of patterns, one that requires no instructional video to understand: a horse on the downgrade. No Dispute's figures had declined steadily from race to race, from 58

to 56 to 48. Based on the three-race decline pattern, a handicapper might have looked for an improvement in his next start, but
No Dispute declined again, to a 46. Perhaps some students of
patterns would now again anticipate an improvement; other handicappers might think the trend suggests that the horse is suffering
a serious physical decline — one seemingly confirmed by the assessment of his trainer, who has lowered him from stakes company
to allowance company to $25,000 claiming races and now to
$11,500. But all of these analyses miss the point. On September
15 No Dispute broke in the air, came out of the gate four lengths
behind the field, and never had a chance. On September 27, he
raced on a sloppy track at Pimlico, where horses fighting for the
lead won eight of ten races; with his stretch-running style, he
didn't have a chance. On both October 9 and 20 he found himself
on extremely biased, rail-favoring tracks at Laurel, and he was
five-wide in one race, four-wide in another. His form was not
declining at all; he had been a victim of circumstances. In his next
start, he proceeded to blow away his overmatched $11,500 rivals,
earning a figure of 66. An analysis of the patterns of his previous
figures might have been a fascinating and seductive exercise, but
it had been utterly irrelevant.

As an ardent champion of speed figures, I would love to be able
to claim that they do more than tell how fast a horse has run in
the past, and that they can magically predict what he will do in his
next race. But fluctuations in horses' form and figures are caused
more by the way races are run than by some kind of determinism
springing from their past figures. It is unrealistic to try to judge
horses' form cycles and foretell the future by looking only at their
figures — at a fraction of the evidence that indicates whether they
ran well or poorly in their recent races. Any attempt to understand
horses' past performances and form cycles must take into account
the way their previous races were run. Len Ragozin's early perception is right: The key question in handicapping is not necessarily
"Who has the best numbers?" And he is probably right that there
are cases where a handicapper must ask who has the best patterns.
But an even more important question is this: Under what circumstances did the horses earn those numbers?

THREE

How Was the Figure Earned?

As computers have become more powerful and human knowledge has increased in the last third of the twentieth century, experts in many fields have sought to use mathematics to solve the great mysteries that have baffled mankind. Meteorologists employ computers to develop mathematical models that attempt to predict worldwide weather patterns. Economists try to construct models that can explain and predict anything from the rate of growth in the Third World to the price of bread at a mom-and-pop store. Physicists seek to understand the very nature of the universe. And horse-race handicappers seek, too, to use mathematics to understand their little corner of the universe. Devotees of the Sheets believe their numbers express not only a horse's speed but his total capabilities, and that patterns of those numbers can predict the cycles of a horse's form. Pace-oriented handicappers are using complicated abstract numbers, based on a horse's velocity at different stages of a race, as the ultimate measurement of a horse's performance. I, too, had once believed that my speed figures, alone, fully defined a horse's ability. But my hope of reducing the whole game to a system of numbers was exploded in a testing ground of handicapping theory called the Triple Crown.

Although the Kentucky Derby, Preakness, and Belmont Stakes are not typical races by any means, they offer a handicapper the rare opportunity to study a race knowing every bit of important information about every horse. Whenever a bettor's opinion is proved wrong in an ordinary race, he may suspect that his loss is due not to a fundamental defect in his handicapping but to one of the many factors in horse racing that are largely unknowable. Was a horse suffering from physical problems that might have hurt his performance? Did a trainer fail to prepare a horse for a maximum effort because he was aiming at some future goal? Was, perhaps, some larceny involved? Such nagging questions accompany almost every losing bet, but they don't apply in the Triple Crown, as racing fans are deluged with more information about the horses than they could ever use.

As a journalist, I follow the development of the country's top 3-year-olds throughout the winter, and in the spring I tromp through the stable areas at Churchill Downs, Pimlico, and Belmont Park, interviewing their trainers, owners, and jockeys. If a contender has a physical problem, I know it. So if I am wrong about a Triple Crown race, I can't rationalize my mistake. And when I was relying exclusively on my speed figures, I was wrong — frequently. My public record in handicapping the Kentucky Derby was humiliatingly bad; readers who liked a particular 3-year-old would sometimes write and plead with me not to pick their horse and thus apply the Beyer kiss of death. And if I was often wrong about the Derby, I was frequently bewildered by the contrast between it and the Preakness. Here were two races, two weeks apart, run at virtually the same distance and often with virtually the same cast of characters. Yet their results could be radically different. The majority of Derby winners lost the Preakness, even though, in most cases, they had the top speed figure. Horses trounced in the Derby often won the Preakness. I couldn't ignore these apparent inconsistencies, and as I gradually came to understand them, they not only shed light on the Triple Crown but also revealed some of the fundamental truths of handicapping.

In 1974 I learned an expensive lesson that now seems so obvious that I am embarrassed to recall it. On the Churchill Downs card that featured the centennial Kentucky Derby was an allowance race, the Twin Spires Purse, for the not-ready-for-prime-time 3-year-olds. A colt named Silver Florin won it, running 1$\frac{1}{16}$ miles in 1:43$\frac{2}{5}$; later that afternoon, Cannonade required 2:04 to cover a mile and one quarter in the Derby. On anybody's speed rating chart, Silver Florin had run the faster race. (On mine, he was four points superior.) True to my belief in the figures, I picked him in print to win the Preakness and bet him enthusiastically. Only after he finished tenth did I realize that there must have been a difference between the way he had earned his figure and the way the Derby runners had earned theirs. Silver Florin had encountered barely a straw in his path as he dominated the Twin Spires Purse, while virtually everybody in that 23-horse Derby cavalry charge had been jostled or bumped or forced wide. Little Current had been stopped cold as he was trying to accelerate, and he improved his figure by nearly 30 points when he won the Preakness. Obviously, the way those races at Churchill Downs unfolded had greatly affected the horses' performances — and their speed figures. Welcome to Handicapping 101.

I still believed, however, that if a horse encountered no physical obstructions he should be able to run his normal figure regardless of the early pace of the race. If, for example, a sprinter was capable of running six furlongs in 1:10, he ought to be able to do it whether the first half mile of the race was run in :44 or :46. The 1976 Triple Crown series, dominated by the brilliant speedsters Bold Forbes and Honest Pleasure, was Handicapping 102. When Honest Pleasure's jockey, Braulio Baeza, chose not to contest his rival for the early lead in the Derby, Bold Forbes opened a five-length advantage, set a fast pace, and held on to win by a length. Smarting from the defeat, trainer LeRoy Jolley vowed that he wasn't going to lose the Preakness in the same passive way, and he instructed his rider to fight for the lead at Pimlico. Following orders, Baeza forced a pace of 1:09 for six furlongs that proved suicidal for both colts. Elocutionist, who had been soundly beaten at Churchill Downs, rallied past the tired pacesetters to win the Preakness, with Bold

Forbes a badly beaten third. Honest Pleasure now went to the sidelines, leaving Bold Forbes as the lone speed horse in the Belmont Stakes, where Angel Cordero Jr. nursed him to a wire-to-wire victory. Bold Forbes's performances and wildly fluctuating speed figures in the Triple Crown series had been determined almost solely by pace.

By 1984, when Swale scored a much-acclaimed victory in the Kentucky Derby, I was able to recognize that he had benefited greatly by controlling a slow pace. He had enjoyed optimal racing conditions while many of his rivals had experienced difficult trips in the twenty-horse field — notably Gate Dancer, who had broken poorly from post 20 and raced wide all the way. I detested Swale and disparaged him in print before the Preakness; indeed, he was trounced in the second leg of the Triple Crown. But this time he was the victim of all the bad racing luck. On a Pimlico track whose rail-favoring bias had become legendary and which on this day was stronger than ever, Swale was parked four-wide most of the way and wound up finishing seventh, while Gate Dancer won with a perfect ground-saving trip. In fact, the first three finishers were the three horses who did most of their running on the rail. But when this group of horses went to the Belmont Stakes, the pen-dulum of racing luck seemed likely to swing the other way. Swale was now the lone speed horse against ten runners who came from off the pace; he was going to control this race more easily than he had controlled the Derby. Gate Dancer wasn't going to get lucky here. Reviewing the Preakness films, I saw that Swale was not the only horse who had been hindered by the Pimlico bias. Pine Circle had also been forced to race wide and hadn't run too badly under the circumstances, but he was going to be an extreme longshot in the Belmont Stakes.

As the race approached, I worked myself into a lather of enthu-siasm for the possibilities of the Swale–Pine Circle exacta, and when I rode to the track with the New York Racing Association's Harvey Pack that morning, I bubbled over, "You know, I could win $100,000 today!" I didn't — not quite — but when Swale led all the way and Pine Circle rallied to complete a $125.80 exacta, I enjoyed the most profitable day of my gambling life to that time, atoning for all of my previous debacles in the Triple Crown. A lesson accompanied the windfall. In the three Triple Crown races, Swale had earned figures of 117, 106, and 114. Gate Dancer's numbers had been 108, 118, and 102. Yet all the evidence suggested that the two colts — both managed by Hall of Fame trainers — had gone through the campaign in unvarying physical condition. The horses hadn't changed; the races had been run differently, accounting for the sharp variations in the horses' performances and their speed figures.

This fact may seem so obvious that belaboring the point is unnecessary. Yet some of the most sophisticated bettors in America employ methods which do not acknowledge that important events in the running of a race will affect horses' numbers. The calculations in the Sheets do not take pace or track biases into account. The calculations of the new high-tech pace handicappers, whom we will meet in later chapters, do not consider biases, nor do they recognize that head-and-head pressure is an important element of pace. It is virtually impossible to quantify track biases or to quantify the fact that Bold Forbes could run better when Honest Pleasure wasn't looking him in the eye, and the mathematicians of handicapping would prefer to disregard those factors that don't fit neatly into their system of numbers.

These widespread efforts to quantify the racing universe are a relatively new development. There were no numerical ratings in Tom Ainslie's *The Compleat Horseplayer,* the book that introduced many members of my generation to serious handicapping. Nor were there many numbers in the works of Robert Saunders Dowst, the most influential author of the 1930s and 1940s. Undoubtedly, it was the popularity and effectiveness of speed handicapping and speed figures which prompted many students of the game to seek better and better ratings systems, but they were often misguided. Speed figures are a way of expressing a relatively simple fact: how fast a horse ran, taking into account the condition of the track. Numbers are used only because it is more convenient to say that a horse earned an 85 than to say he ran six furlongs in 1:11 over a track three-fifths of a second fast. But trying to develop systems that include many elements — which try to establish mathematical relationships between complex factors such as final time, pace, weight, and ground loss on turns — is dauntingly difficult. This is essentially what the meteorologists and the economists are trying to do with their mathematical models, and it might be noted that neither weathermen nor economic forecasters have become infallible.

In one of the most thoughtful and literate books on horse racing, *Handicapping Speed,* an archaeologist named Charles Carroll reflected on the nature of recent intellectual inquiries into the game: "Horse race handicapping turned from an art to a science, along with such unrelated, formerly academic arts as sociology and anthropology. It was the spirit of the times. . . . Handicappers borrowed from science, and scientists became handicappers. All of it was based on the clear vision that the universe was orderly and that the laws of Newton and thermodynamics hold, whether you are looking at wrinkles in a distant galaxy or thoroughbreds running out of gas." But, Carroll wrote, in virtually every field of intellectual endeavor, these high-powered attempts to use mathematics to explain the universe eventually plunged into an abyss. It was an MIT meteorologist, Edward Lorenz, who contemplated these failed efforts and launched a whole new area of scientific inquiry, one that bore some fancy academic names but dealt basically with the nature of chaos. "It became one of the hallmarks of a revolution in science," Carroll wrote, that "chaos is as much a part of reality as order. . . . Scientists in many fields have accepted two new fundamentals: You can't know all the parameters, and the ones you do know probably aren't connected in any linear fashion." To find an example of a universe that doesn't conform to neat mathematical descriptions, Carroll said, you don't have to look at the relationship between the earth and the atmosphere. "You could look at the steam rising from a cup of tea. Or you could look at a horse race."

Handicappers who are trying to quantify everything in the sport, or are ignoring the things they can't neatly quantify, are engaged in a futile exercise. Horse racing is an exceptionally complex game, and anyone who plays it must recognize and accept that complexity. For those of us who are speed handicappers, this means we must understand that a horse's figure will be influenced by an infinite variety of events that can occur during a race and that we won't have the comfort of translating all those events into a number that we can relate to the speed figure. Instead, we must look at the circumstances of a race and ask, generally, how did the horse earn his figure? Did the horse have favorable circumstances that permitted him to run a superior figure? Did he encounter adversity which depressed his number? Is his speed figure a fair reflection of his ability?

Fortunately, this task is more manageable than it sounds when we look at the seemingly chaotic nature of horse races. The factors that most affect horses' performances fall into three broad categories: pace, track biases, and trips. The last category includes trouble in a race and ground loss on the turns. If we understand these factors, we will understand how horses earn their speed figures, making those numbers even more potent as a handicapping tool.

PACE

The complexity of horse racing foils not only mathematicians but also the handicappers who try to reduce the game to rules and dictums. Yet there is one aspect of racing and speed handicapping for which a dogmatic statement is appropriate: When a horse is able to take a clear early lead, running at a moderate or slow pace, he will almost always earn the best speed figure of which he is capable.

This makes sense logically. A front-runner will have nobody in his path; he can't get into trouble. Moreover, he will usually race near the rail; he won't lose any ground by going wide. And, in contrast to a horse in a head-and-head duel who must expend energy to keep his rival from pulling away, a solitary front-runner can use his energy in the most efficient way, as he and his jockey choose.

The optimal way for a horse to run is to get clear, to set a pace

well within his capacity, to conserve energy and release it in the
final stages of a race. The biggest figures are usually earned this
way. Groovy recorded the highest back-to-back figures we have
ever assigned a horse when he ran 131 and 134 in his first two
starts of 1987, the Roseben and True North Handicaps at Belmont
Park. There were no sprinters in New York who could match
Groovy's speed, and the brilliant colt was able to get an unchallenged lead in both those races. In the True North, against only
three rivals, he got clear of the field by running a quarter mile in
22 seconds. Claiming horses can run that fast, and :22 for Groovy
was the equivalent of a canter in Central Park. He reached the
half mile in :44 flat, then sped an exceptional final quarter to draw
away from his rivals and set Belmont's six-furlong track record of
1:07⅘. He won with such apparent ease that many observers
might have been tempted to think that he would have gone faster
if he had been pressed. But that is rarely the case for "easy"
winners — and it was not for Groovy. In the Breeders' Cup Sprint
the year before, he had been outrun for the lead by rivals who set
fractions of :21⅕ and :43⅗, and he delivered a poor performance.
In the 1987 Sprint, Very Subtle sped a quarter in :21⅕ to get in
front of him, and Groovy could not muster a big figure under
those circumstances; he was soundly beaten.

At classic distances, too, horses run their best when they can get
to the lead, control a moderate pace, and save their energy for the
stretch. Affirmed earned his biggest figure, a 128, with his front-
running victory over Spectacular Bid in the 1979 Jockey Club Gold
Cup at Belmont Park. His fractions for the quarters of that 1½-
mile race were :25, :24, :24⅕, :24, :25⅕, and :25. General Assem-
bly soared into the stratosphere of the 130s when he won the 1979
Travers Stakes at Saratoga. He, too, was loose on the lead, setting
efficient fractions: :23⅗, :24, :23⅗, :24⅗, :24⅕.

If the best and classiest thoroughbreds are so affected by early
pressure or the lack thereof, then this factor ought to apply even
more forcefully to the ordinary animals who populate everyday
races. And, of course, it does. The first dependable winning angle
I ever discovered was one that enabled me to win consistently on

the cheapest races at Charles Town: Find a horse who showed speed in his last start but couldn't get the lead; if he appears likely to get the lead today, bet him. In every issue of the *Racing Form*, dozens of horses will illustrate the benefits of being the front-runner, and their speed figures further underscore the value of a clear early lead.

Chumming Galla — B. f. 3(May), by Chumming—Shofoose, by Silent Doon
$2,500 Br.—Cohn Seymour (NY)
Own.—Espaillat Nelson S — Tr.—Correa Alex (56 4 2 4 .07) — 118

Lifetime						
13 2 1 2	1992	13	2	1	2	$7,442
$7,442	1991	0	M	0	0	
	Wet	2	0	0	1	$526

28Oct92- 7Del	fst	1^{70}	:48	1:14	1:46^{1}	3↑ⒻClm 4000	46	1	1	1^{2}	1^{5}	1^{7}	1^{4}	Dentici A	Lb	113	16.80	71-25	ChummingGll113^{4}Luren'sSecret116^{2}Coolkrn116	Driving	12
19Oct92- 3Del	fst	1	:47^{4}	1:14^{2}	1:42^{3}	3↑ⒻClm 4000	25	3	1	2½	3^{5}	6^{9}	3^{12}¼	Dentici A	Lb	113	14.50	57-29	SpicyTale116^{2}½Ephesos115^{9}¾ChummingGll113	Held 3rd	10
16Sep92- 4Del	fst	1 1/16	:47^{2}	1:14^{1}	1:50	3↑ⒻClm 4000	16	1	3	3^{8}	2^{4}	7^{9}	7^{13}	Petersen J L	Lb	116	*3.00	49-27	NuticlVenture122¾HowYouGo113¾Lunistic116	Bore out	11
7Sep92- 7Del	my	1^{70}	:47^{2}	1:14^{2}	1:47^{3}	3↑ⒻClm 4000	33	4	3	2½	2^{3}	3^{6}½	3^{4}½	Petersen J L	Lb	116	16.10	59-42	AsmDstnctn110^{4}WndrflRddl108½ChmmngGll116	Faded	10
26Aug92- 9Atl	sly	1 1/16	:48^{3}	1:15	1:50	3↑ⒻClm 5000	18	5	4	4^{3}½	6^{8}	6^{12}	6^{14}¾	Kamada E J	Lb	115	5.50	45-34	SmnthDncer113^{1}½PinkPirouett110^{hd}BlltBilli117	No rally	9
19Aug92- 1Atl	fst	1 1/16	:49^{4}	1:15^{3}	1:48^{4}	3↑ⒻMd 7000	49	6	1	1^{1}	1^{6}	1^{12}	1^{20}¼	Kamada E J	Lb	111	8.80	66-34	ChmnGll111^{20}¼[D]VcsPrl110^{4}ChpnFln122	Wide, rdn out	6
7Aug92- 4Atl	fst	1 1/16	:48^{3}	1:15^{3}	1:50^{4}	3↑ⒻMd 7000	8	10	5	3^{1}½	4^{2}¼	7^{14}	7^{17}¼	Kamada E J	b	112	10.00	39-33	NeedleLittleGold114^{2}¼Zacjck122½Vicki'sPerl106	Outrun	12
30Jly92- 5Atl	fst	1 1/16	:48	1:14^{3}	1:50^{4}	3↑ⒻMd 7000	19	7	3	3^{4}½	2^{2}½	1^{hd}	2^{1}¼	Kamada E J	b	110	12.40	55-27	HlthLd122^{1}¼ChmmngGll110^{nk}LsLrgStp105	Outfinished	7

Chumming Galla is a cheap claimer without much talent, but twice in her career she found herself in races where she was able to get loose on the lead without much exertion — once in a six-horse field at Atlantic City and once when she broke from the rail against a moderate field at Delaware Park. Both times she ran away to easy victories, earning figures of 46 and 49. The best number she ever recorded without the early lead was a 33.

Crafty Gus — Ch. g. 5, by Crafty Prospector—Honey Witch, by Honey Jay
$16,000 Br.—Petrucione Joseph (Fla)
Own.—Bailey Kathleen E — Tr.—Bailey George A (32 5 6 2 .16) — 116

Lifetime						
41 13 5 0	1992	27	10	5	0	$35,087
$64,319	1991	12	1	0	0	$2,232
	Turf	1	0	0	0	$92
	Wet	10	4	1	0	$12,354

7Nov92- 8Suf	gd	1	:47^{3}	1:13^{1}	1:39^{4}	3↑Alw 5000s	81	6	1	1^{3}	1^{1}½	1½	2^{2}½	Caraballo J C	LBb	119	4.00	93-14	AnothrStryn119^{2}½CrftyGs119¾ChrFrSnny119	No match	8
12Oct92- 3Suf	my	1^{70}	:46^{4}	1:12^{4}	1:44^{2}	3↑Clm 6250	81	2	1	1^{1}	1^{2}	1^{4}	1^{9}¾	Caraballo J C	LBb	116	*2.30	91-17	CrftyGus116^{9}¾Hrbourfront114^{hd}Mtt'sSchtck114	Driving	9
5Oct92-11Suf	fst	1 1/16	:46^{4}	1:12^{1}	1:45^{3}	3↑Clm 4000	81	11	1	1^{3}	1^{4}	1^{5}	1^{7}½	Caraballo J C	LBb	116	4.10	94-14	CrftyGus116^{7}½DownBoy116^{1}¼Rex'sCourt117	Ridden out	12
23Sep92- 6Rkm	my	1 1/16	:49^{1}	1:14^{3}	1:49^{3}	3↑Clm 5000	54	2	2	1½	4^{7}	5^{12}	6^{16}½	Vargas J L	LBb	116	4.20	54-40	LnchtmPowr119^{2}¼VgorosRply116^{2}¼DsrtDvl116	stopped	8
13Sep92- 4Rkm	fst	1 1/16	:47	1:12	1:46^{2}	3↑Clm 5000	70	7	1	1^{3}	1^{2}	1^{2}½	2^{1}½	Caraballo J C	LBb	116	2.20	85-14	LnchtmPowr116^{1}½CrftyGs116^{hd}RsFool116	Couldn't last	7
7Sep92- 9Rkm	fm	1	Ⓣ:47^{4}	1:13^{4}	1:40^{2}	3↑Alw 9200	39	8	1	3½	8^{13}	9^{18}	9^{21}½	Caraballo J C	Bb	118	18.80	62-23	HppySlew116½Pm'sFllow114^{2}½LndingCourt116	Stopped	10
2Sep92-11Rkm	fst	1 1/16	:47^{1}	1:12^{3}	1:47^{1}	3↑Clm 3750	81	8	1	1^{3}	1^{3}½	1^{4}	1^{5}	Caraballo J C	LBb	117	21.30	83-30	CrftyGus117^{5}LunchtimePower119^{1}DownBoy116	Driving	10
26Aug92-12Rkm	fst	1 1/16	:46^{3}	1:12^{2}	1:47^{2}	3↑Clm 5000	49	7	2	2^{hd}	3^{5}½	11^{20}	11^{18}¾	Caraballo J C	LB	117	11.40	63-21	Scrtch'sBrothr116^{1}¾Hlo'sSplndor116^{3}¾RsFl116	Stopped	12

Crafty Gus is the quintessential one-dimensional front-runner. He has abundant speed, which has enabled him to win many races in a productive career, but if any rival so much as breathes on him, he's dead. On a muddy track at Rockingham on September 23, Crafty Gus was pressed for the lead and wound up losing a $5,000 claiming race by 16½ lengths. On a muddy track at Suffolk Downs on October 12, he got clear by a length and drew away to win a $6,250 claimer by nearly ten lengths. His loose-on-the-lead figures in these past performances are 81, 81, 81, 70, and 81. His figures after dueling for the lead are 54, 39, and 49.

Crafty Gus exemplifies the difficulty of trying to express this aspect of racing according to a formula that says a clear lead is worth X points. While some horses may show a neat, reasonably definable improvement in races where they get loose, the figures of a pure front-runner will often gyrate wildly because of the effects of pace. It is hard to measure a horse's competitive spirit with mathematical precision. Nevertheless, handicappers using speed figures should always look with a measure of skepticism on any figure that a horse earned while loose on the lead. Unless he gets an early advantage again, he is unlikely to run as well.

If an easy lead helps front-runners and a contentious early pace hurts them, it stands to reason that the horses behind the leaders are going to be affected in some way, too. A horse may struggle if he is chasing a solitary front-runner; he may benefit if he is sitting behind two leaders engaged in a suicidal duel. But it is not always possible to discern, from his past-performance lines, just how a horse ran his previous race. If the past performances show that a horse's position after a quarter mile was 4^4, he might have been chasing a front-runner who was loose on the lead, or he might have been sitting behind three rivals who were battling for the early advantage. The distinction is crucial. Therefore it is essential for even a mildly serious handicapper to keep a set of result charts for the tracks he follows. The chart can sometimes paint a picture of a race that is very different from the past performances, as in the case of a colt in the 1992 Laurel Futurity:

Lord of the Bay	Ch. c. 2(Jan), by Lord Avie—Lituya Bay, by Empery		Lifetime	1992	5	3	0	0	$43,654
	Br.—Four Horsemens Ranch (Fla)		5 3 0 0						
Own.—Port Sidney L Trust	Tr.—Salzman J Edwin Jr (12 1 2 1 .08)	**122**	$43,654	Turf	2	1	0	0	$24,454
2Oct92- 8Med fm 1 ⊤:464 1:112 1:37	World Appeal	74 14 2 11 11½ 13½ 12¾ Wilson R	L 117	31.00	85–10 LordofthBy1172¾IrshHrbor115noMschvsMsc115 Driving 14
13Sep92-11Pim fm 1 ⊤:47 1:114 1:38	Vanland'm	62 3 8 78 89½ 613 415¼ Chavez S N	L 110	18.90	63–27 StormFlight1106SecretOdds111²¼Qizilbsh115 No threat 11
29Jly92- 8Mth fst 5½f :224 :464 1:061	Alw 16500	60 4 2 1½ 1hd 1½ 12 Chavez S N	L 117	*.80e	83–19 LordoftheBy117²ProofsEcho117⁴½VeiledVin113 Driving 8
5Jly92- 6Lrl fst 5½f :222 :463 1:061	Md Sp Wt	47 3 4 3² 32½ 4² 1nk Chavez S N	L 120	12.80	88–13 LordofthBy120nkBubbC120½PointTkr115 Blocked, drvg 9
21May92- 6Pim fst 5f :222 :461 :59	Md Sp Wt	37 4 5 67½ 67½ 67½ 68 Prado E S	120	6.00	85–12 StrFlht1204½InsdCnnctn1201¾MdrTrbdr120 Lck rm late 8
LATEST WORKOUTS ●Sep 25 Lrl 6f fst 1:16 H		●Sep 8 Lrl 3f fst :35 H	Sep 1 Lrl ⊤ 6f fm 1:15 H (d)		●Aug 20 Lrl 6f fst 1:13³ H

Lord of the Bay had an inferior speed figure, and the past performances suggested that he had earned it with the aid of an easy front-running victory at the Meadowlands. In that case, he was an automatic throw-out. Yet the chart of his previous race conveyed a different impression.

EIGHTH RACE **Meadowlands** **OCTOBER 2, 1992**

1 MILE.(Turf). (1.34) 8th Running WORLD APPEAL STAKES. Purse $35,000. 2-year-olds. Free nominations close Saturday, September 26. $100 Supplementary nominations close Wednesday, September 30. $300 to pass the entry box, $300 to start. Weight, 120 lbs. Non-winners of a sweepstakes, allowed 3 lbs. Two races other than claiming, 5 lbs. One such race, 7 lbs. Maidens, 9 lbs. The owner of the winner to receive a trophy. Closed September 26, 1992, with 29 nominations and Supplemental Nomination of Dam Handsome.

Value of race $35,000; value to winner $21,000; second $6,300; third $3,500; fourth $1,400; balance of starters $280 each. Mutuel pool $116,193. Exacta Pool $149,023

Last Raced	Horse	M/Eqt.	A.	Wt	PP	St	¼	½	¾	Str	Fin	Jockey	Odds $1
13Sep92^{11}Pim^{4}	Lord of the Bay	L	2	117	14	10	$2^{3\frac{1}{2}}$	1^{1}	$1^{1\frac{1}{2}}$	$1^{3\frac{1}{2}}$	$1^{2\frac{3}{4}}$	Wilson R	31.00
16Sep92 ^{6}Med^{1}	Irish Harbour		2	115	4	9	13^{hd}	11^{1}	8^{3}	$5^{3\frac{1}{2}}$	2no	Ferrer J C	4.40
24Sep92 ^{4}Bel^{1}	Mischevious Music		2	115	9	13	$11^{2\frac{1}{2}}$	10^{1}	7^{hd}	3^{hd}	$3^{1\frac{3}{4}}$	Romero R P	3.80
16Sep92 ^{6}Med^{2}	Eridge		2	111	6	7	6^{hd}	$8^{1\frac{1}{2}}$	$5^{1\frac{1}{2}}$	4^{hd}	4^{2}	Cruguet J	5.60
5Sep92 ^{6}Mth^{4}	Thatsa Cakewalk	L	2	115	10	5	3^{2}	3^{2}	3^{2}	$2^{1\frac{1}{2}}$	5^{1}	Marquez C H Jr	10.20
22Sep92 ^{8}Med^{1}	Timeforathrill		2	117	12	14	$12^{\frac{1}{2}}$	12^{hd}	12^{2}	8^{3}	$6^{\frac{1}{2}}$	Gavidia W	5.30
13Sep92^{11}Pim^{8}	My Impression	L	2	120	2	2	8^{hd}	$7^{\frac{1}{2}}$	$6^{\frac{1}{2}}$	$7^{\frac{1}{2}}$	$7^{\frac{3}{4}}$	Luzzi M J	a-10.40
24Sep92 ^{3}Bel^{1}	Dam Handsome		2	113	3	3	$5^{\frac{1}{2}}$	$5^{\frac{1}{2}}$	4^{hd}	6^{hd}	$8^{3\frac{3}{4}}$	Gryder A T	11.70
15Sep92 ^{1}Med^{1}	Krispy Peach	L	2	115	8	8	7^{2}	6^{hd}	$10^{\frac{1}{2}}$	$9^{\frac{1}{2}}$	9^{3}	Madrigal R Jr	6.90
13Sep92^{11}Pim^{6}	Perkin's Run	b	2	115	11	11	9^{1}	9^{hd}	11^{1}	$11^{2\frac{1}{2}}$	$10^{1\frac{1}{2}}$	Krone J A	a-10.40
19Sep92 ^{3}Med^{1}	Armagh County		2	115	7	4	1^{hd}	$2^{\frac{1}{2}}$	2^{hd}	10^{2}	11^{1}	Bravo J	15.20
19Sep92 ^{3}Med^{2}	Fired On	b	2	112	1	1	$10^{\frac{1}{2}}$	14	14	$13^{\frac{1}{2}}$	12^{nk}	Nelson D	f-27.80
22Sep92 ^{8}Med^{5}	Count Buckley		2	115	5	6	$4^{\frac{1}{2}}$	$4^{\frac{1}{2}}$	9^{2}	$12^{\frac{1}{2}}$	13^{1}	Conner S E	f-27.80
9Sep92 ^{6}Med^{4}	Class First		2	112	13	12	14	13^{2}	13^{2}	14	14	Santagata N	f-27.80

a–Coupled: My Impression and Perkin's Run.
f—Mutuel field.

OFF AT 10:34 Start good, Won driving. Time, :22^{3}, :46^{4}, 1:11^{2}, 1:37 Course firm.

$2 Mutuel Prices:			
11–LORD OF THE BAY	64.00	25.60	7.80
3–IRISH HARBOUR		6.80	4.40
8–MISCHEVIOUS MUSIC			3.20

$2 EXACTA 11–3 PAID $701.60

Ch. c, (Jan), by Lord Avie—Lituya Bay, by Empery. Trainer Salzman J Edwin Jr. Bred by Four Horsemens Ranch (Fla).

LORD OF THE BAY, vied for the early lead outside of ARMAGH COUNTY, drew clear on the backstretch, responded when challenged on the final turn and came away again, widened into upper stretch under right handed pressure and remained well clear to the wire. IRISH HARBOUR saved ground entering the far turn, moved between rivals nearing the top of the lane, raced between foes again through midstretch then earned the place. MISCHEVIOUS MUSIC, between rivals nearing the top of the lane, moved out for the drive and finished willingly. ERIDGE, between horses turning for home advanced into upper stretch then weakened late. THATSA CAKEWALK, always a factor, lodged a bid outside on the final turn and loomed a threat into midstretch then tired. TIMEFORATHRILL, raced out in the course on the final turn and lacked a solid bid. MY IMPRESSION advanced some on the final turn and lacked a further response. DAM HANDSOME saved ground while forwardly placed to the drive and tired. KRISPY PECH dropped back on the final turn. PERKIN'S RUN raced wide into the lane and faded. ARMAGH COUNTY vied for the early lead, came again on the final turn then gave way in the drive. COUNT BUCKLEY raced forwardly placed to the far turn and gave way.

Owners— 1, Four Horsemens Ranch; 2, Delaney Austin; 3, Pelligrino Peter; 4, Augustin Stables; 5, Canonie Anthony C; 6, Debral Stable; 7, Bailey Morris; 8, Winbound Farms; 9, Bernstein Carl H; 10, Gaudet Linda S; 11, Equity Horse Farm; 12, Davis Ron; 13, Frosta Joseph; 14, Mede Cahaba Stable.

Trainers— 1, Salzman J Edwin Jr; 2, O'Brien Leo; 3, Kelly Patrick J; 4, Sheppard Jonathan E; 5, Velez Roberto; 6, Stoklosa Richard; 7, Gaudet Edmond D; 8, Contessa Gary C; 9, Correnti Anthony; 10, Gaudet Edmond D; 11, Thrasher Clint D; 12, Santucci Frank; 13, Clark Sharon B; 14, Miller Patrice.

Corrected weight: Eridge 111 pounds; Class First 111. **Overweight:** Fired On 1 pound; Class First 1.

Scratched—Cadence Count (21Sep92 ^{7}Bel^{4}); Awad (26Sep92^{12}Pim^{2}); Whyme (20Sep92 ^{4}Pha$^{?}$).

The first call in past performances for route races is the half-mile mark, and there Lord of the Bay had been first by a length. But the chart shows that after a quarter mile he was second, a head behind the leader. (For the uninitiated, the exponential numbers in result charts show how far a horse was ahead of the horse immediately behind him.) Armagh County's 1^{hd} denotes that he was a head in front of Lord of the Bay, whose $2^{3\,1/2}$ indicates that he had sped away from the third-place horse by 3½ lengths. Obviously, the two leaders must have been in high gear in that first quarter, as their time of 22⅗ seconds confirms. Lord of the Bay proceeded to race Armagh County into defeat; the other speedster collapsed and finished eleventh. When Lord of the Bay led all the way to win the Laurel Futurity at odds of 16 to 1, his virtues would have been apparent only to people who had been at the Meadowlands for his last start — or to those who study result charts. They are an indispensable part of a horseplayer's library.

When a handicapper looks at any horse's past performances, he should note whether the horse is coming out of a race with an unusually fast, contentious pace or whether he is coming out of a race dominated by a sole front-runner or characterized by a very slow pace. In Chapter Five we will examine mathematical methods for evaluating fractional times, but in most cases a horseplayer doesn't need sophisticated calculations to make these judgments — just a little common sense and a set of *Daily Racing Form* charts at hand.

Slow-Pace Races A front-runner who sets a slow pace will usually deliver his maximum performance. But what about stretch-running types in that same field? Suppose that a come-from-behind runner rallied from fifteen lengths behind a fast six-furlong pace of 1:10 and won a 1⅛-mile race in 1:48. Now he is in a race devoid of speed, where the front-runner crawls the first six furlongs in 1:13. Shouldn't this horse be able to run his same race, only this time sitting abreast of the leader, and proceed to finish in 1:48 again? As logical as this may sound, it almost never happens. Often a jockey will drop fifteen lengths behind the leaders, anyway, because he knows that is his horse's style. But if he does react to the slow pace and sits close to the front-runner, that pacesetter will, at some point, use his superior speed to kick away and leave his rival in the dust. One-dimensional stretch-runners can almost never overcome the disadvantage of a slow pace — and their figures will usually decline as a result.

Strike the Gold — **Ch. c. 4, by Alydar—Majestic Gold, by Hatchet Man**

Own.—C C W Gold Stable — **Br.—Calumet Farm (Ky)** — **Tr.—Zito Nicholas P (—)** — **120**

Lifetime								
23 5 7 4	1992	8	2	4	1	$923,176
$2,384,426	1991	12	2	3	3	$1,443,850
	Wet	1	1	0	0	$300,000

18Jly92- 8Bel	fst	1¼	:46	1:35^{2}	2:00^{1}	3↑ Suburban H	**110**	4	7	7^{21}	4$^{3\frac{1}{2}}$	3$^{2\frac{1}{2}}$	2$^{1\frac{1}{2}}$	Perret C		119	*1.50e	88-16	PlsntTp119$^{1\frac{1}{2}}$StrikthGold119$^{1\frac{1}{2}}$DfnsvPly115	Rallied wide	7
18Jly92-Grade I																					
6Jun92- 7Bel	my	1⅛	:44^{4}	1:08^{2}	1:46^{3}	3↑ Nassau Co H	**111**	5	9	9^{15}	9$^{5\frac{3}{4}}$	2$^{\frac{1}{2}}$	1^{nk}	Perret C		116	4.80	96-08	StrikthGold116^{nk}PlsntTp119$^{1\frac{1}{2}}$SultrySong111	Wide drvg	9
6Jun92-Grade II																					
9May92-10Pim	fst	1$\frac{3}{16}$	:47^{3}	1:11^{2}	1:54^{4}	Pim Specl H	**111**	4	7	7^{11}	7$^{8\frac{1}{4}}$	3^{2}	1$^{\frac{3}{4}}$	Perret C		114	6.30	88-23	StrkthGld114$^{\frac{3}{4}}$FlySFr116$^{1\frac{1}{4}}$TlghtAgnd122	Wide, driving	7
9May92-Grade I																					
4Apr92- 7Aqu	fst	1$\frac{3}{16}$	:48^{1}	1:12	1:55^{3}	3↑ Thrty Six Rd	**101**	3	4	4^{13}	4^{13}	3^{7}	2^{6}	Antley C W		117	*.80	90-21	RedPine119^{6}StriketheGold117^{hd}Alyten117	Up for place	4
7Mar92-10GP	fst	1¼	:47^{3}	1:36^{3}	2:01^{3}	3↑ Gulf Park H	**110**	6	5	5^{18}	5^{11}	4^{8}	2^{7}	Krone J A		115	2.00	86-14	SeCdet119^{7}StrikthGold115$^{2\frac{1}{2}}$SunnySunris114	4 wide str	6
7Mar92-Grade I																					
17Feb92-10GP	fst	1⅛	:47^{2}	1:11^{2}	1:49^{2}	3↑ Broward H	**107**	3	6	6^{14}	5^{8}	4^{4}	3^{1}	Krone J A		117	*.80	89-21	HnstEnsgn109^{no}PntBttrOnt114^{1}StrkthGld117	4 wide str	7
17Feb92-Grade III																					
1Feb92- 9GP	fst	1⅛	:46^{4}	1:10^{1}	1:48	3↑ Donn H	**104**	6	8	8^{18}	8^{15}	7^{11}	6^{7}	Antley C W		116	*1.30	90-12	SeCdet115^{3}OutofPlc114^{nk}SunnySunris115	Vry wide str	8
1Feb92-Grade I																					
8Jan92- 7GP	fst	7f	:23^{4}	:46^{2}	1:24^{1}	Alw 22900	**99**	11	9	12^{14}	9^{11}	5^{5}	2$^{\frac{3}{4}}$	Antley C W		120	*.70	84-16	ByShrk112$^{\frac{3}{4}}$StriketheGold120$^{\frac{1}{2}}$PerfctFit114	Wide bckstr	12
2Nov91- 8CD	fst	1¼	:48^{2}	1:38	2:02^{4}	3↑ Br Cp Class	**113**	10	9	9^{15}	9$^{7\frac{3}{4}}$	6^{7}	5$^{4\frac{1}{2}}$	Valenzuela P A	B	122	6.20	91-09	BlackTieAffir-Ir126$^{1\frac{1}{4}}$TwilightAgend126$^{2\frac{1}{2}}$Unbridled126		11
2Nov91-Grade I; 7-wide in stretch, late rally																					
5Oct91- 7Bel	fst	1¼	:47^{3}	1:36	2:00^{3}	3↑ J C Gold Cp	**112**	4	5	5$^{8\frac{1}{2}}$	3$^{2\frac{1}{2}}$	2^{hd}	3$^{1\frac{1}{2}}$	Valenzuela P A		121	2.80	92-07	Fstn-Ar126$^{1\frac{1}{4}}$ChfHonch126^{nk}StrkthGld121	Inside, wknd	5
5Oct91-Grade I																					

LATEST WORKOUTS **Aug 5 Sar 4f gd :51^{2} B** **Jly 31 Sar 5f fst 1:00^{1} H** **Jly 25 Sar 4f fst :51^{1} B** **●Jly 16 Bel 3f gd :35 H**

Strike the Gold was an admirably consistent horse who would run speed figures in the 110–112 range, and that level of performance was occasionally good enough to beat the best horses in the country. But when he encountered an extremely slow pace in the Thirty Six Red Stakes at Aqueduct, he couldn't beat an allowance-class runner named Red Pine. In a four-horse field otherwise devoid of speed, Red Pine opened a big lead while crawling the first half mile in 48⅕ seconds, a ridiculously slow time on a lightning-fast Aqueduct strip. Strike the Gold couldn't adjust, and he wound up running a figure of 101, some 10 points below his normal level. (Meanwhile, Red Pine, whose previous five numbers had been 104-96-97-93-97, exploded to run a 110 while loose on the lead — a figure he would never approach for the rest of his life.) The moral is that a habitual off-the-pace runner may be forgiven for running a poor figure if he has been compromised by a very slow pace in front of him.

Fast-Pace Races An unusually fast, contentious pace will often hurt the chances of speed horses. Capable handicappers usually won't need high-tech calculations to tell what constitutes a fast pace at their track; a glance at result charts will indicate how a particular fractional time compared with those of other races at the same distance on the same day. But fractional times alone don't always indicate the severity of a fight for the early lead. A four- or five-horse battle may take a toll on the horses even if the fractions are moderate. (Again, the occurrence of such a battle may be learned only from the charts — if, say, the first call showed horses bunched in this fashion: 1^{nk}, 2no, 3^{hd}, $4^{1/2}$.)

One way to gauge the destructiveness of a fight for the lead is to look at the number of survivors. If four horses were head-and-head for the lead and all of them wound up out of the money, that is evidence of a destructive pace. If one of the four won, however, the others are not so easily forgiven. In the example cited earlier, Lord of the Bay's performance was especially credible because he had dueled for the lead and raced the other speed horse, Armagh County, into defeat. If Armagh County had managed to hold on and finish second, however, that would suggest the speed duel wasn't so destructive, and Lord of the Bay's effort would be less impressive.

In most races that involve a duel for the early lead, the horses in the optimal position are the stalkers, the ones in the second flight just behind the pace. Aside from being loose on the lead, a horse's best possible tactical position is to be sitting third, by himself, behind a pair of dueling speed horses. A horse who finds himself in this garden spot will often win and almost always will be able to earn a good figure. Again, the exact nature of a horse's trip can be deduced only from the result charts. If a handicapper was studying Superstrike's past performances and saw his early position was 3^2 in the Frank J. De Francis Memorial Dash, he might refer to the chart and see this:

EIGHTH RACE
Laurel
JULY 18, 1992

6 FURLONGS. (1.08) 3d Running THE FRANK J DEFRANCIS MEMORIAL DASH (Grade II). Purse $300,000 Guaranteed. 3-year-olds and upward. By subscription of $500 each, which should accompany the nomination. Pre-entry accompanied by a $2,750 pre-entry fee must be made by Thursday, July 9, 1992, $2,750 to enter and start with $300,000 Guaranteed of which 605 to the winner, 20% to second, 10% to third, 6% to fourth and 4% to fifth. Field will be limited to fourteen (14) starters. High weights on the scale preferred. The field and also eligibles, in order of preference shall be released on or before 12 noon, Friday, July 10, 1992. Weights: 3-year-olds 119 lbs. Older, 126 lbs. Fillies and Mares, allowed 5 lbs. Non-winners of $100,000 twice since September 1, 1991, allowed 3 lbs. Once 5 lbs. $75,000 twice since September 1, 1991, 7 lbs. $75,000 once or %50,000 twice, 9 lbs. $50,000 once, 12 lbs. Starters to be named through the entry box Thursday, July 16, 1992 by the usual time of closing. In the event that more than fourteen (14) horses pass the entry box, the also eligibles will be refunded their pre-entry and entry fees. Trophies to the winning owner, trainer and jockey. Supplementary nominations at a fee of $15,000 each closed Thursday, July 16, 1992 by the usual time of closing with 1 nomination. Nominations closed Friday, June 26, 1992 with 21 nominations. Value of race $300,000; value to winner $180,000; second $60,000; third $30,000; fourth $18,000; fifth $12,000. Mutuel pool $111,079. Exacta Pool $124,556 Triple Pool $63,164

Last Raced	Horse	M/Eqt.	A.Wt	PP	St	¼	½	Str	Fin	Jockey	Odds $1
28Jun92 ^{4}Atl^{2}	Superstrike-GB		3 112	12	5	3^{2}	$2^{1\frac{1}{2}}$	1^{1}	$1^{4\frac{3}{4}}$	Sorenson D	13.10
12Jly92 ^{9}LaD^{2}	Parisian Flight		4 114	11	1	1^{hd}	$1^{\frac{1}{2}}$	2^{5}	$2^{\frac{3}{4}}$	Prado E S	a-11.40
5Jly92 ^{4}WO^{2}	King Corrie		4 117	2	4	4^{3}	$4^{\frac{1}{2}}$	$3^{1\frac{1}{2}}$	$3^{1\frac{1}{2}}$	Sabourin R B	4.60
4Jly92^{10}FL^{2}	Burn Fair	b	5 114	4	9	11^{2}	12	9^{hd}	4no	Chavez J F	19.10
11Jly92 ^{8}Lrl^{1}	Hooliganisim	Lb	5 114	10	12	9^{hd}	8^{2}	7^{1}	$5^{1\frac{1}{2}}$	Chavez S N	9.50
2Jly92 ^{9}Lrl^{3}	Smart Alec	b	4 117	3	11	12	$11^{\frac{1}{2}}$	11^{2}	$6^{1\frac{1}{4}}$	Pino M G	23.40
13Jun92 ^{3}Hol^{1}	Dolly's Fortune	L	3 114	7	7	7^{1}	6^{1}	$5^{1\frac{1}{2}}$	7^{hd}	Desormeaux K J	6.80
5Jly92^{10}Lrl^{2}	Sunny Sunrise	Lb	5 123	9	10	10^{4}	$10^{1\frac{1}{2}}$	$10^{1\frac{1}{2}}$	$8^{\frac{1}{2}}$	Luzzi M J	3.80
4Jly92^{10}FL^{3}	(S)Key Spirit	L	6 119	5	6	$5^{\frac{1}{2}}$	7^{1}	$8^{\frac{1}{2}}$	$9^{\frac{1}{2}}$	Penna D	a-11.40
20Jun92 ^{8}Bel^{3}	To Freedom	Lb	4 117	6	8	$6^{\frac{1}{2}}$	5^{1}	6^{hd}	$10^{3\frac{1}{2}}$	Madrid A Jr	9.20
3Jly92^{10}Hol^{1}	Fabulous Champ		3 112	8	3	$8^{\frac{1}{2}}$	9^{hd}	12	11^{1}	Nakatani C S	9.90
20Jun92 ^{8}Bel^{5}	Southern Justice	Lb	4 117	1	2	2^{2}	3^{4}	$4^{\frac{1}{2}}$	12	Solis A	4.90

a-Coupled: Parisian Flight and Key Spirit.
(S) Supplementary nomination.

OFF AT 4:16 Start good Won driving Time, :21^{3}, :45 , :57^{2}, 1:09^{4} Track fast.

$2 Mutuel Prices:

11-SUPERSTRIKE-GB	28.20	7.20	4.20
1-PARISIAN FLIGHT (a-entry)		8.40	4.80
3-KING CORRIE			4.00

$2 EXACTA 11-1 PAID $361.80 $2 TRIPLE 11-1-3 PAID $4,225.20

B. g, (May), by Superlative—Marista, by Mansingh. Trainer Jackson Bruce L. Bred by Red House Stud (GB).

SUPERSTRIKE forwardly placed, advanced three wide on turn, secured command in upper stretch and drew off under brisk urging. PARISIAN FLIGHT sped to front, disputed pace racing off rail and held the place. KING CORRIE never far back, rallied mildy. BURN FAIR taken very wide entering stretch, passed tired ones. HOOLIGANISIM broke in air and finished gamely. SMART ALEC blocked much of stretch run, finished gamely when clear. DOLLY'S FORTUNE raced wide and weakened. SUNNY SUNRISE raced close to rail while outrun. KEY SPIRIT saved ground and weakened. TO FREEDOM weakened. FABULOUS CHAMP raced wide. SOUTHERN JUSTICE had speed along rail and faltered.

Owners— 1, Kruse David R; 2, Franks John; 3, Minshall Aubrey W; 4, Perez Robert; 5, Waverly on Chester; 6, Tuttle Mrs Wylie F; 7, Sherry Margaret J; 8, Meyerhoff Harry & Tom; 9, Franks John; 10, Prestonwood Farm & Einlein Herman; 11, Dutton & Lerch; 12, Biszantz Gary E.

Trainers— 1, Jackson Bruce L; 2, Barnett Bobby C; 3, Noakes Sherry; 4, Callejas Alfredo; 5, Groves W Fred; 6, Delp Richard W; 7, Peterson Douglas R; 8, Delp Grover G; 9, DePaulo Michael P; 10, Tammaro John J; 11, Dutton Jerry; 12, Sadler John W.

Overweight: Superstrike-GB 2 pounds; Dolly's Fortune 4; Fabulous Champ 2.

At the quarter-mile mark, Parisian Flight's position is shown as 1^{hd}, with Southern Justice 2^{2} and Superstrike 3^{2} — the chart paints a vivid picture of the race. The two speed horses were dueling, a head apart, through an extremely fast quarter in $21\frac{3}{5}$ seconds. Superstrike was two lengths behind them, and he was sitting there by himself, as he was two lengths in front of the fourth horse. The garden spot. The perfect trip. Under the circumstances, Superstrike not only scored the biggest victory of his life but also earned the biggest speed figure of his life.

In American racing, one-dimensional, come-from-a-mile-behind runners almost always find themselves at a disadvantage, even in a race like the one Superstrike won. But occasionally the early pace is so extraordinarily fast that it takes a toll not only on speed horses but also on the stalkers just behind the leaders, and the beneficiaries are the horses who rally from the rear of the pack. There is one American race in which this happens with some regularity. The Kentucky Derby is often populated by sprinters who are unable to go a mile and a quarter but are in the race because their owners can't resist temptation. The Derby often draws a full field of twenty that forces the jockeys to hustle their horses early so that they can secure a decent tactical position by the first turn. Frequently, the pace will be devastatingly fast, the speed horses will collapse, and the closers will swoop past the field. In 1982, the horses who were running 19-18-16-14 after the first half mile of the Derby finished 1-2-3-4, led by Gato del Sol, who never won a race of consequence thereafter. In 1986, the horses running 15-14-7-11 after the first quarter mile finished 1-2-3-4. When the race develops in such a fashion, many of these plodders will run the best figure of their lives. An exceptional number earned by a come-from-behind runner should be discounted if it was earned in a race with a super-fast pace that caused all the speed to collapse.

There is no magic formula for interpreting all of the effects of a fast or a slow pace. But handicappers should remain constantly aware of the possibility that horses' previous figures may have been influenced by pace. This was the case in the 1992 Breeders' Cup Juvenile, which was widely seen as a two-horse race involving Gilded Time and Sea Hero.

Gilded Time — **Ch. c. 2(Feb), by Timeless Moment—Gilded Lilly, by What a Pleasure** — Lifetime 3 3 0 0 $335,980 — 1992 3 3 0 0 $335,980
MCCARRON C J (—) — **Br.—Mangurian Mr–Mrs H T Jr (Fla)** — **122**
Own.—Milch & Silverman & Silverman — **Tr.—Vienna Darrell (—)** — **Wet 1 1 0 0 $200,580**

26Sep92- 9AP sly 1 :45^{2} 1:10^{3} 1:37^{4} Arl Fut **91** 3 2 2^{1} 2^{hd} 1^{5} 15½ McCarron C J L 121 *1.10 77–29 GildedTime1215½Boundlssly1214Rockmundo121 Handily 6
26Sep92-Grade II
8Aug92-10Mth fst 6f :21^{2} :44 1:07^{4} Sapling **102** 5 6 4^{1} 3½ 2½ 1½ McCarron C J L 122 *1.10 102–05 GilddTim122½WldZon1227½GrtNvgtor122 Wide str,drvng 8
8Aug92-Grade II
15Jly92- 4Hol fst 6f :22^{1} :45^{2} 1:10^{1} Md Sp Wt **79** 5 8 4^{5} 2½ 1^{1} 1^{4} Stevens G L B 117 *.70 89–12 Gilded Time1174 Chayim1172¼ Gulable117 8
15Jly92-Poor start, wide, early, handily
LATEST WORKOUTS Oct 26 GP 5f fst 1:02 B ●Oct 18 SA 6f fst 1:11^{4} B Oct 5 SA Ⓣ 4f fm :50^{4} H (d) Sep 18 AP Ⓣ 6f sf 1:21^{3} B

Sea Hero — **B. c. 2(Mar), by Polish Navy—Glowing Tribute, by Graustark** — Lifetime 6 3 1 0 $339,720 — 1992 6 3 1 0 $339,720
BAILEY J D (—) — **Br.—Mellon Paul (Va)** — **122** — **Turf 2 2 0 0 $33,000**
Own.—Rokeby Stables — **Tr.—Miller Mack (—)**

10Oct92- 7Bel gd 1 :44^{3} 1:09 1:34^{4} Champagne **97** 1 5 3^{2} 2^{hd} 1½ 15¾ Bailey J D b 122 8.80 96–04 SeaHero1225¾SecretOdds1225¾PressCard122 Drew away 10
10Oct92-Grade I
21Sep92- 7Bel fm 1 Ⓣ:45^{3} 1:09^{3} 1:34^{3} Alw 29000 **86** 7 4 42½ 3½ 11½ 13¾ Bailey J D b 122 *.70 89–11 Sea Hero1223¾ SimilarStar117¾Compadre117 Mild drive 7
7Sep92- 5Bel fm 1 Ⓣ:46^{2} 1:10^{2} 1:35^{2} Md Sp Wt **83** 1 5 31½ 3½ 1½ 12¼ Bailey J D 118 *.90 85–19 Sea Hero1182¼ Halissee1182½ Awad118 Driving 11
21Aug92- 6Sar fst 7f :23 :46 1:24 Md Sp Wt **69** 4 8 74½ 64½ 42½ 21¼ Madrid A Jr 118 3.00 84–14 ThrillerChiller1181¼SeHero118nkAllGon118 Rallied wide 10
2Aug92- 4Sar fst 6f :22^{2} :45^{4} 1:10^{2} Md Sp Wt **63** 5 3 83¾ 8^{6} 75½ 57¼ Madrid A Jr 118 6.80 85–10 Wallenda1182 All Gone1184 D'Orazio118 Stead sharply 12
13Jly92- 5Bel fst 5½f :22^{1} :45^{2} 1:03 Md Sp Wt **56** 5 6 6^{8} 6^{8} 4^{8} 413¼ Bailey J D 118 *1.30 87–10 StrollngAlng1182½DvlshlyYrs1188½Dr.Alfs118 No threat 10
LATEST WORKOUTS Oct 28 GP 3f fst :35 H Oct 22 Bel 6f fst 1:13 H Oct 17 Bel 4f fst :47^{1} B Oct 7 Bel 4f fst :47 H

Strictly on the basis of figures, a handicapper might have preferred Sea Hero, who had earned a 97 in the Champagne Stakes. Gilded Time had run a 102 in the Sapling Stakes, but that was a sprint, and his most recent figure at a mile — his only attempt at a distance — was a 91. These numbers suggested he might be primarily a sprinter. But the nature of the colts' last races clouded this interpretation. Sea Hero had sat third, in the garden spot, behind two one-dimensional speedballs who had sizzled their first quarter in :22 flat. Gilded Time, however, had dueled with another well-regarded speedster, Wild Zone, and they had set a swift pace; their half mile in :45⅖ was a full second faster than the comparable fraction for any of the other three one-mile races at Arlington Park that day. Wild Zone collapsed, as did a colt who had been sitting third, stalking the leaders. So even though Gilded Time's final time wasn't exceptional, he was evidently a better horse than the 91 suggested. His figure of 102 in the sprint might be a more accurate gauge of his ability. He won the Breeders' Cup and established himself as the champion of his generation, while Sea Hero never got into contention.

Here is another virtual two-horse race, a six-furlong allowance event at Del Mar, in which one horse's apparent superiority was not nearly so great as the speed figures would suggest:

Superstrike-GB B. g. 3(May), by Superlative—Marista, by Mansingh
SORENSON D (45 0 1 4 .00) Br.—Red House Stud (GB)
Own.—Kruse David R Tr.—Jackson Bruce L (4 0 0 1 .00) **114**
Lifetime 6 3 2 1 $296,361 — 1992 5 2 2 1 $292,986 — 1991 1 1 0 0 $3,375 — Wet 2 1 1 0 $76,960
18Jly92- 8Lrl fst 6f :21^{3} :45 1:09^{4} 3↑F De Frncis **110** 12 5 3^{2} 2½ 1^{1} 14¾ Sorenson D 112 13.10 92-17 Suprstrik-GB112^{4¾}PrisinFlight114¾KingCorr117 Driving 12
18Jly92-Grade III
28Jun92- 4Atl fst 7f :22^{1} :44^{4} 1:21^{4} Jersey Shore **102** 7 1 1^{hd} 1^{hd} 1^{1½} 2½ Santos J A 122 *1.50 97-06 SurelySix112½Superstrike-GB122^{3}SltLk119 Bid, missed 8
6Jun92- 6Bel my 7f :21^{3} :44^{1} 1:22^{2} Riva Ridge **103** 1 7 2½ 1^{hd} 1^{2½} 1^{1¼} Santos J A 115 12.30 92-08 Sprstrk-GB115^{1¼}ThrPt122^{2½}Wndndrmywngs115 Driving 7
6Jun92-Grade III
6May92- 8Bel fst 1 :44^{2} 1:08^{4} 1:33^{3} Withers **86** 6 4 5^{4} 5^{3} 4^{4½} 3^{11¼} Santos J A 126 7.60 91 – DxBrss126^{8¼}BgSur126^{3}Suprstrk-GB126 Altered path 1/8 8
6May92-Grade II
1Apr92- 7SA sly 6f :21^{3} :44^{4} 1:10^{2} Alw 32000 **99** 2 1 2^{hd} 2^{hd} 2^{hd} 2^{1} Stevens G L B 120 6.50 83-24 Pdrnls117^{1}Suprstrk-GB120^{3½}SprngLnch120 Best of rest 6
31Jly91♦4Southwell(Eng) fst 6f 1:13^{4} Paris Stks(Mdn) 1^{7} Ives T 126 6.00 – – Suprstrk126^{7} PlcgtRcng126^{7} ElysnSprt126 Prom,easily 12
31Jly91-Raced on an all-weather Fibersand course
LATEST WORKOUTS ●Aug 7 Dmr 4f fst :45^{4} H

Star Of The Crop B. c. 3(Mar), by Relaunch—Circular, by What a Pleasure
STEVENS G L (119 24 20 18 .20) Br.—Glen Hill Farm (Fla)
Own.—Glen Hill Farm Tr.—Proctor Willard L (8 2 0 3 .25) **114**
Lifetime 9 3 1 3 $146,300 — 1992 5 1 1 2 $70,350 — 1991 4 2 0 1 $75,950
29Jly92- 7Dmr fst 6f :21^{4} :44^{3} 1:08^{4} 3↑Alw 37000 **99** 7 2 1^{hd} 2^{hd} 1^{2} 1^{2½} Stevens G L B 114 *1.10 95-07 StrOfThCrp114^{2½}LprdLd117^{2¾}TTA117 Wide, ridden out 7
9May92- 5Hol fst 7f :21^{4} :44^{2} 1:21^{4} Harry Henson **97** 3 3 3^{1½} 2^{hd} 1^{1½} 3^{1} Stevens G L 121 2.30 94-08 Slerp121¾NvrRound118^{nk}StrOfThCrop121 Bumped start 6
11Apr92- 8SA fst 6½f :21^{1} :44 1:15^{4} San Pedro **52** 5 4 5^{3½} 4^{4} 5^{12} 5^{19} Sorenson D 119 *.90 72-14 Slerp115½Scherndo119^{5½}NvrRound117 Steadied hard1/4 7
11Apr92-Placed fourth through disqualification
26Feb92- 8SA fst 6f :21^{1} :44 1:08^{2} ⓇBolsa Chica **94** 1 8 5^{3½} 5^{5} 4^{5½} 3^{5} Delahoussaye E 119 *1.80 89-15 Arp117½ Three Peat116^{4½} Star Of The Crop119 8
26Feb92-Off slowly, steadied 3/8
9Feb92- 5SA fst 7f :22 :44^{2} 1:21^{1} Sn Vcnt B C **104** 1 6 3^{1½} 1^{hd} 1^{hd} 2no Delahoussaye E B 116 4.60 97-06 Mineral Wells116^{no} Star OfTheCrop116^{5}PrinceWild118 7
9Feb92-Grade III; Bumped 3/16, brushed late
22Dec91- 5Hol fst 1$\frac{1}{16}$:46^{4} 1:11 1:42^{4} Hol Fut **65** 10 4 3^{1½} 2^{1½} 8^{7¾}11^{17½} Stevens G L 121 3.20 69-17 A.P.Indy121^{nk}DnceFloor121^{5½}CsulLis121 4-wide stretch 14
22Dec91-Grade I
16Nov91- 8Hol fst 7f :22^{2} :45 1:22^{1} Prevue B C **94** 1 3 2^{1} 2½ 1^{hd} 1^{3½} Stevens G L 114 3.80 93-12 StrOfThCrop114^{3½}ShwkGold121^{1¾}SltLk121 Checked 1/4 5
16Nov91-Grade III
20Oct91- 4SA fst 6f :21^{2} :44^{3} 1:10^{2} Md Sp Wt **79** 3 6 5^{6} 5^{4} 2^{1} 1½ Stevens G L 117 2.50 84-16 Star Of The Crop117½ Old Master117^{nk} CapeRoyale117 10
20Oct91-Off a bit awkwardly, 4-wide stretch
LATEST WORKOUTS Aug 15 Dmr 4f fst :50^{1} H Aug 3 Dmr 4f fst :50^{1} H Jly 28 Dmr 3f fst :36 H Jly 22 Hol 6f fst 1:12^{1} H

Superstrike, as we saw earlier, earned his imposing figure of 110 in the Frank J. De Francis Memorial Dash with the aid of a perfect, stalking trip. Star of the Crop might seem overmatched, but the chart of his last race suggests that the effort was much better than it looks in the past performances.

SEVENTH RACE
Del Mar
JULY 29, 1992

6 FURLONGS. (1.07³) ALLOWANCE. Purse $37,000. 3-year-olds and upward which are non-winners of $3,000 twice other than maiden or claiming. Weights, 3-year-olds, 116 lbs.; older, 121 lbs. Non-winners of two races other than claiming since June 1 allowed 2 lbs.; of a race other than maiden or claiming since then, 4 lbs.

Value of race $37,000; value to winner $20,350; second $7,400; third $5,550; fourth $2,775; fifth $925. Mutuel pool $394,134. Exacta pool $404,118.

Last Raced	Horse	M/Eqt.A.Wt	PP St	¼	½	Str	Fin	Jockey	Odds $1
9May92 5Hol³	Star Of The Crop	B 3 114	7 2	1hd	2¹	1²	12½	Stevens G L	1.10
3Jly92 5Hol⁵	Lyphard Legend	LB 3 117	3 7	7	7	3½	22½	Pincay L Jr	15.60
4Jly92 7Hol²	Tax Time Again	LB 4 117	1 6	6¹	6hd	5²	31¾	Delahoussaye E	9.40
4Jly92 5Hol¹	Ruff Hombre	LBb 6 117	6 1	3hd	4¹½	4hd	4¾	McCarron C J	3.90
6Jly92 8Hol¹	Bet On The Bay	B 3 114	4 4	4hd	1hd	2¹	54½	Flores D R	5.70
22Jun92 8Hol⁶	Blue Neon	LBb 4 117	5 3	5²	5hd	7	62½	Sorenson D	8.30
3Jun92 8Hol⁴	Rocket Roger	Bb 3 113	2 5	2½	3hd	61½	7	Solis A	8.80

OFF AT 5:34 Start good. Won ridden out. Time, :21⁴, :44³, :56², 1:08⁴ Track fast.

$2 Mutuel Prices:

Hand Timed

8-STAR OF THE CROP	4.20	3.40	2.60
4-LYPHARD LEGEND		9.20	5.00
1-TAX TIME AGAIN			4.00

$2 EXACTA 8-4 PAID $47.40.

B. c, (Mar), by Relaunch—Circular, by What a Pleasure. Trainer Proctor Willard L. Bred by Glen Hill Farm (Fla).

STAR OF THE CROP dueled for the early lead, raced wide down the backstretch, brushed with RUFF HOMBRE going into the far turn, shook clear after a half, maintained a clear advantage through the final furlong and was shown the whip right handed in the last sixteenth. LYPHARD LEGEND lacked early speed, came into the stretch four wide and rallied for the place. TAX TIME AGAIN, outrun early, improved his position after a half but did not have the needed punch in the final furlong. RUFF HOMBRE, an early pace factor and wide down the backstretch, brushed with STAR OF THE CROP going into the far turn and weakened in the drive. BET ON THE BAY, an early pace factor, also weakened in the drive. BLUE NEON, an early pace factor, faltered. ROCKET ROGER, also an early pace factor, faltered. EL TOREO (3) WAS SCRATCHED BY THE STEWARDS. ALL WAGERS ON HIM IN THE REGULAR AND EXACTA POOLS WERE ORDERED REFUNDED AND ALL OF HIS PICK SIX AND LATE TRIPLE SELECTIONS WERE SWITCHED TO THE FAVORITE, STAR OF THE CROP (8).

Owners— 1, Glen Hill Farm; 2, Hawn W R; 3, Honeyman Steven B; 4, Carey&Gldmn&RidgwdRcgStInc; 5, McCaffery & Toffan; 6, Albrecq Charles & Gilbert; 7, 505 Farms.

Trainers— 1, Proctor Willard L; 2, MacDonald Mark: 3, Jones Gary; 4, Hronec Philip; 5, Gonzalez Juan; 6, Baffert Bob; 7, Headley Bruce.

Overweight: Lyphard Legend 5 pounds; Rocket Roger 1.

Scratched—Tark The Shark (3Jly92¹²Hol¹); El Toreo (15May92 8Hol⁵).

Star of the Crop had engaged in a five-horse battle for the early lead, parked five-wide, in fast fractions. (Note the positions in the chart after a quarter mile: Star of the Crop 1ʰᵈ, Rocket Roger 2¹/², Ruff Hombre 3ʰᵈ, Bet on the Bay 4ʰᵈ, Blue Neon.) He disposed of the other four horses, who wound up finishing fourth, fifth, sixth, and seventh in the field of seven. It was a powerful effort, certainly better than the figure of 99 suggests. Is Star of the Crop good enough to beat Superstrike? Even though Superstrike encountered ideal conditions at Laurel, he is no phony; he had previously earned figures of 102 and 103 under seemingly honest circumstances while dueling for the lead. Star of the Crop's lifetime best, earned six months earlier, was a 104. This is a tough call, but at least a pace-oriented handicapper would be aware that Superstrike is not a cinch, not a horse to single in the pick six, despite his big figure.

Star of the Crop dueled with Superstrike around the turn and through the stretch and prevailed by a half-length, paying $6.60. Superstrike, who had been bearing out badly in the early stages, was disqualified after finishing second.

An exceptionally interesting, illuminating, and (for me) profitable illustration of the interplay between speed figures and pace occurred in the 1991 American Championship Racing Series, dominated by Farma Way and Festin. Farma Way was a versatile runner with tactical speed; Festin was a plodder who almost always started from last place and made a bold late charge. In such confrontations, horses with tactical speed have the advantage, and Farma Way had the edge over Festin. He typically ran figures in the 113–116 range, and he had beaten Festin twice in three meetings before they went to Baltimore for the Pimlico Special. In the field was a formidably fast horse, Jolie's Halo, who might have dueled with Farma Way, but when he didn't, Farma Way inherited an easy lead. On a track that was very speed-favoring, anyway, he was permitted to set the pace while running his first half mile in a dawdling 46⅘ seconds. Under the circumstances, he figured to be unbeatable and to run a maximum figure — and he did just that. Farma Way scored by three lengths, broke the track record, and earned a figure of 122. Because the early pace had been so slow, Farma Way had been running strong in the last half mile, and it was hard to make up any ground on him. Yet Festin had gained nearly a dozen lengths to finish fourth and had outkicked another of the country's most vaunted stretch-runners, Unbridled, in the process. He had delivered an impressive effort even though he hadn't threatened the winner.

Three weeks later, Farma Way, Festin, and Jolie's Halo were meeting again in the next stop on the American Championship Racing Series circuit, the Nassau County Handicap at Belmont Park. As the lineup for the race took shape, I thought of an old handicapping lesson — the 1976 Preakness, in which Honest Pleasure, having once ceded an easy lead to Bold Forbes, wasn't going to do it again and instigated the speed duel that destroyed them both. Trainer Happy Alter had been so unhappy about the way Jolie's Halo lost the Pimlico Special that he fired his jockey: he wasn't going to lose passively again. The stage was set for a speed duel that would benefit Festin, and the race developed just as I had envisioned. Farma Way and Jolie's Halo came rocketing out of the gate and dueled in a breathtaking $44\frac{2}{5}$ seconds, and then Festin flew past them as if they were standing still. He won by seven lengths, paying $13.60 to win, and earned a speed figure of 121. Just as Farma Way's Pimlico number had been a once-in-a-lifetime effort produced by a favorable pace, so was Festin's. He lost as a 1-to-2 favorite the next time he ran, and he reverted to his usual figures, in the 110–113 range, for the rest of the season. The horses had not changed and miraculously improved when they scored their big victories, nor had they bounced when they ran poorly in their subsequent starts. They had simply run exceptional figures when they encountered exceptional pace situations. Most thoroughbreds will do the same.

TRACK BIASES

The 1986 Breeders' Cup at Santa Anita was a day of championship performances. Lady's Secret clinched the Horse of the Year title with her runaway victory in the Distaff. Smile earned an Eclipse Award because of the way he won the Sprint, running six furlongs in $1:08\frac{2}{5}$. Brave Raj was hailed as the best of her age and sex after trouncing a field of 2-year-old fillies by more than five lengths. And Capote was acclaimed racing's brightest star of the future after his victory in the Juvenile. Despite a lack of experience, the magnificently bred 2-year-old colt had led all the way to defeat an outstanding field that included Alysheba, Bet Twice, and Gulch, and he had established himself as the early favorite for the next year's Kentucky Derby. Yet knowledgeable racegoers at Santa Anita suspected that what they were seeing was partly an illusion. These were not true championship performances; on this day, the Santa Anita racing strip gave an insuperable advantage to horses who raced on the rail, while dooming anybody who tried to rally wide.

Capote had led all the way on the rail while Alysheba's wide rally fell short. Brave Raj stalked the leaders and got through along the inside to win the Juvenile Fillies. Smile broke from post position 1 and stayed on the rail to win a duel with Pine Tree Lane. Lady's Secret led all the way. In the main event, the Breeders' Cup Classic, Skywalker stayed close to the lead and held off the six-wide rally of the country's best racehorse, Turkoman, depriving him of a chance to become Horse of the Year.

Some people might have argued that these were the best horses, anyway, and the similarity of their victories was a coincidence, but subsequent events demolished that notion. Brave Raj made her next start a month later in the Hollywood Juvenile, where she had the top speed figure and was favored at 8 to 5, and she was soundly beaten. Pine Tree Lane had the top speed figure when she ran in a sprint stakes a few weeks later, but she was trounced by a stretch-runner who hadn't been able to threaten her in the Breeders' Cup. Smile never won another race of consequence. Skywalker's career demonstrated that his victory had been a fluke; he finished dead last in the next year's Classic. And the greatest phony of all was Capote. He was such a flop as a 3-year-old that he became a laughingstock. He was trounced in both of his prep races for the Kentucky Derby; then, in the Derby itself, he tired so badly that jockey Angel Cordero Jr. pulled him up in the stretch.

There is no factor in horse racing which can conceal and distort the true ability of horses so much as a track bias. No factor can render speed figures so meaningless. The greatest of horses can be defeated by a bias; ordinary horses can be turned into champions by a bias; championship races can be turned into farces by a bias. All serious bettors therefore pay keen attention to this aspect of the game.

Yet few handicapping factors are so misunderstood and misused. Before *Picking Winners* was published, neither the term nor the concept of track bias had ever appeared in print. Steve Davidowitz had coined the phrase and taught me about biases; he later gave the subject an excellent treatment in *Betting Thorough-*

breds. But since those not-so-long-ago days when horseplayers were oblivious to the tendencies of racing surfaces, bettors today have become bias-obsessed. It is now rare to hear a racetrack described as normal or even. When a 3-to-5 shot wins the first race on a card by leading all the way, horseplayers will be chorusing, "Speed is good today! There's a bias!" When a favorite loses, many will immediately conclude that a bias was responsible. Such hasty judgments are very dangerous. If there is any aspect of the game which demands clear-eyed analysis, it is track bias, because this one factor can so radically alter a handicapper's interpretation of a horse's record or a whole race. If anybody using speed figures is going to disregard a performance in which a horse earned a standout number, he had better be right.

I divide biases into four basic categories and keep a record of them either in a notebook or in my racing programs:

Tracks with a good rail: (GR)
Tracks with a bad rail: (BR)
Speed-favoring tracks: (S)
Closer-favoring tracks: (C)

It is not possible to gauge the strength of biases with precision, but it is necessary to draw some distinction between those that dictate the outcome of races and those that merely influence the outcome. So I divide biases into three gradations; in the case of good rails, I would designate them in my notes as GR+, GR and GR-.

To determine whether a bias exists, it is ideal to watch the races and to know something about the ability of the horses in them. Often, however, horseplayers must rely on the information in the *Daily Racing Form* charts, especially the footnotes, which may vary in their usefulness depending on the thoroughness of the trackmen who make the comments. Fortunately, most of them are fairly good about designating horses' location on the track, drawing the crucial distinction between "rallied along the rail" and "rallied four wide." When they merely write "rallied," I want to scream. Whether a handicapper is evaluating possible biases on the basis of his own observation or a study of the *Daily Racing Form* charts, however, I recommend the following guidelines.

Do not make a final judgment about a track bias during the races themselves. Wait until the heat of battle has cooled and analyze the relevant data dispassionately.

Bear in mind that a substantial majority of racetracks are normal and bias-free. Don't search for biases that aren't there.

Look at the way the top two or three finishers in each race ran. If a reasonable number of horses did well showing speed on the inside and a reasonable number managed to close on the outside, the analysis is done. The track was normal.

If horses with a particular style dominated the races, do not jump to the conclusion that a bias existed. The laws of random distribution suggest that even on a perfectly normal track there will be days when, say, six races are won by front-runners — because those horses happened to be the best in the race or because they were the sole speed horses. (When stretch-runners dominate a day's program, the track may very well have been normal; American racing strips rarely give a genuine advantage to closers.) But when the results do seem to be skewed in a particular direction, study further.

Try to judge whether the results contradicted normal handicapping logic. If there were six front-running winners on a card and some of them were longshots who upset short-priced favorites, that is evidence of a speed-favoring bias. One particularly revealing sign of a speed- or rail-favoring bias is an unusual number of large margins separating horses at the finish. When a single horse benefits from a speed- or rail-favoring bias, he is apt to draw off and win by five or ten lengths, with everybody else struggling against the bias. Another indication of a speed-favoring bias is the ability of horses to withstand a pace that ordinarily would be destructive. When Smile and Pine Tree Lane battled through fractions of :21⅕ and :43⅗ in the Breeders' Cup Sprint but nobody could gain on them in the stretch, their performance was a persuasive piece of evidence that a bias existed at Santa Anita.

Tracks with a bad rail have a distinguishing characteristic of their own. When several horses are racing on or near the lead, they'll "peel off" and drop out of contention from the inside out. If, say, numbers 1, 2, 3, and 4 are racing abreast, number 1 drops back, forcing number 2 to inherit the inside position. Then he tires, and number 3 inherits the inside position, etc.

When it is clear that a bias exists, take special care to define just what type of bias it is. Rail- and speed-favoring tracks can be easily confused, because most front-runners go to the rail, but the distinction is crucial. The key is this: How do outside horses in speed duels perform? If a track has a rail-favoring bias, a horse parked in a three-wide battle for the lead is as good as dead. If the bias purely favors speed, however, the horse three-wide has as good a chance as the dueler on the rail.

Bear in mind that, when judging biases, the eye can deceive. At virtually every track in America, horseplayers will insist that inside posts are a disadvantage in races run out of a chute on the backstretch — particularly at seven furlongs. But people in the grandstand watch these races from an extreme angle, which makes it appear that the horses on the rail are breaking tardily. Even track announcers and *Racing Form* trackmen are regularly fooled by the angle.

Recognize, too, that while biases usually appear in easily definable form, they occasionally defy the neat GR, BR, S, and C categories. A bias may affect sprint races but not route races, or vice versa. (One year at Gulfstream Park, speed horses were doing very well at sprints, but in a span of seventy route races, only one front-runner was able to win.) The southern California tracks sometimes manifest an odd condition: the rail isn't bad, but inside posts can't win at sprints. Post position 1 might be death at six furlongs, but a horse could break from a middle post at seven furlongs, drop to the rail by the point where the six-furlong races begin, stay on the inside, and win without any difficulty. Horses in inside posts may be at a disadvantage in the fast-paced California sprints because jockeys have to hustle them continuously to maintain a decent tactical position.

When there is doubt about the existence of a bias, monitor the results of horses who raced on the questionable day when they run again. If, for example, there is ambiguous evidence of a bad rail, watch for the horses who were on the rail when they make their next starts. If they improve sharply, the bias is confirmed.

If there is no doubt about the existence of a bias, interpret the performance of every horse who ran on that racetrack accordingly. Good speed figures earned with the aid of a bias should be discounted. Horses who earned poor speed figures while running against the bias may be forgiven. And horses who earned competitive figures while racing against the bias will be viewed as potentially sensational betting opportunities when they run again.

The importance of evaluating the effect of biases on horses' past performances was vividly illustrated in the 1992 Mother Goose Stakes at Belmont Park, where Prospectors Delite faced a rematch with Turnback the Alarm.

Prospectors Delite **Ch. f. 3(Mar), by Mr Prospector—Up the Flagpole, by Hoist the Flag** Lifetime 7 6 0 1 $424,343 — 1992 7 6 0 1 $424,343 — 1991 0 M 0 0
DAY P (1 1 0 0 1.00) **Br.—W. S. Farish (Ky)** **121**
Own.—Farish William S **Tr.—Howard Neil J (1 1 0 0 1.00)**

23May92- 8Bel fst 1 :453 1:10 1:35 ⒻAcorn **98** 7 4 42 21 1hd 12 Day P 121 3.10 95-07 PrspctrsDlt1212PlsntStg1211½TrnbckThAlrm121.. Driving 12
23May92-Grade I
1May92- 9CD fst 1⅛ :481 1:122 1:512 ⒻKy Oaks **88** 5 4 3½ 2hd 2½ 31 Day P B 121 *.50 86-13 LvMLvMNt121½PlsntStg121½PrspctrsDlt121 Weakened 6
1May92-Grade I
18Apr92- 8Kee fst 1 1/16 :464 1:11 1:423 ⒻAshland **97** 1 1 11½ 11½ 12 12½ Perret C B 121 3.30 91-15 ProspctorsDlt1212½SpnnngRound1211LuvMLvMNot121 10
18Apr92-Grade I; Grade I; Ridden out, sharp effort;
29Mar92- 9FG fst 1 1/16 :471 1:12 1:441 ⒻF G Oaks **92** 2 1 1½ 1½ 14 18¾ Day P 118 *.30 93-14 ProspectorsDlit1188¾GlitziBj118hdDsrtRdinc118 Handily 7
29Mar92-Grade III
14Mar92-10FG fst 1 1/16 :483 1:124 1:434 ⒻDavona Dale **93** 2 2 21½ 2½ 11 13¼ Walker B J Jr 117 *.30 95-12 ProspectorsDelite1172¼RoylMd1129¼ClitziBj119 Driving 7
14Feb92-10FG gd 140 :471 1:131 1:432 ⒻAlw 11500 **74** 5 4 31 13½ 15 110 Walker B J Jr 119 *.30 80-27 ProspectorsDelite11910MimiMehmt11610WildrBrry119 6
14Feb92-Rider misjudged the finish and stood up final sixteenth
23Jan92- 9FG fst 6f :22 :462 1:121 ⒻAlw 11500 **82** 7 9 55 31 2hd 1nk Walker B J Jr 114 *.70 83-24 ProspctorsDlt114nkO'Hr'sScrt1191¾HpflAlc116 Hit gate 9
LATEST WORKOUTS Jun 3 Bel 4f fst :481 H May 19 Bel 5f fst 1:002 H ●May 14 CD 6f fst 1:132 H May 8 CD 4f fst :501 B

Turnback The Alarm **Ro. f. 3(Mar), by Darn That Alarm—Boomie's Girl E, by Figonero** Lifetime 12 3 5 2 $295,684 — 1992 3 1 1 1 $66,496 — 1991 9 2 4 1 $229,188
ANTLEY C W (118 21 6 13 .18) **Br.—Burke Walter J (Fla)** **121**
Own.—Valley View Farm **Tr.—Terrill William V (21 3 3 3 .14)** **Wet 1 1 0 0 $31,980**

23May92- 8Bel fst 1 :453 1:10 1:35 ⒻAcorn **91** 1 1 1½ 11 2hd 33½ Antley C W b 121 3.40 91-07 PrspctrsDlt1212PlsntSt1211½TrbcThAlr121 Speed, wknd 12
23May92-Grade I
2May92- 7Aqu fst 7f :214 :434 1:214 ⒻFamily Style **103** 1 5 2½ 21 21½ 2nk Carr D 118 2.80 96-07 AmrcnRl121nkTrnbckThAlrm11816LkngfrWn116 Gamely 5
18Apr92- 3Aqu my 6f :213 :442 1:10 ⒻAlthea **84** 3 1 32 32½ 2hd 11¾ Antley C W 116 *.60 91-06 TrnbcThAlr1161¾MssCrGrl1161½TddsTpT116 Mild drive 5
8Dec91- 8Aqu fst 1 1/16 ⊡:483 1:132 1:463 ⒻTempted **82** 5 1 1hd 2hd 2½ 23 Santos J A b 121 *.70 72-30 Dputton1143TurnbckThAlrm1213BlssOrHom114 Gamely 9
8Dec91-Grade III; Stumbled start, dueled, tired
17Nov91- 8Aqu fst 1⅛ :47 1:122 1:52 ⒻDemoiselle **91** 2 1 1½ 2hd 1hd 2¾ Santos J A b 116 7.90 75-32 StolnButy113¾TurnbckThAlrm116nkEsyNow116 Gamely 6
17Nov91-Grade II
13Oct91-11Crc fst 1 1/16 :474 1:14 1:49 ⒻⓇFlaStallion **54** 10 5 42 43½ 610 610¼ Santos J A 120 *1.60 67-17 MissJlski120½RunforBby120nkSubtlDncr120 Bmpd in str 15
13Oct91-My Dear Girl Division
28Sep91-10Crc fst 170 :47 1:144 1:472 ⒻGardenia Bc **57** 2 4 44½ 21 32 21 Carr D 116 *1.40 75-15 PttsPrcss1131TrbcTAlr1161ApplTGlr112Lost whip gamely 8
15Sep91-11Crc fst 7f :222 :453 1:262 ⒻⓇFlaStallion **65** 7 4 1hd 21 76¾ 53¾ Carr D 118 *.50 79-16 SbtlDncr1181PrrEprss1182FrtFrtFr118 Bumped on turn 10
15Sep91-Susan's Girl Division
26Aug91- 8Sar fst 6f :21 :45 1:103 ⒻSpinaway **84** 6 2 32 31 31½ 2no Carr D 119 7.20 91-10 MssIronSmok119noTrnbckThAlrm1193¼Prch119 Gamely 10
26Aug91-Grade I
LATEST WORKOUTS Jun 3 Bel tr.t 5f fst 1:011 B May 18 Bel tr.t 5f fst :594 B ●May 12 Bel 5f fst :581 H Apr 29 Bel tr.t 4f fst :49 B

Prospectors Delite had been regarded as one of the nation's top 3-year-old fillies, and she lived up to her reputation when she went to New York and won the Acorn Stakes, the first leg of the "Filly Triple Crown" series. She defeated Turnback the Alarm in that race, and the result seemed to suggest that Turnback the Alarm was principally a sprinter. She had earned a figure of 103 at seven furlongs and now, in the one-mile Acorn, she had tired and her figure had declined to a 91. In the 1⅛-mile Mother Goose, Prospectors Delite might appear to have an even greater edge. Or so it would seem to anyone who didn't know that a significant bias had existed on the day of the Acorn.

The rail had been disadvantageous that day, and Turnback the Alarm had engaged in a duel from the inside, running the first half mile in a fast 45⅗ seconds before she weakened. Prospectors Delite, racing in the best part of the track, rallied outside the leaders to score her victory. She was certainly no better than the figure of 98 that she had earned under ideal conditions. But Turnback the Alarm's poor figure of 91 was excusable because of the bias; the 103 she had earned in her previous start might indeed be the proper indication of her ability. If so, she was a better filly than Prospectors Delite. She proved this in the Mother Goose, rallying to win by 2¼ lengths and pay $16.40, while Prospectors Delite was soundly beaten as the 4-to-5 favorite.

TRIPS

If speed handicapping was the revolution of the 1970s in American horse betting, trip handicapping was the revolution of the 1980s. This new approach to the game originated at harness tracks, where even neophytes realize that the way a race unfolds tactically will determine winners and losers as much as the raw ability of the horses. Ground loss on the turns is overwhelmingly important; a horse parked three-wide for a substantial portion of a race is doomed. Many harness bettors who converted to thoroughbred racing brought with them a heightened sense of the importance of the way a race is run, and they talked routinely about horses' performances as having been easy or tough trips. In fact, they defined horses in terms of their trips as I defined them with speed figures. I was initially dubious about their approach, but I learned that when the trip handicappers' opinions conflicted with my figures, their assessments were often right. Moreover, the trip handicappers had a great advantage in the parimutuel competition. While the popularity of speed handicapping was reducing the odds on top-figure horses, the trip handicappers were using information that was often subjective and well hidden. They could hope to see something — a subtle bit of trouble, a jockey strangling a horse — that virtually nobody else at the track had observed, and to collect big payoffs as a result. I was converted to their methods, which I use in conjunction with my speed figures. So whenever I am making an all-out assault on a racetrack, I devote a large percentage of my time to the gathering of trip information. I will study the films of every race and make notes on every horse. It is a demanding, time-consuming way to approach the game, and for most fans that is its drawback.

Some important components of horses' trips — notably, pace and track bias — can be assessed fairly well from the *Daily Racing Form* charts. But many other aspects of the race — trouble, and ground loss on the turns — cannot be judged well from the footnotes. If the footnotes say that a horse "raced wide," what does that mean? Was he three horses wide or a disastrous ten-wide? If the footnote says "off slow," did the horse break a stride slow or was he left standing flat-footed in the gate, five lengths behind the field? If a horse is said to be "steadied," did the jockey stop riding for a split-second or encounter serious trouble that cost him the race? If I am gambling seriously, I want to be able to assess, firsthand, the degree to which such events may have affected a horse's figure. With race-replay shows on television in most areas, fans have the chance to study the races even if they are not everyday racegoers. Bettors must decide whether it is worth their time and effort to secure the edge that comes from a more acute understanding of the factors that make up horses' trips.

Ground Loss It should be self-evident that horses are hindered by racing wide on turns; they have to travel farther than the horses inside them. This factor is so important that all trip handicappers will regularly note horses' positions on the turn. They envision a racetrack as a track for human runners, on which every athlete has his own lane. If horses are racing tightly abreast of one another, with the innermost horse close to the rail, that inside horse is said to be on the rail, the horse outside him is in the 2-path, the next horse is in the 3-path, and so on. When making notes on a race, handicappers will commonly designate the horses' positions when they are at the midpoint of a turn as well as when the field fans out into the stretch. In my notations, a designation of "2T 4E" would indicate that a horse was in the 2-path on the turn and the 4-path when he entered the stretch. A horse parked five-wide on the first turn of a route race would be "5FT." (Racing far out from the rail doesn't force a horse to travel extra ground when he is running a straight line, on the backstretch or in the stretch, but I will note his position in case a track bias exists — such as "3B" or "Rail S.") In many situations, a horse's position on the turn will be the deciding factor in handicapping a race. If two horses have similar figures, and I know that one of them earned his with a four-wide move while the other got through along the rail, I may strongly prefer the wider horse.

In theory, at least, loss of ground on the turns lends itself to precise mathematical measurement. If a horse has been traveling an additional X extra feet by going wide, it should be possible to adjust his figure according to the extra ground he traveled. This, in fact, is the most distinguishing feature of the Sheets' calculations; employees at each track note how wide the horses ran on the turns so that this ground loss can be incorporated into the numbers. Roughly speaking, a horse travels an extra length for each path that he is removed from the rail on a turn. If he is in the 2-path all the way around a turn, he has lost one length. If he is in the 4-path around both turns of a route race, he has gone an additional six lengths — three around each turn.

But if these calculations sound unassailable in theory, they often collapse in practice. The significance of ground loss on turns varies according to different situations in a race; sometimes going four-wide is fatal; sometimes going six-wide is irrelevant. In route races, for example, ground lost on the first turn always seems more significant than ground lost on the stretch turn. Although plenty of horses win races by swooping around the field as they enter the stretch, horses who are parked wide all the way around the first turn are invariably doomed. Outside posts rarely win route races starting very close to the first turn — such as the $1\frac{1}{16}$-mile races at $1\frac{1}{8}$-mile tracks like Laurel, Hollywood Park, and Hialeah.

The mathematics of ground loss is complicated by its relationship to the pace of a race. When a hot pace has taken its toll on front-runners, horses regularly circle the field with success. This is a frequent Kentucky Derby scenario: Strike the Gold swooped wide around the field to win the 1991 Derby; Gato Del Sol swooped to win in 1982. Did their performances deserve to be upgraded because they were in the 7-path or thereabouts? Would they be able to run faster by several lengths, thus earning much bigger figures, if they subsequently benefited from rail trips? Not likely. Both Strike the Gold and Gato del Sol ran the very best races of which they were capable when they raced wide in the Derby. (Strike the Gold, in fact, stayed on the rail in the Preakness, and his figure dropped from 107 to 97.)

The effects of pace can be more important than those of ground loss; if one horse is engaged in a hot battle for the early lead and a rival swoops wide past him, the battler has probably run the better race. This principle was demonstrated in a $1\frac{1}{16}$-mile race at Del Mar:

Pass Me Lypheor — Dk. b. or br. g. 5, by Lypheor (Eng)—Pass Me, by Pass

DELAHOUSSAYE E (162 31 30 18 .19) — **$10,000** Br.—Hughes Farm Inc (Fla) — **120**

Own.—Ellison Spearl (Trust) — Tr.—Hess R B Jr (58 15 8 10 .26)

Lifetime						
44 3 2 4	1992	10	1	1	0	$10,925
$68,025	1991	12	1	0	1	$20,000
	Turf	20	0	0	3	$23,325
	Wet	1	0	0	0	

10Aug92- 9Dmr	fst	1 1/16	:461	1:104	1:431	3↑Clm 10000	84	5	12	99¼	73¾	3½	11¼	Delahoussaye E	LBb	116	9.80	85–15 PssMLyphr1161¼DnSpt1162¼GBgAl116	Off slowly, wide	12
28Jun92- 9GG	fm	1 1/16 Ⓣ	:474	1:113	1:43	+ Clm 12500	76	7	6	66	87	88½	85½	Martinez O AJr	LBb	117	17.80	91–04 CrolinNorth117hdBrryVersus117hdEvrStdy117	No threat	9
13Jun92-10GG	fm	1 1/16 Ⓣ	:463	1:112	1:43	+ Clm 12500	82	3	6	78½	64	43	41	Noguez A M	LBb	117	41.00	96 — PrivtJt117hdBrryVrsus117noSoltu117	Lacked room late	9
31May92- 7GG	fst	1	:454	1:094	1:36	Clm 12500	75	2	6	712	88¾	810	85½	Kaenel J L	LBb	117	53.60	84–17 Generator1171¾ Power Full119hd Kayoed117	Outrun	9
16May92- 9GG	fst	1	:451	1:092	1:354	Clm 10000	52	6	8	817	918	822	717¾	Espindola M A	LBb	117	12.40	73–12 Gnrtor1171½WoodnWishs1195PowrFull119	Showed little	10
3May92- 1GG	fst	1 1/16	:462	1:102	1:423	Clm 18000	65	5	6	610	611	612	613½	Espindola M A	LBb	116	12.30	70–12 SpndingBucks1172SrtogLd1172ViwpointAhd117	Outrun	6
18Apr92- 9GG	fst	1	:454	1:094	1:341	Clm 16000	81	5	5	54¾	56¼	48	28	Espindola M A	LBb	117	27.10	91–06 ArnCmndr1178PssMLphr117½ChlSnd117	Wide late run	7
7Mar92-10GG	fst	1⅛	:464	1:11	1:49	Hcp 12500s	74	2	7	79½	78	811	810	Doocy T T	LB	114	8.50	79–13 Baltistan116hd Strogien1152½ Nice Balloon115	Outrun	8
15Jan92- 9SA	fst	1 1/16	:472	1:121	1:441	Clm c-16000	83	11	10	1011	98½	77¾	55½	Delahoussaye E	LB	116	9.80	76–12 GchAlrt-Ch1151¾GrtRlts1193AMTRbr117	6-wide stretch	11
4Jan92- 9SA	gd	1 1/16	:464	1:103	1:422	Clm 20000	59	1	7	65½	78½	816	922	Valenzuela P A	LB	118	5.20	69–13 ElGranSid1107Bassman1102LtestRelese-Ir115	Wide trip	10

LATEST WORKOUTS Aug 5 Dmr 4f fst :484 H Jly 29 Hol 6f fst 1:144 H Jly 23 Hol 4f fst :511 H

Down Spout — B. c. 4, by Mr Leader—Immortal, by T V Lark

SOLIS A (171 21 21 24 .12) — **$10,000** Br.—Madden P & Morriss Mrs C F (Ky) — **116**

Own.—Gatti Robert J — Tr.—O'Hara John (9 2 0 2 .22)

Lifetime						
15 4 1 1	1992	5	1	1	0	$10,475
$42,625	1991	9	3	0	1	$32,150
	Turf	2	0	0	0	$875

10Aug92- 9Dmr	fst	1 1/16	:461	1:104	1:431	3↑Clm 10000	82	6	1	1½	1hd	2hd	21¼	Solis A	LBb	116	7.50	84–15 PssMLyphor1161¼DownSpt1162¼GBgAl116	Good effort	12
6Jun92- 9Hol	fst	7f	:222	:45	1:232	Clm 10000	67	7	4	1hd	2½	33	75¾	Solis A	LBb	116	*1.80	81–09 CutterSam116½RangeRider116¾ShrpEvent118	Gave way	11
8Mar92- 9SA	fst	1 1/16	:462	1:104	1:432	Clm 12500	88	3	2	2hd	1hd	1½	11¼	Solis A	LBb	115	4.10	86–13 DownSpout1151¼ChiefSssfrs1151¾TurboTrick110	All out	10
17Feb92- 1SA	gd	6½f	:221	:451	1:174	Clm 16000	72	4	5	79	78½	66	52½	Solis A	LBb	114	4.70	78–17 Udino115nkRelAffirmed1151¾Andimo117	Climbing early	7
9Jan92- 7SA	gd	1 1/16	:471	1:121	1:452	Clm 20000	70	1	2	2hd	42¼	64½	712¼	Solis A	LBb	114	5.80	64–29 ThClnrs1203¼TrulyRoyl1172Mr.Winnr116	4-wide stretch	10
26Dec91- 9SA	fst	7f	:224	:454	1:224	3↑Clm 12500	87	7	3	2½	1½	1hd	11½	Solis A	LBb	113	5.80	89–11 DwnSpt1131½GchAlrt-Ch115½WrttnWrds-Au116	Driving	11
9Oct91- 1SA	fst	1 1/16	:463	1:112	1:442	Clm 16000	62	1	1	2hd	3nk	3½	97¼	Solis A	LBb	118	*2.50	74–15 YsCnD116¾OvrssMrt-Ir116no🄳Dr.FstLv114	Took up 1/16	11
9Oct91-Placed eighth through disqualification																				
26Sep91- 7Fpx	fst	1 1/16	:47	1:122	1:441	Clm 16000	77	9	2	1hd	1½	11½	12	Solis A	LBb	114	2.20	87–13 DownSpout1142Dr.FstLove1142OvrssMrkt-Ir114	Driving	9
21Aug91- 5Dmr	fst	1 1/16	:463	1:111	1:43	Clm 16000	71	11	3	2hd	3½	33	34¾	Solis A	LBb	115	7.60	81–16 KlCri1152¾Dr.FstLov1162DownSpout115	4-wide stretch	11
12Aug91- 5Dmr	fst	6½f	:213	:44	1:16	Clm 25000	64	8	6	76¼	98	1010	812¼	Castanon A L	LBb	115	18.10	76–16 NoNewts1152¾FiestaFair1152Fistylee110	5-wide stretch	12

LATEST WORKOUTS Aug 19 Dmr 4f fst :473 H Aug 1 Dmr 5f fst 1:014 H Jly 25 Dmr 4f fst :493 H Jly 15 SA 5f gd 1:03 H

Pass Me Lypheor had rallied to beat Down Spout when they met in their previous start, and now they were matched up again. My notes on Pass Me Lypheor read "5T move past battlers." My comment on Down Spout was "2B battle, Rail T, caught." Down Spout had been engaged in a hard fight for the lead through a half mile in 46⅕ seconds; he had won that fight and gained the lead on the rail. But Pass Me Lypheor rallied five-wide on the turn to catch him in the stretch. Despite their relative positions on the turn, this had been a fairly easy trip for Pass Me Lypheor and a fairly tough trip for Down Spout. In their rematch, the Del Mar crowd made Pass Me Lypheor the 5-to-2 favorite (maybe a lot of Sheet players were there), but with an easier pace Down Spout prevailed and paid $11.60.

Ground loss becomes much more significant when a horse races wide as the pace of the race is hurting him. It can be very difficult for a horse to battle for the lead while racing four-wide around a turn. And it can be even more difficult for a come-from-behind runner to lose ground when he is trying to close against a slow pace. This was the basis of the most clear-cut betting opportunity I have ever seen in a Triple Crown race.

The 1988 Kentucky Derby was an exciting battle of the sexes between the filly Winning Colors and the colt Forty Niner, and between their illustrious trainers, Wayne Lukas and Woody Stephens. Nobody thought that Louie Roussel III, the trainer of Risen Star, belonged in the company of the giants of the profession, and Roussel himself seemed to agree. "What I know about training," he told reporters a few days before the Derby, "you could put under a gnat's armpit. If Risen Star could talk, you know what he'd say? He'd say, 'Get me Whittingham!'" Even though Risen Star had earned speed figures that were close to those of his Derby rivals, it was hard to take him too seriously. But the Derby showed that he deserved to be taken very seriously indeed, even if Louie Roussel III didn't have Hall of Fame credentials.

Winning Colors set a moderate early pace, a half mile in 46⅘ seconds, and opened a four-length lead. Forty Niner was content to stalk her, because Stephens was uncertain about his colt's ability to go the Derby distance and didn't want him subjected to excessive early pressure. Given this relatively easy lead, Winning Colors was able to run the race of her life, and she held on to beat Forty Niner by a neck. But Risen Star had tried hard under impossible conditions. Jockey Eddie Delahoussaye had taken him eight-wide on the backstretch and had stayed that wide on the turn. But despite the ground loss and the adverse pace, the son of Secretariat rallied furiously to finish third, three lengths behind Forty Niner. I saw Roussel the next morning and said, "Congratulations. You had the best horse in the Derby," but he was inconsolable. He'd let down all of the colt's fans back home in New Orleans. He'd let down the nuns who were praying for Risen Star. He didn't know if he wanted to go through this again in the Preakness.

Roussel did take Risen Star to Baltimore, where he continued to fret and vacillate. Four days before the Preakness, he said he was "99 percent certain" that the colt wouldn't run. Then he entered him anyway. While he wavered, I prayed that he would make the right decision. Never had I seen a situation in which the loser of a major race had so clearly been the best horse. Moreover, I thought Risen Star could benefit from a Bold Forbes–Honest

Pleasure scenario, because Woody Stephens was stating firmly that he would not permit Winning Colors to steal away from Forty Niner this time. "We may finish next-to-last," he declared publicly, "but she'll finish last." Nevertheless, there was no groundswell of support for Risen Star, and he was going to be a big price if he ran in the Preakness. He was getting attention at Pimlico not because he was potentially America's best 3-year-old but because of his trainer's indecision about everything. Roussel had decided not to give Risen Star a workout at Pimlico, but then he said, "I saw Mr. Stephens work his horse, I saw Mr. Lukas work his horse, and I started questioning myself. I could see the headlines: 'Dummy Makes Mistake, Skips Workout.'"

The trainer didn't make up his mind to run Risen Star until early on the rainy afternoon of the Preakness. When he did, he created a great gambling opportunity, because the odds in that race bore little relationship to the ability of the horses: Winning Colors 9 to 5, Forty Niner 2 to 1, Risen Star 6 to 1. True to Woody Stephens's vow, Forty Niner came out of the gate on a mission to beat Winning Colors. Jockey Pat Day kept Forty Niner five-wide on the first turn, forcing the filly wider, and stayed in that path all the way around the track, losing a disastrous amount of ground but forcing Winning Colors to lose even more. Seeing what the leaders were doing, Delahoussaye took Risen Star to the rail and stalked the leaders, then accelerated inside them on the final turn to take command of the race. When he won and paid $15.60, the result was a classic illustration of the way ground loss on the turns can sometimes be a race's determining factor. In the Derby, Winning Colors had earned a figure of 111 and Risen Star a 106. In the Preakness, Risen Star earned a 110 and Winnings Colors a 106 — differences almost exclusively due to the effect of running wide.

Trouble If, instead of running wide and being hindered by a slow pace in the Derby, Risen Star had been blocked or checked or had encountered some dramatic instance of trouble, horseplayers would have been keenly aware of it. Television replays would have shown the crucial incident over and over. And Risen Star's odds might have been 3 to 1 instead of 6 to 1. This is why most trip-oriented handicappers restrain their excitement when they see an extremely dramatic incident of trouble during a race. The public invariably overbets such horses when they run again. Subtler types of trips are almost always more productive.

Nevertheless, trouble in a race is obviously important, and any handicapper — whether he is watching races intently or relying on data in the *Daily Racing Form* — has to be aware of it and evaluate how much it might have affected a horse's performance. It is the question of degree that is critical. If the comment in the *Racing Form* says "blocked" and the horse ran a poor figure, does this mean that a low speed figure can be disregarded entirely? Or might the horse have been affected by only a couple of lengths or a few points? When I watch a race and see a horse's progress impeded, I try to review the films and find a horse near him who was moving at a similar rate of speed when the incident occurred. I note the distance between those two horses and estimate how many lengths the troubled horse lost vis-à-vis the other until he regained his momentum. I'll put that estimate into my notes: "Blocked (3L)" or "Steadied (2L)."

One of the subtlest and yet most serious types of trouble occurs when a front-runner tires and starts to drop back abruptly, forcing the horse immediately behind him to drop back, too, to avoid running over the erstwhile leader's heels. If the jockey on the troubled horse doesn't obviously panic and yank the reins, but merely lets his horse drop back, few observers will notice the incident, yet the horse may lose many lengths.

There is one type of trouble that most racing fans — and even many *Racing Form* trackmen — consistently overrate. When a field is bunched on the turn, horses on the inside behind the leaders will commonly have to wait for running room until the field fans out into the stretch. Their jockeys may have to sit as if paralyzed, but they will benefit from saving ground and are probably in a much better position than the horses who are parked three- and four-wide around the turn. Nevertheless, this type of trip will always attract attention and elicit comments like "Steadied, "Lacked room," or "Blocked."

• • •

Slow Starts   As in the case of horses in trouble, there are many types and degrees of bad starts that might earn the comment "Off slowly." Some horses are chronic slow starters, plodders who put themselves at a tactical disadvantage whenever they run. But sometimes a horse will break tardily because he is momentarily unprepared when the gate opens. When that happens, I will estimate the number of lengths the horse broke behind the field — "2 slo," for example. In the case of a horse who is usually a front-runner, coming out of the gate even a step or two slow can disrupt his entire race, forcing a jockey to alter the horse's style entirely or else to gun him hard to get him into contention.

"Easy" Winners   When a horse wins a race with ease, with the jockey restraining him or even standing in the irons at the wire, novice racing fans will invariably assume that the animal could have run much faster if he had been pushed. Every *Daily Racing Form* trackman pays careful attention to the way winners finish, and every chart designates how hard the jockey was riding at the wire. Most horses win all-out and are described as "driving"; those under intermittent pressure earn the comments "handily" or "ridden out"; a few earn the supreme accolade "easily." Few aspects of horse racing are so deceptive.

Once a half-ton animal has reached high gear and taken command of a race, a jockey can't significantly slow his momentum. A horse may give the impression of having energy in reserve, but this is most often an illusion. When Groovy ran six furlongs in 1:07$\frac{4}{5}$ and earned a figure of 134, he was described as being "ridden out." But he never ran faster in races where he was under pressure. When jockeys "wrap up" on horses at the finish, they may look more stylish in the official photograph of the race, and they may please owners and trainers who don't like to see their horses abused unnecessarily, but this late restraint won't have much of an effect on the horse's figure.

The sight of a jockey "wrapping up" on a horse at the wire always evokes for me one of my bitterest memories as a horseplayer. I had been enduring a painful losing streak at Gulfstream Park when I found a horse with a big figure, earned with a tough trip, who was going to reverse my fortunes. I bet him heavily at 6 to 1 and watched excitedly as he surged to the lead in midstretch, a certain winner. But as he approached the wire, jockey David Penna looked as if he had been suddenly stricken by rigor mortis, and a rival on the far outside, presumably out of Penna's view, flew past him in the final stride to win by a nose. As I was watching the television replay in the press box, howling, "What was Penna doing?" a Toronto turf writer standing nearby said, "I can tell you. There's a Canadian camera crew here today doing a piece on Canadians in Florida racing, and this is the race where they were filming Penna. He's kind of a vain guy, and he was striking a nice pose for the camera." And jockeys wonder why we hate them.

When horses win "easily," it is often because they have had easy trips. They may be front-runners who have benefited from a slow early pace, and they won't run better when they are put under pressure and subjected to adversity. The majority of the horses described as easy winners will run inferior figures in their next starts. Four colts came into the 1992 Breeders' Cup Juvenile with comments in the *Racing Form* that denoted comfortable victories in one of their last two starts. These were the horses, their victorious performances, and their subsequent figures at Gulfstream Park:

Horse	Figure	Comment	Breeders' Cup Figure
River Special	93	Ridden Out	85
Sudden Hush	92	Ridden Out	41
Gilded Time	91	Handily	87
Caponostro	85	Ridden Out	74

Handicappers should never assume, on the basis of an easy victory, that a horse is capable of running much faster unless he has done it before. If a horse frequently runs speed figures around 100 and now he toys with a field and gets a 90, I will accept the premise that he might have run a 100 again if he had been asked. But if he has never run a 100 before, he will have to show me that he can do it.

• • •

"Outrun" Figures   The most alert trip handicappers will sometimes watch a horse from start to finish and see him do absolutely
nothing of interest. The animal plods around the track in the back
of the field without going especially wide, without encountering
any trouble, and he gets trounced. But what if that horse subsequently shows up in a field where he has the top figure? Should
he be bet? Is the number credible?

Harness handicappers maintain, correctly, that standardbreds
can be "sucked along" to a fast time: an animal incapable of pacing
a mile in 1:56 under normal circumstances can do it if he is in a
field of champs who are going in 1:52. Yet in thoroughbred racing
this phenomenon does not seem to exist. I believe in the legitimacy of figures earned when a horse was being outrun, and I am
willing to bet a horse who barely appeared to pick up his feet in
his last start if he has the top number in today's race. When such
a situation arises, the horse is probably dropping sharply in class,
with his trainer thinking, "It's now or never," and revving him up
accordingly. Moreover, the jockey probably wasn't asking for an
all-out effort when the horse was so far behind, and he will surely
be more aggressive if the horse is in contention today. Obviously,
I would prefer a badly beaten horse to have shown some faint
signs of life — a flash of speed for an eighth of a mile, an abortive
five-wide move on the turn — but even if he didn't, I am prepared
to live and die by my figures.

Readers who have purchased this book in the hope of finding a
few neat rules for applying Beyer Speed Figures may feel now that
they are sinking into an abyss. Certainly they may feel that they
are on a slippery slope as they try to use speed figures in conjunction with pace, biases, ground loss, and trouble, trying to relate
something quantifiable to something that is not quantifiable. But
it is not so difficult.

I approach each race in what is essentially a simple fashion. On
the basis of speed figures, who are the contenders and noncontent-
ders? Under what circumstances have the contenders earned their
figures? Are some of them perhaps better or worse than their

numbers? This is a realistic way of handicapping with figures, and it is also more satisfying than using numbers blindly. Handicapping is an art, a test of man's creative intelligence, not merely a puzzle to be solved by applying the right formula. When I picked the winner of the eighth race at Laurel on October 27, 1992, I felt a satisfaction that transcended even the joy of collecting a stack of hundred-dollar bills.

1 1/16 MILES. (1.41⁴) ALLOWANCE. Purse $18,500. 2–year–olds, which have not won a race other than maiden or claiming. Weight, 120 lbs. Non–winners of a race at one mile or over since October 1 allowed 3 lbs. Such a race since September 1, 6 lbs.

Coupled—Stelios Art and Wild About Harry.
LASIX—Foxy Bailjumper, Dynamic Brush, Wild About Harry.

Foxy Bailjumper

B. g. 2(May), by Bailjumper—Foxy Naskra, by Naskra
Br.—Halter Constance (Md)
Tr.—Hendricks Franklin J (2 1 0 0 .50)

Own.—A & A Stables

10Oct92- 3Pim fst 1⅟₁₆	:48	1:14	1:47⁴	Md 8500	57	2 2	2³	2²	1²	1⁸	Castillo F⁵	L 115	*2.70	65–29 FoxyBljmpr115⁸Conclmn Jhn115ⁿᵏFrdmtChs120 Driving 11
13Sep92- 5Pim fst 6f	:22³	:47²	1:13³	Md 12000	39	1 1	3²⅟₂	33⅟₂	35⅟₂	66⅟₂	Prado E S	L 120	2.70	70–16 YnFghtg120⅟₂FnrlMrch115⅟₂ShnngWtass1⅟₂ Weakened 12
23Aug92- 5Lrl fst 6f	:22¹	:46²	1:12⁴	Md 12000	36	8 10	11¹⁵	81⁴	67	47⅟₂	Moorefield W T⁵	115	6.90	69–21 Against HllBll⅟₂HnstHrbrt115²⅟₂poses deWn114 14
9Aug92- 3Lrl fm 6f ⊕	:22³	:46²	1:10⁴	Md Sp Wt	26	3 7	71³	71³	71²	71³⅟₂	Reynolds L C	120	6.10	74–13 Clint Coody125⅟₂...byirVrgun120 No Factor 9
21Jly92- 3Lrl fst 6f	:23	:47²	1:06³	Md 16000	23	7 2	46⅟₂	46⅟₂	46	41⁰⅟₂	Delgado A	120	5.90	75–19 JstcTrmphs120⅟₂SwthrtRdor20ⁿRckyPrspctr120 Evenly 10
14Jly92- 3Lrl fst 5⅟₂f	:22²	:47	1:06²	Md 25000	35	8 3	68⅟₂	6⁸	57	47⅟₂	Delgado A	120	9.10	80–15 Cullen120⅟₂ Jorge ofMexic.120⅟₂Orrgrumd120 Steadied 8
26Jun92- 3Pim fst 5f	:22⁴	:47²	1:00¹	Md 25000	21	8 8	97⅟₂	77⅟₂	6⁹	51⁰⅟₂	Prado E S	120	4.30	76–11 Ziggy's Dream120⅟₂ Stelios Art1201⅟₂irValiant120 Wide 9
11Jun92- 5Pim fst 5f	:23¹	:48¹	1:01	Md 16000	30	1 5	85⅟₂	6⁵	4⁴	3¹	Douglas F G	120	10.60	82–13 FrDncngHvs117¹JstcTrmphs120ⁿᵏFxyBljmpr120 Rallied 12

LATEST WORKOUTS   Oct 16 Pim 4f fst :48³ H   Sep 24 Pim 7f fst 1:28⁴ H

Lifetime	1992	8 1 0 1	$6,975
8 1 0 1			
$6,975	Turf	1 0 0 0	$300

109⁵

Sir Valiant

B. c. 2(Apr), by Your Eyes Only, by Exclusive Native
Br.—Oxley John C (Ky)
Tr.—Delp Grover G (7 2 1 1 .29)

Own.—Meyerhoff Harry C

20Oct92- 7Lrl fst 6⅟₂f	:22³	:46¹	1:18³	Md 25000	60	2 2	1hd	1²	16⅟₂	Wilson R		b 120	*1.70	84–14 SirValinty120⅟₂Dvt'sunner120⅟₂osts'Choice120 Driving 9
11Sep92- 7Pim fst 6f	:23³	:47¹	1:12³	Md Sp Wt	51	5 6	4²	53⅟₂	56⅟₂	58⅟₂	Douglas F G	b 120	11.40	74–20 Domus⅟₂pySchrff123⅟₂pnk120 Weakened 11
11Aug92- 5Lrl fst 6f	:22²	:46²	1:12³	Md Sp Wt	47	2 4	3⅟₂	3ⁿᵏ	21⅟₂	2¹	Douglas F G	b 120	4.10	77–18 ForeignConflict120⅟₂irValiant120Crdiologist120 Sharp 10
21Jun92- 3Pim fst 5f	:22⁴	:47²	1:00¹	Md 25000	32	2 4	23⅟₂	2³	3⁵	36⅟₂	Douglas F G	120	6.30	80–11 Ziggy'sDrm120⅟₂StliosArt120¹SrVlnt120 Stumbled start 9

LATEST WORKOUTS   Oct 15 Lrl 4f fst :48² H   Sep 4 Lrl 5f gd 1:02³ B

Lifetime	1992	4 1 1 1	$10,580
4 1 1 1			
$10,580			

114

Down Home Doctor

Gr. c. 2(Mar), by Family Doctor—Keyov, by Zinov
Br.—Patton Charles (Fla)
Tr.—Salzman J Edwin Jr (23 4 5 2 .17)

Own.—Fry Nancy B

8Oct92- 6Lrl fst 6f	:22³	:46²	1:12²	Alw 16800	48	4 3	3²	3¹	66⅟₂	6⁷	Wilson R	b 114	*.50	72–20 GoldenMony112ⁿᵏPointTkr115¹⅟₂Pddy'sFlir120 Fell back 7
27Sep92- 8Pim sly 6f	:22⁴	:46	1:12³	Alw 17100	69	4 3	2hd	2hd	22⅟₂	22⅟₂	Wilson R	b 114	2.40e	79–18 DpprDoc114²⅟₂DownHomDctr114ⁿᵏJrgfMxc114 Held 2nd 8
15Sep92- 6Pim fst 6f	:23	:46²	1:12	Alw 16800	68	6 1	1¹	1²	2hd	2¹	Wilson R	b 114	*.70e	84–15 DprtngClg114¹DynHmDct4⅟₄DpprDc114 Held place 7
7Aug92- 6Lrl fst 6f	:22²	:46³	1:12²	Alw 16800	53	4 5	1⅟₂	11⅟₂	3²	48⅟₂	Prado E S	b 120	2.70e	71–22 StormFlht114⅟₂eiledVet⅟₂114⁵NoDisput114 Gave way 7
17Jly92- 3Lrl fst 5⅟₂f	:22¹	:46²	1:06¹	Md Sp Wt	65	1 2	1⁴	1⁴	1³	11⅟₂	Prado E S	b 120	*1.50	88–15 DownHmDoctor120¹⅟₂BbnCC120⅟₂Jssi'sWnnr120 Driving 8
3Jly92-11Lrl my 5⅟₂f	:22¹	:46¹	1:04³	Primer	40	2 5	2hd	2¹	57⅟₂	51¹⅟₂	Chavez S N	113	2.90e	84–08 WldZnl113⅟₂StrmFlght113¹⅟₂DprtngCld113 Dropped back 6
25Jun92- 5Pim fst 5f	:22²	:46¹	:58²	Md Sp Wt	68	10 8	1⅟₂	1³	1²	2⅟₂	Chavez S N	120	11.10e	95–13 GlRoyle120⅟₂DownHomeDoctor120⁶⅟₂Cchumb120 Gamely 12

LATEST WORKOUTS   Sep 8 Lrl 5f fst 1:01 H   ● Sep 1 Lrl ⊕ 5f fm 1:01 H (d)

Lifetime	1992	7 1 3 0	$21,163
7 1 3 0			
$21,163	Wet	2 0 1 0	$4,108

114

Dynamic Brush

B. c. 2(Feb), by Broad Brush—Dynamic Star, by Silent Screen
Br.—Mayerhoff Robert E (Md)
Tr.—Small Richard W (9 0 4 0 .00)

Own.—Meyerhoff Robert E

17Oct92- 1Pha fst 1 70	:47	1:14	1:46²	Md Sp Wt	66	3 3	1hd	1¹	2hd	1ⁿᵏ	Black A S	L 120	4.40	64–29 DynmicBrush120ⁿᵏHopeOfPc120⁷⅟₂MgicPppr120 Driving 7
27Sep92- 4Pim sly 6f	:23¹	:46³	1:14	Md 25000	52	6 2	42⅟₂	4⁴	31⅟₂	32⅟₂	Moorefield W T⁵	L 115	7.00	73–18 Stv'sFllw120¹³anmacjon120⁰Dtqⁿ brush115 Slight r'ly 8
15Sep92- 7Pim fst 6f	:23²	:47	1:12¹	Md 25000	41	6 7	4²	3³	35⅟₂	41¹⅟₂	MoorefildWT⁵	b 115	*3.10	72–15 JorgofMxico120⅟₂byinnPdro1115⅟₂Fllow118 Faded 12
25Aug92- 6Lrl fm 6f ⊕	:23²	:46	1:12²	Md Sp Wt	36	5 2	21	53⅟₂	57⅟₂	69⅟₂	Seefeldt A J	120	7.10	70–21 OnforthPlot120ⁿᵏMiddlbrpYrk120⅟₂RylSnr120 Weakened 10
28Jly92- 5Lrl fst 5⅟₂f	:23	:47	1:06	Md Sp Wt	43	6 6	54⅟₂	5⁶	4⁷	35⅟₂	Seefeldt A J	120	5.70	83–13 StelosArt120ⁿᵏubbbs⅟₂⅟₂nicBrush1⅟₂d r'ly 10

Lifetime	1992	5 1 0 2	$12,285
5 1 0 2			
$12,285	Turf	1 0 0 0	$310
	Wet	1 0 0 1	$1,150

115⁵

Stelios Art

Ch. c. 2(Mar), by Roo Art—Resoundingly, by Exclusive Native
Br.—Green Willow Farms (Md)
Tr.—Delp Richard W (22 1 3 4 .05)

Own.—Dellis Marcella M

Lifetime	1992	7	2	2	0	$22,505
7 2 2 0						
$22,505	Turf	1	0	0	0	
	Wet	1	1	0	0	$8,265

114

9Oct92- 4Lrl my 6f	:224	:47	1:12		Clm 25000	76 1 2 12 13 15 16½ Pino M G	b 114	6.70	81-22 Stelios Art114⁶½ Silver Key114²½ Granlund114	Driving 8
26Sep92- 5Pim gd 6f	:23	:46¹	1:12		Nursery	53 12 4 55 77¾ 811 99¾ Pino M G	b 122	38.70	75-13 Military Look115 Guru Dude122ⁿᵏ P.J.Higgins122	Wide 12
13Sep92-11Pim fm 1	①:47	1:11⁴	1:38		Vanland'm	34 10 7 10¹¹11¹⁹11²⁵10³⁰½ Prado E S	b 112	57.30	47-27 StormFlight110⁸SecrtOdds111²½Qizilbsh115	Wide early 11
7Aug92- 6Lrl fst 6f	:222	:46³	1:12²		Alw 16800	48 6 6 65½ 68½ 69 610 Pino M G	b 120	7.00	69-22 Storm Flight114ⁿᵏ VeiledVi...114½DispureE114	Outrun 7
28Jly92- 5Lrl fst 5½f	:23	:47	1:06		Md Sp Wt	59 5 4 2ʰᵈ 2ʰᵈ 1ʰᵈ 1ⁿᵏ Luzzi M J	b 120	*1.60e	89-13 Stelios Art120ⁿᵏ BubbaC120ʰᵈDynamicBrush120	Driving 10
3Jly92- 2Lrl fst 5½f	:222	:46¹	1:05²		Md 25000	52 7 2 54½ 55½ 44 2ⁿᵒ Pino M G	b 120	3.10	92-12 No Dispute120ⁿᵒ Stelios Art120¹½ Cullen120	Wide 7
21Jun92- 3Pim fst 5f	:224	:47²	1:00¹		Md 25000	35 9 6 44½ 44½ 24 25¾ Pino M G		120	5.80	81-11 Ziggy's Dream120⁵¾ Stelios Art120¹ SirValiant120	Wide 14

LATEST WORKOUTS   Oct 6 Pim 4f fst :49⁴ B   Sep 24 Pim 3f fst :35² H   Sep 8 Pim 5f sly 1:01³ H   Sep 3 Pim 5f fst 1:00² H

Stevie's Fellow

Dk. b. or br. c. 2, by Play Fellow—Barbie Bev, by Bailjumper
Br.—Brady W James (Ky)
Tr.—Wolfendale Howard E (10 1 1 1 .10)

Own.—Stern Margaret E

Lifetime	1992	3	1	0	1	$9,040
3 1 0 1						
$9,040						
	Wet	1	1	0	0	$6,900

114

17Oct92- 2Lrl fst 6½f	:223	:46⁴	1:20		Alw 16800	50 3 3 41½ 52½ 45 43½ Wilson R	b 114	13.90	73-18 JorgofMxco114½Wh⅜Aberryhry116³PontTkr115	Willingly 7
4Pim sly 6f	:224	:46	1:14		Md 25000	57 1 1 2ʰᵈ 2½ 1½ 11½ Luzzi M J	b 120	5.50	75-18 Stvi'sFllow120¹⅓Cllingtym120³DanzaBrsh120	Driving 8
15Sep92- 7Pim fst 6f	:232	:47	1:12¹		Md 20000	42 9 5 52½ 77½ 6¹¹ 3¹¹¼ Luzzi M J	118	7.60	73-15 JorgofMxico120⁸MyMnfⁱdro115³½Stvi'sFllow118	Rallied 7

LATEST WORKOUTS   Sep 8 Lrl 5f fst 1:02¹ B

Wild About Harry

Dk. b. or br. c. 2(May), by Wild Again—Diamond Tilly, by Alydar
Br.—Calumet Farm (Ky)
Tr.—Delp Richard W (22 1 3 4 .05)

Own.—Capital Racing Stable

Lifetime	1992	8	1	2	0	$16,940
8 1 2 0						
$16,940	Turf	1	0	0	0	
	Wet	1	0	0	0	$300

114

17Oct92- 2Lrl fst 6½f	:223	:46⁴	1:20		Alw 16800	57 4 5 21 1ʰᵈ 2ʰᵈ 2½ Pino M G	Lb 116	*1.50e	76-18 JorgofMxico114½WildAboutHrry116³PointTkr115	Hung 7
27Sep92- 8Pim sly 6f	:224	:46	1:12³		Alw 17100	28 5 6 78¾ 815 822 819½ Pino M G	b 117	6.80	62-18 DpprDoc114²¾DownHomDoctr114ⁿᵏ JrgfMxc114	Outrun 8
13Sep92-11Pim fm 1	①:47	1:11⁴	1:38		Vanland'm	46 9 11 11¹²10¹⁴10²⁰ 92⁴ Pino M G	b 113	14.70	54-27 Storm Flight110⁸ Secret Odd111¹²½Qizilbash115	Outrun 11
9Aug92- 7Lrl fst 6f	:223	:46³	1:12²		Md Sp Wt	68 8 2 21 1½ 12½ 13½ Pino M G	b 120	3.60	79-21 WldAbtHrry120³¼ltry↓120ⁿᵒ Bllgmn116	Driving 8
28Jly92- 5Lrl fst 5½f	:23	:47	1:06		Md Sp Wt	40 4 10 78½ 68 59 57 Pino M G	b 120	*1.60e	82-13 Stelios Art120ⁿᵏBubba120ʰᵈDynmicBrush120	Wide 10
17Jly92- 8Lrl fst 5½f	:222	:46	1:04²		Md Sp Wt	68 4 3 22 22 24 29 Pino M G	b 120	8.20	88-15 ScrtOdds120⁹WildAboutHrry120⁴½TkngRsks120	Gamely 8
5Jly92- 6Lrl fst 5½f	:222	:46³	1:06¹		Md Sp Wt	38 7 2 42 55 68½ 63½ Pino M G	b 120	16.20	84-13 LordofthBy120⁶BubbC120³PointTkr115	Wide, willingly 8
25Jun92- 5Pim fst 5f	:222	:46¹	:58²		Md Sp Wt	12 1 7 12¹⁹12²²¹22⁶11¹⁸¾ Pino M G		120	11.00	77-13 GlRoyle120¹DownHomDoctor120⁶½Cchumb120	Steadied 12

LATEST WORKOUTS   Oct 6 Pim 5f fst 1:02 B   Sep 24 Pim 4f fst :49 B   Sep 8 Pim 5f sly 1:01⁴ H   Sep 3 Pim 5f fst 1:00² H

Hasty Jaune

B. g. 2(Mar), by John Alden—Ocre Jaune, by Wittgenstein
Br.—Hidden Lane Stable (Md)
Tr.—Boniface J William (9 1 1 2 .11)

Own.—Meadow Bridge Farm

Lifetime	1992	6	1	0	0	$11,413
6 1 0 0						
$11,413	Turf	1	0	0	0	$750
	Wet	1	1	0	0	$8,700

120

9Oct92- 3Pha sly 1	:472	1:13⁴	1:41²		Md Sp Wt	61 1 8 8¹⁴ 74 41½ 1ⁿᵒ Colton R E	b 120	3.90	74-27 Hasty Jaune120ⁿᵒ Magic Pepper120ʰᵈSkiptheRoses120	9
9Oct92-Changed course, steadied, driving										
26Sep92-12Pim gd 1¹⁄₁₆	:472	1:13	1:47⁴		Md Sp Wt	58 4 8 8¹³ 67¾ 45 4½ Reynolds L C	b 122	9.10	64-18 SilentTestmony122ⁿᵏAwd122ⁿᵏTourDMrylnd122	Closed 11
26Sep92-Originally scheduled on turf										
9Sep92- 4Medfm 1	①:472	1:11⁴	1:37³		Md Sp Wt	43 5 9 8¹³ 87¾ 75¾ 49 Diaz L F	b 118	24.10	73-15 Timforthrill118²½Sminr118⁴TriplMnhttn118	Bothered st 9
13Aug92- 3Lrl fst 6f	:23	:47¹	1:13³		Md 12000	32 6 9 10¹⁷ 918 713 48 Reynolds L C	b 120	9.50	65-20 Jen's Beau118½Moycullen120⁴DanzaDelFuego120	Wide 9
18Jly92- 3Del fst 6f	:232	:49	1:15³		Md 20000	-0 5 6 8¹³ 811 612 516¾ Salvaggio M V	b 118	*2.50	52-29 BkndRoses112¹⁵SintlySon116½Jmi'sCbrt112	No threat 8
28Jun92- 2Del fst 5f	:23	:48³	1:01³		Md Sp Wt	0 9 9 65½ 68 67½ 59 Salvaggio M V	b 118	*2.60	64-23 BoldforBlssng118¹¾RDIStr115¼WrghttKnght118	Outrun 9

Strand of Blue

Gr. c. 2(Mar), by Blue Ensign—Strand of Gems, by Accipiter
Br.—Lucas Francis W (Fla)
Tr.—Perkins Ben W Jr (15 2 1 5 .13)

Own.—Char-Mari Stable

Lifetime	1992	4	1	1	2	$15,200
4 1 1 2						
$15,200						

120

10Oct92- 7Medfst 1⁷⁰	:47	1:12³	1:44²		Md Sp Wt	57 3 1 12 14½ 15 14½ Ferrer J C	b 118	*2.10	76-18 StrndofBlu118⁴½NorthBrule120¹MrshlRk118	Driving 8
18Sep92- 6Pim fst 6f	:24	:47¹	1:12⁴		Md Sp Wt	47 7 3 31 33 33 35¾ Wilson R		120	*.80	75-19 Jhn'sBeau120⁴½⁽ ⁾QuickStp118²½Strndf8lu120	Weakened 8
24Jly92- 7Mth fst 5½f	:221	:46¹	1:06¹		Md Sp Wt	52 5 7 44 45½ 31 32½ Wilson R		118	*1.80	81-16 Ingroove118ⁿᵏHighCounty118½½StrndfBl118	Inside bid 10
1Jly92-10Mth fst 5f	:22	:45²	:57³		Md Sp Wt	71 4 7 34½ 35 36½ 28 Wilson R		118	3.50	85-17 GrtNpt120ᵒ⁸Strdf8lu118ⁿᵏ⁽ ⁾DxcHnk118	Earned place 11

LATEST WORKOUTS   ●Oct 6 Bow 4f fst :48³ Hg   Sep 5 Mth 4f fst :50 Bg   Aug 28 Mth 4f fst :49⁴ B

The symbols at the left of past performance lines are my designations of track biases; there had been several strong rail- and speed-favoring days at this meeting. The comments on the right are my trip notes.

In this allowance race for 2-year-olds, one horse had a standout number in his last start: Stelios Art had earned a 76 — ten points higher than the next best last-race figure, Dynamic Brush's 66, and significantly better than the lifetime best of anybody else in the field. Stelios Art was a potential standout. Although he was going a distance for the first time, he would be very hard to beat if that number was legitimate. Was it?

I was certain that it was not. On the day Stelios Art ran, I had designated the track GR — a strong rail bias. The colt had broken from post position 1, and he got loose on the lead while running a half mile in a moderate 47 seconds. Never before had he earned a figure better than 59. Readers of the Sheets might look at the numbers before them and say that Stelios Art was a candidate to bounce, but bouncing was going to have nothing to do with his performance. His last race had been a bias-aided, pace-aided fluke, and under those circumstances I wouldn't touch him.

Several other horses in this field had earned figures in the mid-60s or better, which suggested that it would be safe to eliminate Foxy Bailjumper, Sir Valiant, and Stevie's Fellow, who had never run more than a 60. That left five possibilities.

Strand of Blue had once earned a big figure, but that was in a five-furlong race, and his loose-on-the-lead figure in his last start was a poor 57. He was an easy elimination.

Wild About Harry had a figure of 57 in his last race, and he had earned it honestly, dueling for the lead at a respectable pace. He had run figures in the mid-60s in the past, so he was a possibility.

Down Home Doctor's last was a 48, but his previous race was a 69. Might the higher number better reflect his ability? Actually, the reverse was true. His 48 had come under normal conditions, but he had earned that 69 dueling for the lead on an extremely speed-favoring track.

Dynamic Brush had been beaten by Stevie's Fellow on September 27, but his 52 might be excusable because he had been trying to rally on a speed-favoring track. Subsequently, he won at Philadelphia Park with a good figure of 66. I hadn't seen the race, so I found the *Racing Form* chart.

FIRST RACE

Phila Park

OCTOBER 17, 1992

1 MILE 70 YARDS. (1.39) MAIDEN SPECIAL WEIGHT. Purse $14,500. 2-year-olds. Weights, 120 lbs. (69th DAY WEATHER CLEAR TEMPERATURE 60 DEGREE)

Value of race $14,500; value to winner $8,700; second $2,900; third $1,595; fourth $870; fifth $435. Mutuel pool $32,452. Exacta Pool $39,541 Trifecta Pool $19,838

Last Raced	Horse	M/Eqt.A.Wt	PP	St	1/4	1/2	3/4	Str	Fin	Jockey	Odds $1
27Sep92 4Pim3	Dynamic Brush	L 2 120	3	1	34	1hd	11½	25	1nk	Black A S	4.40
20ct92 7Pim2	Hope Of Peace	2 120	5	4	42	4hd	21	1hd	27½	Colton R E	9.50
90ct92 3Pha2	Magic Pepper	Lb 2 120	1	2	1hd	21½	48	31½	3½	Molina V H	1.30
26Sep9212Pim6	Truly Rowdy	2 120	6	6	68	63	61½	56	42½	Woodhouse R	22.40
90ct92 3Pha3	Skip the Roses	b 2 120	7	7	58	515	3hd	43	52½	Martinez J R Jr	2.00
	Romeo Niner	2 120	4	5	7	7	7	67	612½	Castillo R E	38.70
29Sep92 7Med6	Alinick	2 120	2	3	2½	31	51	7	7	Ryan K	9.50

OFF AT 1:01 Start good Won driving Time, :22³, :47 , 1:14 , 1:41⁴, 1:46² Track fast.

Official Program Numbers\

$2 Mutuel Prices:

3-DYNAMIC BRUSH	10.80	6.80	3.00
6-HOPE OF PEACE		10.60	3.20
1-MAGIC PEPPER			2.40

$2 EXACTA 3-6 PAID $56.60 $2 TRIFECTA 3-6-1 PAID $134.00

B. c, (Feb), by Broad Brush—Dynamic Star, by Silent Screen. Trainer Small Richard W. Bred by Meyerhoff Robert F (Md).

DYNAMIC BRUSH broke sharply, was three wide into the first turn, dueled, gradually moved cloer to the rail, was headed in midstretch but fought back to get the nod. HOPE OF PEACE split rivals when moving, rallied and tookthe lead briefly in midstretch and gave way grudgingly. MAGIC PEPPER vied for command inside, swung out entering the lane and tired. SKIP THE ROSES raced outside and flattened out. ROMEO NINER broke slowly. ALINICK, between top flight, stopped.

Owners— 1, Meyerhoff Robert E; 2, Kintz James; 3, Kenline Stable; 4, Big Board Stable; 5, Appleton Arthur I; 6, Ng Archie; 7, Campbell Gilbert G.

Trainers— 1, Small Richard W; 2, McGreevy James L; 3, Papaycik Edward; 4, Poirier Stephen; 5, Camac Robert W; 6, Frommer Timothy G; 7, Allard Edward T.

Scratched—Colonel's Sonata (100ct92 7Med11); Wedges of Lemon.

Dynamic Brush had been three-wide in a three-horse battle that included the 6-to-5 favorite, Magic Pepper, and the trio had raced the first quarter mile in a fast 22⅗ seconds. Dynamic Brush destroyed the two other speed horses, who wound up losing by 7½ and 25 lengths respectively. Hope of Peace had been stalking the three-horse battle and gained the lead, but according to the footnote, Dynamic Brush "fought back to get the nod." This was not merely an honest effort; the figure of 66 had been hard-earned.

There was another horse in the field who had last raced at Philadelphia Park, Hasty Jaune; while his figure of 61 was not dazzling, the comment in the *Racing Form* said, "Changed course, steadied, driving." I looked up this chart, too:

THIRD RACE   1 MILE. (1.34⁴) MAIDEN SPECIAL WEIGHT. Purse $14,500. 2-year-olds. Weight, 120 lbs.

Phila Park

OCTOBER 9, 1992

Value of race $14,500; value to winner $8,700; second $2,900; third $1,595; fourth $870; fifth $435. Mutuel pool $32,822. Exacta Pool $41,476 Trifecta Pool $26,462

Last Raced	Horse	M/Eqt.A.Wt	PP	St	1/4	1/2	3/4	Str	Fin	Jockey	Odds $1
26Sep92¹²Pim⁴	Hasty Jaune	b 2 120	1	8	8	8	7¹²	4hd	1no	Colton R E	3.90
27Sep92 ⁵Mth²	Magic Pepper	Lb 2 120	2	3	7¹²	5²	4²	3¹	2hd	Vigliotti M J	1.00
9Sep92 ⁴Med⁸	Skip the Roses	b 2 120	4	5	6²	6³	5½	5⁸	32¾	Martinez J R Jr	10.60
11Jun92 ⁵Pha⁶	King Kazar	2 120	3	1	2¹	1hd	1½	2hd	46¾	Somsanith N	12.30
	Disorderly Conduct	2 120	6	4	3hd	3½	3½	1½	56½	Molina V H	29.00
26Sep92 ²Del³	Adakai	2 120	5	2	1½	2hd	2hd	6⁴	6½	Taylor K T	6.70
	Mr Excellerator	b 2 120	8	6	4½	4½	6½	7¹²	710½	Black A S	6.10
22Sep92 ⁶Del⁵	Drums of Victory	b 2 120	7	7	5¹	7⁸	8	8	8	Cruz C	18.20

OFF AT 1:56 Start good Won driving Time, :23³, :47², 1:13⁴, 1:41² Track sloppy.

$2 Mutuel Prices:

1-HASTY JAUNE	9.80	4.00	2.80
2-MAGIC PEPPER		2.80	2.40
4-SKIP THE ROSES			3.80

$2 EXACTA 1-2 PAID $18.40 $2 TRIFECTA 1-2-4 PAID $78.20

B. g, (Mar), by John Alden—Ocre Jaune, by Wittgenstein. Trainer Boniface J William. Bred by Hidden Lane Stable (Md).

HASTY JAUNE came out a bit leaving gate and was badly outrun early saving ground, rallied suddenly and continued inside on final turn, tried to move off rail to secure racing room near stretch but had to angle back to the rail and after steadying briefly in midstretch when KING KAZAR came in, closed determinedly under very strong handling and got up, benefitting from a fine piece of race riding. MAGIC PEPPER was eased back from early speed duel and saved ground under rating, continued inside and awaited racing room when in traffic on the final turn, angled out at the head of the lane, came out and bumped with SKIP THE ROSES in deep stretch and was outfinished. SKIP THE ROSES raced off the rail and just off the pace, rallied wide into and through stretch, came in and contributed to the bumping with MAGIC PEPPER and missed. KING KAZAR moved through along the inside to take the lead on the backstretch, came in slightly in midstretch and weakened. DISORDERLY CONDUCT was forwardly placed between foes and tired. ADAKAI set early pace off the rail, allowed KING KAZAR to rally inside of him and faded. MR. EXCELLERATOR, seven wide on first turn, tired. DRUMS TO VICTORY was also wide and tired.

Owners— 1, Meadow Bridge Farm; 2, Kenline Stable; 3, Appleton Arthur I; 4, Atrium Racing Stable; 5, Humphreys Jerry K; 6, Loving Frank; 7, Nagel Dietmar; 8, Phillips Mrs Richard.

Trainers— 1, Boniface J William; 2, Papaycik Edward; 3, Camac Robert W; 4, Marini Thomas; 5, Voss Ronald L III; 6, Sheppard Jonathan E; 7, Velazquez Alfredo; 8, Campo Salvatore.

Scratched—Wedges of Lemon; Richard's Toy (27Sep92 ⁴Bel⁷); Colonel's Sonata (10Sep92 ⁵Bel⁸); Turning Pro (19Sep92 ³Med⁴).

According to the footnote, Hasty Jaune's trouble hadn't been earth-shaking; he had rallied along the rail most of the way while "steadying briefly" in the midst of this ground-saving trip. What was more enlightening was the way the whole race had been run. Several horses had been battling for the early lead, and all collapsed. The horses who had been running 8-7-6 in this eight-horse field after a quarter mile wound up 1-2-3. The pace had obviously benefited closers, and Hasty Jaune had been the principal beneficiary. He did have the merit of being the one stretch-running distance horse in this speed-laden field, but it was hard to make the case that he was much better than the 61 he had earned in his last start.

Dynamic Brush was the logical horse. If the fluky figure of Stelios Art was ignored, he had the best figure in his most recent start. He had earned it in an impressive fashion. There was no reason to believe that anybody else in the field was ready to run a figure in the mid-60s.

EIGHTH RACE
Laurel
OCTOBER 27, 1992

1 $\frac{1}{16}$ MILES. (1.41^4) ALLOWANCE. Purse $18,500. 2-year-olds, which have not won a race other than maiden or claiming. Weight, 120 lbs. Non-winners of a race at one mile or over since October 1 allowed 3 lbs. Such a race since September 1, 6 lbs.

Value of race $19,400; value to winner $10,545; second $3,885; third $2,035; fourth $1,110; fifth $555; sixth $370; balance of starters $300 each. Mutuel pool $33,000. Exacta Pool $61,427

Last Raced	Horse	M/Eqt.	A.	Wt	PP	St	¼	½	¾	Str	Fin	Jockey	Odds $1
17Oct92 ^{1}Pha^1	Dynamic Brush	L	2	115	4	4	2½	1^{hd}	1½	1^{1½}	1^{nk}	Moorefield W T^5	21.10
17Oct92 ^{2}Lrl^2	Wild About Harry	Lb	2	114	7	6	7^{2½}	6^{hd}	3½	2^1	2no	Pino M G	a-1.70
9Oct92 ^{3}Pha^1	Hasty Jaune	b	2	120	8	9	9	9	9	4^{1½}	3^{1¾}	Reynolds L C	9.20
8Oct92 ^{6}Lrl^6	Down Home Doctor	b	2	114	3	7	8^5	8^6	7^3	3^2	4^{4¼}	Wilson R	4.10
1Oct92 ^{3}Pim^1	Foxy Bailjumper	L	2	109	1	1	6^{1½}	7^3	4^{hd}	5^2	5^{4¾}	Castillo F^5	22.20
17Oct92 ^{2}Lrl^4	Stevie's Fellow	b	2	114	6	3	4^{1½}	4½	6^{hd}	8^6	6^{2½}	Luzzi M J	5.70
9Oct92 ^{4}Lrl^1	Stelios Art	b	2	114	5	5	3^4	3^{1½}	5^2	7½	7^{1¾}	Prado E S	a-1.70
20Oct92 ^{7}Lrl^1	Sir Valiant	b	2	114	2	2	1^{hd}	2½	2^2	6^4	8^{11}	Johnston M T	8.20
10Oct92 ^{7}Med^1	Strand of Blue	b	2	120	9	8	5½	5^2	8^2	9	9	Rocco J	3.70

a-Coupled: Wild About Harry and Stelios Art.

OFF AT 3:46 Start good Won driving Time, :22^4, :46^4, 1:12^2, 1:39^1, 1:46 Track fast.

$2 Mutuel Prices:				
	5-DYNAMIC BRUSH	44.20	12.80	5.60
	1-WILD ABOUT HARRY (a-entry)		3.40	2.60
	7-HASTY JAUNE			3.80
	$2 EXACTA 5-1 PAID $128.40			

B. c, (Feb), by Broad Brush—Dynamic Star, by Silent Screen. Trainer Small Richard W. Bred by Mayerhoff Robert E (Md).

DYNAMIC BRUSH disputed the early pace outside SIR VALIANT, opened up entering the stretch and gamely prevailed. WILD ABOUT HARRY closed between horses. HASTY JAUNE, swung wide entering the stretch, closed strongly. DOWN HOME DOCTOR weakened between rivals. FOXY BAILJUMPER weakened along the rail. STEVIE'S FELLOW, wide, weakened. STELIOS ART circled both turns and tired. SIR VALIANT faltered. STRAND OF BLUE raced wide and fell back.

Owners— 1, Meyerhoff Robert E; 2, Capital Racing Stable; 3, Meadow Bridge Farm; 4, Whip Stable; 5, A & A Stables; 6, Stern Margaret E; 7, Dellis Marcella M; 8, Meyerhoff Harry C; 9, Hesse Charles J.

Trainers— 1, Small Richard W; 2, Delp Richard W; 3, Boniface J William; 4, Salzman J Edwin Jr; 5, Hendricks Franklin J; 6, Wolfendale Howard E; 7, Delp Richard W; 8, Delp Grover G; 9, Perkins Ben W Jr.

Dynamic Brush showed the same kind of gutsiness in this race that he had displayed at Philadelphia Park — and he needed it. He battled for the lead with two other speedsters, including Stelios Art, left them for dead, opened a clear lead, and then held off the late charge of the stretch-runners. The payoff of $44.20 refutes the notion that speed figures never produce large prices anymore. While it is difficult to get big payoffs from the most simplistic applications of figures, speed handicappers can still prosper if they interpret the figures with sound judgment and apply them with a bit of inspiration.

FOUR

How Will He Run Today?

Before the 1991 Breeders' Cup Classic, most handicappers believed that the winner was going to be a stretch-runner, because the 1¼-mile race seemed certain to have a fast, destructive pace. Black Tie Affair was going to Churchill Downs after scoring six straight front-running victories. In Excess had won four straight Grade I stakes while fighting for the lead. Farma Way had led all the way to win the nation's two richest handicap races, the Pimlico Special and the Santa Anita Handicap. It would be difficult for any of these horses to outfight the others and withstand the stretch kick of rivals like Unbridled, Festin, and Strike the Gold.

But then trainer Wayne Lukas regretfully announced that Farma Way had wrenched an ankle and wouldn't be able to run. In Excess's trainer, Bruce Jackson, made the inexplicable decision to pass the Classic and run his horse on the turf instead. Suddenly, the whole character of the world's richest race was changed. Black Tie Affair still had the same six-race winning streak and the same solid speed figures, but now, instead of facing the prospect of a harmful duel for the lead, he looked as if he might be able to control the pace. Unbridled, Festin, and Strike the Gold were still formidable horses, but their running styles were now going to be a liability.

Black Tie Affair set a moderate pace, a half mile in 48⅖ seconds, and led all the way to win at 4 to 1, while the stretch-runners never got into contention. The winner's performance earned him widespread acclaim as well as the Horse of the Year title, but if the composition of the field had been different, it is probable that Black Tie Affair would have ended his career without any fanfare. The outcome of the Classic was not inevitable, nor is the outcome of any race foreordained because of the horses' speed figures or other details of their past performances. Countless factors affecting a race today can cause horses to run better or worse than they have done in the past.

This is a daunting aspect of the game. When a handicapper examines a horse's past performances, considering the possible effects of pace, track biases, and trips, he is at least dealing with a finite number of factors. But when he tries to envision all the things that might happen in today's race, he is confronting the unknown and the infinite. Pace and biases might affect races in unimaginable ways. A horse's performance may vary because his physical condition has changed or because he has been treated with Lasix or some other drug. A horse may be running over a distance or a racing surface that he has never tried before, and these new conditions may drastically affect his performance. So, in addition to analyzing what happened in the past, a handicapper must try to peer into the future and judge how each horse may be helped or hurt by today's conditions.

THE BIAS OF TODAY'S RACETRACK

When a handicapper is evaluating past races, he can decide thoughtfully and dispassionately whether they might have been affected by a bias. But when he is at the track and suspects the existence of a bias, he may have to make a hasty and crucial judgment. Does a bias really exist and, if so, should he jettison his previously held opinions and let the bias dictate whom he bets? If he does this and he is right, he can justifiably congratulate himself for his alertness and his flexibility; he has caught lightning in a bottle. But if he is wrong — and this happens often — he will be fuming because he talked himself out of betting a horse he liked.

My general rule is this: If a bias existed yesterday or if a track has a consistent tendency, I will handicap the card on the presumption that the bias will be there again today. I may bet the first race or two of the day accordingly, and I will, of course, watch those races carefully to determine whether the bias still exists. But if there has been no recent bias, I require a much higher standard of proof before I will conclude that one has suddenly appeared. I need to see two or three races that, say, are totally dominated by horses racing on the rail, with nobody able to accelerate on the outside. Or two or three races where logical horses on the rail collapse while the winners make wide, sweeping moves.

If a strong bias does exist, though, there is one all-important rule that every horseplayer should heed: Don't fight it. Horses' past speed figures and other handicapping factors are rendered relatively unimportant, and the overriding issues are these: How will the race develop? Who will take advantage of the bias? It is easy to deal with pure speed-favoring tracks, because it is often easy to identify the horse in a field with the most early foot. But when the rail is an advantage, the key is to find the one horse who will get the lead on the inside. Horses breaking from inside posts naturally have a great advantage. It is very hard for a horse on the outside to pop clear and get to the rail if inside him there are other speed horses whose jockeys are pushing to maintain their position. In such circumstances, the speedsters in outside posts may wind up parked outside and forced to stay there the whole way. (It is a rare jockey who will be smart and bold enough to break from the outside, yank his horse back, and drop to the rail, like harness drivers leaving from the outside post.) Besides the leader, the horse in the best position will be the stalker who can sit on the rail behind the first flight.

When the rail is bad, there is a greater range of potential winning scenarios, but any speed horse on the inside is in a probable losing position. Even if a jockey is fully aware of the bias and takes a horse several paths off the rail to avoid the worst going, a speedster being pressed from the outside will rarely be able to overcome the adverse conditions.

When I am handicapping on a biased track, I am not slavishly devoted to my speed figures. If a horse merely has competitive numbers and also has a bias in his favor, he may offer an excellent betting opportunity. Of course, the ideal race is one in which the horse with the best speed figures also appears likely to take advantage of the bias. One of the clearest such situations I ever saw was in the 1984 Black-Eyed Susan Stakes, run during a period when a consistent, powerful rail-favoring bias existed at Pimlico — the same bias that would carry Gate Dancer to victory in the Preakness the next day.

Lucky Lucky Lucky, Wayne Lukas's filly, was going to be the heavy favorite on the strength of her front-running victory in the Kentucky Oaks, but I had seen her run at Churchill Downs and had not been impressed. Lucky Lucky Lucky had indeed been lucky to set a slow pace and lead all the way over a speed-favoring track, earning a figure of 100. A few days earlier at Churchill, I had been dazzled by another 3-year-old filly, Sintra, who made an eye-catching move to win a minor stakes with a figure of 106. Both were going to Pimlico, and while this would have been an interesting betting situation under any circumstances, it became almost perfect when entries were drawn for the Black-Eyed Susan, and Sintra got post position 1.

I couldn't contain my enthusiasm, and on the morning of the race I advised readers of the *Washington Post*, "There is a three-star mortal lock, an empty-the-wallet, mortgage-the-house betting opportunity at Pimlico this afternoon." I explained Sintra's virtues and said that the only way she could possibly lose was if her jockey, Keith Allen, didn't heed the bias. I suggested that Sintra's trainer give Allen these instructions: "Keith, you've got the best horse, but the best horse can lose here if the jockey doesn't understand how important the rail is. Stay close to the leaders, but don't try to swing out and go around them on the backstretch. Stay on the rail around the turn and look for an opening. Do your best because there's a nut who may jump off the press box roof if you blow it."

I bet with gusto, then watched in abject horror as Allen blew it.

He took hold of Sintra coming out of the gate, surrendered position, then rushed up on the inside, attempting to test the law of physics that says two solid masses cannot occupy the same space at the same time. He virtually ran Sintra into another rival's rear end and dropped back a couple of lengths. Even so, he would have been all right if he had stayed on the rail, because a hole was about to open for him, but he panicked and swung wide. It got worse from there, and Sintra wound up losing by a half-length to Lucky Lucky Lucky.

It was a demonstration of the one great pitfall of betting track biases. Bettors are totally at the mercy of jockeys' tactics, and the little pinheads are usually the last people at the racetrack to recognize a bias. Of course, I didn't let my financial drubbing affect the objectivity of my report on the race for the *Post:*

"When historians are chronicling examples of the folly and perversity of mankind during the 20th century, they will start with this list:

"1. Vietnam.

"2. Keith Allen's ride on Sintra in the Black-Eyed Susan Stakes."

THE PACE OF TODAY'S RACE

A horse's past performances may show atypically high figures in races where he was loose on the lead; other figures may have been affected by extreme pace situations. But what about today? Is it reasonable to anticipate improvement or decline in a horse's figure based on what the pace of today's race is likely to be?

The answer, indisputably, is yes. Many handicappers use mathematical methods to predict the probable pace of a race and to identify the horse or horses with superior speed; such methods will be discussed in the next chapter. Yet this is one of the few areas in the complex game of handicapping which is sometimes better approached simply. Horseplayers who get too sophisticated may overlook the central question: How many horses in today's race are habitual front-runners? An analysis of fractional times may be much less significant than the established tendency of horses who almost always contest the lead. In *Winning at the Races*, William

Quirin presented a system for awarding "speed points" to horses according to whether they were running 1-2-3 early in recent races, and it's probably as reliable as any high-tech method of judging how today's race will unfold.

If there are three or more horses in a field who are habitual front-runners, I would be wary of them all and would ignore any good figures they have earned loose on the lead. I would assume that off-the-pace runners will have the chance to deliver their maximum performance.

If there is evidently a lone front-runner in the field, I will expect that horse to deliver the top performance of which he is capable. If he is already competitive on the basis of figures where he has not had a clear lead, he is an excellent bet. If he already has superior figures, he represents virtually the best betting situation in all of racing. And if the lone front-runner with the superior figure also happens to find himself on a track with a speed- or rail-favoring bias, he's a three-star mortal lock, an empty-the-wallet, mortgage-the-house opportunity.

In races with two distinct front-running types, it is often impossible to predict how the race will develop. The speedsters can run one-two around the track, as Bold Forbes and Honest Pleasure did in the Kentucky Derby, or duel each other into extinction, as the same two horses did in the Preakness. If one of the two doesn't show his speed, an anticipated duel can turn into an unforeseeable one-horse runaway — as happened in the 1985 Derby when the widely anticipated Spend a Buck–Eternal Prince suicide pact turned into a tour de force for Spend a Buck. A handicapper cannot reasonably predict the way all races will unfold — not when racing luck and jockeys' intentions can be so important. But there are enough races when a bettor can anticipate that there will be either a sole front-runner or a destructive battle for the lead, and those races can be very profitable.

CHANGE OF DISTANCE

A speed figure earned at one distance represents the same level of ability as a number earned at another. The average winning figure for Santa Anita's $10,000 claiming races at six furlongs is 85; at route distances it is also 85. In a recent banner year for thoroughbred competition, 1986, the country's Eclipse Award–winning sprinter, Phone Trick, earned a figure of 128 on his best day, and the champion older horse, Precisionist, recorded a 128 running nine furlongs. But this, of course, does not mean that Phone Trick could have competed with Precisionist at a long distance; he might have had a heart attack if he had tried. Every horse has distances at which he is more or less effective. Sometimes it is relatively easy to predict how a horse will fare when he attempts to go a longer distance, and sometimes it is not.

In March 1992, the speedster Dixie Brass won Aqueduct's six-furlong Swift Stakes, an early prep race on the road to the Kentucky Derby, with a figure of 106. If he were able to produce figures of that magnitude at longer distances, he would be one of the stars of his generation. But would Dixie Brass be effective going as far as a mile? A mile and one eighth? A mile and one quarter? Not even his trainer, Dennis Brida, could answer those questions confidently until the colt actually tried the longer distances.

Dixie Brass — **Dk. b. or br. c. 3(Mar), by Dixieland Band—Petite Diable, by Sham**

PEZUA J M (5 1 1 0 .20) — **Br.—Rooker John W (Ky)**

Own.—Watral Michael — **Tr.—Brida Dennis J (—)** — **122**

Lifetime						
11 6 1 1	1992	7	3	1	1	$539,763
$602,763	1991	4	3	0	0	$63,000
	Wet	2	2	0	0	$68,040

22Aug92- 7Sar	fst	1¼	:46^{4}	1:35^{2}	2:00^{4}		Travers	**95**	1	1	1^{2}	1½	21½	49¼	Pezua J M	126	3.90	91 –	ThundrRmbl1264½DvlHsD1264½DncFloor126	Speed,tired	10
22Aug92-Grade I																					
2Aug92- 8Sar	fst	1⅛	:46^{1}	1:09^{2}	1:47^{2}		Jim Dandy	**109**	1	1	1^{1}	1^{1}	1^{1}	2½	Pezua J M	126	2.80	99 –	ThundrRumbl117½DixiBrss1267½DvlHsDu126	Drftd, gmly	8
2Aug92-Grade II																					
25May92- 8Bel	fst	1	:44^{4}	1:08^{2}	1:33^{3}	3↑	Metropoln H	**111**	6	1	1½	11½	1^{1}	12¼	Pezua J M	107	4.50	102-05	DixieBrass1072¼PleasantTp1191¾InExcess-Ir121	Driving	11
25May92-Grade I																					
6May92- 8Bel	fst	1	:44^{2}	1:08^{4}	1:33^{3}		Withers	**108**	3	1	1^{2}	11½	1^{3}	18¼	Pezua J M	126	7.50	102 –	DixiBrss1268¼BigSur1263Suprstrik-GB126	Wide,driving	8
6May92-Grade II																					
18Apr92- 7Aqu	gd	6f	:22	:44^{2}	1:09^{1}		Best Turn	**87**	4	6	2½	41½	43½	43½	Migliore R	122	*1.40	91-05	BlongtoM1152NinsWld1171½RomnChorus115	Brk slowly	6
18Apr92-Grade III																					
28Mar92- 8GS	gd	1	:48^{1}	1:13^{2}	1:39		Cherry Hill	**96**	5	2	2^{hd}	1^{1}	2½	31¾	Mojica R Jr	117	*.80	84-19	PieinYourEye115noSurelySix1151¾DixiBrss117	Bid, tired	7
28Mar92-Grade III																					
7Mar92- 8Aqu	sly	6f	⊡:22	:45	1:10^{2}		Swift	**106**	8	1	2^{hd}	1^{1}	1^{2}	13¼	Mojica R Jr	120	2.70	91-17	DixieBrss1203¼AmericnChnce1202¼GoldnPhs114	Driving	8
19Dec91- 8Aqu	fst	6f	⊡:22^{3}	:47^{1}	1:13^{2}		Copelan Stk	**88**	7	5	11½	1^{1}	11½	13¼	Mojica R Jr	117	*1.20	76-29	DixBrss1173¼TruDutch117noSlngOnApryr115	Ridden out	9
18Nov91- 1Aqu	fst	6f	:22	:45^{1}	1:10^{3}		Alw 27000	**91**	1	4	21½	2^{1}	1^{hd}	1no	Mojica R Jr	117	2.90	88-18	DixieBrss117noBstDcortd1195½Chpito119	Drifted, drvng	5
23Oct91- 8Aqu	fst	7f	:21^{4}	:44	1:22^{3}		Cowdin	**72**	2	5	42½	4^{4}	99½	811¾	Migliore R	122	7.30	77-13	Salt Lake1226½MontrealMarty122nkOffbeat122	Bmpd st	9
23Oct91-Grade II																					

LATEST WORKOUTS ●Sep 4 Bel 3f sly :33 H (d) Aug 30 Sar tr.t 4f fst :48^{4} B ●Aug 18 Sar tr.t 4f gd :47^{4} B ●Jly 29 Sar 4f fst :46^{2} B

Dixie Brass passed both of his tests at one mile with flying colors, winning the Withers Stakes and the Metropolitan Handicap with figures of 108 and 111. He ran well at 1⅛ miles in the Jim Dandy Stakes, earning a figure of 109. But 1¼ miles was too far for him; even though he got a clear lead in the Travers Stakes at Saratoga, he faded, and his figure declined to 95. Speed figures did indicate how good Dixie Brass would be if he translated his six-furlong ability to longer distances, but they could not have predicted his successes or failures with certainty.

As a general rule, however, when a horse is trying to go a longer distance and his speed figures are superior to those of his rivals, he will be very formidable. A horse moving from a sprint to a route will almost always display speed, and the essential speed-favoring nature of American racing will be on his side. If such a horse can get loose on the lead, he will be hard to beat even if, genetically, he is not a natural distance runner. The classic horse of this type was Bold Forbes, who, while fundamentally a sprinter, managed to win the Kentucky Derby and the Belmont Stakes by virtue of his sheer superior speed. If a horse going from sprint to route has inferior figures, however, he ought to give some indications that he may be a natural distance runner or that he will get loose on the lead. A sprinter who has inferior figures and faces a probable fight for the lead in a route race is a dismal betting proposition.

When a router turns back to a shorter distance, bettors will properly shun him if he has displayed no tactical speed in his longer races. Plodders don't win many sprints in America, although such horses will occasionally succeed if they have superior figures that they earned in routes. Turkoman was the most exciting stretch-running router of the 1980s, but he managed to come from sixteen lengths behind and win a six-furlong stakes at Hialeah in 1:08⅕. Unbridled, the winner of the Kentucky Derby and Breeders' Cup Classic, was a surprisingly effective sprinter and once blew past the champion Housebuster at seven furlongs. Nevertheless, in most cases a horse must have shown some early speed in route races in order to have much chance in a sprint. Many pace-oriented handicappers try to assess a horse's six-furlong fractional time in a distance race to determine whether he can sprint effectively, but there is a danger here. A horse may have run fast fractions while loose on the lead in a route race, but when he returns to a sprint he is apt to find himself in a battle for the lead, and he may crack from the more intense pressure. I prefer a horse who has fought for the lead in a route race and managed to earn a final speed figure competitive with those of the sprinters he is facing today.

DIRT TO TURF, AND VICE VERSA

Speed figures earned in sprints and routes represent the same level of ability, and so, too, do numbers earned on turf and dirt. The average winning figure for a $50,000 claiming race on the dirt at Santa Anita is 98. The average for the same class on the turf is 98 as well. So, just as figures are an important clue to a horse's prospects at a longer distance, one might suppose that they would tell something about a dirt runner when he makes his debut in grass competition. But they don't.

Trying to relate dirt and turf figures is a largely futile exercise because dirt and turf racing are fundamentally different games. The distinctive nature of turf racing is the subject of Chapter 6. While it is true that a theoretical horse with the same level of talent on both grass and dirt will run the same speed figure on each, it is a pure coincidence if a horse is equally gifted on each surface — like finding a person who has precisely the same level of skill as a poet and as a bricklayer.

The 1992 Breeders' Cup demonstrated how little correlation there may be between a horse's ability on grass and his ability on dirt. In the early years of the Breeders' Cup, Europeans had fared dismally in their sporadic attempts to win dirt races. But they constructed dirt training tracks to prepare their horses, and they finally made a breakthrough in 1991, when both Sheikh Albadou and Arazi won on the main track at Churchill Downs. Sheikh Albadou was a grandson of one of America's greatest speedsters, Danzig, and Arazi was a Kentucky-bred with a solid dirt pedigree, but the Europeans now assumed that virtually any of their top-class grass runners could win on dirt. So they made an all-out assault on the dirt races at Gulfstream Park. Marling, a brilliant filly with a purely European turf pedigree, went into the Breeders'

Cup Distaff on the dirt. So did Culture Vulture, even though she had flopped on dirt in the Breeders' Cup the year before. Rodrigo De Triano, winner of five Grade I stakes in England, skipped logical opportunities in the turf races and made his dirt debut in the Classic. In many cases, these European runners were more accomplished than their American rivals; if speed figures had been available for them, they probably would have been standouts. But at the end of the day, the Europeans' record on dirt was 11 starts, 0 wins, 0 seconds, 1 third, 1 horse dead. Their superiority didn't matter because turf form doesn't translate into dirt form, although the European trainers still didn't understand that fact. They blamed the Florida heat for the debacle.

When I handicap a race, I normally look first at each horse's most recent figure; the one with the best number in his most recent start is nominally the "top figure." But if a horse's last race was run on a different surface, I disregard it. I look instead at his most recent start on today's surface. Since the Beyer Speed Figures have been incorporated in the *Daily Racing Form,* many readers have tinkered with systems and mechanical approaches for using them. But they should ignore figures earned on grass if today's race is on the dirt, and vice versa.

I pay attention to figures on a different surface only as a general indication of a horse's current form. If, in the past, a horse was running in the 80s on both turf and dirt but now has been competing mainly on dirt and earning figures around 100, it is possible that his overall form has improved and he might be able to run 100 on grass now, too. When Sea Hero went into the 1992 Champagne Stakes, he had run in the 60s in a couple of dirt sprints, but then had earned figures in the 80s, winning two routes on the turf; now he was back on dirt. He might be a pure turf specialist, but it was also possible that he had been improving because of maturity and because he was more effective in longer races. I would not have taken a short price on this proposition, but Sea Hero was 8 to 1, and he continued his improvement, earning a 97 in his runaway victory on dirt.

To my dictum about the difference between turf and dirt racing

I offer one footnote: Horses in California seem to make the dirt-to-grass and grass-to-dirt transitions more easily than those in other parts of the country, perhaps because all of their sun-baked racing surfaces are hard and fast. Many California horses (such as Prized, Perrault, and Greinton) have been equally effective on both surfaces, and California horseplayers often bet races as if they think dirt and turf form are interchangeable. But even in the West this is generally not the case, as a horseplayer named Red Tucker can attest.

Readers may have noted that I have a perverse fascination with traumatic racetrack experiences. Just as some people can't divert their eyes from a grisly automobile wreck, I am mesmerized by horrible disqualifications, photo finishes, and other twists of racing fortune. And the most terrible such story I have ever heard was the disaster that befell Tucker in a turf race on Christmas Eve, 1987.

It was the final day of the Hollywood Park meeting, and more than $1 million that had accumulated in the track's pick-nine jackpot was going to be distributed. Tucker spent seven hours handicapping the card and decided on a $256 pick nine play. He drove from his Oxnard, California, home to the off-track betting facility in Ventura to place his wager, then went to his construction company's Christmas party. Late in the afternoon, he excused himself to go to his car so he could listen to the race results on the radio. His excitement grew as he heard he had picked eight winners in a row, and his heart was pounding as he waited to hear whether one of his two selections — Gypsy Prophecy and The Great Prize — had won the final race on the turf. "The reception was poor," Tucker told me, "but I did hear the announcer say that the last race had been switched from the turf to the main track, and that Gypsy Prophecy was scratched. I couldn't understand it because there hadn't been any rain, and the turf should have been in good shape." He also learned that his horse, The Great Prize, had finished second. The winner, Fiction, paid $6, completing a pick nine that returned $571,873 to four ticketholders. Under the rules of the pick nine, a wager on a scratched horse is switched to the favorite, and if Fiction was the favorite, Tucker had a $571,873 ticket in his pocket. He immediately phoned a friend who had been at the track and asked who had been the favorite in the ninth race. "Fiction was the favorite," the friend said. "I should know. I bet him."

Tucker started to celebrate and to plan his new life. But before he got too carried away, he decided to call the track and double-check that Fiction had indeed been the favorite. He spent an agonizing fifteen minutes on the phone while the track's switchboard operator tried to locate somebody with the chart for the final race of the meeting. Finally Tucker got the official results. Fiction had gone off at 2.00 to 1. A horse named Breakfast Table was 1.90 to 1, the favorite. Tucker's near-perfect ticket was worth nothing.

"I still didn't believe it," Tucker said. "I got up at three in the morning to go out and get the paper with the race results." He confirmed that Fiction had not been the favorite and learned the rest of the day's events. A sprinkler had broken and water had saturated the Hollywood turf course, making a portion of it unsafe. When the jockeys complained, the race was switched to the dirt, and five horses were scratched. Fiction had been the only horse in the field with any dirt form; he never would have beaten The Great Prize on turf. If this was devastating information, Tucker's pain would be even greater a couple of weeks later. A turf race for the same group of horses was run at Santa Anita, and the winner, at 9 to 1, was Gypsy Prophecy, Tucker's horse who had been scratched. If he had run and won on December 24, Tucker might have collected the whole $2.2 million pool. But because turf and dirt racing are different games, and because the Goddess of Wagering is a cruel deity, Tucker had nothing.

LAYOFFS

Handicappers of the past were always wary of horses who had been laid off for weeks or months. Books and systems contained rules that dictated, "Never bet a horse who has not raced in 30 days." But in the sport today, horses often produce top performances — and top speed figures — after a layoff. At the upper echelon of the game, the current fashion among trainers is to run horses "fresh," to bring them into major stakes after three- or four-week layoffs that would have been unthinkable in the past. Improved veterinary techniques have enabled horses to recover from injuries that sideline them for a year, and to come back to win at first asking. Bettors trying to evaluate a laid-off horse should pay careful attention to the trainer's record under such circumstances and, of course, to the horse's workouts, assuming they are in California or some area where workout information is reasonably reliable.

Handicappers using speed figures should remember one special caution when evaluating laid-off horses. The figures of young horses tend to improve as they age — typically, about 1 to 1½ points per month. If a young horse is idle for six months and returns to competition in sharp form, his speed figure might improve 6 to 9 points because he is more mature.

Paradise Creek					Dk. b. or br. c. 3(Feb), by Irish River–Fr—North Of Eden, by Northfields					Lifetime	1992	2	2	0	0	$36,000
SMITH M E (35 6 5 6 .17)					Br.—Firestone Mr–Mrs B R (Va)					4 3 0 0	1991	2	1	0	0	$26,400
Own.—Firestone B R					Tr.—Mott William I (9 4 2 0 .44)				115	$62,400	Turf	3	0	0	0	$50,400
22Jly92- 7Bel fm 1⅛ ⊕:46³ 1:10 1:40			3+Alw 31000		99 5 2 2½ 2¹ 1hd 12½ Smith M E		113	*.50		96-15 PrdiseCreek113²½VictoryCross117⁶TimberCt111 Driving 9
18Jun92- 7Bel fm 1⅛ ⊕:46¹ 1:10 1:40²			3+Alw 29000		97 10 2 2¹ 1¹ 1⁴ 1⁴ Perret C		b 112	*1.00		94-11 Paradise Creek112⁴Scuffleburg113⁶Alfaares117 Handily 11
24Aug91- 8Sar fst 6½f :21³ :44² 1:17³			Hopeful		74 9 2 6⁶ 5⁸¾ 3⁶ 49½ Cordero A Jr		122	3.40		78-14 Salt Lake122⁹ Slew's Ghost122hd Caller I. D.122 4-wide 9
24Aug91-Grade I											
19Jly91- 5Bel fm 7f ⊕:22⁴ :45⁴ 1:22³			Md Sp Wt		86 2 12 52½ 41½ 1² 1¹¹ Smith M E		118	3.00		92-08 PrdiseCreek118¹¹ForeverFighting118ndJyGe118 Handily 12
LATEST WORKOUTS	Aug 2 Sar 5f fst 1:02³ B				Jly 10 Bel 1 fst 1:49 B			Jly 2 Bel ⊤ 6f fm 1:16² B (d)			Jun 11 Bel ⊤ 6f fm 1:14³ H (d)

Paradise Creek had won his debut in a turf race with a figure of 86 but was sidelined with physical problems for nearly a year. When he returned after working well for trainer Bill Mott, he was eligible to run a much bigger number. I wouldn't necessarily bet him on the assumption that this was certain to happen, but I would recognize that as a 3-year-old in midseason he was much more mature than he had been when he earned the 86 as a 2-year-old. Paradise Creek did make that improvement, running a figure of 97, improving 11 points in the 11 months since his previous turf race.

WEIGHT

Of all handicapping factors, weight is the one that ought to lend itself most readily to mathematical analysis. If a horse is carrying X pounds more than he did in his last start and he is racing at a distance of Y furlongs, the additional burden should lower his Beyer Speed Figure by Z points. But in two decades of fiddling with numbers, I have never been able to discern what X, Y, and Z are, because weight is a relatively tiny component among all the factors that affect horses' performances. If a horse is carrying ten pounds more than he did in his previous start and his speed figure drops by three points, how much of this decline is due to weight and how much to pace, trips, track bias, and the horse's general level of fitness? (Under the conditions of most races, horses carry higher weight if they have won recently, so the small disadvantage of added weight is often negated by the animal's current sharpness.) It seems almost impossible to measure accurately the effect of weight. Fortunately, American horses are seldom asked to carry huge imposts, so bettors can usually afford to ignore the factor.

High weight assignments are much more common in other countries. If a horse abroad carried 110 pounds in his last start and totes 130 pounds today, handicappers must attempt to judge how the extra 20 pounds will affect him, and they learn about the significance of weight by dealing repeatedly with such extreme cases. In Australia, the majority of races are handicaps in which the best horses are severely penalized; top-weighted horses may carry as much as 61 kilograms, or 134 pounds. Before launching my effort — chronicled in Chapter Six — to employ speed figures Down Under, I analyzed the most significant weight shifts and also studied the way the Australian experts deal with them. I arrived at a satisfactory and simple equation: One kilogram equals one point in my speed figures, regardless of the distance of the race. A kilogram is 2.2 pounds, which means that a weight shift of one pound equals 0.45 points.

When the *Daily Racing Form* undertook its computer analysis of the Beyer Speed Figures in early 1993, I decided to take one more crack at the subject of weight. The programmers asked the computer to look for horses who carried six pounds more or less than they did in their previous start and to compare each one's change in weight with the change in his speed figure. The study produced a seemingly aberrant result. Added weight did cause horses to run slower, but decreased weight did not enable them to run faster. In fact, the horses who shed weight ran slightly slower than they had in their previous start under a higher impost. These were the results:

Speed figures of the 2,953 horses carrying more weight than in their last start declined by 0.79 points for each additional pound.

Speed figures of the 3,084 horses carrying less weight than in their previous start dropped by 0.20 points per pound.

Logically, a decrease in weight cannot make a horse run slower, so other factors had to be responsible. In the case of the 3,084 horses in the latter group, these other factors obviously overwhelmed any benefit of lower weight and made it impossible to discern the effect of weight on the horses' performances. If this large sample produced such an aberration, it is easy to be suspicious of the evidence provided by the other group of 2,953.

In trying to make some sense of this data, I hesitantly accepted the statistic that these 2,953 horses were affected at the rate of 0.79 points per pound, and I assumed that the effect of weight on the second group was nil. If the two samples are lumped together, the conclusion is that a one-pound change in weight will affect a horse's Beyer Speed Figure by 0.39 points. This is very close to the equation I found to be valid in Australia. I still do not believe that the effect of weight in U.S. racing can be measured accurately, but handicappers who are hell-bent on making weight adjustments may reasonably do this: Subtract four-tenths of a point from a horse's previous Beyer Speed Figure for each additional pound that he is carrying today and add four-tenths of a point per pound if he is carrying less weight.

MUD

Before the *Daily Racing Form*'s past performances included a horse's record on wet tracks, handicappers would rummage through back issues of the newspaper to ferret out information about "hidden" mud form. Now readers need only to glance at the upper-right-hand corner of each horse's past performances to see how a horse has fared on such surfaces. Since the Beyer Speed Figures have been incorporated into the past performances, it is possible to get an even more accurate measurement of a horse's off-track ability. Horses may win in the mud, even if they don't particularly like it, because they are simply better than their competition; they may like mud but lose because they are overmatched. So when a handicapper is studying a race that will be run on an off track, he should note the figures that a horse has previously earned on such a surface. Moreover, he should note whether a horse's numbers improved or declined the last time he was in the mud — as an indication of whether he may run better or worse today than he has in his most recent races.

These two fillies were matched against each other on a sloppy track at Monmouth Park:

Dusty Roads Girl — B. f. 3(Feb), by Proud Truth—Northern Pine, by Far North

$8,000 — Br.—Guilting Stud (Ky)

Own.—Martucci William C — Tr.—Crupi James J (127 27 20 26 .21) — 111

Lifetime 8 2 1 1 $9,550 — 1992 4 1 0 1 $4,670 — 1991 4 1 1 0 $4,880 — Wet 1 0 0 1 $660

4Aug92- 4Mth	fst	6f	$:22^1$	:46	$1:12^3$	ⓕClm 7500	57	7	2	$5^{2\frac{1}{4}}$	2^{hd}	$3^{\frac{1}{2}}$	$1^{\frac{1}{2}}$	Marquez C HJr	b	115	4.00	78-16	DstRdsGrl115½DmndsOnmMnd111^{nk}WrngSn115	Driving 8
4Jly92-10Mth	gd	6f	$:22^2$	:46	$1:13^4$	ⓕClm 8500	36	8	3	$8^{5\frac{1}{2}}$	6^7	4^6	$4^{4\frac{3}{4}}$	Marquez C HJr	b	114	5.50	67-18	Xube115^{hd}SweetScm115$^{4\frac{1}{2}}$JmminBbe115	Wide into lane 9
23Jun92- 2Mth	fst	6f	$:22^2$	$:46^2$	1:13	ⓕClm 7500	37	8	2	6^5	$7^{5\frac{3}{4}}$	6^6	$5^{6\frac{1}{4}}$	Homeister RBJr^5		110	2.40	70-16	LndthLmt116$^{1\frac{3}{4}}$ShsRmntc113$^{1\frac{1}{2}}$GGAll111	Wide into lane 8
2Jun92- 2Mth	sly	6f	$:22^2$	:46	1:12	ⓕClm 7500	47	1	8	$4^{2\frac{1}{4}}$	2^2	2^2	$3^{3\frac{1}{4}}$	HomistrRBJr^5	b	110	6.40	78-17	FshonLst106$^{1\frac{3}{4}}$Ambrdor114$^{1\frac{1}{2}}$DstyRdsGrl110	Bobbld str 8
1Dec91- 7Med	gd	6f	$:22^1$	$:46^1$	$1:12^1$	ⓕClm 12500	40	5	1	$5^{8\frac{1}{2}}$	$5^{8\frac{1}{2}}$	$5^{6\frac{3}{4}}$	$4^{5\frac{3}{4}}$	Marquez C HJr	b	115	3.40	75-12	Jetta Zetta115$^{1\frac{1}{2}}$ Palarca111$^{1\frac{1}{4}}$PerfectGold115	Even trip 7
25Nov91-10Med	fst	6f	$:22^4$	$:47^1$	$1:13^2$	ⓕMd 10000	50	4	2	3^1	1^1	1^7	$1^{9\frac{1}{2}}$	Marquez C HJr	b	117	*2.40	75-19	DstRdsGrl117$^{9\frac{1}{2}}$DndlsDhtr112$^{1\frac{3}{4}}$MbsChc117	Ridden out 9
14Nov91- 4Med	fst	1^{70}	$:48^3$	$1:14^2$	$1:45^4$	ⓕMd 16000	—	6	7	7^{13}	8^{12}	—	—	Marquez C HJr	b	117	2.20	— —	April Sport113^1 Chay113$^{2\frac{1}{2}}$ Jean McWard109	Eased 8
23Oct91-10Med	fst	6f	$:22^3$	$:46^2$	$1:12^3$	ⓕMd 16000	44	5	3	$4^{1\frac{1}{4}}$	2^1	$2^{3\frac{1}{2}}$	$2^{3\frac{1}{2}}$	Marquez C HJr	b	117	5.80	75-18	RomnticSprk117$^{3\frac{1}{2}}$DustyRodsGrl117^{6}Kmmr117	2nd best 12

LATEST WORKOUTS Jly 25 Mth 4f fst $:49^4$ B — Jly 17 Mth 3f fst $:37^2$ B — Jun 19 Mth 4f fst :49 H

Proud Clare — B. f. 3(Mar), by Tank's Prospect—Proud Clarioness, by Tri Jet
$10,000 Br.—Lou-Roe Farms (Ky)
Own.—Montauri Marion — Tr.—Reading John F (1 0 0 0 .00) — **115**

Lifetime					
	1992	11 1 1 3			$8,334
17 1 1 3	1991	6 M 0 0			
$8,334	Turf	2 0 0 0			$540
	Wet	2 1 1 0			$5,100

31Jly92- 4Del	my	6f	:214	:46	1:131	3↑ⒻClm 10000	55	2	6	1½	2hd	21½	22¼	Sellers M S	Lb	112	2.40	79-23	RuntoShelter1132¼ProudClre112½NecyBby111	Held well	7
12Jly92- 6Pha	fst	6f	:22	:454	1:122	ⒻClm 10000	54	4	4	52	2hd	32	31	Verge M E	Lb	116	11.80	78-17	Felicia D.114¾ Page Four117nk ProudClare116	Held well	7
21Jun92- 5Pha	fst	5½f	:222	:463	1:061	ⒻClm 20000	50	2	3	65½	64¼	58	46½	Lloyd J S	Lb	114	9.00	75-19	MggsPrspct122nkBrdyShr1143AmzngMrcl112	No threat	7
7Jun92-10Del	fm	5f	Ⓣ:22	:462	:592	ⒻAlw 9000	67	1	5	52	43½	25	42¾	Salvaggio M V	Lb	119	8.20	84-12	IDoDzzel1141CleverSlote119nkCrol'sEcho114	Mild rally	10
10May92- 1Pha	sly	5½f	:223	:47	1:064	3↑ⒻMd 12500	52	4	3	21½	11½	18	16½	Lloyd J S	Lb	113	*1.90	80-19	ProudClr1136½BrigidsCross1205OurVlnor120	Ridden out	7
1May92- 7Pha	fst	6f	:22	:443	1:093	ⒻMd Sp Wt	51	5	6	31½	33	46	79¾	Lloyd J S	Lb	122	9.10	83-08	VerblVolley122nkGroovyFeling1226½PrincssZhr122	Tired	11
20Apr92- 6Pha	fst	6f	:22	:46	1:124	ⒻMd Sp Wt	34	3	1	3nk	2hd	55½	77¾	Madrigal R Jr	Lb	122	12.30	69-20	Alvear1221 Dial A Babe1222 Gillingham122	Tired	11
29Mar92- 8Tam	fst	6f	:223	:462	1:131	ⒻMd Sp Wt	46	5	7	42¼	2½	22	35½	Blackstun K M	Lb	118	*2.20	74-14	Npl'sLndng1181½SvrgnLn1184PrdClr118	Bid, weakened	12
1Mar92- 9Tam	fst	6f	:224	:47	1:134	ⒻMd Sp Wt	51	5	1	42	2½	2hd	44	Allen R D Jr	b	118	3.10	73-19	LkSurpror118hdSouxLookot1181JockyJIK118	Hung late	12
16Feb92- 8Tam	fst	6f	:224	:464	1:131	ⒻMd Sp Wt	55	4	5	1hd	1hd	11	43½	Blackstun K M		118	*1.40	76-17	Cohom1181½SoxLookt118½SprklnChmpgn118	Weakened	11

LATEST WORKOUTS Jly 7 Pha 4f fst :491 B

Proud Clare had run twice in the mud, with a second-place finish in her last start and an earlier 6½-length runaway. Dusty Roads Girl had finished third in her only start over a sloppy track, earning a moderate figure. So Proud Clare was the better mud runner, right? The Jersey bettors thought so, making her the 2-to-1 favorite.

But Proud Clare didn't really move up in the mud. When she scored that 6½-length victory, she earned a figure of 52 — after getting a 51 on a fast track in her previous start. And her last mud race was only one point higher than her prior fast-track number. She is not a mud freak but a filly equally capable on either surface, with figures in the low to mid-50s.

When Dusty Roads Girl ran in the slop, though, earning her 47, it was her first start after a six-month layoff, and she fared worse in her next two races, running figures of 37 and 36. She may actually be better on mud than she is on dry going. She has now hit (for her) peak form, running a figure of 57 on a fast track in her last start. This gave her a narrow edge in the figures over Proud Clare and the rest of the fillies in this Monmouth race, and she seemed likely to run at least as well in the slop. Dusty Roads Girl did so, beating Proud Clare to win and pay $13.20.

NEGATIVE CLASS DROPS

If a horse has been running well recently but is entered for a sharply lower claiming price today, he deserves to be viewed with suspicion — even if his speed figures suggest that he is a standout. Owners and trainers will rarely risk losing a healthy thoroughbred for less money than he is worth. An erstwhile $15,000 horse who is now entered for a $10,000 price tag undoubtedly has a physical ailment that makes the owner willing to lose him cheaply. But even if a handicapper knows this, evaluating such a dropdown can be tricky. Sometimes the negative class drop indicates that an infirm animal won't be able to stagger around the track. Sometimes it means that the horse is two or three races away from being seriously afflicted by his ailments; the owner and trainer may have decided to win quickly whatever purse money they can, and they won't mind if somebody takes this future problem off their hands.

Bettors trying to judge such horses should view the steepest drops in class as potentially the most negative. They should be aware that certain stables — usually the larger and more aggressive ones — make a habit of dropping horses in class to grab a purse. And they should always pay close attention to the message of the tote board. When a horse with superior class is ready to run a good race, insiders will usually know it and wager accordingly. Conversely, if a dropdown appears ice-cold in the betting, his problems have probably caught up with him already.

Many tracks have begun to card more and more conditioned claiming races — those that limit the eligibility of entrants — and the class labels of those races can be very deceptive. Aqueduct, for example, offers $25,000 claiming races for horses who have never won more than one previous start; the bad animals who meet those conditions usually aren't worth half of that designated price. So if a horse wins such a $25,000 race and is next entered for $15,000, he doesn't necessarily have a problem; he has a realistic trainer. When a horse takes a sharp class drop into a restricted race, the drop may not be negative; it may mean that the trainer wants to take advantage of some easy pickings. The trainer of a decent $10,000 claimer may risk losing him in a $6,500 race for "nonwinners of two lifetimes" because he knows the horse will be virtually unbeatable in such a spot.

While there are few hard-and-fast rules for judging negative dropdowns, there is one generally sound guideline. If a horse is taking a suspicious drop in class but still doesn't have a top speed figure, he can be eliminated. Such a horse may be able to muster a performance equal to his recent starts, but he will rarely improve on his latest form.

PHYSICAL APPEARANCE

If a horse with speed figures in the 90s runs a disappointing race today and earns a figure of 75, the explanation may not be the pace or the track bias or any of the other factors that students of the *Daily Racing Form* regularly consider. It may be that a trouble-some ankle has now started to bother the animal seriously, or that he was running a slight fever and felt listless. Conversely, a horse may improve sharply because an old knee problem is bothering him less or because the trainer "tapped" him — drained fluid from the affected joint and injected it with corticosteroids.

Judging the physical condition of racehorses and the way it may change from race to race is the most neglected important area of handicapping. Certainly, I have neglected it. Keeping records of horses' appearance is an extremely demanding, time-consuming task, and a bettor can only do so much; moreover, this is an area where a little knowledge can be a dangerous thing. Yet I have observed enough skilled professionals to appreciate how valuable such expertise can be. I know one New York bettor who goes to the paddock before every race and notes the condition of the ankle and knee of every horse; if a left front ankle is puffier today than it was in the horse's last start, this bettor will know it and assess the race accordingly. But the most impressive student of horse-flesh I have ever seen is my friend Al Torch, who can call on his past experience as a harness trainer to sense how horses feel when they warm up before a race.

When Torch broke into the game as a youngster, a veterinarian offered some help which Torch was eager to accept. The vet's instructions would be explicit: "Give the horse a 10cc injection from the red vial three days before the race; work him two hard miles two days before the race; give him a 5cc injection from the blue vial one day before the race. . . ." Torch was an instant success as a harness trainer, and he came to appreciate how changeable racehorses are. Moreover, he was convinced that drugs, both legal and illegal, are a crucial factor in racing, and when he looks at horses on the track, he distinguishes between a good-looking, energetic horse whose merits are "natural" and one whose exuberance may be chemically induced. I had always thought Torch's view of the game was tinged with paranoia until a day when I was sitting next to him during a post parade at Gulfstream Park. Torch is the consummate pro who almost never manifests emotions or nerves, but I saw that he was almost shaking with excitement as he watched the horses through his 30-power binoculars. "Beautiful!" Torch exclaimed. "Beautiful! You know, most trainers who use drugs really don't know what they're doing. But there's a horse out there who's the best drug job I've seen since New York in the late '70s. They've done it just right!" My suspicions about Torch's paranoia evaporated when the 6-to-1 shot, an ex-claimer, ran away from the field and earned a figure of 110.

Gamblers like Al Torch, who base their wagers on horses' appearance, benefit from a view of the game that is subjective and distinctive. The prices on horses they see as standouts are not going to be depressed in the way that speed and pace handicappers have seen their methods become less profitable. Because the crucial judgments have to be made in the ten minutes before post time, this is one aspect of handicapping that is never going to be commercialized and mass-marketed.

If a youthful horseplayer asked me how he should go about learning the game, I would recommend that he concentrate on studying horses' appearance and relating it to their level of performance and their speed figures. Fortunately for would-be students, several good videos offer basic instruction in assessing horses in the paddock and post parade: Joe Takach's *Spotting the Ready to Win Racehorse,* Trillis Parker's *Horses Talk,* and the late Bonnie Ledbetter's *The Body Language of Racehorses.* Ideally, students of physical appearance and speed figures should want to reach the point where they can say, "This horse has been running in the 70s, but he hasn't looked so good since six races ago, when he ran a 90, and he ought to be able to run a 90 again today."

LASIX

In the mid-1970s, I was confounded by the racing in Maryland. Horses were performing in ways that defied all handicapping logic; indeed, they seemed to defy the laws of nature. Faint-hearted sprinters were miraculously turning into stouthearted distance runners. Certain trainers were claiming horses and improving them overnight by twenty lengths. These phenomena were so striking that I made them the centerpiece of the chapter in *Picking Winners* that dealt with understanding the methodology of trainers. I did not know at the time that the factor behind these form reversals was not the skill of trainers. It was Lasix. The diuretic was being introduced to American racing, illegally, in Maryland; eventually its use got so out of hand that the state's racing commission capitulated and made the antibleeding medication legal.

That was the beginning of a national debate over the politics, ethics, and medical benefits of Lasix use, which, two decades later, still has not been resolved. Handicappers are still often confounded by the drug and its effects. Its mysteries aren't as unfathomable as they used to be, when most tracks did not identify the horses who were racing on Lasix and when the *Daily Racing Form* had not yet included the crucial L symbol in its past performances. But even with all of the relevant information at hand, what do we do in a race where the top horses run speed figures of 90 and a rival with a figure of 80 is getting Lasix for the first time?

I have wrestled with this question for twenty years, and the answer has varied according to the place and time. In the early 1980s, I studied the drug's effects and found a recurring pattern. Horses did tend to improve sharply when they were treated with Lasix for the first time — but it was a predictable improvement. Usually, a horse's form would steadily deteriorate until he gave a terrible effort; when he got Lasix, he would rebound sharply to the level of his previous best form. My friend Tom Aronson, a consultant to racetracks who has studied the Lasix issue, offered a common-sense explanation of what happened in this scenario: "A horse starts to race worse and worse, and then he throws in a real clinker. The trainer says, 'Something's got to be wrong; let's have him 'scoped.' [The horse's throat and lungs are examined with a device called an endoscope to determine if he has been bleeding internally.] Now they find he's a bleeder. They give him a little time off, put him on Lasix, and put him in a race. The trainer tells the jock, 'This horse has been bleeding, but he's going to do a lot better today. Let's give him a good run.'" In my study, two-thirds of the horses given Lasix for the first time ran a speed figure higher than that of their previous race, but now the whole process seemed demystified. Lasix didn't induce miracles; it cleared up a respiratory problem and enabled a horse to recapture his best form.

That's the way Lasix works — or, at least, the way it used to work. As American trainers have become more and more Lasix-conscious, or, some would say, Lasix-obsessed, few wait until a horse's form goes through a steady deterioration until they say, "Something's got to be wrong; let's have him 'scoped." Many fear that they will be losing an edge of some sort if they run a horse without Lasix, and they may give a horse the medication whether he needs it or not, which is easily possible in the many states where regulations are lax. Nowadays, handicappers won't see many horses who endure a long downhill slide before they are given Lasix for the first time. Usually, a horse will throw in one clinker and be given the drug:

Private Access had earned figures of 71, 78, and 76 before he ran a dismal race and got a figure of 63. Undoubtedly, his new trainer had him 'scoped, found that he had bled, and gave him Lasix for the first time. And handicappers could reasonably assume that this is what happened. The combination of a single poor race followed by first-time Lasix usually means that the horse bled and that the poor performance can be excused. Private Access rebounded from his poor showing and returned to his usual form, winning with a figure of 78.

While all handicappers recognize that the administration of first-time Lasix is potentially significant, many believe that second-time Lasix is important, too. There is no medical basis for this idea, and I have never been persuaded of its validity, except in the cases when there was a reason that a horse didn't run well the first time he received it.

Nasdette — B. m. 7, by Spring Double—Ask No Questions, by Nearctic
$6,000 Br.—Questroyal Farm (NY)
Own.—Wallace Waldyn — Tr.—Wallace Waldyn (49 4 3 5 .08) — **112**

Lifetime								
85 7 8 4	1992	21	3	1	0	$9,208
$74,585	1991	18	2	2	1	$7,912
	Turf	3	0	0	0	
	Wet	11	0	2	0	$8,685

10Oct92-15Del	fst	1	$:48^4$	$1:14^2$	$1:41^3$	3↑ⒻClm 4000	49	5	6	$7^{3\frac{1}{2}}$	$5^{3\frac{1}{2}}$	4^5	$1^{\frac{1}{2}}$	Rodriguez A	Lb	119	8.90	74-31	Nsdette119$^{\frac{1}{2}}$NeverSoSly113$^{4\frac{1}{4}}$DoublyFoolish116	Up late	8
1Oct92- 3Pha	fst	6f	$:22^4$	$:47^2$	$1:13^2$	3↑ⒻClm 4000	33	1	12	4^2	6^4	$9^{8\frac{1}{4}}$	$7^{10\frac{1}{2}}$	Bisono J	Lb	119	16.60	63-24	CuttingWay116$^{4\frac{1}{4}}$SecretBlend115$^{1\frac{1}{2}}$PagnRitul119	Faded	12
13Sep92- 4Pha	fst	$1\frac{1}{16}$	:48	$1:13^3$	1:48	3↑ⒻClm 4000	32	9	6	$6^{6\frac{1}{4}}$	6^9	8^{13}	8^{15}	Melchor V	b	119	73.00	54-28	[D]Imabaygirl119$^{1\frac{1}{4}}$Berty'sGlory119^{4}JanetPlnet116	Wide	9
30Aug92- 1Pha	fst	$1\frac{1}{16}$	$:47^3$	1:13	$1:47^3$	3↑ⒻClm 4000	38	6	8	$8^{7\frac{1}{4}}$	$7^{8\frac{1}{4}}$	$7^{8\frac{1}{2}}$	$7^{13\frac{1}{4}}$	Bisono C V^7	b	112	15.50	58-23	Imabaygirl116$^{1\frac{1}{2}}$ Nine Grand116$^{1\frac{1}{2}}$BiteofGold115	Outrun	8
13Aug92- 4Atl	gd	$1\frac{1}{16}$	:48	$1:14^4$	$1:48^3$	3↑ⒻClm 4000	44	8	4	4^7	3^2	2^3	$2^{4\frac{1}{2}}$	Gavidia W	b	122	5.00	62-31	Dromara112$^{4\frac{1}{2}}$ Nasdette122$^{2\frac{3}{4}}$ Celebreath122	2nd best	9
5Aug92- 2Atl	fst	$1\frac{1}{16}$	$:48^2$	$1:14^4$	$1:49^1$	3↑ⒻClm 4000	52	3	3	3^3	1^1	$1^{3\frac{1}{2}}$	$1^{1\frac{1}{2}}$	Gavidia W	b	117	6.80	64-21	Nasdette117$^{1\frac{1}{2}}$SladyJaney117$^{6\frac{1}{2}}$Starkey'sGirl117	Driving	8
24Jly92- 4Mth	gd	6f	$:22^2$	$:46^2$	$1:12^3$	3↑ⒻClm 5000	49	6	7	7^{11}	$7^{7\frac{3}{4}}$	7^6	$7^{4\frac{3}{4}}$	Gavidia W	b	116	52.20	73-16	SmoldringEmbrs111^{no}HppyKy116$^{\frac{3}{4}}$ArForbsGl116	Outrun	7
30Jun92- 2Mth	fst	1^{70}	$:47^1$	$1:12^2$	1:45	3↑ⒻClm 5000	38	3	8	$8^{8\frac{1}{2}}$	7^{13}	5^{13}	$4^{17\frac{1}{4}}$	Gavidia W	b	115	27.60e	54-25	JntPlnt115$^{7\frac{3}{4}}$GlowingWld117^{8}DrngJmny115	No solid bid	9
19Jun92- 4Mth	sly	$1\frac{1}{16}$	$:48^1$	$1:13^1$	$1:46^2$	3↑ⒻClm 5000	25	8	9	9^{10}	9^{12}	9^{16}	$9^{25\frac{3}{4}}$	Vega A	b	115	76.60	51-27	Farrus115^7 Meetmenow115$^{\frac{3}{4}}$ Glowing Wild117	Outrun	9
10Jun92- 4Mth	fst	6f	:22	$:45^2$	$1:11^1$	3↑ⒻClm 5000	32	1	7	7^8	10^{12}	9^{16}	$9^{17\frac{1}{4}}$	Emmolo O^5	b	112	85.00	68-18	GLssG116$^{6\frac{1}{2}}$SmldrngEmbrs116$^{1\frac{3}{4}}$Shyl'sPrspct111	Outrun	10

Nasdette was treated with Lasix for the first time on October 1, but that day she was in an obviously inappropriate spot. A distance runner with little tactical speed, she was entered in a six-furlong race. Nine days later she was back in a route, where she belonged, and her figure improved sharply to a 49 — about the same level she was running before her form started to deteriorate. This improvement is better seen in the light of handicapping logic than of a second-time Lasix mystique.

Lasix tends to produce improvement more reliably in horses with early speed than in those who come off the pace, and this, too, makes sense in view of the drug's properties. Although Lasix is known for its ability to help horses who bleed through the nostrils, it works on the lungs — where most bleeding originates.

Within a few minutes of being administered, the diuretic clears any excess fluid out of the lungs. It works on obstructed airways. It helps horses breathe better. Many horses who show speed and tire may be doing so not because of a genetic inability to go a distance but because they are failing to breathe properly. Once they get Lasix, they can carry their speed farther.

Because horses now rarely go through a sustained period of decline until a trainer decides to give them Lasix, older horses tend not to produce the shocking wakeups they used to. But young horses do. If a horse has had only one or two starts in his career and now gets Lasix, a handicapper can only guess what his potential may be with it. And if the horse flashed speed before getting Lasix, the possibility for an explosive wakeup is even greater:

Speedy Frog	Ch. c. 3(Jan), by Lyphard's Wish—Etoile d'Orient, by Targowice—Fr		Lifetime	1992	3	1	0	0	$7,150
				3 1 0 0	1991	0	M	0	0	
TORRES H (27 1 1 0 .04)	$16,000	Br.—Clovely Farms (Ky)		$7,150					
Own.—Wiles Dennis & Robert A		Tr.—Mulhall Richard W (8 1 1 2 .13)	**117**						
28Sep92- 5Fpx fst 6½f :221 :45⁴ 1:18³ 3+Md 16000	59 1 1 1½ 1½ 1¹ 1½ Torres H	L 114	7.00	83-12 Speedy Frog114½ Inception Said1181½ Booth N Bob114	10
28Sep92-Lugged out drive, brushed late				
4Sep92- 2Dmr fst 6f :22 :45² 1:10² 3+Md 32000	37 2 4 41½ 66½ 712 717½ Torres H	B 118	96.30	69-13 ConqstdorSx118³½Shmoon116²ColtnPrtnrs118 Faltered 8
17Aug92- 9Dmr fst 6f :22 :44⁴ 1:10¹ 3+Md 32000	34 6 3 63½ 96½111311117½ Torres H	B 118	57.00	70-10 PeceMongr122²¾RoylDixi118¹½DvNz118 Stumbled start 11
LATEST WORKOUTS	Oct 6 SA 4f fst :47² H	Sep 25 SA 5f fst 1:03⁴ H	Sep 20 SA 4f fst :48⁴ H	Sep 14 Dmr 5f fst 1:00¹ H

This colt showed brief speed at Del Mar, chasing a :22-flat first quarter, before he tired badly and lost by more than seventeen lengths. Could pulmonary troubles have been stopping him? Could Lasix be the answer? In this case, first-time Lasix was good for a 22-point improvement in the figures.

My general rule for assessing first-time Lasix users is this: In the case of an experienced horse who has run a bad recent race or two, I will consider it likely that he will now duplicate his best recent figure before those bad races. If the horse gets Lasix after a good effort, I am less likely to upgrade him. (Perhaps he delivered his optimal effort in that race but bled in a workout thereafter.) If the horse is lightly raced, and in particular if he has flashed speed, I will entertain the possibility that he could improve sharply. I will look at a horse's entire past-performance picture with an awareness of the time he started using Lasix, and I may be willing to forgive some shortcomings he displayed in his pre-

Lasix days. For example, a horse who ran poorly in past distance races may deserve another chance at a route now that he is using the medication.

When horses are taken off Lasix — as often happens with shippers to New York, where the drug remains illegal — handicappers are faced with a dilemma. Many regular Lasix users don't really need the drug and can run perfectly well without it. Others will sometimes give disastrous performances if they are taken off Lasix. One factor that seems to affect the performance of such horses is weather. Thoroughbreds with respiratory problems may find it harder to run without Lasix in hot, muggy summer weather than they do in cooler climates. Unbridled was trounced without Lasix in June, in the 1990 Belmont Stakes, but returned to New York and won the Breeders' Cup Classic on a brisk October day.

The unpredictability of horses' performances when they go off and on Lasix was the the crucial factor in one of the most painful betting experiences of my life, on the final day of the Hialeah meeting in March 1987. That year the track had offered a ridiculously impossible jackpot wager, the pick ten; with so many wide-open races on every card, few people tried to hit it and nobody did. But on closing day the accrued jackpot of $200,000 would have to be paid out, and I wanted it. Susan Vallon and I were going to be married two weeks later and we were beginning to furnish our marble-floored dream house; I was learning, to my astonishment, that a sofa can cost $10,000. I pored over the record of every entrant in the pick ten and worked out a tentative betting strategy, but there was one horse on the card about whom I couldn't make up my mind. Glaros had run well on the turf in California before coming to Hialeah for a race in February. The program indicated that he was running on Lasix, though I presumed he had been running on it in California, too — this was before the information was shown in Daily Racing Form past performances. I had bet him enthusiastically — but Glaros ran dismally. Now he had reappeared in the eighth race of the pick ten, where I already had two solid contenders. If I included him, the cost of my ticket would jump from $2,160 to $3,240. I wrestled with the decision for hours, but I couldn't find any way to excuse the terrible recent race. I threw out Glaros, invested $2,160, and proceeded to savor one of my all-time great handicapping performances. I had five of the first seven winners, and the two I missed were impossible longshots that nobody could have used. I knew I had the ninth and tenth events locked up, and so the eighth race would be decisive. As one of my horses, Kings River, stalked the leaders, looking strong, I noted with relief that Glaros wasn't even showing any of his customary speed and was a dozen lengths behind. Kings River surged to the front entering the stretch and looked as if he had taken command in the race — until a chestnut horse came flying on the outside and nailed him in the last stride. Glaros had beaten me out of the pick ten. I wound up with seven winners, and one person — who had used Glaros on his ticket — picked eight.

I was stunned and disheartened, but mostly I was perplexed. Why had Glaros run such a smashing race after performing so dismally in his previous start? I knew trainer Tom Skiffington slightly, and I called him to ask him the question point-blank. "Charlie Whittingham sent the horse to me from California," Skiffington said, "and I entered him to run on Lasix because I had a certificate from California saying he was a bleeder. But the racing commission wouldn't accept the certificate because they have a very antiquated rule saying the horse has to bleed from the nostrils before he can get Lasix. We argued back and forth until four hours before the race when they told me he couldn't run with Lasix. I went ahead and ran him anyway, and, sure enough, when he came back to the barn he was bleeding from the nostrils. That's why he ran so badly. We showed the state vet, and so the horse qualified to run on Lasix the next time. There's no doubt that was the reason he improved so much." Because of all the bureaucratic confusion, though, the Hialeah program didn't show that Glaros was back on Lasix today. Goodbye, $200,000. Hello, $10,000 sofa.

Even in this maddening situation, Lasix had worked the way it is supposed to: a horse runs poorly, gets the drug and reverts to his normal level of performance. If this were always the case, Lasix would be no more mysterious a handicapping factor than "blinkers on." But there are still times and places where Lasix horses seem to defy the laws of nature. Shortly after I had done my study in Maryland which seemed to clarify the workings of the drug, I went to Florida for the winter season and saw, time after time, horses with Lasix exploding to run races of which they had never been capable in their lives. What was the difference between the two states? In Florida, Lasix was administered by private vets, not in a state-run detention barn, raising the possibility that the diuretic might be used to disguise the presence of more potent illegal drugs. This has been an important topic in the industry's debate over Lasix ever since it began. While experts insist that Lasix can't "mask" the presence of illegal drugs, it does greatly dilute their presence in a horse's urine, making detection much more difficult.

Whatever the reason, improbable form reversals accompanied by Lasix tend to occur in clusters, not as isolated incidents. Sometimes a few stables will appear to be working miracles of which Lasix is a regular component.

Troubled Emperor — Dk. b. or br. g. 3(Apr), by Hail Emperor—Nasca, by Hold Your Peace
Br.—Olsson Sture G (Md)
Own.—Alecci John V — Tr.—Patty Karen A (35 7 6 3 .20) — 115
Lifetime 4 1 1 0 $7,359 — 1992 4 1 1 0 $7,359 — 1991 0 M 0 0

6Nov92- 7Lrl	fst	6f	:221	:452	1:094	3↑Alw 17100	92	2	4	1½	1hd	2hd	21	Reynolds L C	Lb	115	4.80e	91-18	MdHst1151TroubldEmpror1154¾SqntmPont117	Gamely	8
24Oct92- 5Lrl	fst	6f	:223	:462	1:103	3↑Md 8500	80	2	4	11	1½	1hd	12	Reynolds L C	Lb	119	*2.50	88-14	TroubledEmperor1192MstrMkr1195OhStrikr117	Driving	14
8Mar92- 5Lrl	fst	6f	:224	:473	1:132	Md c-8500	37	12	7	52¾	74¼	32½	42½	Prado E S		120	*1.90	71-17	BrotherRoberts1201½HighBemr120¾KnIntntion115	Hung	14
21Feb92- 5Lrl	fst	6½f	:23	:472	1:211	Md 12000	33	5	14	1410	1110	98¾	78¼	Prado E S		120	4.10	63-20	Crown Mist120¾ Chip'NMe1201½SkunkFoot120	Off slow	14

LATEST WORKOUTS ●Oct 6 Pim 6f fst 1:133 B ●Sep 29 Pim 6f gd 1:16 Hg

Partially Literate — Ch. f. 2(May), by Parfaitement—Literary Lark, by Arts and Letters
$11,500 Br.—Bonita Farm (Md)
Own.—Supchak Leonard P — Tr.—Patty Karen A (39 9 7 3 .23) — 1095
Lifetime 4 1 0 0 $3,929 — 1992 4 1 0 0 $3,929

17Nov92- 5Lrl	fst	6f	:224	:471	1:141	ⒻMd 8500	31	12	11	1115	913	56	1½	MoorefildWT5	Lb	114	12.80	70-16	PrtillyLtrt114½LghtlyLndng1171¼MondyClub119	Driving	13
29Sep92- 5Pim	fst	6f	:234	:482	1:144	Md 8500	3	8	3	86¾	710	1014	1017	Reynolds L C	b	117	11.80	54-25	ArtDancer118½RitchiePark1151HurriedWhisper120	Wide	10
19Sep92- 3Pim	fst	6f	:241	:492	1:154	ⒻMd 8500	13	5	5	42½	87¼	77¾	87¼	Reynolds L C		119	10.60	59-23	MoodIndigo1192½Gil'sProtg1191½Kyl'sGrl119	Weakened	11
31Aug92- 3Pha	fst	6f	:231	:48	1:141	ⒻMd 16000	1	7	7	86¾	811	714	514¾	Vigliotti M J		119	8.30	55-21	Alom'sDobl1221¾AmznglyBl1191½RM'sGrl116	No threat	9

LATEST WORKOUTS Oct 22 Pim 5f fst 1:03 B

Buck Be a Lady — Dk. b. or br. f. 2(Mar), by Buckfinder—Promising Gal, by Blade
Br.—Pearlstein Leonard (Ky)
Own.—Alecci John V — Tr.—Patty Karen A (55 12 11 4 .22) — 113
Lifetime 5 1 1 0 $12,890 — 1992 5 1 1 0 $12,890

3Dec92- 7Lrl	fst	6f	:222	:462	1:121	ⒻMd Sp Wt	60	3	7	42½	11½	11½	16	Reynolds L C	Lb	119	3.30e	80-19	BuckBLdy1196BusyWomn1194Forgottnvlntn119	Driving	12
22Nov92- 7Lrl	gd	6f	:224	:463	1:123	ⒻMd Sp Wt	65	7	3	31	1½	1hd	22	Reynolds L C	Lb	119	13.80	76-20	Allepia1192BuckBeaLady1197FoulisAlicia119	Lugged in	13
22Oct92- 3Lrl	fst	6½f	:224	:47	1:20	ⒻMd c-25000	28	8	3	11½	1hd	32½	117½	Delgado A	b	119	11.30	69-20	GoldSprkl1191MissIvy1191¾Justyouwitnds119	Fell back	11
22Oct92-Claimed from Pearlstein Leonard, Benshoff Ronald L Trainer																					
11Oct92- 7Lrl	fst	6½f	:222	:462	1:184	ⒻMd Sp Wt	42	5	8	52½	65	79¼	89¾	Delgado A		119	29.90	73-17	Lily of theNorth119½Booly1194½BuckRoll119	Weakened	13
18Aug92- 7Lrl	fst	6f	:223	:462	1:122	ⒻMd Sp Wt	-0	5	7	21	69	722	838¼	Luzzi M J		119	2.80	41-18	ProsprousLdy1195¼Crcd1192½Cod'sBlossom119	Faltered	8

When Troubled Emperor improved by 43 points with first-time Lasix, when the inept Partially Literate finished like a wild horse with first-time Lasix, when Buck Be a Lady improved by 37 points after being claimed, many Marylanders concluded trainer Karen Patty was a miracle-worker whose horses were defying the laws of nature. I concluded that not a great deal had changed in the two decades since Lasix made its first appearance on the American racing scene.

The performances of the above horses may be atypical, and downright bizarre, but they underscore an important truth of handicapping. There is no way that any system of handicapping could ever take into account the fact that horses in Maryland trained by Karen Patty are apt to improve wildly when they are administered Lasix for the first time. Successful bettors are the ones who are observant and flexible, who can adjust to changing conditions in the sport instead of being imprisoned by rigid ideas. This is a particular danger for those of us who use speed figures. Because figures are usually so reliable, it is easy for a handicapper to grow complacent and bet mechanically on the horses with the best recent numbers, instead of watching vigilantly for the innumerable factors which might cause a horse to run very differently today. There was an excellent test of such vigilance at Belmont Park on October 10, 1992, a day of stakes events billed as Breeders' Cup Preview Day. These were the past performances for the five-horse Beldame Stakes.

6

1 ⅛ MILES. **(1.45^{2}) 53rd Running THE BELDAME (Grade I). Purse $250,000. Fillies and Mares, 3-year-olds and upward. By subscription of $500 each which should accompany the nomination; $2,000 to pass the entry box; $2,000 to start. The purse to be divided 60% to the winner, 22% to second, 12% to third and 6% to fourth. Weight for age. Weight: 3-year-olds 119 lbs. Older 123 lbs. Starters to be named at the closing time of entries. Mrs. John E. Cowdin has donated a perpetual cup to be held by the owner of the winner for one year. A permanent trophy will be presented to the owner of the winner and trophies will be presented to the winning trainer and jockey. Closed with 19 Nominations Wednesday, September 23.**

Saratoga Dew — **B. f. 3(Apr), by Cormorant—Super Luna, by In Reality**

MCCAULEY W H (126 24 19 12 .19) — **Br.—Chenery Helen B (NY)**

Own.—Engel Charles F — **Tr.—Sciacca Gary (29 3 2 3 .10)** — **119**

Lifetime 9 7 1 0 $391,580 — 1992 9 7 1 0 $391,580 — 1991 0 M 0 0 — Wet 1 0 1 0 $44,000

2Sep92- 8Bel	fst	1⅛	:46	1:10^{1}	1:47^{3}	ⒻGazelle H	101	2	2	$2^{3\frac{1}{2}}$	2^{2}	1^{hd}	$1^{1\frac{1}{4}}$	McCauley W H	120	*1.00	91-10	SaratogaDew120$^{1\frac{1}{4}}$Vivano114$^{4\frac{1}{4}}$TineyTost113	Mild drive	6	
2Sep92-Grade I																					
15Aug92- 8Sar	my	1¼	:47^{1}	1:36^{2}	2:02^{3}	ⒻAlabama	99	5	1	1^{1}	$1^{1\frac{1}{2}}$	1^{1}	2no	McCauley W H	121	6.70	91-09	NovmbrSnow121^{no}SrtogDw121$^{1\frac{3}{4}}$PcificSqull121	Gamely	7	
15Aug92-Grade I																					
25Jly92-10FL	gd	1$\frac{1}{16}$	:47^{3}	1:12^{1}	1:46^{4}	ⒻⓈN Y Oaks	101	5	2	$2^{\frac{1}{2}}$	$1^{\frac{1}{2}}$	1^{2}	$1^{6\frac{1}{2}}$	McCauley W H	112	*.40	92-25	SrtogDew112$^{6\frac{1}{2}}$Noble'sHoney109^{27}She'sQun112	Handily	6	
27Jun92-10Mth	fst	1^{70}	:45^{4}	1:10^{2}	1:41^{3}	ⒻPost Deb	80	7	11	9^{10}	$6^{9\frac{1}{4}}$	$6^{8\frac{1}{2}}$	$6^{9\frac{1}{4}}$	McCauley W H	119	2.70	79-16	DmondD113^{nk}C.C.'sRtrn115^{6}MssLglty121	No solid rally	12	
27Jun92-Grade II																					
3Jun92- 8Bel	fst	7f	:22^{4}	:45^{4}	1:23^{2}	3↑ⒻⓈHydePrkH	96	5	6	$1^{\frac{1}{2}}$	$2^{\frac{1}{2}}$	1^{hd}	1^{nk}	McCauley W H	114	2.40	87-12	SrtogDw114^{nk}MissIronSmok114$^{\frac{3}{4}}$Bn'sMomnt112	Driving	7	
28Mar92- 8Aqu	fst	1	:46^{2}	1:11^{2}	1:37^{1}	ⒻComely	93	7	2	2^{1}	2^{1}	2^{hd}	1^{1}	McCauley W H	114	*.80	76-31	SrtogDw114^{1}CityDnc112$^{\frac{1}{2}}$LookingforWin114	Hard drive	7	
28Mar92-Grade II																					
16Mar92- 8Aqu	fst	7f	:22^{4}	:46^{2}	1:24^{3}	ⒻOver All	93	8	4	$2^{\frac{1}{2}}$	$2^{\frac{1}{2}}$	1^{3}	$1^{4\frac{3}{4}}$	McCauley W H	116	*1.60	82-25	SrtogDew116$^{4\frac{3}{4}}$MissCoverGirl116^{hd}GivNotic118	Driving	9	
8Feb92- 6Aqu	fst	6f	⊡:23	:46^{4}	1:11^{4}	ⒻⓈAlw 27000	91	4	2	$1^{\frac{1}{2}}$	1^{hd}	1^{6}	$1^{11\frac{1}{2}}$	McCauley W H	121	*.70	84-22	SrtogDew121$^{11\frac{1}{2}}$BeSpcil116$^{1\frac{1}{2}}$Ain'tShNic116	Ridden out	6	
19Jan92- 6Aqu	fst	6f	⊡:23^{3}	:48^{2}	1:14	ⒻⓈMd Sp Wt	70	11	9	5^{3}	$1^{\frac{1}{2}}$	1^{4}	$1^{5\frac{3}{4}}$	McCauley W H	121	8.90	73-27	SaratogDew121$^{5\frac{3}{4}}$MontnGl121^{2}Kyle'sKreem121	Handily	11	

LATEST WORKOUTS **Oct 6 Bel 4f fst :47^{2} B** **●Oct 1 Bel 5f fst :59 H** **Sep 25 Bel 5f fst 1:00^{2} B** **●Aug 28 Sar tr.t 4f fst :47^{1} B**

A Gal For Gordo — B. f. 4, by Geiger Counter—Tantalizingly, by Val de l'Orne
KRONE J A (133 24 14 18 .18)
Own.—Bankuti Tibor I
Br.—Foxdale Farm (Ont-C)
Tr.—Attfield Roger (2 1 0 0 .50)
123
Lifetime 15 7 1 2 $270,655 | 1992 5 3 1 1 $180,620 | 1991 7 3 0 0 $75,780 | Turf 1 0 0 1 $12,100 | Wet 1 1 0 0 $65,100

26Sep92- 9WO fst 1⅛ :464 1:122 1:532 3+ⒻⓈBelMhone 87 1 1 1hd 12 2½ 2nk Seymour D J L 124 1.25 79-22 PltnmPws114nkAGlForGordo124nkBllyVghn116 Gamely 5
26Sep92-Grade I-C
6Sep92- 7WO fst 1 1/16 :474 1:122 1:442 ⒻⓈAlgoma 100 3 1 1½ 13½ 110 113 Seymour D J L 118 *.50 92-12 AGlForGordo11813Gydel'Orne114nkLdyRgncy112 Easily 6
8Aug92-10WO sly 1 1/16 :473 1:12 1:454 ⒻⓇOntMatron 94 6 1 1½ 2hd 11 12½ Seymour D J L 114 3.55 85-17 AGlFrGrd1142½WldrnssSn1251½CntOCh115 Ears pricked 6
8Aug92-Grade II-C
18Jly92- 6WO fst 7f :224 :454 1:242 3+ⒻAlw 30900 83 5 3 3nk 1½ 13 16 Seymour D J L 117 1.80 89-14 A Gal ForGordo1176QuietCleo1173½Illeria117 Hand ride 7
18Jly92-Originally scheduled on turf
1Jly92- 4WO fm 1 1/16 Ⓣ:464 1:101 1:413 3+ⒻⓇVictoriana 86 4 1 1½ 11 11½ 32½ Seymour D J L 119 13.50 93-04 CountryStg117½HopForABrz1172AGlForGordo119 Tired 10
24Nov91-10Hia fst 7f :231 :461 1:224 ⒻJasmine 69 3 4 1½ 3nk 64½ 710½ Penna D L 121 5.80 78-19 PrivteTresur1213½ForignAid116½Fullofstuff118 Faltered 10
2Nov91-11Grd fst 7f :23 :463 1:263 ⒻJmmedLovly 75 2 2 11½ 12 16 15¾ Fenech S C L 120 13.35 75-23 AGlForGrd1205¾Mnnpls118noStlthThndr116 Ridden out 8
2Nov91-Run in Two Divisions
12Oct91- 8WO fst 6f :223 :464 1:111 3+ⒻⓈOntario 71 4 3 4¾ 41¼ 710 710½ Walls M K L 111 4.10 78-19 Illeria1194 Bees 'N' Honey114¾ Areydne112 Gave way 8
12Oct91-Grade II-C
31Aug91- 6WO fst 1 1/16 :463 1:122 1:454 ⒻⓈW'dbineSl 70 8 1 13 2½ 37½ 512¼ McKnight J 110 6.35 73-18 PlatinumPaws1106LdyRegency1114Gydel'Orne114 Tired 14
17Aug91- 2WO fst 6½f :222 :452 1:172 ⒻⓈAlw 22900 85 2 2 11½ 11 12 11 Walls M K5 113 *.55 88-19 AGlForGordo1131PltnmPws1184Mstoyo118 Ridden out 5
LATEST WORKOUTS ●Oct 7 WO 5f fst :594 B ●Sep 23 WO tr.t 5f gd 1:003 B ●Sep 17 WO 5f fst :593 B Sep 2 WO 5f fst 1:002 B

Train Robbery — Ch. m. 5, by Alydar—Track Robbery, by No Robbery
DAY P (28 10 4 8 .36)
Own.—Houng William T
Br.—Gussin F & P (Ky)
Tr.—Lukas D Wayne (29 2 4 3 .07)
123
Lifetime 40 8 12 2 $586,897 | 1992 9 2 4 1 $203,825 | 1991 14 1 4 1 $170,744 | Turf 4 0 2 0 $24,273 | Wet 5 1 1 1 $136,583

20Sep92-10TP fst 1 1/16 :472 1:111 1:431 3+ⒻBud Brd Cp 87 5 2 2½ 32 47 712½ Migliore R B 120 3.10 78-25 Fit for a Queen1232 Auto Dial1207½ Hitch112 In tight 9
20Sep92-Grade II
6Sep92- 8Bel fst 1 :46 1:102 1:36 3+ⒻGo ForWand 92 3 1 1½ 1hd 1hd 31¾ Migliore R 118 7.30 88-12 Easy Now1111 ⒹNannerl123¾ Train Robbery118 Gamely 5
6Sep92-Grade I; Placed second through disqualification
15Aug92- 9Mth sly 170 :461 1:11 1:421 3+ⒻBud Bred H 95 3 3 2½ 1hd 12 12¾ Gryder A T 112 5.20 85-19 TrinRobbry1122¾Concord'sGold1111½Crownd115 Driving 7
15Aug92-Grade III
19Jly92-11Del fst 1¼ :50 1:393 2:03 3+ⒻDelaware H 97 3 1 11 1hd 1hd 21¾ Velazquez J R 111 10.60 89-21 BrillintBrss1171¾TrinRobbery1117RisnColony113 Sharp 6
19Jly92-Grade II
6Jun92-11CD fst 1⅛ :47 1:12 1:504 3+ⒻFlr D Ls H 81 3 8 77 53 106 78 Lopez R D B 113 11.50 82-12 Bunglow1141TilForbid113nkBethBelivs112 Bid, faltered 12
6Jun92-Grade III
24May92- 9CD fst 1 1/16 :473 1:13 1:453 3+ⒻAlw 38050 85 3 3 31 2hd 1½ 1nk Allen K K B 119 *.80Ⓓ 86-12 ⒹTrnRobbry119nkGdfrHr1222MgnlRvnl117 Drft out, dq 6
24May92-Disqualified and placed third
30Apr92- 6CD fst 1 1/16 :491 1:141 1:444 3+ⒻAlw 40850 83 5 3 1hd 2hd 22 23 Stevens G L B 119 *1.30 87-14 CrtnsDrn1173TrnRbbr119nkCrtHstss122 Fully extended 6
2Apr92- 9TP fst 1 1/16 :481 1:131 1:442 ⒻAlw 27400 96 1 4 41½ 31 21½ 21¼ Allen K K B 121 *.40 83-24 BthBlivs1121¼TrnRobbry1218Nnzng115 Bid, second best 5
20Mar92- 9TP fst 1 :47 1:131 1:391 ⒻAlw 27400 92 6 2 23 21½ 1hd 14½ Allen K K B 113 *.90 81-26 TrnRbbry1134½JsThghts1146SttlWv115 Ridden out best 6
28Nov91- 9CD fst 1⅛ :482 1:124 1:511 3+ⒻFalls City 76 9 6 54½ 55 711 918¼ McDowell M B 110 20.40 74-23 ScreenProspect1172½FitforQueen1244Bunglow112 Tired 11
LATEST WORKOUTS Aug 28 Mth 4f fst :523 B Aug 21 Mth 5f fst 1:041 B Aug 11 Mth 4f fst :504 B

Coxwold — B. f. 4, by Cox's Ridge—Egyptian Rose, by Sir Ivor
ANTLEY C W (92 22 5 12 .24)
Own.—Maktoum Mohammed Al
Br.—Miller Mr-Mrs & West Mr-Mrs (Ky)
Tr.—Clement Christopher (12 3 2 0 .25)
123
Lifetime 6 3 0 0 $55,206 | 1992 3 2 0 0 $46,800 | 1991 3 1 0 0 $8,406 | Turf 4 1 0 0 $8,406

25Sep92- 8Bel fst 1 :47 1:112 1:361 3+ⒻHandicap 98 3 6 52 51½ 2½ 1¾ Krone J A b 108 3.50 89-15 Coxwold108¾HeyBabLulu1115½LdyD'Accord119 Driving 7
24Aug92- 8Sar fm 1⅜ Ⓣ:471 1:364 2:131 3+ⒻWaya 70 8 3 24 42½ 79½ 717¾ Antley C W b 115 *1.80 86-02 Fairy Garden115¾PillowMint1155BigBigAffair115 Faded 10
24Aug92-New Course Record
9Aug92- 3Sar gd 1⅛ :462 1:103 1:484 3+ⒻAlw 31000 92 1 3 1½ 1½ 12 14 Antley C W b 117 18.40 93-07 Coxwold1174 Buck SomeBelle1123½BiancaD.114 Driving 7
6Aug91♦4Deauville(Fra) gd*1⅛ 2:42 ⓉⒻPrix De Thiberville 12 Cauthen S 121 22.00 — — Crnagor 1214 Lunar Quest 121nk Numidie121 No threat 15
28Jly91♦4Clairfont'e(Fra) gd*1⅜ :00 ⓉⒻPrix De Trouville 12½ Guillot S 120 8.10 — — Coxwld1202½ Sphnsb1231½ AllnsEnfnts123 Prom, clear 18
28Jly91-No time taken
9Jly91♦3StCloud(Fra) gd*1⅛ 2:154 Ⓣ Prix Madrigal(Mdn) 14 Tellier C 114 *1.75e — — NorhtenrSprite1141½ TienAnMen120¾ SirnBlu120 Tired 16
LATEST WORKOUTS Sep 23 Bel 3f gd :371 B Sep 13 Bel 4f fst :50 B Aug 21 Sar tr.t 3f fst :391 B

Versailles Treaty — B. f. 4, by Danzig—Ten Cents a Dance, by Buckpasser
SMITH M E (168 24 30 19 .14)
Own.—Phipps Cynthia
Br.—Phipps Cynthia (Ky)
Tr.—McGaughey Claude III (32 14 6 5 .44)
123
Lifetime 18 9 7 2 $1,016,154 | 1992 6 2 2 2 $310,318 | 1991 11 6 5 0 $689,636 | Wet 2 0 1 1 $35,726

20Sep92- 8Bel fst. 1 1/16 :464 1:10 1:412 3+ⒻRuffian H 106 5 2 21 2hd 1hd 1½ Smith M E 120 *1.20 95-15 VersillesTrety120½QuickMischief1163Nnnerl119 Driving 6
20Sep92-Grade I
23Aug92- 8Sar fst 1⅛ :483 1:114 1:474 3+ⒻJohn Morris 95 4 4 42 31½ 42½ 26¾ Smith M E 122 *.70 91-02 QuickMischief1135¾VrsillsTrty122½ShrdIntrst111 4 wide 7
23Aug92-Grade I
4Jly92- 9Mth gd 1 1/16 :454 1:102 1:43 3+ⒻM Pitcher H 105 6 5 55½ 22 1hd 14¼ Smith M E 120 *.40 94-12 VrsllsTrty1204¼QckMschf1153½Czn'sWsh113 Ridden out 6
4Jly92-Grade II
31May92- 8Bel sly 1⅛ :451 1:084 1:47 3+ⒻHempsteadH 104 1 4 32 42 32 33¼ Smith M E 119 *1.20 91-09 Mssy'sMrg1183HrbrClb110nkVrsllsTrty119 Evenly inside 6
31May92-Grade I
9May92- 8Bel gd 1 1/16 :451 1:091 1:403 3+ⒻShuvee H 100 4 4 21½ 21 32 3nk Smith M E 119 *.50 99-07 Mssy'sMrg116noHrbourClb110nkVrsllsTrty119 Willingly 6
9May92-Grade I
18Apr92- 5Aqu my 7f :23 :454 1:204 3+ⒻLife's Magic 104 1 4 43½ 43 22 21¾ Smith M E 117 *.60 99-06 Mssy'sMrg1191¾VrsllsTrty11713Brchn'sLss119 Willingly 4
2Nov91- 4CD fst 1⅛ :471 1:114 1:504 3+ⒻBr Cp Dstff 105 9 7 78 64 42½ 21½ Cordero A Jr 120 4.80 92-09 DncSrtl1201½VrsllsTrt1202¾BrhtTMd123 Wide, 2nd best 13
2Nov91-Grade I
6Oct91- 7Bel gd 1⅛ :464 1:104 1:48 3+ⒻBeldame 101 1 3 23 1hd 2hd 2no Cordero A Jr 119 *1.20 89-11 ShrpDnce123noVersillsTrty1199LdyD'Accord123 Gamely 6
6Oct91-Grade I
31Aug91- 8Bel fst 1⅛ :464 1:104 1:472 ⒻGazelle H 95 7 3 57¾ 2hd 11 1½ Cordero A Jr 123 *.90 92-08 VersillesTrety123½GrndGirlfrind1151½Immrs112 Driving 8
31Aug91-Grade I
10Aug91- 9Sar gd 1¼ :471 1:361 2:022 ⒻAlabama 96 2 3 21½ 1½ 12 14½ Cordero A Jr 121 *.90 92-15 VersillesTrty1214½TilForbid1211DsigntdDncr121 Driving 6
10Aug91-Grade I
LATEST WORKOUTS ●Oct 4 Bel 5f fst :59 H Sep 30 Bel 4f fst :484 B ●Sep 19 Bel tr.t 3f fst :344 H Sep 14 Bel 5f fst 1:00 H

Versailles Treaty and Saratoga Dew were obviously the out-standing fillies in this field, and Versailles Treaty was the more accomplished of the two. She had been second in the Breeders' Cup Distaff the previous year, and as a 4-year-old she had been running consistently well against the East's best older fillies and mares. She had never been out of the money in an 18-race career. Saratoga Dew, too, had an exemplary record, but she had done most of her racing against other 3-year-olds and this was not an exceptional 3-year-old filly crop. Speed figures reflected the fact that Versailles Treaty was the better filly. She regularly ran numbers in the 104–106 range.

Moreover, the pace of the Beldame seemed certain to benefit Versailles Treaty. Saratoga Dew possessed a sprinter's speed and she always contested the early lead. So, too, did the Canadian filly A Gal for Gordo, who was a habitual front-runner and whose record showed a couple of wire-to-wire sprint victories. The tough mare Train Robbery was a speedster, too. This race seemed likely to have a three-way battle for the lead that would benefit Versailles Treaty. The versatile filly not only possessed tactical speed but also a decent stretch kick, as she had shown with her rally in the 1991 Breeders' Cup. With all of these virtues, Versailles Treaty was the most solid favorite of the day — an obvious "single" in the pick six and the pick three. Or at least she was on paper. But when the first few races were run that day, handicappers had to reassess their opinions. These were the charts of the first two dirt races on the card:

FIRST RACE
Belmont
OCTOBER 10, 1992

6 FURLONGS. (1.07^4) 1st Running THE GULCH STAKE. $50,000 Added. 3–year–olds. Weight, 122 lbs. Non-winners of four races other than maiden or claiming allowed 3 lbs.; of three races other than maiden or claiming, 5 lbs.; of two races other than maiden or claiming, 7 lbs. A trophy will be presented to the owner of the winner. $100 to nominate; $100 to enter and $200 to start. Closed Friday, October 2 with 23 Nominations. (34TH DAY. WEATHER CLEAR. TEMPERATURE 71 DEGREES.)

Value of race $54,600; value to winner $32,760; second $12,012; third $6,552; fourth $3,276. Mutuel pool $249,447, Minus show pool $1,485.17. Exacta Pool $440,611

Last Raced	Horse	M/Eqt.A.Wt	PP	St	¼	½	Str	Fin	Jockey	Odds $1
20Sep92 ^{7}Bel^2	Detox	b 3 115	2	1	$1^{\frac{1}{2}}$	$1^{\frac{1}{2}}$	1^{hd}	$1^{3\frac{3}{4}}$	Perret C	3.90
13Sep92 ^{8}Bel^3	Belong to Me	b 3 122	4	3	2^1	$2^{1\frac{1}{2}}$	2^5	$2^{5\frac{1}{2}}$	Maple E	.80
18Sep92 ^{6}Med^1	Border Cat	b 3 119	1	2	3^2	3^5	3^3	3^3	Smith M E	a-1.50
27Sep92 ^{2}Bel^4	Permit	b 3 115	6	5	$5^{\frac{1}{2}}$	5^1	$5^{2\frac{1}{2}}$	$4^{\frac{1}{2}}$	Migliore R	24.40
22Aug92 ^{8}Sar^{10}	Big Sur	3 117	5	4	$4^{2\frac{1}{2}}$	4^1	$4^{\frac{1}{2}}$	$5^{3\frac{1}{4}}$	Day P	a-1.50
3Oct92 ^{5}Bel^8	Federal Funds	b 3 117	3	6	6	6	6	6	Chavez J F	26.00

a–Coupled: Border Cat and Big Sur.

OFF AT 1:30 Start Good, Won driving. Time, :22 , :44^2, :56^1, 1:08^2 Track muddy.

Official Program Numbers↘

$2 Mutuel Prices:				
	2–(B)–DETOX	9.80	3.20	2.10
	5–(E)–BELONG TO ME		2.60	2.10
	1–(A)–BORDER CAT (a-entry)			2.10
	$2 EXACTA 2–5 PAID $22.80			

Dk. b. or br. c, (Apr), by Dr Blum—Cornish Art, by Cornish Prince. Trainer Downing Michael W. Bred by Iselin & Lippert (NY).

DETOX outsprinted rivals for the early advantage, dug in when challenged by BELONG TO ME in upper stretch then drew clear under brisk urging. BELONG TO ME stalked the pace from outside for a half, drew on nearly even terms with the winner in midstretch but couldn't stay with that one through the final eighth. BORDER CAT raced in close contention just behind the leaders to the turn and lacked a strong closing response. PERMIT was never a serious threat. BIG SUR was never a factor. FEDER FUNDS was always outrun. FEDERAL FUNDS and BELONG TO ME wore mud caulks.

Owners— 1, Murphy Charles J Jr; 2, Middletown Stables; 3, Young William T; 4, Shields Joseph V Jr; 5, Young William T; 6, Garren Murray M.

Trainers— 1, Downing Michael W; 2, Jerkens H Allen; 3, Lukas D Wayne; 4, Galluscio Dominic V; 5, Lukas D Wayne; 6, Garren Murray M.

Scratched—Riddle's King (17Sep92 ^{3}Med^1); Sticks and Bricks (18Sep92 ^{6}Med^3); Wardrobe Test (18Sep92 ^{6}Med^2); Thelastcrusade (25Sep92 ^{10}Med^{10}); Concorde's Tune (26Sep92 ^{7}Med^1).

THIRD RACE
Belmont
OCTOBER 10, 1992

7 FURLONGS. (1.20^2) 15th Running THE FIRST FLIGHT HANDICAP (Grade II). Purse $200,000. Fillies and Mares, 3–year–olds and upward. By subscription of $400 each which should accompany the nomination: $1,600 to pass the entry box; $1,600 to start. The purse to be divided 60% to the winner, 22% to second, 12% to third and 6% to fourth. Weights, Monday, October 5. Starters to be named at the closing time of entries. Trophies will be presented to the winning owner, trainer and jockey. Closed Wednesday September 23 with 22 nominations.

Value of race $200,000; value to winner $120,000; second $44,000; third $24,000; fourth $12,000. Mutuel pool $379,402.

Last Raced	Horse	M/Eqt.A.Wt	PP	St	¼	½	Str	Fin	Jockey	Odds $1
20Sep92 ^{8}Bel^4	Shared Interest	4 111	1	3	2^3	$2^{2\frac{1}{2}}$	$2^{1\frac{1}{2}}$	$1^{1\frac{1}{2}}$	Bailey J D	a-3.50
19Sep92 ^{4}Bel^1	Missy's Mirage	4 121	2	4	1^{hd}	1^1	$1^{\frac{1}{2}}$	$2^{4\frac{3}{4}}$	Maple E	.40
20Sep92 ^{8}Bel^3	Nannerl	5 119	3	5	$4^{2\frac{1}{2}}$	4^8	$3^{3\frac{1}{2}}$	3^5	Smith M E	a-3.50
30Aug92 ^{7}Sar^2	Preach	3 112	5	1	3^4	3^2	$4^{2\frac{1}{2}}$	$4^{\frac{3}{4}}$	Krone J A	4.20
19Sep92 ^{1}Bel^1	Ben's Moment	4 111	4	2	5	5	5	5	Day P	10.00

a–Coupled: Shared Interest and Nannerl.

OFF AT 2:42 Start Good, Won driving. Time, :22^1, :44^3, 1:08^2, 1:20^3 Track muddy.

$2 Mutuel Prices:				
	1–(A)–SHARED INTEREST (a–entry)	9.00	2.40	—
	2–(B)–MISSY'S MIRAGE		2.20	—
	3–(A)–NANNERL (a–entry)		—	—
	(No Show Wagering)			

B. f, by Pleasant Colony—Surgery, by Dr Fager. Trainer Schulhofer Flint S. Bred by Folsom Robert S (N.Y.).

SHARED INTEREST, dueled heads apart for the early lead while saving ground, eased back a bit nearing the far turn, angled to the outside to launch her bid leaving the three-eighths pole, drew along side MISSY'S MIRAGE to challenge in midstretch then drew clear under right hand encouragement. MISSY'S MIRAGE battled outside the winner along the backstretch, opened a clear advantage on the far turn, continued on the front while slightly off the rail entering the stretch, yielded to shared interest a furlong out then continued on well to clearly best the others. NANNERL, outrun for a half after breaking a bit slowly, made a run along the rail to reach contention in upper stretch but was no match for the top two. PREACH raced within striking distance to the turn and lacked a strong closing response. BEN'S MOMENT was never a factor. MISSY'S MIRAGE and BEN'S MOMENT wore mud caulks.

Owners— 1, Evans Robert S; 2, Middletown Stable; 3, Marablue Farm; 4, Claiborne Farm; 5, Double Brook Farm.

Trainers— 1, Schulhofer Flint S; 2, Jerkens H Allen; 3, Schulhofer Flint S; 4, McGaughey Claude III; 5, Alpers Sue P.

Overweight: Shared Interest 2 pounds.

Scratched—My Treasure (3Oct92 ^{6}Med^2); Harbour Club (9Aug92 ^{8}Sar^2).

In the first race of the day, a colt named Belong to Me looked like a standout, and he dueled for the lead outside Detox around the track and into the stretch. The pace was sizzling — a half mile in :44⅖ — but Detox kissed his rival goodbye and drew away along the rail to an easy win. A formidable horse who was sitting third behind these duellers, Border Cat, never made any headway in the stretch. Could there be a speed-favoring or rail-favoring bias in effect here?

In the next dirt race, Shared Interest broke from post 1, dueled with the 2-to-5 Missy's Mirage, dropped back, surged alongside the favorite again, and dueled to the half-mile mark in a sizzling :44⅗. This hot pace should have provided a perfect set-up for the one formidable stretch-runner in the race, Nannerl, but she couldn't make up any ground on Shared Interest in the stretch.

The fourth race further confirmed the impression of these two races. Educated Risk led all the way on the rail while the favorite, the stretch-running Beal Street Blues, tried to circle the field and never got untracked, finishing a distant third.

Those were the only three dirt races run before the Beldame, but the evidence seemed overwhelming. This muddy track was extremely speed-favoring, and it also favored horses who were on or near the rail. Suddenly, the complexion of the Beldame Stakes was altered. Yes, there were three habitual front-runners in the field, but even seemingly suicidal speed duels hadn't hurt Detox and Shared Interest on this track. Saratoga Dew would almost certainly benefit from the bias, while Versailles Treaty's versatility — her tactical speed combined with a decent stretch kick — now looked like a liability instead of an asset. She wasn't quick enough to get the lead, and she wasn't so slow that she'd fall way back and drop to the rail behind a speed duel. She figured to be sitting four-wide, just off the leaders — a disastrous position on this bi-ased racetrack. This race was clearly not going to offer great win-betting possibilities regardless of the result, but it was part of a pick three in which the public at large would be singling Versailles Treaty, and as such it became a good test for handicappers' alertness and adaptability. Bettors who singled Versailles Treaty anyway would deserve an F in this handicapping test. Those who decided it was now prudent to use Saratoga Dew and Versailles Treaty in equal strength get a B. Those who concluded that Saratoga Dew had become a virtual cinch score an A.

SIXTH RACE

Belmont

OCTOBER 10, 1992

1 ⅛ MILES. (1.45²) 53rd Running THE BELDAME (Grade I). Purse $250,000. Fillies and Mares, 3-year-olds and upward. By subscription of $500 each which should accompany the nomination; $2,000 to pass the entry box; $2,000 to start. The purse to be divided 60% to the winner, 22% to second, 12% to third and 6% to fourth. Weight for age. Weight: 3-year-olds 119 lbs. Older 123 lbs. Starters to be named at the closing time of entries. Mrs. John E. Cowdin has donated a perpetual cup to be held by the owner of the winner for one year. A permanent trophy will be presented to the owner of the winner and trophies will be presented to the winning trainer and jockey. Closed with 19 Nominations Wednesday, September 23.

Value of race $250,000; value to winner $150,000; second $55,000; third $30,000; fourth $15,000. Mutuel pool $371,629, Minus show pool $3,992.58. Exacta Pool $713,279

Last Raced	Horse	M/Eqt.A.Wt	PP	St	¼	½	¾	Str	Fin	Jockey	Odds $1
2Sep92 8Bel¹	Saratoga Dew	3 119	1	4	1hd	11	1½	13	16	McCauley W H	2.00
20Sep92 8Bel¹	Versailles Treaty	4 123	5	2	44	32	2½1½	22½	26	Smith M E	.60
25Sep92 8Bel¹	Coxwold	b 4 123	4	5	5	5	44	3hd	36¼	Antley C W	12.50
20Sep92 10TP7	Train Robbery	5 123	3	3	3½	2hd	31	48	45	Day P	17.80
26Sep92 9WO²	A Gal For Gordo	4 123	2	1	2¹	43	5	5	5	Krone J A	6.50

OFF AT 4:36 Start Good, Won driving. Time, :22⁴, :45³, 1:09³, 1:34¹, 1:46⁴ Track good.

$2 Mutuel Prices:

1-(A)-SARATOGA DEW	6.00	2.20	2.10
6-(F)-VERSAILLES TREATY		2.10	2.10
5-(E)-COXWOLD			2.10

$2 EXACTA 1-6 PAID $10.20

B. f, (Apr), by Cormorant—Super Luna, by In Reality. Trainer Sciacca Gary. Bred by Chenery Helen B (NY).

SARATOGA DEW, moved through along the inside to gain a narrow lead in the early stages, widened her margin a bit along the backstretch, set a brisk pace while in hand for six furlongs, dug in when challenged by VERSAILLES TREATY on the turn, shook off that one to gain a comfortable advantage in midstretch then drew off under mild encouragement. VERSAILLES TREATY stalked the pace from the outside for five furlongs, made a run outside the winner to threaten on the turn but couldn't stay with that one through the stretch. COXWORLD was never a serious threat. TRAIN ROBBERY raced in close contention just inside VERSAILLES TREATY to the far turn then lacked a further response. A GAL FOR GORDO showed only brief speed.

Owners— 1, Engel Charles F; 2, Phipps Cynthia; 3, Maktoum Mohammed Al; 4, Houng William T; 5, Bankuti Tibor I.

Trainers— 1, Sciacca Gary; 2, McGaughey Claude III; 3, Clement Christopher; 4, Lukas D Wayne; 5, Attfield Roger.

Scratched—Quick Mischief (20Sep92 8Bel²).

As expected, Saratoga Dew went to the lead, pressed by A Gal for Gordo and Train Robbery, with Versailles Treaty parked four-wide throughout the long run down the backstretch. The front-runner shook off her pursuers, stayed near the rail, and drew away to a six-length victory; Versailles Treaty couldn't threaten her. The win price of $6 in the five-horse field was nothing fancy, but the defeat of the 3-to-5 favorite produced a pick three bonanza, with logical horses in the other two legs (Roman Envoy in the Kelso Handicap and Sea Hero in the Champagne Stakes) accounting for a $378 payoff. If there were any doubts that a bias had determined the outcome of the Beldame Stakes, they were dispelled three weeks later at Gulfstream Park. Bettors at the Breeders' Cup were so impressed by Saratoga Dew's six-length runaway that they made her the 2-to-1 favorite in the Distaff. She finished twelfth.

FIVE

The Mathematics of Pace

My early racing experiences, like those of most horseplayers, were limited by geography. I bet exclusively at tracks on the East Coast, but as I mastered the game, I assumed I was learning universal truths, and so I felt no trepidation when I planned my first trip to the West at the end of 1982. I was eager to see — and to conquer — California. To all but the most chauvinistic Easterners, it was apparent that racing in the West was the best in America. The huge, enthusiastic crowds at Santa Anita were a mocking contrast to the dwindling on-track business in New York. And the headline-making payoffs produced by the pick six had made California irresistibly exciting for a gambler.

I spent months developing and honing a set of speed figures for southern California, and I used my own experience to illustrate in *The Winning Horseplayer* the step-by-step process of calculating figures. "Having compiled these figures," I wrote, "I knew that I would be able to walk into Santa Anita on opening day with an understanding of the ability of the horses and the nature of racing in the state, even though I had never set foot in Arcadia, California, before. . . . I would be in complete command of everything that was happening at Santa Anita."

How wrong I was. I not only lost that winter at Santa Anita; the sport seemed as foreign to me as if I were at a track on the moon. Racing in the West was so different from racing in the East — or anywhere else in the world, for that matter — that authors like me had erred badly in thinking that we could postulate universal truths about handicapping.

Other first-time visitors to Arcadia might be entranced by the beauty of the San Gabriel Mountains, but my fixation was that black Santa Anita racing strip. I had never seen a racing surface that looked like this one, nor had I ever seen horses run as they did over it. On my first day at Santa Anita a speed horse zipped the first quarter mile in 21 seconds flat and a half mile in :43⅗ — and still didn't get tired; he sustained this breathtaking pace and completed six furlongs in 1:07⅗. A few days later I had a chance to meet the track superintendent, who explained to me that this track was indeed fundamentally different from the ones I knew. While racing surfaces in the East are sandy, the soil at Santa Anita contains silt and clay, which bind the track together to make it faster, more resilient, and less tiring.

Just as humans can run farther and faster on an asphalt track than on a sandy beach, horses can sustain their speed longer on these hard surfaces. In my first season at Santa Anita, I was amazed by the number of fainthearted sprinters who would win at a mile or more — and how the crowd would bet them without any concern for their lack of stamina. Eastern horseplayers have always been taught to ask "Can he go the distance?" whenever they assess horses in longer races; in the West, under the right circumstances, almost any horse can go any distance. I was surprised, too, by the frequency with which races in California are won by first-time starters and horses who had been laid off for months. In the East, bettors assume such horses are at a disadvantage because of their lack of fitness.

Trainers in the West recognize that speed, not stamina and fitness, wins races, and they drill their horses accordingly. Even routers will have a regimen of five-furlong works in :58 or :59 instead of the stamina-building breezes — such as a mile in 1:41

— that are fashionable in the East. Having been trained to develop this essential speed, the horses are ridden to use it. When the gate opens for a sprint in California, virtually every horse will be in an all-out drive. A jockey who comes out of the gate tentatively and tries to assess the tactical situation before he commits himself — that is, one who rides as if he is in the East — will be hopelessly out of the race. Jeff Siegel, editor of the newsletter *Handicapper's Report,* summed up for me the way to approach this style of racing: "You don't have to be a front-runner to win here, but you must have tactical speed — the ability to leave the gate and get position in the first eighth of a mile. You don't swoop around the field on the turn the way horses do in the East. If you're a plodder, the only way you can win a race is by default."

For all horseplayers in California, an awareness of horses' early speed is instinctive. Many make speed and pace the main focus of their handicapping. While Easterners may look superficially at a field and conclude that a particular horse appears to be the probable front-runner, Westerners will analyze fractional times meticulously and, perhaps, conclude that one horse figures to be 1½ lengths faster than his rivals over the first half mile.

Literature on handicapping reflects these regional perspectives. I had breezily dismissed the importance of pace in *Picking Winners.* Len Ragozin's calculations ignore pace. Steve Davidowitz's *Betting Thoroughbreds,* one of the best handicapping primers ever written, barely mentioned the word. Meanwhile, in California, Howard Sartin developed a pace-oriented method that attracted a rabid group of followers. His disciple, Tom Brohamer, wrote the most advanced book on the subject, *Modern Pace Handicapping,* with virtually every illustration drawn from tracks in the West. James Quinn, another Californian, staunchly advocated pace analysis and the use of pace figures in *Figure Handicapping.*

To some extent, these Californians were looking at the game from a viewpoint whose provincialism they didn't recognize. Except for the West, there is no place on earth where early speed is so all-powerful that an ordinary horse can battle head-and-head for the lead in :44 flat and hold on to win. There is no other place where handicappers can look at a horse's past fractional times and take them at face value without wondering if the jockey was urging him hard or rating him. But the distinctive nature of California racing has provided handicappers with the perfect laboratory in which to study pace, and has given them a heightened sensitivity to the importance of a factor that so many Easterners overlook. It's not as if speed and pace are irrelevant everywhere else. For *Winning at the Races,* William Quirin analyzed thousands of races and found a direct correlation between a horse's chances of winning and his position at the first call of a race in the *Daily Racing Form's* charts. The horse who took the early lead won 26 percent of all races; the horse who was running second early won 16 percent of the time; the third horse 13 percent; and so on. The advantage of early speed, Quirin wrote, was "the universal track bias."

The effort to understand, analyze, and quantify the importance of early speed and pace, led by the aforementioned California experts, has been the most significant new intellectual development in the world of handicapping. I have been intrigued by this quest because of the possibility of relating the effects of pace to a horse's final time and his speed figure. Consider this common scenario: A plodder runs a race in which he is ten lengths behind the leader at every stage and earns a speed figure of 70. In the same field, a speedster fights for the lead for a half mile, tires, loses by ten lengths, and earns a figure of 70. There is absolutely no doubt that the latter ran the better race. He was a contender and he exerted himself hard while the plodder did virtually nothing. Yet their final figures are the same. Might there be some way to express, mathematically, the difference between their performances? Could a number be calculated to show that the speedster is really better than a 70 while the plodder is worse than a 70?

Whenever I contemplate or observe efforts to make such a calculation, I am dogged by questions that won't go away. Is it realistic to look for some universal mathematical system when there are clearly such great regional differences in the effects of speed and pace? Are the experts in pace analysis perhaps trying to quantify something that is ultimately unquantifiable?

Amid all the complexities of this issue, there is at least one piece of common ground that may serve as a starting point in a study of pace. Horses A and B are front-runners who both fought for the lead in their last starts and who both ran six furlongs in 1:11. These were their fractional times:

Horse A	:22	:45	1:11
Horse B	:23	:46	1:11

Now the two are facing each other. What will happen? Despite their equal final times, Horse A will beat B. In fact, he will probably annihilate his rival. As B tries to make the early lead, he will struggle to keep up with A's faster pace and will be exhausted by the effort. This is as close to a universal truth as anybody will find in handicapping: When two front-runners have recorded the same final time, the one who has run faster early fractions is superior and will prevail in a head-to-head confrontation.

The example might be changed slightly:

Horse A	:22	:45	$1:11^{2}/_{5}$
Horse B	:23	:46	1:11

Now the choice between the two front-runners is considerably tougher. Is A's superior early speed more significant than B's faster final time? There is no automatic answer here, but even though I am philosophically committed to the importance of final time, I would lean strongly toward Horse A, because B may crack from the pressure of chasing the quicker horse. Here is a real-life example:

Air Corps One

Gr. c. 2(May), by Air Forbes Won—Aspenglo, by Raise a Native
Br.—Clay Albert G (Ky)
Tr.—Salzman J Edwin Jr (48 9 11 6 .19)

Own.—Whip Stable

Lifetime 1992 3 2 1 0 $14,490
3 2 1 0
$14,490
114

6Nov92- 8Lrl fst 6f	:22	:45³ 1:10⁴	Alw 16800	76 6 6 4¹½ 11 13½ 22	Castillo F⁵	Lb 109	2.00	85-18 Olney120²AirCorpsOn109²¼AsstImprssion117	Lugged in 7
29Oct92- 2Lrl fst 6f	:22¹	:46 1:10⁴	Clm 18500	78 1 7 56¼ 44 12 111½	Castillo F⁵	Lb 109	3.30	87-15 AirCorpsOn109¹¹½Chilos114¾Moycullin115	Wide, drvng 7
30Aug92- 10Tim fst 4f	.23	:46⁴	Md Sp Wt	64 6 9 66½ 32½ 11½	Juarez C	Lb 120	1.90	90-16 ArCrpsOn120¹½JhnsAmbtn120²KtAmbtn115	Going away 9

LATEST WORKOUTS   Oct 17 Lrl 4f fst :50 B

Gold Candy Too

B. c. 2(Apr), by Goldlust—Candy Too, by Fast Hilarious
Br.—William Kenan Rand Jr (NC)
Tr.—Perkins Benjamin W (—)

Own.—Kennan Rand W

Lifetime 1992 1 1 0 0 $3,990
1 1 0 0
$3,990
114

Wet 1 1 0 0 $3,990

31Oct92- 1Lrl my 6f	:23¹	:47¹ 1:11⁴	Md 11500	84 7 3 1² 1⁵ 1⁶ 114	Rocco J	120	2.00	82-19 GoldCndyTo120¹⁴FnrlMrch120¹¼SlrAngli120	Ridden out 8

LATEST WORKOUTS   Nov 12 Bow 3f fst :37 B   Oct 24 Bow 5f fst 1:03 Bg   Oct 17 Bow 4f fst :50¹ Bg   Oct 9 Bow 5f my 1:02¹ B

These 2-year-olds faced each other in a six-furlong allowance race at Laurel that was essentially a two-horse affair. Nobody else in the field had the figures or early speed to make an impact on the race. Gold Candy Too had a figure of 84, which was superior to the 76 his rival had earned in his last start. But Air Corps One had run clearly faster fractions — a half mile in :45⅗ versus a half in :47⅕. He had been running over a faster racing surface, but even when that was taken into account, he was more than a full second faster to the half-mile mark. When the two colts met, Air Corps One's speed enabled him to control the race. He set sizzling fractions of :21⅘ and :45 as Gold Candy Too pressed him, and maintained his lead all the way to prevail by three-quarters of a length. As in so many situations, a horse's early speed proved to be more important than his final time and speed figure.

It is obviously important to know which horse in a field possesses the superior early speed. In California it is essential, because even a slim one-length advantage over the first half mile can sometimes enable a horse to seize control of a race. Therefore, many handicappers calculate pace figures to measure how fast a horse has run his early fractions. Most employ a speed rating and track variant to measure a horse's half-mile speed in sprint races. (Fractional times in route races are much less meaningful because all horses in those races will be under a measure of early restraint by their riders.)

Readers of the *Daily Racing Form* can calculate their own pace figures expressed in the same numerical language as the Beyer Speed Figures. The method I recommend may not satisfy the most meticulous pace handicappers, but it has the advantage of ease and practicality. Serviceable pace figures can be derived from the information in the past performances, without any need for poring over result charts and making day-to-day calculations. As with our speed figures, they are based on a speed rating and track variant. On page 132 is a speed-rating chart for four-furlong fractions and, beside it, our standard chart for six furlongs.

Four Furlongs		Six Furlongs	
:44	128	1:08	135
:44$\frac{1}{5}$	124	1:08$\frac{1}{5}$	132
:44$\frac{2}{5}$	119	1:08$\frac{2}{5}$	129
:44$\frac{3}{5}$	115	1:08$\frac{3}{5}$	126
:44$\frac{4}{5}$	110	1:08$\frac{4}{5}$	123
:45	106	1:09	120
:45$\frac{1}{5}$	101	1:09$\frac{1}{5}$	118
:45$\frac{2}{5}$	97	1:09$\frac{2}{5}$	115
:45$\frac{3}{5}$	92	1:09$\frac{3}{5}$	112
:45$\frac{4}{5}$	88	1:09$\frac{4}{5}$	109
:46	84	1:10	106
:46$\frac{1}{5}$	79	1:10$\frac{1}{5}$	103
:46$\frac{2}{5}$	75	1:10$\frac{2}{5}$	100
:46$\frac{3}{5}$	71	1:10$\frac{3}{5}$	98
:46$\frac{4}{5}$	66	1:10$\frac{4}{5}$	95
:47	62	1:11	92
:47$\frac{1}{5}$	58	1:11$\frac{1}{5}$	89
:47$\frac{2}{5}$	53	1:11$\frac{2}{5}$	86
:47$\frac{3}{5}$	49	1:11$\frac{3}{5}$	83
:47$\frac{4}{5}$	45	1:11$\frac{4}{5}$	81
:48	41	1:12	78
		1:12$\frac{1}{5}$	75
		1:12$\frac{2}{5}$	72
		1:12$\frac{3}{5}$	70
		1:12$\frac{4}{5}$	67
		1:13	64
		1:13$\frac{1}{5}$	61
		1:13$\frac{2}{5}$	59
		1:13$\frac{3}{5}$	56
		1:13$\frac{4}{5}$	53
		1:14	51

The numbers indicate that, at a typical track, a six-furlong race run in 1:10 (a rating of 106) would normally be run with a half-mile time of :45 flat (also a rating of 106). Unfortunately, the relationship of fractional times to final times can vary greatly from track to track. The clocking of races does not begin until one horse reaches a beam activating the electric timer, and the distance of the running start will greatly affect fractional times. At Monmouth Park, horses are in high gear by the time they reach the official start of a race, and half-mile times of :44-and-change are common. At Pimlico, where the horses get almost no running start, nobody breaks :45. If a handicapper has no need to compare fractions at different tracks, he can use the four-furlong chart above as it appears. Otherwise, he needs to adjust it for each track.

This is the procedure: Get a set of results for a track and compile a few decent-size samples of six-furlong races that were run in specific final times — say, exactly 1:10, exactly 1:11, exactly 1:12. Calculate the average half-mile time in each of these samples. Then compare the half-mile rating on the above chart with the six-furlong rating, as follows:

Final Time	Rating	Average Fractional Time	Rating	Difference
1:10	106	:45$\frac{1}{5}$	101	Slow by 5
1:11	92	:45$\frac{4}{5}$	88	Slow by 4
1:12	78	:46$\frac{3}{5}$	71	Slow by 7

The average half-mile fraction in this case is slightly more than five points slower than the norm. Add five points to the above chart for four-furlong times and the chart will now be tailored to this particular track. Handicappers who don't want to tally the necessary data may want to purchase the list of par times compiled by Gordon Pine (Cynthia Publishing Co., 11390 Ventura Boulevard, #5, Studio City, California 91604). It shows the average winning times and fractional times for various classes at virtually every track in North America.

When the 4-furlong chart is established for a given track, I recommend using it for races at 6½ and 7 furlongs, too. James Quinn advocates adding points to a horse's pace rating at these distances, because fractions at 6½ and 7 furlongs are usually slower than at 6 furlongs. That is true, but only because jockeys tend to rate their horses more; with a longer straightaway, horses can actually run faster fractions at 6½ and 7 furlongs if they are urged. They don't deserve extra credit for having raced at those distances.

For horses who are racing behind the leaders, points are subtracted according to this lengths-behind chart for four furlongs:

Margin	Points	Margin	Points
hd	0	2¾	8
nk	1	3	9
½	1	3¼	10
¾	2	3½	11
1	3	3¾	11
1¼	4	4	12
1½	5	4¼	13
1¾	5	4½	14
2	6	4¾	14
2¼	7	5	15
2½	8		

The track variant must now be applied to these ratings. Although our variants do not appear in the *Daily Racing Form,* any reader can deduce them. Our speed figures are calculated by taking the speed rating for the winner, adding or subtracting the variant, and then subtracting points according to the number of lengths a horse was beaten. To find the variant, work backward:

1. Note the number of lengths by which a horse was beaten and refer to the chart in the Appendix to translate the margin into points.

2. Add those points to the horse's Beyer Speed Figure to find the figure for the winner of the race.

3. Note the winner's time and find the corresponding speed rating in the Appendix.

4. Subtract this raw speed rating from the winner's actual figure, and that's the variant.

Look again at the past performances of Air Corps One. He earned a Beyer Speed Figure of 76 in his prior start while losing a six-furlong race by two lengths. On the beaten lengths chart, two lengths at six furlongs equals five points. Therefore, the winner of the race earned an 81. The winning time for the race was 1:10⅘, which translates to a speed rating of 95. The track variant for the day had been −14. When this variant is applied to Air Corps One's half-mile time of :45⅗, which has a value of 92 on the above chart, the horse gets a pace figure of 78.

Similarly, Gold Candy Too earned a figure of 84 by running six furlongs in 1:11⅘, which has a rating of 81 on the chart. The track variant was therefore +3. Gold Candy Too's fraction of :47⅕ has a rating of 58 on the four-furlong chart. Adding the variant gives him a pace figure of 61 — making vivid the disadvantage he faces against Air Corps One, despite his superior speed figure.

This process is much, much easier than it may sound, because a handicapper who wants to use our variants need only make this calculation once for each race. He should keep the daily variants in a notebook so that he can apply them at a glance without having to do the arithmetic whenever he wants a pace figure.*

Some purists will object that it is more accurate to calculate a separate variant for fractional times. This is true for windy days and for tiring, muddy tracks, but overall the results do not justify the extra effort. When I am looking at pace figures earned in the mud,

---

* There is one possible source of confusion in deducing and using our track variant. The beaten-lengths calculation we use to produce our figures for the *Racing Form* is affected by the final time of a race, so there may be slight variations from the beaten-lengths chart in the Appendix. But those differences will never be more than a point or two. A one- or two-point discrepancy in the track variant will not significantly affect the accuracy of pace figures it is used to produce.

I will be wary of them and may prefer to judge a horse on the basis of a different performance.

The virtues of pace figures are obvious — more so than their defects. They will reveal at a glance whether one horse in a field possesses superior early speed that may enable him to take control of a race. Sometimes they will point out a probable front-runner who isn't at all obvious, who has been two or three lengths behind the leaders in his recent races, but who has the quickness to set the pace today. Californians relish such situations, because they can be confident that their speed-oriented jockeys will get such a horse to the front. But bettors elsewhere know that an idiotic rider is apt to take the horse two or three lengths off the lead, anyway, because that's the way he usually runs. Californians who are spoiled by watching Valenzuela, Stevens, Desormeaux, et al., should visit Maryland and join me for the experience of betting on a supposed speed horse being ridden by Mario Pino. They will quickly learn some of the pitfalls of pace handicapping.

Most pace handicappers believe that there is a direct correlation between a horse's pace figure and speed figure. Bill Quirin argues that the relationship between the two is symmetrical for most horses; when the pace number increases, the final figure decreases, and vice versa. James Quinn uses pace figures based on Quirin's methods, and years of experience have taught him the validity of this idea. "I find that it's true, especially for claiming horses," he said. "You'll have a horse who runs a pace figure of 98 and a final figure of 102. Next time he runs a pace figure of 102 — and he runs a final figure of 98." For some types of races, Quinn said, he simply adds the two numbers together to get his final evaluation of a horse. The relationship between speed and pace figures may not be as neat as Quinn suggests, but the idea is logical. When a front-runner is forced to exert himself hard in the early stages of a race, his final performance will suffer; when he gets a comfortable lead, he'll run big.

All of these situations involving pace have dealt, conveniently, with front-runners. But what happens when a handicapper attempts to compare some horses with early speed, some who stalk the pace, and some who come from far behind? Consider this hypothetical situation. Horse X opens a clear lead, runs a quarter mile in 22⅖ seconds, a half-mile in 45⅕ seconds, and finishes six furlongs in 1:11. Horse Y, who customarily stalks the pace, displays his usual style, sits three lengths behind the leader throughout the first half mile, and then rallies to finish within a nose of X. This is presumably a good performance by Y, because it is not easy to catch a solitary front-runner. Now the two horses are meeting each other again, and in pace analysis they will look like this on paper:

Horse X	:22²⁄₅	:45¹⁄₅	1:11
Horse Y	:23	:45⁴⁄₅	1:11

To handicappers using pace figures, they may look like this:

	Pace Figure	Final Figure
Horse X	100	92
Horse Y	87	92

Either way, Horse Y looks exactly like another of those over-matched front-runners who will crack from the pressure applied by a superior speed horse. And this — in my view, at least — is where most pace-handicapping theory collapses into a heap of contradictions, illogic, and provincialism. Horse Y is viewed as an inferior horse just because he doesn't have a front-running style.

I have often discussed this problem with Quinn, who believes that Horse Y does indeed deserve his lower pace ratings. He argues, "By the time the field hits the second call of a race — the half-mile mark in sprints — horses will have moved into whatever striking position they're going to be in." In other words, if a horse is three lengths behind the leaders at this point, he is in that position because he has been outrun in the dash from the gate. His lack of raw speed makes him inferior to the front-runners — not just a horse with a different but effective style. It's a distinctly Californian view of the world. Quinn does concede that pace figures are meaningless when applied to the horses he calls "deep closers." In this respect, too, pace handicapping seems very much a product of California, where it is usually safe to disregard one-dimensional come-from-behind runners. But I find it hard to imagine handicappers at Belmont Park or Hawthorne or the Fair Grounds developing an intricate, time-consuming method that cannot take into account the ability of horses who make their moves in the stretch. For years I have sought a pace-rating concept that could deal effectively with front-runners, stalkers, and stretch-runners, and I never found one that was satisfactory. But by far the most promising efforts in this direction are the ones inspired by a psychotherapist named Howard Sartin. Even though I do not practice the Sartin methodology and I have many reservations about it, it is the most interesting development in the handicapping world since . . . well, since speed figures.

The genesis of the method is now legendary among its devotees. Sartin was conducting a therapy session for eight truck drivers who were compulsive gamblers. The traditional way to deal with the compulsion is to stop gambling, but this was California, and Sartin had a novel idea. "The cure for losing is winning," he said. "So I suggested that none of us place a bet until we established a method that picked 45 percent winners, betting two horses to win in each race." The patients plunged into a study of handicapping, but none of them was more avid about the project than Sartin himself.

"It didn't take us long to isolate the importance of early speed," he recalled. "In the writings of Pittsburgh Phil and Colonel Bradley [two legendary gamblers of the early twentieth century], both mentioned measuring horses' speed in feet per second. So we translated a horse's time into his velocity." In the case of our aforementioned Horse A, who had run fractions of :22, :45, and 1:11, Sartin would divide the animal's performance into its quarter-mile components — the first quarter was run in :22, second quarter in :23, third quarter in :26 — and would express each fraction in feet per second. Then he would compute the average of the velocity rates to determine what he called Average Pace.

1st quarter	:22	60.00 feet per second
2nd quarter	:23	57.38 feet per second
3rd quarter	:26	50.76 feet per second

Average Pace = 56.05 feet per second

Compare this, now, with our Horse B, who had run :23, :46 on the way to the same final time of 1:11:

1st quarter	:23	57.38 feet per second
2nd quarter	:23	57.38 feet per second
3rd quarter	:25	52.80 feet per second

Average Pace = 55.86 feet per second

These calculations express, mathematically, the fact that Horse A's six furlongs in 1:11 was a better performance than B's 1:11 because A had exerted himself more during the early stages of the race. But the very same methodology can evaluate any horse with any style. Suppose that a horse was ten lengths behind Horse B after the first and second quarter, then rallied furiously to lose by a nose. Applying the rough equation of one length with one-fifth of a second, this horse would have run the first quarter in :25 and the last two in :23 each, and his Average Pace will reflect that this was a strong effort. The method properly gives more credit to horses who show speed and sustain it throughout a race, but it can reward exceptional stretch-runners.

As innovative and sophisticated as the Average Pace calculation is, it is only a small part of Sartin's mathematical repertoire, in which horses' velocity serves as the basis of innumerable measurements. Early Pace is a horse's velocity to the half-mile mark in sprints or the six-furlong mark in routes. Sustained Pace is the average of Early Pace with the velocity of the final fraction.

The horseplayers attracted to this approach were understandably a serious, mathematically oriented breed. (When Sartin made a presentation on his method at the National Conference on Thoroughbred Handicapping in 1984, the title of his paper was

"The Dynamics of Incremental Velocity and Energy Distribution." Nobody ever accused Doc Sartin of trying to pander to a mass audience.) Among the most avid students of the new method was Tom Brohamer, a Pacific Bell executive who had spent most of his professional life involved with computers and data. He had started playing the horses by using speed figures but concluded that final time doesn't tell enough about horses' ability. "So many high-figure horses kept getting beat," he said, "and it was almost always a matter of their not being able to keep up early." Brohamer inevitably gravitated to the Sartin theories. He not only added many refinements to the method but eventually became its most prominent teacher and spokesman.

Brohamer looked at all of the potential Sartin measurements — Early Pace, Sustained Pace, Average Pace, and other esoterica — and recognized that each might be supremely important, depending on the track over which a race was being run. Neanderthals in the game (like Beyer) might characterize tracks as favoring speed or favoring stretch-runners. Brohamer would define them in a wholly new, mathematical way. He would look at the feet per second for the early stage of a race (Early Pace), the feet per second for the final fraction, and compare the two. If, for example, he found a race that looked like this —

Early Pace	**56.0 feet per second**
Last Fraction	**50.0 feet per second**

— he would add the two numbers to get an artificial measurement that Sartin had called Total Energy, which in this case was 106.0. Now he would calculate the percentage of this total that the Early Pace represented, which here is $^{56}/_{106}$ or 52.8 percent. Brohamer would say that a horse had expended 52.8 percent of his energy in the first fraction; this was his Energy Distribution. He proceeded to define horses' running styles in terms of their typical Energy Distribution and to define racetracks in terms of the typical energy requirements that won there. In *Modern Pace Handicapping* he discussed a sprint race at Del Mar in these terms: "The energy range for the meeting was consistently between 51.7 and 52.8

percent, with the ideal expenditure around 52.35 percent. . . .
Behind the Scenes is not really in her best form, and the early
energy (49.87 percent) is more likely to win on the turf course.
She may want to route. . . . Table Frolic's 51.46 percent is too late
an expenditure to be effective. At Belmont Park she might be
tough but [not] in southern California. . . . Kool Arrival, at 52.55
percent . . . is very close to the target par of 52.35 percent. She's
almost a perfect fit for the race."

Brohamer conceived, too, what he called a decision model,
which was a numerical ranking of the contenders in a given race
according to the various Sartin measurements — Average Pace,
Early Pace, Sustained Pace — and which also noted whether a
horse's Energy Distribution was suitable to the race. It might look
like this:

	AP	EP	SP	%E
Akinemod	1	1	2	Yes
Miss Tawpie	2	2	1	Yes
A Penny Is a Penny	3	2	4	Yes
Linda Card	4	4	5	Yes
Survive	5	5	3	No

Brohamer would examine these rankings and make his judgments
according to the requirements of the track. If Sustained Pace was
the dominant factor where this race was being run, he might
prefer Miss Tawpie; otherwise, Akinemod would be his horse.

As I have watched Sartin devotees use their decision models
with these 1-2-3-4-5 rankings, I am troubled that they seem preoccupied more by abstract numbers than by the horses and the
race itself. Instead of using their numbers to help them understand the real world of racing, they sometimes seem to twist and
mold reality so that it will fit their system of numbers. The Sartin
handicappers pick a single race from a horse's recent past performances to which they will apply their various measurements, and
there is a lot of discussion among the faithful about techniques for
choosing the right "paceline." Of course, it is a dubious premise

that a single previous race can be used to represent the total capabilities of each horse. Sartin handicappers might choose to dismiss a horse's last race because the *Daily Racing Form* gives a trouble call like "bumped," but most of these people won't know whether that was a serious, excusable instance of trouble or just an inconsequential jostle: they were probably too busy studying their numbers to have paid attention to the race.

Indeed, in most literature on pace handicapping, there are few indications that the experts know or care what actually happens in horse races, that they recognize a qualitative as well as a quantitative aspect to pace. If a horse has run six furlongs in fractions of :22, :45, and 1:11, that's a given Early Pace, Average Pace, and Energy Distribution regardless of what was happening around the animal. But consider these different possible scenarios:

The horse was engaged in a head-and-head battle with two rivals and ran the first half mile in 45 seconds flat.

The horse popped out of the gate to take a quick early lead and was never challenged as he set the pace in :45 flat.

The horse sat third, in the garden spot, three lengths behind two speedballs who were dueling through fractions in :21⅖ and :44⅖.

The difference in these performances is enormous. The first horse, the one in the three-way battle, delivered the best performance from the standpoint of pace, yet all of the mathematical pace ratings fail to recognize that truth.

There is another great defect inherent in the Sartin approach — and in most other mathematical pace-handicapping methods — and it is one that horseplayers and authors of books on handicapping rarely mention, perhaps because it is too painful to address: These precise, meticulously crafted methods are based on data that is woefully imprecise.

Virtually all calculations of horses' times — except for those of the horses in front — are derived from the number of lengths by which they trail the leader. Casual handicappers will look at the leader's time and arrive at the time of any horse behind him according to the equation that one length equals one-fifth of a second. Serious pace and speed handicappers will employ more refined calculations, but they will all be based on the beaten-lengths number.

Lunch Connection

	B. g. 2(May), by Linkage—Parisian Honey, by Honey Jay	Lifetime 1992 1 M 0 0 $300
	Br.—Audley Farm Inc. (Va)	1 0 0 0
Own.—Hemsley & Radford	Tr.—Bailes W Robert (7 0 0 0 .00)	**120** $300
7Nov92- 7Lrl fst 6f :22³ :47 1:12³ Md Sp Wt	44 3 10 10¹² 97¼ 88¾ 86¼ Pino M G	b 120 7.10 72-21 LovingCorkey120ⁿᵒBubbC120ⁿᵒGoodGms120 No factor 10
LATEST WORKOUTS Nov 23 Bow 5f sly 1:02 B	Nov 15 Bow 7f fst 1:29⁴ H	Oct 31 Bow 5f sly 1:02 B Oct 22 Bow 6f fst 1:14³ H

At the first call — the quarter-mile mark — Lunch Connection was twelve lengths behind the leader, who was running in :22⅗. He was twelve fifths, or 2⅖ seconds behind, so his actual time was :25. After a half mile in :47, he was roughly seven lengths behind and his time was :48⅖. Similarly, Lunch Connection's own final time was 1:13⅘. Pace handicappers might break down the components into quarters that look like this:

First quarter	:25
Second quarter	:23⅖
Third quarter	:25⅖

The smaller the unit being measured, the more important precision is; that's why heroin dealers don't weigh their wares on bathroom scales. For a handicapper basing decisions on horses' times over a quarter mile, an error of even a fifth of a second or so could be critical, so it is essential that the beaten lengths are accurate. Are they?

Well, what's a length? The basic unit of racetrack measurement has no real meaning. Horses comes in different sizes, and common estimates of a "standard" length range anywhere from eight to ten feet. Fast horses will cover a given number of feet in less time than slow horses. Therefore, the meaning of a length varies according to the animals' velocity at the moment the length is being measured. One length doesn't even have a definite meaning in the "official" margins of finish that are determined by the photo-finish camera, because the operators of those cameras determine a length in different ways. Five lengths at Thistledown is not the same distance as five lengths at Pimlico.

The *Daily Racing Form*'s trackmen determine the margins at

fractional points of call with the naked eye — by rattling off the names of horses and the margins to an assistant, who is writing frantically. The skill of these professionals always astonishes me. The trackman in Maryland, Bill Brasaemle, will call the positions of all the horses at five points in the race and then, immediately afterward, mention a subtle instance of trouble or a jockey's strangulation of a horse that I might miss after repeatedly scrutinizing films of the race. But the methodology of the chart-callers is still fundamentally flawed. They are not taking a mental still photograph of a race; they are calling positions and lengths while the horses are in motion. During the time they are making the half-mile call, for example, a horse may be accelerating or dropping back sharply, and his margin will vary according to the split second in which the chart caller sees him.

I had been only dimly aware of these problems before the summer of 1992, when a pile of computer and video equipment appeared one day in the press box at Laurel. It was the creation of a midwesterner named Cary Charlson, who was trying to time horses in a manner appropriate to the latter portion of the twentieth century. Wasn't it absurd that we could know, in hundredths of a second, the time for the last-place Ivory Coast relay team in the Olympics, but we could only estimate Arazi's time in the Kentucky Derby to the nearest fifth of a second?

Charlson's company, Turf Sciences Inc., was filming the Laurel races, and each frame of the film corresponded to a certain number of hundredths of a second. A computer allowed the operator to draw a line across a television screen, marking the quarter- or half-mile point and then to advance the film, frame by frame, until a horse's nose touched the line. Each horse's individual fractional time was then recorded in hundredths of a second. Turf Sciences achieved further accuracy by timing races from the instant the gate opened instead of the moment a horse broke an electronic beam at the "official" starting point. The results of the venture were both enlightening and depressing.

The fractional times on which Sartin's disciples and others had based their calculations were routinely off by three-fifths of a second, four-fifths of a second, a full second — an eternity to a pace handicapper. In the case of Lunch Connection, above, his middle fraction was actually 24.08 seconds — more than three-fifths of a second slower than the :23⅖ calculated according to the lengths by which he was trailing. The discrepancies had a small effect on horses' final times and speed figures, but they were serious enough to destroy pace handicappers' attempts to rate horses who were several lengths behind the leaders. And that had seemed to be one of the greatest strengths of the Sartin methodology. The day will surely come when Charlson's system for timing races, or something like it, will be standard at American tracks. Until that time, however, any efforts to use fractional times with precision are going to be based on shaky ground.

I view pace handicapping as I do the Republican party. I believe in its principles, and I believe that it holds the promise of delivering some very important answers. I'm just never satisfied with the way it works in practice. Therefore, my only applications of pace handicapping techniques are limited and modest. I will use pace figures, but only in the limited function for which they are indisputably effective: in judging and comparing the past performances of speed horses. I want to know if a field contains one horse with superior speed that will enable him to dominate the race. Pace figures will indicate, too, whether a front-running type has earned his previous speed figures by contesting a fast pace or benefiting from a soft pace.

A handicapper also needs to know whether any horse, regardless of his style, was previously in a race whose pace was so fast or slow that it might have affected his performance. But what constitutes a fast or slow pace? If a horse is coming out of a six-furlong race where the half mile was run in :44 flat, the answer is obvious. But what about a 1¹⁄₁₆-mile race run in 1:46, with a six-furlong fraction of 1:12? Is that pace fast, slow, or average? I would like to be able to answer that important question without getting tangled in an enormously complicated system of pace analysis. If I know, for example, that for 1¹⁄₁₆-mile races run in 1:46 the average six-furlong fraction is 1:13⅕, I will know that the race run with a 1:12 fraction had a quick pace. Handicappers can find the data for such an analysis in Gordon Pine's *Par Times,* or they can compile it themselves very easily. If I am examining $1\frac{1}{16}$-mile races at Laurel, where the fastest races might be run in 1:44 and the slowest in 1:49, I would take a large sheet of paper and make vertical columns for ranges of final times that might look like this:

$$1:44-1:44^2/_5 \quad 1:44^3/_5-1:45 \quad 1:45^1/_5-1:45^3/_5 \quad 1:45^4/_5-1:46^1/_5, \text{ etc.}$$

I would go through a few weeks of results and write the six-furlong fraction for each route race in the appropriate column. Then I would average the fractions, and my calculations might look like this:

Final Time Range	Average 6-Furlong Fraction
$1:44-1:44^2/_5$	$1:12^3/_5$
$1:44^3/_5-1:45$	$1:12^4/_5$
$1:45^1/_5-1:45^3/_5$	$1:13$
$1:45^4/_5-1:46^1/_5$	$1:13^1/_5$
$1:46^2/_5-1:46^4/_5$	$1:13^3/_5$
$1:47-1:47^2/_5$	$1:13^4/_5$
$1:47^3/_5-1:48$	$1:14$
$1:48^1/_5-1:48^3/_5$	$1:14^2/_5$

With such data before me, I can judge at a glance the pace of a horse's previous races. I simply look at the fractional and final times of a race, refer to this chart, and note how many fifths of a second faster or slower than average the pace was. I will designate the pace by writing F6 or S1 or F3 on a horse's past performances. This number doesn't necessarily indicate who is going to be faster than whom today; pace figures are needed for that. But it neatly expresses what pace handicappers call the shape of a horse's last race and makes it easy to assess his performance. If, for example, a horse won with an impressive-looking rally in his last start but the pace was F7, his victory might be discounted because he took advantage of a hot pace in front of him. If a stretch-runner gave a dull-looking effort in a race denoted S10, he was undoubtedly compromised by the slow pace.

As useful as this method is, I feel hopelessly old-fashioned writing "F4" on my *Racing Form* with a red Flair pen while the Sartin methodologists are unfolding their computer printouts of velocity rates, energy profiles, and decision models. And I remain confused by many of the issues of pace handicapping that smart men like Sartin, Brohamer, and Quinn address with such certitude. Stricken with feelings of inadequacy, I turned for counsel to my former racetrack mentor. Steve Davidowitz was the first successful professional bettor I ever met, and he set me on the path to enlightenment. His philosophy of handicapping is that he has no philosophy, no dogmas; he is an eclectic who is always ready to learn, to adapt, to incorporate new methods into his repertoire. Since he moved to northern California I knew that he had paid increasing attention to pace, and I asked him his current view of this subject, which he had once largely ignored. His answer made me decide that I'd rather have Steve Davidowitz than Doc Sartin as my psychotherapist.

"I look at pace the way we always have looked at biases," he said. "I look at each individual race as having conditions which may have benefited some horses and hindered others. If you know what a reasonable pace is for a given time on a given track, then you can relate horses' performances to it. Maybe there's a way to quantify this, and it may not be quite as elusive as the urge to turn base metal into gold, but it's almost as difficult. Since I've been in California I've seen a lot of the mathematical approaches to pace and there seem to be problems associated with all of them, even though the principles they're trying to apply are extremely valid. All of the mathematicians have good ideas, but they wind up getting hung up in their own mathematics. I think the conceptualists like you and me are going to get to the finish line ahead of them."

Davidowitz is probably right, at least for now, but the day may come when the mathematicians beat the conceptualists to the finish line. The early practitioners of speed handicapping, too, used figures in ways that were often clumsy and confused, but they eventually developed those figures into a phenomenally effective tool. High-tech pace handicapping is still in its nascency, and in the future it may revolutionize the game.

SIX

Turf Racing: Lessons from Two Continents

It was in a sleazy bar in a town called Alice that I first entertained the idea that would turn into my obsession: I wanted to become the greatest gambler in the Southern Hemisphere. In 1988 my wife and I had taken a vacation in Australia, where we visited all the standard tourist attractions, from the Great Barrier Reef to the Sydney Opera House. I always consider racetracks to be important tourist destinations, and thus we spent an afternoon at Melbourne's Sandown Racecourse. In the featured Sandown Cup, a pair of fillies finished first and second, defeating fifteen male rivals; afterward I noticed that the two of them had run 1-2 just a week earlier in an ordinary race for members of their own sex. I noted, too, that the time of their previous race had been very fast relative to other races at the same distance on the same day. In American terminology, this was a key race and a big figure, and so I fixed in my mind the name of the third-place finisher in that filly race: Papal Princess.

On the day she was entered, our travels had taken us to Alice Springs, in the arid heart of the continent, but in Australia there are off-track betting facilities even in outposts of civilization. The one I found consisted of a single ticket-selling machine in the corner of a dusty barroom largely populated by Aborigines drinking 50-cent draft beers. But I got down my bet on Papal Princess and watched excitedly on a big-screen television as she led all the way to win at odds of 15 to 1. When I presented my winning tickets, the seller did a double-take, excused herself, and disappeared. When she reappeared a half-hour later, she counted out a large stack of filthy, crumpled twenties, tens, and fives. I had evidently broken the bank. Today, Alice Springs, I thought. One day, Sydney.

Could American handicapping techniques be used to beat the races in Australia? On visits to other countries, I had rejected similar thoughts almost instantly. Racing in England and France, in particular, is utterly foreign to an American; horses gallop along in a tight pack in virtual slow motion during the early stages of a race and don't accelerate in earnest until they turn into the stretch. As a result, their final times are unimportant, and speed figures would be useless as a handicapping tool. But racing in Australia, despite its British roots, seemed very speed-oriented; jockeys urged their horses from the gate, and the pace was usually fast from start to finish. Yet none of the newspaper selectors made any references to horses' times; they all were preoccupied by class and weight — just as Americans were in the era before speed handicapping came into vogue. I picked up a copy of the definitive Australian book on handicapping, in which the author, Don Scott, declared, "I see no value in times at all." He pointed out that "times at different tracks vary greatly because no two tracks are identical" and that "track conditions are never exactly the same from day to day." These were the identical arguments that Americans had once used to support the belief that time is only important when you're in jail. I had often dreamed of being able to go back to the 1950s and 1960s, when almost nobody in the United States believed in speed handicapping. Maybe it would be possible to make the equivalent of a trip back in time by going to Australia, where I could be the only person on a great continent armed with a set of speed figures.

By 1990 I had become so preoccupied by this vision that I was determined to try. Susan and I scheduled a 3½-month stay in Sydney, to begin that November; I persuaded the *Washington Post* to let me write my column from Down Under. Five months before our departure, I went to work on the Australian speed figures. The country doesn't have a daily racing paper with all of the results from major tracks, but a twice-a-week publication called the *Sportsman* contained most of the data I needed, and I acquired a year of back copies for my research.

Race distances in Australia are comparable to those in the United States, but the country uses the metric system; it was not difficult to convert my six-furlong speed chart into one for 1,200 meters, with the times in tenths rather than fifths of a second. Nor was it too difficult to create par figures for classes of Australian races, though the typical races there are handicaps rather than claiming events. What was daunting, though, was the different configuration of the tracks. At most American tracks, six- and seven-furlong races are run around one turn on an oval track, and there is a fixed relationship between times at those distances. At Rosehill in Sydney, 1,200-meter races start in the infield and are contested over a hairpin-shape course; the 1,400-meter races start on the backstretch and are run over a course that looks like a semicircle. Races in Sydney are all run clockwise; Melbourne races are run counterclockwise. As the author Don Scott had warned, no two tracks are alike. And there are so many tracks! In my home base, the Maryland circuit, I have to deal with three: Laurel, Pimlico, and Timonium. In the state of New South Wales, of which Sydney is the capital, there are more than a hundred. I narrowed my focus to the major dozen and struggled to establish the relationships between the different distances at each; I would wake up in the middle of the night fretting about the peculiarities of 1,290-meter races at Canterbury or the configuration of the 2,000-meter course at Kembla Grange.

But I finally constructed all of the necessary speed charts, then started maintaining my day-to-day variants and figures from information in the daily newspapers at the Australian Embassy library in Washington. Soon, everything started to make sense. I was beginning to understand the relative strengths and weaknesses of horses at different class levels and at different tracks, just as I had when I began to use speed figures at home in the early 1970s. During one day's work at the library, I saw that a horse with a ten-point edge in the figures had won a race at Rosehill at odds of 20 to 1. I told Susan seriously over dinner that night that our trip might turn into a permanent stay; we might win so much money in Australia that we couldn't afford to leave.

My optimism was not dampened by the awareness that Australia's thoroughbred sport is conducted entirely on grass, and I had never done particularly well betting turf races. The reason for my poor performance, I assumed, is the fact that speed figures cannot be as accurate for U.S. grass races as they are on the dirt. With only one or two races run each day on a given course, there isn't enough evidence on which to base an accurate track variant. Moreover, some American tracks don't have electric timers on their turf courses; even at Belmont Park, races were clocked by stopwatch before 1991, and the "official" times were often preposterous. It is these obstacles, not the nature of grass racing itself, that make turf racing difficult for a speed handicapper. But in Australia all of the major tracks time races electronically — most in hundredths of a second. Speed figures would be as effective on the grass in Australia as they were on the dirt in the United States. Or so I thought.

Susan and I settled into the top floor of a duplex in the town of Kirribilli, by Sydney Harbor. Adjusting to daily life in Australia was easy, once we got over the shock of seeing an occasional brown spider, the size of a large fist, clinging to the ceiling. ("No worries, mate," a neighbor advised. "We get rid of 'em by sucking 'em into the vacuum cleaner.") Adjusting to handicapping was a bit more difficult. Except on Wednesdays and Saturdays, the major racing days, complete past performances were not available in any newspaper. The Australian Associated Press compiles all of the country's racing data, and serious punters — as the Aussies call horseplayers — can subscribe to its computer service, downloading the necessary information each day. I would do the form — as they call handicapping a card — on an unwieldy computer printout instead of a newspaper. The shortcomings of the data would make any American realize how much we are spoiled by the *Daily Racing Form*. The running lines, which indicate a horse's position at various early stages of a race, are either inadequate or nonexistent. And as speed-oriented as Australian racing is, it can be hard to tell whether there are ten front-runners in a field or none at all. Fortunately, films of races are readily available by subscription. A courier would arrive at our door at seven o'clock every Monday morning with the tapes of the previous week's action, and I would proceed to make notes on every horse in every race — an exhausting job when there were eighteen horses in a field.

If I was slightly unprepared for some of the difficulties involved in handicapping, I was utterly stunned by the sophistication of the Australian racing industry — and of the local punters who would be my rivals. When I arrived in Sydney, I thought of myself as a wise guy coming to a backward country. But after my first Saturday at Rosehill racecourse, I realized that the backward racing industry was the United States'. The track program at Rosehill was about the size of Chairman Mao's little red book, because Australia's off-track betting system links all of the metropolitan tracks with each other in a well-coordinated fashion; the 1:00 P.M. race in Sydney would be followed by a simulcast from Melbourne at 1:10, from Brisbane at 1:20, and from Adelaide at 1:30, and then by the next live race at 1:40. The ultramodern tote system offers quinellas and trifectas on every race, plus an assortment of doubles and other exotica. But because of its British traditions, Australia also has a well-entrenched system of legal on-track bookmakers. Dozens of bookies in the betting ring would be constantly adjusting their odds and generally offering more attractive prices than the tote in order to lure business.

The crowd of 12,000 at the spacious Rosehill facility was a diverse mix — from well-dressed types in the champagne bar to a surprising number of families and college-age youths in the grandstand — but it looked like a fairly ordinary racetrack crowd. What was extraordinary was the way these people bet. The crowd wagered the equivalent of $6 million in U.S. dollars with the book-makers and another $2.5 million through the tote machines — more than $700 per capita. In addition, the off-track betting system in New South Wales generated $6 million on the Rosehill card and another $12 million on other tracks in Australia. The figures dwarfed anything ever seen in U.S. racing.

The sheer quantity of money in the game created the possibility for scores that are unimaginable in America. On a metropolitan Saturday race, a gambler who plotted his attack meticulously could put himself in position to win $1 million. (Moreover, under the country's civilized laws, the winnings would be exempt from taxation.) So the bookmakers had to be extremely smart in order to survive. As I watched the rapid movement of odds in the betting ring I was somewhat dazed, but one example of the bookies' sharpness amazed me. A race for 3-year-olds included two first-time starters; one came from an obscure country track and elicited no positive comments from any newspaper analyst; another had won a nonbetting trial race in Sydney. But when the bookmakers posted their prices, the country horse was 5 to 1 or thereabouts around the betting ring; the other first-time starter was 200 to 1 on many bookies' boards. And they were right: the short-priced horse proved to be a contender while the other barely picked up his feet. If the bookmakers knew so much about horses who had never run, how astute might they be about horses with established form?

I would learn, in the coming weeks, that they were uncannily accurate and that punters would follow their lead; odds on the tote board would generally fall into line with the prices in the betting ring. With my speed figures, however, I was looking at races from a unique and unorthodox perspective, and there were several occasions when the price on my top figure was 50 to 1 or more. I would walk up to the bookies with the swaggering confidence that I knew something they didn't. And yet, in every single case, my horse performed like a true 50-to-1 shot, running miserably. My speed figures did pick their share of winners — but they were usually short-priced winners that other punters were picking, too, with orthodox Australian methods. During my first month I had only one notably successful day, when I spotted and capitalized on a bad-rail bias at Warwick Farm, but otherwise I was paying a high tuition for my Australian racing education.

As I came to appreciate the sophistication of the battle between punters and bookmakers, I had the chance to meet some of the principals on both sides of the combat lines. Long before this trip I had received a note from a man in Sydney named Robbie Waterhouse, who said he had read and enjoyed *Picking Winners*. I wrote and told him of my planned trip and asked if we might go to the races together one day; he responded that he would like to meet me, but that a misunderstanding with the authorities had caused him to be barred from all racetracks in the country. I soon learned that the Waterhouse name was well known throughout the continent. Before his "misunderstanding" with officialdom, Robbie had been one of Australia's most successful and controversial bookmakers. His father, Bill Waterhouse, had once been the most prominent member of his profession in the world, described by his biographer as "the first of the glamour bookies." I became their friend and sat spellbound for hours as Bill Waterhouse told stories of his bookmaking career — such as how he met the man who would become his fiercest adversary in the betting ring.

Waterhouse received a phone call from a man who introduced himself as Felipe "Babe" Ysmael and said he had moved to Australia from the Philippines because it was the only place in the world where he could bet on the scale he wanted. Could they meet? Waterhouse went to Ysmael's hotel that day and chatted with him until the gambler proposed, innocently, "Could we have a bet?" The only racing that day was at an obscure country track. Ysmael glanced at a newspaper, scanned the entries for the first race, picked the 2-to-1 favorite, and told Waterhouse, "Make it $20,000." When the bookmaker assented, they turned on the radio to hear the call of the race, and the favored horse lost. Ysmael kept upping his bets and losing them, and by late afternoon he had lost more than $500,000. Even so, Waterhouse was wary. Was this a setup of some kind? Indeed it was, for Ysmael secretly owned a filly in the next race who had been training brilliantly at a private track. She was the 1-to-2 favorite, and Ysmael said quietly, "I want a chance to get out with a big bet." Waterhouse said, "All right. You can have a million dollars on." They listened as the filly won easily, and Ysmael's $1 million bet cut his losses for the day to a few thousand dollars.

That was the way Waterhouse always did business: fearlessly. Whenever he mounted his stand in the betting ring, he wore a perpetual frown and projected an attitude that said, "Take your best shot at me." He entered the combat with more than psychological strength, though. He had the numbers on his side. Bookies work on a very narrow profit margin — only about 5 percent, less taxes and overhead — and so their odds have to be extraordinarily accurate. Waterhouse's were. "There's not a market in the world — the stock market or the commodities market — as accurate as the starting price [i.e., the final odds] of bookmakers here," Waterhouse said. "If you get a bet above that price, you'll beat the bookmaker. If the favorite is 2 to 1 but you get 9 to 4 on him, and you do that regularly, you've got a good shot at finishing ahead at the end of the year."

When Robbie Waterhouse grew up to carry on the family tradition, he brought to it even more refined methods of gauging odds. His staff would assemble vast quantities of information and feed it into a computer that would generate estimates of each horse's "true" odds. In addition to his mathematical bent, Robbie had a roguish streak, and he liked to say, "Bookmaking is the last business in which you can be a buccaneer." He told me one story about himself that illustrated what a cutthroat buccaneer he was.

Robbie was willing to work at the most humble race meetings, and he occasionally went to a small track in Canberra, where his presence both annoyed and intimidated the amateurish local bookies. In the first race one day, his numbers told him that the low-weighted horse in a handicap race deserved to be the favorite, but when he posted his odds — an hour before anybody else — he put that horse at 33 to 1. He took not a single bet, but when the other bookies put up their own prices, they basically copied the odds of the big-city sharpie. Robbie proceeded to have his agents go around the ring betting the 33-to-1 shot — and inflicted a beating on all of his rivals when the horse won.

Robbie ultimately proved to be too much of a wise guy for his own good, though. When he learned that an abundance of "smart money" was flowing onto a horse named Fine Cotton in a minor race at Brisbane, he sought to capitalize on the information and bet heavily himself. The wagering had originated with a group of desperadoes, who planned to run a look-alike, high-class horse in Fine Cotton's name. But when the high-class horse was injured, the perpetrators didn't want to abandon their scheme; they acquired another horse, who didn't look anything like Fine Cotton, and clumsily tried to dye him. The attempted coup was so inept that as soon as Fine Cotton crossed the finish line first — having been bet down from 33-to-1 odds to 5 to 2 — the chief steward summoned the trainer and asked, "Doesn't this horse look a bit lighter in color than the last time you raced it?" Fine Cotton was disqualified and a nationwide scandal erupted. Robbie was implicated because of his peripheral involvement, and both he and his father were ultimately banned from the sport. It was the only time anyone had ever been able to defeat the Waterhouses.

The sophistication of the men who set the odds obviously demanded enormous sophistication from the bettors who were their rivals. I got the chance to observe the other side of the combat when a bookmaker arranged an introduction to a punter he described as "the best form man in Australia." Mr. D. was no flashy high-roller like Babe Ysmael; he was affable and modest, little known even by the sport's insiders. He operated out of a complex of offices in a small industrial park, where he employed a clerical staff of three, who entered data into his computer system; and several part-time workers, who telephoned his bets on busy racing days. The computer analyzed each race and translated each horse's chances into a figure that represented his percentage chances of winning; 15 minutes before each race, Mr. D. received, via computer, the tote odds on the race as well as a telephone report on bookmaker odds at the track. He compared those prices with his own, looking for horses he considered slightly overvalued or undervalued. Then he typed into the computer the numbers of the horses he wished to use in the trifecta, and the machine did the rest. It printed out a list of trifectas for Mr. D. to play — often more than a hundred combinations in a single race. The computer specified the amount that he should wager on each one so that he could win 5 percent of the total wagering pool on the event. Now Mr. D.'s staff swung into action, calling the wagers into his telephone betting accounts. There are separate off-track betting systems in Australia's different states, and Mr. D. was betting into all of them.

As I watched this operation, one thing perplexed me. Mr. D.'s method of playing so many trifecta combinations in every race was clearly geared toward grinding out a narrow margin of profit. But with his expertise, he should be ferreting out horses who could generate windfall profits. In the United States, after all, every handicapper strives to find horses he thinks are superior and are going off at long odds. Why didn't Mr. D. simply wait for horses that, say, ought be 2 to 1 but are going off at 10 to 1 or more? "Because," he answered, "that never happens. Never, ever. If you had a horse at 2 to 1 and he went off at 5 to 2, that would be a luxury. If you got 3 to 1, you'd think that Christmas had come early."

The professional punters were looking for narrow edges and trying to grind out narrow margins of profit, perhaps as little as 2 or 3 percent on their total investment. (They could beat the game only because parimutuel percentages weren't heavily stacked against them. The takeout from the tote was only 16 percent, and bookmakers worked on considerably smaller margins. Most bettors were astonished that any American horseplayer could survive our country's rate of taxation.) To make a 2 or 3 percent edge worthwhile, of course, professional gamblers would have to bet heavily — and they did. One day I was visiting a country track called Gosford, which might have been comparable in its ambience and quality of racing to Delaware Park, and I mentioned to a local journalist that I had always liked little tracks that were as quaint and charming as this one. He said, "Well, it's not as quaint as you may think," and led me to an unmarked white door in the grandstand. I peeked in and saw about about a dozen bettors, mostly men in their thirties, each with a portable computer, each with his own ticket seller. The journalist gestured toward one of them. "See that chap?" he said. "He'll bet about $150,000 through the tote today — and he might run outside to bet $10,000 with a bookmaker occasionally. Of course, this is just a small meeting. He'll bet $500,000 on a Saturday in the city."

I would have been elated if I could have ground out even a slim margin of profit. Despite all the time I had spent making figures and scrutinizing the films of races, my first 2½ months in Australia produced a net loss. In my final weeks, however, I made a comeback. I cashed a $6,000 superfecta — a wager requiring the bettor to pick the first six finishers in order — based on a combination of figures and trips. One day at Rosehill I observed a strong speed-favoring bias, and the top-figure horse in one of the races, Glenhaven Boy, also happened to be the principal speed horse in the field. His running style couldn't be gleaned from the past performances; I knew this only from watching the films of his races at a minor track. When he led all the way at 4 to 1 and other speed horses ran second and third, I collected more than $10,000, and my ledger showed a profit for the first time. I had one other chance, during those final days, to make a substantial score. I had spotted a horse named Moville Peter making a big eight-wide move in a race at a bush league track, and the race had earned a big speed figure. The number was verified when another horse in the field came back to win. Now Moville Peter was entered in a stakes race at Tamworth, a remote track. Because he was seemingly outclassed, he was 55 to 1. I had been chastened for thinking that I could be very right when the public was very wrong, but all handicapping logic pointed to Moville Peter, and so I bet $400 at an off-track outlet. I watched the longshot bobble at the start, then rally furiously to finish second — missing by a half-length. And with his defeat ended my chances for a triumphant assault on Australia.

At the end of our visit, I had netted a profit of $500 — before expenses. Given the competitive nature of the gambling game in Australia, I suppose I could have rationalized that this was a respectable performance, but I felt both disappointed and confused. I did not ascribe my lack of success to the foreignness of the racing; the nature of the game Down Under was recognizable and comprehensible to an American. Trips were important, pace was important, biases were important, and speed figures were useful, but I still didn't understand the game fully. One possible explanation occurred to me. Perhaps the critical factor did not lie with the differences between the two continents, but between turf racing and the dirt racing with which I was more familiar. Were there, perhaps, some elements of grass racing that I didn't recognize because I had learned virtually all my lessons about handicapping from dirt races?

Because of a coincidental set of events, I was about to gain a small insight into turf racing. While I was in Australia, the *Racing Times* was gearing up its operation, which was going to include Beyer Speed Figures. When the paper began publication in the spring, it was the first time my associates and I had seen our numbers incorporated into a horse's complete past performances. In the past, when we were writing the figures on the *Racing Form,* we would transcribe only a horse's last three or four figures, and we wouldn't bother to calculate and write the numbers for horses who had been trounced by twenty or thirty lengths. But in the *Racing Times,* and then in the *Racing Form,* every figure for every horse appeared in print, and repeatedly, in turf races, we encountered an oddity like this one:

Daria's Brother — **Ch. c. 4, by Leematt—Floway, by Freeway**

$45,000 **Br.—Richman Jerold D (Pa)**

Own.—Kaminsky Carol Ann — **Tr.—Kaminsky Carol Ann (16 1 1 0 .06)** — **120**

Lifetime						
12 0 0 0	1992	11	M	0	0	$180
$180	1991	1	M	0	0	
	Turf	5	0	0	0	$140
	Wet	1	0	0	0	

28Aug92- 9Pha	fm	*1⅛ Ⓣ			1:53¹	3↑Md 45000	**31**	7	9	9¹⁴	8¹⁵	7²²	727¾	Harvey B	b	120	172.80	57–18	PlmthGntlmn114¹⁴[D]ImprssvAppl113ⁿᵏMGrn113	Outrun	10
6Aug92- 9Pha	fm	*1 1/16 Ⓣ			1:47²	3↑Md 45000	**31**	8	8	65¼	66½	6¹⁶	629½	Navedo E	b	120	92.60	53–17	PhonixForc120¹⁷½IsldMujrs1134¼Kingfish120	No threat	8
30Jly92-10Atl	fm	*1½ Ⓣ	:51		2:37¹	3↑Md Sp Wt	**19**	2	6	6⁸	66¼	9²⁶	9⁴⁸	Mendez J P	b	122	156.50	— —	Isaiah122¹ Nobelium10912¼ ContareMan122	No menace	10
24Jly92- 4Atl	yl	*1 Ⓣ	:48²	1:14⁴	1:41²	3↑Md Sp Wt	**34**	8	6	9¹²	9¹⁰	7¹⁴	7²²	Navedo E	b	122	189.90	65–14	SpiceTrde1222¾WildBuck117ⁿᵒSddletheWind114	Outrun	10
2Jly92- 7Pha	fm	1⅛ Ⓣ	:49	1:14²	1:53	3↑Md 45000	**33**	8	11	11¹¹	11¹³	11¹⁹	1226½	Harvey B	Lb	120	176.20	52–21	Royal Duty114ⁿᵒ Destimony114⁵ Be Helpful113	Dull	12
19Jun92- 2Atl	fst	7f	:23	:46³	1:26³	3↑Md 6000	**7**	7	6	99½	9¹³	8¹⁴	818¼	Harvey B	b	118	71.30	56–17	CptnHoochd1175¼DncnDoblTm118½BlzthLrd112	Outrun	9
6Jun92-12Pha	fst	1 70	:46²	1:11³	1:43⁴	3↑Md 8000	**12**	3	8	8¹⁷	9¹⁹	8²²	927¾	Harvey B	b	122	95.90	49–15	TigerWithin114ʰᵈRascalRbbit1134½LordFlirt113	Outrun	11
31May92- 1Pha	sly	1 1/16	:47⁴	1:13⁴	1:49⁴	3↑Md 8000	**–0**	1	7	8¹⁹	9²⁴	9²³	931¾	Harvey B	b	122	41.50	28–27	Gato Bay114² Superbird1201½ Tiger Within114	Outrun	9
2Apr92- 9GS	fst	1 1/16	:49	1:16¹	1:51²	3↑Md 7500	**10**	3	4	7¹³	8¹⁷	9²³	925½	Harvey B	b	122	86.30	31–34	Contactor116½ Secret Bay1222¼ RallyingMan122	Outrun	12
5Feb92- 9GS	fst	1 1/16	:48⁴	1:16²	1:51⁴	Md 7500	**–0**	3	9	9²¹	10¹⁷	9¹⁷	924¼	Harvey B	b	122	45.90	— —	BrokenAllinc122ⁿᵏCochMss122ⁿᵏEskimoCov117	Outrun	10

LATEST WORKOUTS **Sep 7 Pha 5f fst 1:07 B**

Theoretically, a horse with the same level of ability on turf and dirt is supposed to run similar figures on each surface. Daria's Brother was horrible on both turf and dirt, losing by twenty lengths or more every time he ran. In races from 1 mile to 1$\frac{1}{16}$ miles on the dirt, he had run figures of 12 and 10, plus two that were below zero. But on the turf, in the same distance range, his figures had been 31, 31, 34, and 33. This one case might have been dismissed as an aberration — and, indeed, I did dismiss many such examples until I had seen hundreds of horses just like Daria's Brother. Why did bad horses always run much bigger speed figures on the grass?

The answer involved a technical aspect of making figures, but it led to an important truth. In calculating figures for horses behind the winner, we deduct a certain number of points for each beaten length, according to the distance of a race. Margins of victory will generally be narrower in a shorter race than in a longer race, so a length will be proportionately more significant. (In a six-furlong race, we subtract from the winner's figure 2.4 points for each length that a horse is beaten; in a 1$\frac{1}{8}$-mile race, we subtract 1.7 points per length.) But it seemed that we were not deducting enough in these route races on the grass, permitting horses like Daria's Brother to earn inflated figures. Was a length more significant on turf than on dirt? Most racing fans have probably observed that turf races seem to be closer and more exciting than races on the dirt. Mark Hopkins and I tested this notion by tallying the average margins that separate horses in turf races versus dirt races, and we found that grass races are indeed tighter. Horses were bunched at the finish of turf races as closely as they are bunched in sprints. We finally decided to reflect this fact in our figures by deducting 2.2 points per length in turf races, the same as we did at 6$\frac{1}{2}$ furlongs on the dirt, and to make other revisions in the mathematical underpinnings of our turf numbers. When we made those changes in 1993, Daria's Brother's turf figures would become 7, 7, 11, and 10, reflecting the same level of incompetence on the grass that he showed on the dirt.

What made our discovery so interesting was not its effect on the technical aspects of speed figures but its implications about the essential nature of turf racing. What did it mean that horses were bunched at the end of a grass race as if they had been running a sprint? It was as if the horses had bided their time, doing nothing, staying together in a pack, and then sprinted the last few furlongs of the race. And why did this sound so familiar? This is the way races are regularly run in Europe. With typical American arrogance, I had always thought that England and France had developed ridiculous styles of training and riding because nobody in European racing has a brain, and that anybody who ever appreciated the value of speed, American style, would dominate the sport there. But the British have been racing thoroughbreds for more than two centuries, and in that time some of the world's most famous trainers and jockeys might have learned a thing or two about the optimal strategy for winning races. Perhaps the determining factor in turf races is the horses' finishing kick. Perhaps speed figures have limited usefulness because they measure a horse's overall performance, from start to finish, instead of placing an emphasis on the final fraction.

This, I would learn, was not an original insight. The California pace handicappers, whose methods I had thought were so provincial, were way ahead of me. James Quinn had been mulling over the distinctive nature of turf racing for a long time, and he was going to devote much of his book *Figure Handicapping* to this very subject. In it he wrote, "Grass races are distinct. The courses are different. . . . The pace is different. . . . The horses are different too. Conformation favors shorter, more angular pasterns and dishlike feet. The turf stride is straight, gliding over the ground in a forward paddling motion, with less up and down curling movement of the front legs. . . . So why, in the face of obvious differences, do handicappers expect the same rating methods that work well on the dirt to work equally well on the turf? Why do figure handicappers, in particular, expect their methods will be perfectly transportable to the turf? Of course, the methods are not very transportable at all." And he had figured this out without spending 3½ months on the other side of the world.

Quinn examined turf racing from the special perspective of the Sartin methodology, and he looked at horses' performances in terms of their Energy Distribution, as described in the previous chapter. Over a ten-week period at Santa Anita in 1990, he found that the winners of routes had an Energy Distribution of 51.72 percent in the early stages of dirt races and 50.60 percent in turf races — a huge difference in the Sartin calculations. Even on Santa Anita's fast new turf course, where front-runners were having considerable success, horses won by conserving their energy and using it late. The essential nature of turf races, Quinn concluded, was "a relatively slow pace, followed by a furious all-out finish."

My own understanding of turf racing crystallized in California, too, at the 1992 Del Mar meeting. It was with mixed emotions that I had decided to spend the summer there. Three years earlier I gone to Del Mar for the first time, and I loved the ambience of the track and town, loved the climate, loved my morning bike rides on the Pacific Coast Highway — loved it all so much that my two decades of fervent loyalty to Saratoga immediately eroded. Unfortunately, my travel guide to this resort could have been called *Del Mar on $1,500 a Day*, because my performance at the betting windows had been nothing short of disastrous.

So I returned with a sense of trepidation, and I was eager to solicit whatever counsel I could from the resident experts I knew. One was Andy Cylke, an accountant turned professional bettor. Ordinarily, I might not have listened attentively to Cylke's opinions; he used the Sartin methodology, and I have the same instinctive reaction to Sartin disciples that I do to Moonies and other cultists. But my friend Roxy Roxborough, the Las Vegas oddsmaker, knew Cylke well and regularly split pick six investments with him. Roxborough has seen thousands of aspiring young gamblers come and go, and he is skeptical of anybody with an angle or a system, but he described Cylke as "the best handicapper I've ever seen." His confidence would be admirably rewarded later in the year. On the day of the California Cup at Santa Anita, Cylke loved the card and cut Roxborough in for half of his pick nine investment. The ticket cost $24, and after Cylke swept the card it was worth $88,337.

At Del Mar, I observed that Cylke's opinions in turf races were not merely good, they were almost infallible. He was relying largely on a single Sartin measurement, Sustained Pace, which he said was usually the most important factor on grass, and the top S.P. horses were winning regularly. If I had been a racing neophyte seeing the performance of this rating, I might have thought I had stumbled onto the magic Secret of Beating the Races and probably would have sworn a blood oath to Doc Sartin. Being more jaded, I recognized that the conditions at Del Mar were ideal for a mechanical system of rating turf races: There were virtually no shippers with which to contend, the condition of the course changed little from day to day, and the races happened to be uncommonly formful. Even so, I gained a whole new respect for the Sartin methodology, and I wanted to understand the meaning and implications of Sustained Pace.

In route races, this rating is an average of a horse's velocity for the first six furlongs of the race and his velocity for the final fraction. With the velocity expressed in feet per second, it seemed like mumbo-jumbo to me, but I grasped it better by thinking of it in terms of straightforward fractional times. Consider a horse who runs a mile on the turf with a six-furlong fraction of 1:13⅕ and a final time of 1:37. His three-quarter fraction is the same as 73.2 seconds; divided by 3, this is a rate of 24.4 seconds per quarter — or :24⅖. Since Sustained Pace is not concerned with varying rates of speed in the early quarters, only the average rate, the horse's race, broken down by quarters, was the equivalent of this:

Time per Quarter	Final Time
:24⅖ :24⅖ :24⅖ :23⅘	1:37

The Sartin practitioners, however, took these rates of Early Speed and Late Speed and weighted them equally to create a new (and wholly artificial) measurement of the horse's performance. Instead of the final quarter mile counting one-quarter of a horse's whole performance, it now counted for one-half. It was as if the horse's performance was now being recalculated like this:

Time per Quarter	Final Time
:24²/₅ :24²/₅ :23⁴/₅ :23⁴/₅	1:36²/₅

In other words, the final fraction counted more heavily than the early fractions, but it didn't count exclusively. A horse's final time and speed figure were not unimportant, but they needed to be viewed beside his closing fraction.

So, in an elementary and admittedly crude fashion, I began to do that. Although I was well aware of the potential inaccuracies involved, I would calculate a horse's final fraction in basically the same way the Sartin people did: by looking at the leader's final quarter and then adjusting it by one-fifth of a second for each length that the horse gained or lost from the six-furlong mark to the wire. If the fractions of the race were 1:13⅕ and 1:37, the final quarter was :23⁴/₅. If a horse had dropped from two to five lengths behind over this stage of the race, he had lost three lengths, or three-fifths of a second. His own fraction was :24²/₅. The only complication in this simplified version of pace analysis is the fact that final fractions commonly come in three different sizes: a quarter mile, five-sixteenths of a mile (in 1¹/₁₆-mile races), and three-eighths of a mile (in 1⅛-mile races). For easy comparison, I translated the latter two distances into their quarter-mile equivalents, according to the chart on the facing page.

Crude as this pace analysis might have been, it was often a revelation for me. Turf races are generally so competitive, so evenly matched, that they rarely produce standouts with 10- or 15-point advantages in the figures, as are frequently found on the dirt. On the grass, the contenders are often clustered within a few points of each other. Suddenly I had a way to separate these contenders, as in the case of the two fillies, Her Elegant Ways and Lyin to the Moon, who constituted a virtual two-horse race at Del Mar. Their past performances appear on page 166.

$5/16$ fraction in $1\frac{1}{16}$-mile races	Quarter-mile equivalent	$3/8$ fraction in $1\frac{1}{8}$-mile races	Quarter-mile equivalent
:29	:23$\frac{1}{5}$	:35	:23$\frac{2}{5}$
:29$\frac{1}{5}$	:23$\frac{2}{5}$	:35$\frac{1}{5}$	:23$\frac{2}{5}$
:29$\frac{2}{5}$	:23$\frac{3}{5}$	:35$\frac{2}{5}$	:23$\frac{3}{5}$
:29$\frac{3}{5}$	:23$\frac{3}{5}$	:35$\frac{3}{5}$	:23$\frac{4}{5}$
:29$\frac{4}{5}$	:23$\frac{4}{5}$	:35$\frac{4}{5}$	:23$\frac{4}{5}$
:30	:24	:36	:24
:30$\frac{1}{5}$	:24$\frac{1}{5}$	:36$\frac{1}{5}$	:24$\frac{1}{5}$
:30$\frac{2}{5}$	:24$\frac{2}{5}$	:36$\frac{2}{5}$	:24$\frac{1}{5}$
:30$\frac{3}{5}$	:24$\frac{2}{5}$	:36$\frac{3}{5}$	:24$\frac{2}{5}$
:30$\frac{4}{5}$	:24$\frac{3}{5}$	:36$\frac{4}{5}$	:24$\frac{3}{5}$
:31	:24$\frac{4}{5}$	:37	:24$\frac{3}{5}$
:31$\frac{1}{5}$	:25	:37$\frac{1}{5}$	:24$\frac{4}{5}$
:31$\frac{2}{5}$	:25$\frac{1}{5}$	:37$\frac{2}{5}$	:25
:31$\frac{3}{5}$	:25$\frac{1}{5}$	:37$\frac{3}{5}$	:25
:31$\frac{4}{5}$	:25$\frac{2}{5}$	:37$\frac{4}{5}$	:25$\frac{1}{5}$
:32	:25$\frac{3}{5}$	:38	:25$\frac{1}{5}$
:32$\frac{1}{5}$	:25$\frac{4}{5}$	:38$\frac{1}{5}$	:25$\frac{2}{5}$
:32$\frac{2}{5}$	:26	:38$\frac{2}{5}$	:25$\frac{3}{5}$
:32$\frac{3}{5}$	:26	:38$\frac{3}{5}$	:25$\frac{4}{5}$
:32$\frac{4}{5}$	:26$\frac{1}{5}$	:38$\frac{4}{5}$	:25$\frac{4}{5}$
:33	:26$\frac{2}{5}$	:39	:26

Her Elegant Ways — Dk. b. or br. f. 3(Jan), by Habitony—Laura's Star, by Key to the Kingdom

VALENZUELA P A (132 24 25 14 .18) — Br.—Mabee Mr-Mrs John C (Ky)

Own.—Golden Eagle Farm — Tr.—Cenicola Lewis (15 2 0 2 .13) — 117

Lifetime 11 1 1 7 $54,975 — 1992 4 0 0 3 $15,300 — 1991 7 1 1 4 $39,675 — Turf 2 0 0 2 $10,500

```
21Aug92- 7Dmr fm 1 1/16 Ⓣ:474 1:12  1:43   ⒻAlw 36000    89 6 4 32  2½  11  3½  Valenzuela P A LBb 117  3.80  90-09 CrtDM117½SnAdShd-GB117hdHrEltWs117 Broke slowly 8
16Jly92- 8Hol fm 1 1/16 Ⓣ:473 1:111 1:424  ⒻAlw 34000    82 3 2 44½ 75½ 65  31¼ Pincay L Jr    LBb 117 10.70  80-17 Klwd118hdSovereignLiz1201½HrElgntWys117 Rough trip 8
24Jun92- 8Hol fst 1 1/16 :47  1:112 1:432  ⒻAlw 34000    73 1 5 42½ 42  54  64¼ Pincay L Jr    LBb 117 *.80e  80-16 Omjii I119nk Terre Haute117nk Sovereign Liz119 7
      24Jun92-Bumped break, rank 7/8, checked 3/4
31May92- 7Hol fst 6½f :22  :441 1:154 3↑ⒻAlw 32000  81 3 5 54¼ 47  44  33¾ Pincay L Jr     Bb 117  6.90  89-06 Mnplt1182ShootngThMon1151¾HrElgntWys117 Mild bid 7
30ct91- 5SA fst 6½f  :212 :442 1:154   ⒻAlw 32000    75 8 1 33½ 35½ 35½ 24  Pincay L Jr     Bb 117 20.80  87-11 Cptivnt1184HrElgntWys1171¼ChrryALMod118 2nd best 8
12Sep91-10Fpx fst 6½f :214 :461 1:19    ⒻBstls &Bows  68 8 6 74½ 64¼ 34  35½ Desormeaux KJ   Bb 114  1.90  75-17 FllTFrnd1144½DrllDncr1141HrEltWs114 Not enough late 9
14Aug91- 8Dmr fst 7f  :23  :452 1:221   ⒻSorrento     77 3 4 3½  31  44½ 47  Desormeaux KJ   Bb 115  7.00  82-15 SovitSojourn1211¼LSp1171½Sh'sTops117 4-wide stretch 4
      14Aug91-Grade III
26Jly91- 6Dmr fst 6f  :22  :46  1:103   ⒻMd 50000     81 6 7 54½ 21  15  17  Desormeaux KJ   Bb 117 *2.80  86-14 HrElgntWys1177Win'NMusc1173FltRj115 Bumped start 10
27Jun91- 6Hol fst 5½f :22  :453 1:041   ⒻMd 62500     57 1 2 1½  2hd 31½ 34¼ McCarron C J    Bb 117  6.60  88-11 FllTFrnd1173½ChrrALMd117¾HrEltWs117 Saved ground 12
29May91- 6Hol fst 5f  :221 :453 :58     ⒻMd 62500     58 5 7 43  34  38  37¼ Pincay L Jr      B 118  3.50  85-12 ForDix1187AllWorld118nkHrElgntWys118 Bumped start 10
LATEST WORKOUTS   Aug 30 Dmr 4f fst :48 H   ●Aug 17 Dmr Ⓣ 5f fm 1:014 H (d)   Aug 10 Dmr 5f fst 1:004 H   Jly 26 Hol 4f fst :471 H
```

Lyin To The Moon — B. f. 3(Jan), by Kris S—Telferner, by Tell

DELAHOUSSAYE E (162 31 30 18 .19) — Br.—Meadowbrook Farms Inc (Fla)

Own.—Allred & Hubbard — Tr.—Mandella Richard (41 6 10 8 .15) — 117

Lifetime 3 1 1 0 $21,700 — 1992 3 1 1 0 $21,700 — 1991 0 M 0 0 — Turf 1 0 1 0 $6,300 — Wet 1 1 0 0 $15,400

```
6Aug92- 7Dmr fm 1 1/16 Ⓣ:484 1:131 1:432 3↑ⒻAlw 36000 86 2 6 77  75½ 52  2nk Delahoussaye E LB 116  4.50  89-11 BllCt-NZ119nk[DH]LTTM116[DH]RrPtrl-GB122 Rank, wide 7
      6Aug92- Dead heat
29Mar92- 4SA sl 6f    :22  :454 1:113   ⒻMd Sp Wt     71 12 1 84¾ 63¼ 32 1hd Delahoussaye E LB 117 *1.60  78-19 Lyin ToTheMoon117hdTurkFury117noSwill117 Wide trip 12
16Feb92- 6SA fst 6½f  :221 :451 1:161   ⒻMd Sp Wt     73 8 4 63¾ 43  31½ 34½ Delahoussaye E  B 117  2.40[D] 84-10 ChinBll1174Mm'm117½[D]LyinToThMoon117 Came in 3/8 8
      16Feb92-Disqualified and placed seventh
LATEST WORKOUTS   Aug 29 Dmr 6f fst 1:124 H   Aug 23 Dmr Ⓣ 6f fm 1:161 H   Aug 17 Dmr 3f fst :361 B   Jly 28 Hol 6f fst 1:15 H
```

With my normal methods of analysis, these fillies looked almost equal in ability. Her Elegant Ways had earned a slightly better speed figure. Both had impressed me visually; certainly, neither had benefited from an easy trip. But the fractional times told a different story. The fractions of Her Elegant Ways' last race had been 1:12 and 1:43. She had been a half-length behind at the six-furlong mark and the finish, so her five-sixteenths fraction had been the same as the leader's, 31 seconds. On the above chart, that was the equivalent of a quarter mile in :24⅘. The fractions of Lyin to the Moon's last race had been 1:13⅕ and 1:43⅖ — or a closing fraction of :30⅕. She had rallied from 5½ lengths behind to a neck behind — a gain of slightly more than five lengths. Since five lengths equals one second, her own last fraction had been :29⅕. This was the equivalent of a final quarter mile in a spectacular :23⅖. On the basis of this measurement, she appeared to be much superior to Her Elegant Ways. And she was. The two of them were abreast after three-quarters of a mile, when Lyin to the Moon proceeded to run away from the field to score a six-length victory over Her Elegant Ways.

Another turf event for fillies turned out to be the crucial race of the whole Del Mar meeting for me, the one that ensured me of a winning meeting at a track I had once found inscrutable.

These were the horses with the top turf figures in the Grade II Del Mar Oaks:

Golden Treat — Ch. f. 3(Feb), by Theatrical—Golden Dust, by Dusty Canyon

DESORMEAUX K J (161 38 22 31 .24) — Br.—Offutt-Cole Farm (Ky)

Own.—Golden Eagle Farm — Tr.—Mandella Richard (37 5 10 7 .14) — **120**

Lifetime 10 3 4 1 $329,963 — 1992 6 2 3 0 $287,685 — 1991 4 1 1 1 $42,278 — Turf 1 1 0 0 $49,350 — Wet 2 0 0 0

8Aug92- 5Dmr fm 1 Ⓣ:463 1:102 1:351 ⒻSnClemnteH 92 8 2 1hd 1½ 1½ 1¾ Desormeaux K J LB 121 *2.00 95-14 GoldenTret121¾MorristonBelle118 1½Alysbell118 All out 8

1May92- 9CD fst 1⅛ :481 1:122 1:512 ⒻKy Oaks 88 3 3 4¾ 41¾ 31 41¼ Desormeaux K J LB 121 4.50 86-13 LMLMNt121½PlstSt121½PrspctrsDlt121 Brushed,weakened 6
1May92-Grade I

12Apr92- 9OP fst 1 1/16 :464 1:114 1:433 ⒻFantasy 99 6 8 65½ 21 22 2½ Desormeaux K J L 121 1.80 82-21 RcThWldWnd117½GoldnTrt1216NwDnc117 Carried wide 8
12Apr92-Grade II

8Mar92- 8SA fst 1 1/16 :464 1:11 1:431 ⒻS A Oaks 90 2 2 2½ 2hd 1hd 1no Desormeaux K J LB 117 2.70 87-13 GoldnTrt117noMgiclMidn1171QunsCourtQun117 Gamely 8
8Mar92-Grade I

16Feb92- 8SA fst 1 :464 1:103 1:361 ⒻLas Virgnes 91 6 8 86¾ 64¾ 23 2nk Desormeaux K J LB 115 3.80 86-13 MgiclMiden121nkGoldenTret1154½RedBndn115 Good try 10
16Feb92-Grade I

22Jan92- 8SA fst 1 1/16 :463 1:113 1:441 ⒻⓇSantYsbel 84 1 7 63 63¼ 62½ 2hd Solis A LB 114 2.60 82-21 Crownett116hdGoldnTrt1141¾LooiCpot114 Troubled trip 9

21Dec91- 8Hol fst 1 1/16 :463 1:11 1:423 ⒻHol Starlet 81 5 6 41½ 31 55½ 57¼ McCarron C J LB 120 5.20 81-15 Magical Maiden1201LooieCapote1201SovietSojourn120 8
21Dec91-Grade I; Bothered, carried wide 1st turn, 4-wide stretch

13Nov91- 8Hol fst 7f :22 :444 1:23 ⒻMcsnBrsCup 82 1 6 43½ 32½ 42½ 32½ McCarron C J B 115 4.60 86-14 MloMlody113hdMgclMdn1142½GoldnTrt115 Steadied 1/4 6

18Oct91- 7SA fst 7f :221 :452 1:23 ⒻAlw 28000 81 3 4 43¾ 21½ 21½ 22 Nakatani C S B 118 *.60 86-17 AlNsrStr1182GldTrt1181DBsPrcss118 Wide backstretch 6

15May91- 6Hol fst 4½f :22 :452 :513 ⒻMd Sp Wt 77 6 3 32 31 1¾ McCarron C J B 117 *1.00 — — GoldenTreat117¾PeacefulRod1173½Flyctcher117 Driving 8

LATEST WORKOUTS Aug 22 Dmr 6f fst 1:112 H — Aug 5 Dmr 4f fst :473 H — Jly 30 Dmr Ⓣ 7f fm 1:27 H (d) — ●Jly 24 Hol 1 fst 1:40 H

Suivi — Ch. f. 3(May), by Diesis-GB—Quarrel Over, by One for All

SOLIS A (154 17 18 22 .11) — Br.—Whitaker Fms Inc&Mill Ridge Fm Ltd (Ky)

Own.—Broccoli Mr-Mrs Albert — Tr.—Winick Randy (5 1 1 0 .20) — **120**

Lifetime 5 2 2 0 $48,200 — 1992 5 2 2 0 $48,200 — 1991 0 M 0 0 — Turf 2 2 0 0 $36,300

7Aug92- 4Dmr fm 1 1/16 Ⓣ:473 1:121 1:423 ⒻAlw 36000 89 8 7 64 52¼ 22 1¾ Solis A LB 120 1.90 93-08 Suivi120¾CertmDeMy1175ConceptSttmnt117 5-wide 1/4 8

20Jun92- 6Hol fm 1 1/16 Ⓣ:464 1:104 1:411 3↑ⒻMd Sp Wt 88 9 5 53½ 31 11½ 12¼ Solis A LB 115 5.90 89-08 Suivi1152¼ Happy Wife1225½ Pattimech115 Rough start 12

25May92- 6Hol fst 6f :213 :444 1:093 3↑ⒻMd Sp Wt 75 6 5 46 46 55 26 Solis A LB 115 4.00 86-09 ArchsOfGold1156Sv1152GlowBrghtly115 Lugged out 3/8 11

8Apr92- 3SA fst 6½f :214 :451 1:163 ⒻMd Sp Wt 73 7 1 2½ 2½ 53 57½ Solis A B 117 *1.00 79-19 Hollyfrnkie1171¼ScondStop1174DsrtScndl117 Gave way 7

8Mar92- 4SA fst 6½f :214 :452 1:163 ⒻMd Sp Wt 81 2 4 2hd 2hd 2hd 2¾ Solis A B 117 2.90 86-08 MissionPss117¾Suivi1176½GoldenRosie117 Sharp effort 6

LATEST WORKOUTS Aug 24 Dmr Ⓣ 6f fm 1:17 H (d) — Aug 17 Dmr Ⓣ 6f fm 1:153 H (d) — Jly 30 Dmr Ⓣ 6f fm 1:144 H (d) — Jly 24 Hol 3f fst :364 B

Morriston Belle — B. f. 3(Mar), by Herat—Barkerville Belle, by Ruthie's Native

NAKATANI C S (141 15 14 12 .11) — Br.—Franks John (Ont-C)

Own.—Tucker Paula J — Tr.—Drysdale Neil (12 0 3 0 .00) — **120**

Lifetime 16 3 5 2 $182,204 — 1992 7 1 3 2 $97,565 — 1991 9 2 2 0 $84,639 — Turf 7 2 2 2 $131,600 — Wet 1 0 0 0

8Aug92- 5Dmr fm 1 Ⓣ:463 1:102 1:351 ⒻSnClemnteH 89 2 3 31½ 32 21½ 21¾ Delahoussaye E Bb 118 3.30 93-14 GoldnTrt1211¾MorristonBll1181½Alysbll118 Good effort 8

6Jun92- 8Hol fm 1 1/16 Ⓣ:463 1:101 1:41 ⒻHonymoonH 88 5 1 1½ 1hd 1hd 31½ Nakatani C S B 118 11.00 88-05 PcificSqull1151MissTurkn119½MorrstonBll118 Held well 10
6Jun92-Grade III

16May92- 8Hol fm 1 Ⓣ:46 1:092 1:333 ⒻSnrta Br Cp 88 4 2 21 21½ 21½ 31 Valenzuela P A B 118 16.30 96 — ChrAGndr116½MlhtElc116½MrrstBll118 Weakened a bit 13
16May92-Grade III

12Apr92-11Crc gd 1⅛ :501 1:144 1:544 ⒻTropPkOaks 72 1 2 31½ 32½ 25 27½ Vasquez J 122 3.20 81-11 SilntGrtnss1137½MorristonBll1221½CptivMss114 Gamely 8
12Apr92-Originally scheduled on turf

29Mar92- 9Crc fm *1 1/16 Ⓣ 1:433 ⒻAlw 23000 88 3 1 1½ 11 12 2½ Vasquez J 120 *2.20 — — FvordLdy112½MorrstnBll1201¾LnktPlsr112 Couldn't last 8

11Mar92- 9GP fm *1⅛ Ⓣ 1:50 + ⒻSwtstChnt 87 1 1 13 1½ 1½ 31 Penna D 121 *.80Ⓓ — — ChineseEmpress1141FvoredLdy114noⒹMorristonBll121 8
11Mar92-Disqualified and placed fifth

19Jan92-10GP fm 1 1/16 Ⓣ:481 1:12 1:421 + ⒻHrcsthbrd 87 6 1 12 11 12 14 Penna D 118 6.50 — — MorristonBll1184SnzzlDzzl1131MissJlsk116 Pulled away 11

30Nov91- 9Grd sly 1 :484 1:141 1:422 ⒻⓈOnt Lassie 36 1 2 2hd 76¾ 720 721¼ Dos Ramos R A 121 5.05 37-44 Prsnthsprng1161¼VllgDncr1192½VctrsLi115 Early speed 8
30Nov91- Grade III-C

16Nov91- 9Grd fst 7f :233 :472 1:253 ⒻⓇGlorosSng 63 2 3 21½ 21½ 46 46 Dos Ramos R A 122 11.35 74-22 DbrsVctr1251½Prsnthsprn114hdBcsSltn128 Not keep up 10

LATEST WORKOUTS Aug 26 Dmr Ⓣ 5f fm 1:05 H (d) — Aug 20 Dmr Ⓣ 7f fm 1:312 H (d) — Aug 1 Dmr Ⓣ 7f fm 1:281 H (d) — Jly 27 Dmr 4f fst :52 B

Each of these fillies had made one start on the Del Mar turf course, with these final fractions:

	Final Fraction	Quarter-Mile Equivalent
Golden Treat	:24⁴/₅	:24⁴/₅
Suivi	:30	:24
Morriston Belle	:24⁴/₅	:24⁴/₅

Suivi's speed figures may have been slightly inferior, but she possessed much the best finishing kick in the field. And this was a case, too, where the numbers were fully confirmed by my visual observations. Golden Treat and Morriston Belle had enjoyed easy rail trips in the San Clemente Handicap, while my notes on Suivi said she had gone five-wide on the turn and finished "like a wild horse." I singled her in the pick three and keyed her in exactas, and when she closed like a wild horse, again, to win and pay $10.60, I had broken my Del Mar hex.

And I had taken my turf-racing education a significant step further. After observing the relationship of fractional times to horses' performances, I learned that turf races are not merely different from dirt races; in many crucial respects, their nature is antithetical. Consider, for example, a horse who runs a mile on the dirt, sets the pace while running six furlongs in 1:12, then accelerates to finish with a final time of 1:36 and a solid Beyer Speed Figure. A good handicapper will not be impressed by that performance and, most likely, will throw the bum out when he runs again. A speed horse who gets the lead with a slow early pace is benefiting from the most optimal of trips, and he will usually run a deceptively fast final time. Subjected to more pressure, he will never duplicate it. But if a horse races at a mile on the turf, sets a fraction of 1:12, and finishes in 1:36, he has delivered a performance that any pace-oriented handicapper will love. He has displayed the critical ability to run a final quarter mile in 24 seconds, the kind of acceleration that usually wins races on the grass; at the same time, he has shown enough tactical speed to stay in contention early. It's a devastatingly effective combination of talents.

Conversely, consider a speedster who battles for the lead in 1:09 and tires badly to finish in 1:36 on dirt. Most handicappers would view him very favorably when he runs again. If he can avoid a similarly suicidal pace and — best of all — if he can get a clear lead, he has the potential to deliver a powerful, dominating performance. That is an elementary lesson from Handicapping 101. Yet if a horse runs the same 1:09 and 1:36 on the grass, he may not be so formidable in his next start. Yes, he may get loose and control the race by sheer virtue of his superior early speed, but raw speed doesn't translate into victory on turf nearly as often as on the dirt. If the horse doesn't have some ability to run a respectable final quarter mile, he may well get caught anyway.

The distinctive nature of turf racing and the importance of late speed are fundamental truths of handicapping, but some mathematical analysis is essential to put them to practical use. A horse may make a visually impressive run through the stretch, but whether he does it in :23⅘ or :24⅘ is the difference between excellence and mediocrity. The crude method I used at Del Mar was at least serviceable. But can horses' turf performances be measured with exactitude, as the Sartin handicappers try to do? Can a single number, based on a combination of fractional and final time, be concocted to define horses' turf performances as accurately as final-time speed figures define their dirt performances?

After a two-year intellectual odyssey that began in Australia and climaxed in Del Mar, I arrived at my answer to this critical question: I don't know. Dealing effectively with horses' closing fractions requires great precision, because a mere fifth of a second can be so significant. Trying to refine those measurements to permit comparison of fractional times on different turf courses is dauntingly difficult. Quinn's efforts to do so in *Figure Handicapping* may be instructive. Quinn is an extraordinarily diligent student of handicapping; he holds a Ph.D. in educational psychology and applies academic rigor to every phase of the game. Once he was about to implement a new money management strategy, and when I asked him about his expectations, he leafed to the bottom line of a computer analysis and said he expected to win $431,199.10. He didn't, but the point is made: Jim Quinn is not a guy who tolerates imprecision. But when he painstakingly constructed the turf-figure charts for his book, which give numerical ratings for final fractions on grass courses at the nation's tracks, he sank into a swamp of complexities. A horse who travels a quarter mile in :24 is moving at a rate of 6 seconds per sixteenth and thus should go ⁵⁄₁₆ of a mile in :30. At Aqueduct, however, Quinn's charts equate :24 with :30⅘ — a horse who is going at 6 seconds per sixteenth abruptly slows down to :6⅘. At Hollywood Park, :24 does indeed equal :30. But this same chart shows that a pitiful last quarter in :27 is the equivalent of :32⅖, suggesting that a slow horse will miraculously accelerate a sixteenth of a mile in 5⅖ seconds. Secretariat couldn't have done that.

Even if I knew how to improve significantly on Quinn's mathematics, I'm not sure the effort would be worthwhile, because any attempts to treat turf-course fractions with precision crash headlong into the same obstacles I discussed in the previous chapter: the deficiencies of the available data. The problems with the inaccuracy of beaten-lengths measurements become especially critical on the turf, where handicappers are most interested in horses who are making up a lot of ground over the final fraction. And the timing of turf races is plagued by inaccuracies. Some tracks utilize hand-timing for fractions on the grass. But the major problem is that tracks frequently put up temporary rails — which are, say, ten feet outside the normal rail — so that horses aren't always running over and digging up the same sod. When the configuration of the course is altered in this fashion, the half-mile and six-furlong points are in a new location, and electronic timing systems often are unable to measure fractional times exactly. Temporary rails were in place when a horse named Finder's Choice ran 1⅛ miles in 1:46 to set a course record at Laurel, speeding the final three eighths in 36⅗ seconds. But Turf Sciences clocked Finder's Choice's final fraction in 37.65 and, in fact, found that the race was 19 feet short of a mile and one-eighth.

These inaccuracies abound from coast to coast, and they are a great pity, because I can envision some exciting possibilities for the analysis of turf races. I have toyed with ideas for relating a horse's final quarter-mile fraction to his Beyer Speed Figure — for example, deducting two points for each fifth of a second slower than :24. It has occurred to me that the Sartin disciples and other pace handicappers may have erred by focusing on the fraction of the race from the six-furlong mark to the finish; perhaps the closing fraction should be measured from the half-mile mark to the finish. But trying to develop a precise system of analysis that is based on imprecise data is not only futile; it is dangerous. I don't want to develop a system of numbers that might tempt me to make bets on the basis of narrow edges when in fact there are so many flaws built into the system. At least when I am using my crude final fractions in conjunction with my speed figures I am conscious of their limitations. I am satisfied to use them for unambiguous situations like the Suivi race, where a horse has an edge so large that it overwhelms any inaccuracies that might go into the calculations. And I am happy, too, to benefit from understanding that a horse's finishing ability is a crucial factor on the turf, even if I don't have perfect numbers to express that ability. That concept is so important, so valuable, that an idea has been germinating in my mind: Perhaps, armed with an understanding of the distinct character of turf racing, I could go back to Australia . . .

SEVEN

Exotic Betting Strategy

Mark O'Keeffe moved to New York with the hope of getting a break in the music business, but he could never have dreamed how that break would materialize. He had played first trumpet in the all–New Mexico concert band and came east to study his instrument under a top teacher. He played at weddings and bar mitzvahs while hoping to get more serious opportunities, and, as he struggled, his main form of entertainment was the racetrack. One day at Belmont Park O'Keeffe observed that the track's bugler was so hopelessly inept that he could barely get air through his horn; New York's horseplayers, not a sympathetic breed, booed the bugler mercilessly. O'Keeffe introduced himself to a track executive, asked for an audition, and got a job, making nine appearances a day wearing a red coat. It might not have been Carnegie Hall, and the salary might have been lousy, but in one respect he had realized every racing fan's ambition: He was getting paid to go to the track.

O'Keeffe was happy that this chance to play the horses on a regular basis had coincided with the birth of the *Racing Times*. He liked betting with speed figures and had dabbled at making his own, but now, with access to the Beyer Speed Figures in this new paper, he said, "I seemed to be raking in the money." On the rainy day of January 23, 1992 — a day he will never forget — O'Keeffe thought that some of the races in Aqueduct's pick six were "no-brainers," such as the one where the horses' most recent figures looked like this:

Country Lake	56
Cyclonic Girl	47
Ballet Princess	35
Easy Magic	35
Divided Statement	30
Bejila Rose	24
Kashki	19
Gypsy Gina	12

O'Keeffe decided to risk $168 in the pick six, using several horses in three of the races and standing alone with a single horse in each of the other three. Country Lake was one of these key horses, as was a more venturesome selection named Twenty Flags, who had poor recent form but had earned good figures every time she ran in the mud. The pick six started promisingly when an 11-to-1 shot emerged from the fog to win one of the races in which he had played all of the contenders. Country Lake won easily at odds of 6 to 5, and then Twenty Flags scored at 12 to 1. O'Keeffe hit two more short-priced winners, and for the final race his ticket included four horses in a five-horse field. "I knew I had a 99 percent chance," O'Keeffe said, "and then I bumped into Bruce Levine, who trained the one horse I didn't use. He told me, 'Don't worry, I can't win.'" So it was almost anticlimactic when O'Keeffe hit the pick six; when the payoff appeared on the tote board, he saw that he had won $12,842 — approximately what he had expected. But then he heard a horseplayer near him exclaim, "One winner!" and he looked again. He had misread the price. The pick six had in fact returned $128,420, and the only winning ticket was in the bugler's pocket. "I was in control," he said. "It surprised me. I've felt more emotion with $50 on an 8-to-5 shot. I guess maybe I couldn't believe it."

O'Keeffe treated himself to a trip to New Mexico, where he visited friends and made a trip to Santa Fe Downs. He asked, "Where's the bugler?" and he soon found himself discussing job possibilities with track executives. They couldn't afford to hire him solely as a bugler, but they were impressed by the story of his pick six triumph, and they offered him a job that would include writing an analysis of races in the track program, serving as co-host of the track's in-house television program, and bugling at both Santa Fe Downs and Albuquerque Downs. O'Keeffe loved the whole idea. He used some of his pick six winnings to buy a house in New Mexico, moved there in December 1992, and started his new career. The pick six had conferred professional legitimacy on him and changed his life.

This is every horseplayer's dream. For much of my gambling life I would think, whenever I sat down to handicap a day's races, "This could be the *Racing Form* that changes my life." Some of them did. As the racing industry offers increasing numbers of high-paying exotic wagers — which are defined as bets involving three or more horses — the opportunities for spectacular wins have increased greatly. Of course, the vast majority of racing fans will never collect a six-digit payoff, and many will never win in five digits, either, but the possibility is what makes racetrack betting much more exciting today than it was in the win-place-and-show era. And, I would argue, it is the one aspect of the modern game which makes playing the horses a rational financial activity.

Obviously, most of us bet because we love the game. I have never heard of anyone trudging into a racetrack, grumbling, "I hate this place but I've got to earn a living somehow." If Mark O'Keeffe had never won $128,420 in an afternoon, he still would be an enthusiastic horseplayer who enjoys going to the track every day. But if playing the horses was no more fun than, say, being a corporate lawyer, would there be any reason to go to the track? Can an expert bettor expect to earn a dependable, healthy income that justifies all the work involved in serious handicapping? Certainly, the answer to that question used to be affirmative. Legendary gamblers like Pittsburgh Phil reportedly made fortunes at the track. My friend Al Torch, whose professional gambling experience antedates mine by a decade, says that in the 1960s an expert handicapper could reasonably expect to make as much as the president of the United States. I can attest that in the late 1970s and early 1980s, I would start each year confident of earning at least a healthy upper-middle-class income. But I feel no such confidence today, and if Pittsburgh Phil were resurrected, he too would probably say that playing the horses is a much less attractive game than it used to be. The main reason for the change is the oppressive level of taxation that horseplayers face.

For most of my gambling life, I was only dimly conscious of the effect of the parimutuel takeout on a horseplayer's bottom line. But now I am keenly aware of it. Imagine a professional gambler who starts a year with a $15,000 bankroll. He goes to the track every day, bets an average of $300 on every race, and quadruples his money by the end of the year, showing a profit of $45,000. He will feel justifiably proud that he has mastered a difficult game, and he may feel that his mastery is unshakable. But his success is in fact very tenuous. He has been putting some $900,000 a year through the mutuel windows and is earning a profit of 5 percent on his total turnover. If a track takes an extra 1 percent from his (and everybody else's) handle, his annual profit decreases by $9,000. If the takeout rises 3 percent, his profits will diminish to the point that he can no longer support himself by gambling. If the takeout increases 5 percent, he will no longer be a winner. And if the takeout were to go up 7 percent, his initial bankroll would be wiped out and he would be broke.

America's horseplayers have all been affected by such cruel arithmetic. In 1970 the total takeout on all racetrack wagers was 16 percent. In 1992 it had risen to approximately 20 percent. When I was enjoying such great success in Florida in the 1970s, the takeout was 17 percent. At the 1993 Gulfstream Park meeting, the takeout on exactas and trifectas had soared to 24 percent. Across the country, tracks were confiscating higher and higher percentages, especially from multiple wagers. Tampa Bay Downs blazed new trails in 1993 by imposing a 28 percent takeout on exactas. Philadelphia Park took a 30 percent bite from trifectas.

Economist Maury Wolff compiled irrefutable evidence that a

higher takeout almost always winds up hurting racetracks because their customers are knocked out of action; indeed, business was disastrously bad at Tampa Bay and Philadelphia Park. But track managements don't get the message, and state legislatures don't care about it. The trend in takeout has been up, up, up. Its harmful effects have been compounded by the federal withholding tax on certain gambling winnings and also by an ever-growing number of state withholding taxes. (A customer at a New York City off-track betting parlor who hits a large trifecta, having already been subjected to a 25 percent takeout plus a 5 percent surcharge, will be assessed a 4.46 percent city withholding tax and a 7.59 percent state withholding tax on top of the 28 percent federal withholding tax.) And, of course, this escalation of taxation has occurred at a time when the sophistication of bettors has increased dramatically, when the population of hunch players at the track has diminished, when the parimutuel competition has grown so fierce that it is hard for good handicappers to find a significant edge even if the takeout were low. If eight world-class poker players sat down at a table in which the house took even a modest cut out of every pot, none of them could reasonably expect to win — or even to survive — over a game of reasonable duration. That is the situation in which horseplayers find themselves today.

Racing industry executives constantly complain about the competition their sport faces from other forms of gambling, and rightly so, because some other forms of gambling are more attractive than playing the horses. Twice as much money is bet illegally on sports in America than is bet on horses, and the reason is easy to understand. Bettors are working at a 4½ percent disadvantage when they wager with their local bookie on a football game, not 17 to 25 percent. An able handicapper has a decent chance to surmount those odds, for betting on sports is a game of skill and judgment, and a game considerably more honest than horse racing. Moreover, bookies offer credit, don't charge admission, don't charge two bucks for a Coke, and don't withhold 28 percent when a customer hits a six-team parlay. They may even send their clients a bottle of booze for Christmas.

Despite the harsh realities of horse betting today, most authors and academic experts continue to counsel betting strategies that seem rooted in the 1960s, when it was possible to grind out a slow, steady profit at the track and when, in the win-place-and-show era, that was the only way to play the game, anyway. For Howard Sartin's disciples, the orthodox method is to bet two horses to win in the same race. Among sophisticated students of betting strategy, the favored approach is the Kelly Criterion, in which a gambler wagers a certain percentage of his total bankroll according to the proved percentages of winners that he picks and the average mutuel price that they pay. (In this era of exotic betting, I don't know any people who define themselves as horseplayers by saying, "I pick 28 percent winners at an average win mutuel of $8.40," but among the academics they evidently exist.) The Sartin disciples and the Kelly Criterionists were much in evidence at the 1984 National Conference on Thoroughbred Handicapping, where I participated in a money management seminar, and they all tittered when I proposed a strategy for them: "If you want a steady, dependable source of income, get a job."

I wasn't joking. As the parimutuel takeout has increased and the sophistication of the betting public has grown, winning at the track has become most difficult for the conservatives who aspire to grind out steady profits by finding solid opportunities day after day. Yet, despite all its present drawbacks, the horse-betting game still has one unmatchable virtue, which people engaged in other forms of gambling and more conventional forms of investment can only envy: It offers a chance to turn moderate capital into spectacular profits. Mark O'Keeffe wouldn't have bought his house in New Mexico by laying 11-to-10 odds on a football game. A single bet can sometimes change a horseplayer's life, and it can often make his whole year a success. Many excellent handicappers acknowledge that their profits are more apt to come from occasional windfalls than from day-in, day-out success, and they play the game accordingly. They direct much of their effort and their bankroll toward exotic wagers, and while this may seem very risky, there are in fact sound mathematical arguments for such a strategy.

A bettor gets more value for his money by playing several horses or several races at a single high takeout than by betting a single horse to win, place, or show at a lower takeout. American horse-players used to relish the daily double when it was the only form of multiple betting available, because it let them play two horses for the price of one bet and regularly paid more than a two-horse parlay. It was the best bargain that racetracks offered. Now horse-players can play three, six, or more horses for the price of a single bet — and these exotic wagers are a bargain, too. Barry Meadow, a professional gambler and writer from California, explained in *Money Secrets at the Racetrack* the mathematics of this advantage. If three horses are genuine even-money shots, with a 50 percent probability of winning, there is a 1-in-8 chance that they all will win. (The probability is $\frac{1}{2} \times \frac{1}{2} \times \frac{1}{2} = \frac{1}{8}$.) If there were no takeout, a $2 bet on this proposition should return $16. With a 25 percent takeout in a pick three, the return would be $12. But if a bettor played the same three horses in a parlay at a track with a 16 percent takeout from win bets, the return would be a paltry $8.20, because that bite was taken three separate times. Steve Crist, the former editor of the *Racing Times,* makes the same point about his favorite wager, the pick six: "Even on a bad day, the pick six may pay 100 percent higher than a parlay. It offers far more value than any other wager."

Wagers like the pick six may also offer an opportunity that was unimaginable in the gambling world before the creation of carry-over jackpots. The percentages may actually shift in the bettors' favor. On the day Mark O'Keeffe won the pick six at Aqueduct, there was (using round numbers) a modest $48,000 carryover jackpot. Bettors that day wagered a total of $142,000 on the pick six, of which 25 percent — or $35,500 — went to the New York Racing Association and Mario Cuomo. That left $106,500 in the day's pool, plus the $48,000 carryover, to be paid to O'Keefe and to the holders of tickets with five winners — a total of $154,500. There was, on this day, a reverse takeout: Bettors got back 8 percent more than they wagered. The advantage can grow much greater as the carryover becomes larger; on some days, a track will pay out 40 percent more than the public puts in.

Exotic wagers also give a handicapper the chance to capitalize on his strongest opinions, even when a horse's odds are less than spectacular. I do not intend to minimize or abandon speed figures just because so many bettors have recognized their virtues, resulting in lower payoffs. That would seem to be an exercise in throwing out the baby with the bathwater. I would prefer to use speed figures as the basis for exotic wagers that could produce a bonanza. Country Lake, the speed-figure standout on O'Keeffe's memorable day at Aqueduct, was worthless as a win-betting proposition at 6 to 5, but was nevertheless a useful, solid foundation for a pick six wager.

When a handicapper starts playing the exotics, especially the more complex ones like the pick six, he will quickly discover that good handicapping is not necessarily the key to success. I learned this from my association with Steve Crist, the best pick six bettor I know. When we were at the track together in New York and Florida, we would regularly discuss the card, and since Steve is a figure-oriented handicapper, too, we would usually be in general agreement about the horses we liked and didn't like. We would typically invest similar sums in our respective pick six plays. But time after time, Crist would manage to win when I didn't, because he always seemed to have the optimal combination of horses on his ticket or because he had taken a flyer with the one implausible longshot that had busted me out. In exotic betting, the nature of the game changes; there is much less emphasis on the traditional, pure task of doping out a winner and much more on strategy. In a pick six, after all, a handicapper who is confused about a race can always mark the "all" box on his betting slip, eliminating any indecision with the stroke of a pencil. Knowing when to do it is what's important. So before committing a significant part of his bankroll to any exotic wager, a horseplayer had better think about — and master — the appropriate strategy.

THE PICK SIX

Originated at Caliente Race Track in Mexico in the 1950s, the pick six became a mania when it was introduced in California in the early 1980s. This was the first time that horseplayers anywhere had a regular opportunity to win six-figure payoffs, and Californians eagerly studied the intricacies of the new wager, looking for any edge they could find. They learned that the obvious way of playing the pick six is absolutely the wrong way.

It might seem natural for us to analyze the six races, choose our contenders in each, and play one ticket, like this:

Race	Horses
1	3
2	2-7-9
3	1-4
4	2-4-6-8-9-10-12
5	7
6	1-2

The number of combinations on a ticket is calculated by multiplying the number of selections in each race. In this case, with one horse in Race 1, three horses in Race 2, etc., the number of combinations is $1 \times 3 \times 2 \times 7 \times 1 \times 2$, or 84. This total is multiplied by the price of the basic wager, $2: The ticket costs $168. Although it may seem logical and straightforward, a pick six play on a single ticket seriously limits a handicapper's options. Suppose, in the above play, that after deciding to stand alone in the first race with one solid horse, No. 3, we began to perceive some virtues in No. 7, an esoteric 30-to-1 shot. If that horse won, he could eliminate just about everybody else from the pick six and generate a huge payoff. Should this longshot be included on our ticket? If so, the addition of this one horse would now increase the play to $2 \times 3 \times 2 \times 7 \times 1 \times 2$, or 168 combinations, for a cost of $336. One longshot flyer would double the whole cost, and the horse probably doesn't merit such a large investment. So the California bettors conceived a strategy for using horses like No. 7 in a limited capacity. They divided their contenders for each race into two categories, their main horses and their backup horses, in this fashion:

Race	Main	Backup
1	3	7
2	2-7-9	3
3	1-4	2-12
4	2-6	4-8-9-10-12
5	7	5
6	1-2	

Our main ticket, consisting of our prime contenders, the horses in the left-hand column, costs $48 ($1 \times 3 \times 2 \times 2 \times 1 \times 2 \times \$2$). Now we fashion a ticket that includes our longshot, No. 7; we substitute him for our top choice in the first race and use him on a ticket that includes the main contenders in the other races, as follows:

Race	Horse
1	<u>7</u>
2	2-7-9
3	1-4
4	2-6
5	7
6	1-2

This ticket costs $48, too. Now we move on and substitute our backup horse for the main horses in Race 2:

Race	Horse
1	3
2	<u>3</u>
3	1-4
4	2-6
5	7
6	1-2

This ticket costs a mere $16. We proceed to fill out five such backup tickets (we had no backup horses in the sixth race) in addition to the main ticket; the total cost comes to $328.

In every form of exotic wagering, it is important to be able to calculate the cost of an investment readily and accurately. Many a pick six player has had the experience of walking to a mutuel window a few minutes before post time, turning in his betting slips, and seeing that the wager costs hundreds of dollars more than he had reckoned, necessitating a late and panicky revision. To calculate the size of an investment using main and backup horses, first find the cost of the main ticket. The cost of each backup ticket simply depends on how many backup horses are substituted for how many horses on the main ticket. If two backup horses are inserted for one main-ticket horse, the cost of that ticket is double that of the main ticket. If, in the above case, one backup horse is substituted for three main-ticket horses, the cost of that ticket is one-third — or $16 instead of $48.

The virtues of this method ought to be clear. It often takes only one longshot to make a pick six ticket extremely lucrative. Trying to get, say, two 30-to-1 shots on the same ticket is superfluous, implausible, and prohibitively expensive. Attempting to get one marginal, backup horse on a winning ticket gives the player a chance to include many more horses in his total play for less money. There are, of course, many variations on the basic theme. A bettor who thinks his main-ticket horses are particularly vulnerable in two races might fashion an extra ticket in which he plugs in the backup horses for both of those races along with the main-ticket horses in the other four. A bettor might design a combination of tickets which will permit any two backup horses to win in conjunction with four main-ticket horses.

The pick six can be played in even more elaborate ways, and probably it should be, based on my observations of Steve Crist's success. Crist neatly summed up the nature of his often-complex approach by suggesting that the pick six would be better understood if it had a different name: the "avoid one." Anybody who has ever played the pick six knows how difficult it is to survive six races without encountering at least one implausible, unforeseeable result. So, Crist said, "I try to give myself the chance to be wrong on one race if I can be right in enough other spots. If I am right four times, I want to give myself a good chance to win those other two races. And if I'm dead right on three races, I'll use six or seven horses in a couple of the others and hope for something silly to happen." Other players devote all their energy to fine-line handicapping and then curse when one crazy result busts them out. Crist envisions the scenarios in which one crazy horse busts him out, then fills out tickets to cover as many of those scenarios as he can reasonably afford. Indeed, he may spend as much time marking pick six tickets as he does handicapping. His willingness to do so, he thinks, is one source of an edge: "The vast majority of horseplayers, even the good ones, are too lazy to mark twenty-four different pick six tickets."

Anyone who plays the pick six, even a bettor who uses many combinations, will invariably depend heavily on one or two solid horses, standing alone with them on every ticket or at least on the main ticket. In pick six parlance, these key horses are known as singles. Without them, an investment can become impossibly expensive. If there is an odds-on favorite in one of the pick six races, the vast majority of bettors at the track will be thinking, "I'll single this favorite and spread in the other races." The performance of such singles is what principally determines how much pick sixes pay, and accounts for what may seem aberrantly high or low payoffs.

Here were the results on two consecutive days at Santa Anita that were eerily similar:

Race	January 15, 1993	January 16, 1993
4	$8.20	$8.20
5	$7.40	$8.60
6	$4.20	$4.20
7	$5.80	$5.20
8	$5.00	$5.00
9	$86.60	$47.00
Parlay value	$20,001	$11,310
Pick six payoff	$8,443	$11,687

By all rights, the pick six on January 15 should have been worth more than it was the next day; the parlay value of those six winners on January 15 was nearly twice as large as on January 16, yet the pick six in fact paid $3,243 less. The reason lay in the difference between the $8.20 winners who started the pick six each day. On January 15 the winner, George's Buster, was narrowly the favorite and one of four horses who were being well supported in an evenly matched race. Anybody playing the pick six on a serious level would have included him on the ticket. But the next day's fourth race was a four-horse field in which the 3-to-1 winner, Choice Is Clear, nipped a 2-to-5 favorite, Admirallus. The latter was the only odds-on favorite in the pick six races and was, presumably, a single on many tickets. His loss brought about a five-figure payoff even on a day when there was only one slightly implausible winner.

The results of these two days at Santa Anita reflect another important aspect of pick six betting. The longshots in the final race each day did not generate blockbuster payoffs; even with an $86.60 winner, the pick six on January 15 paid a modest $8,443. The explanation is that in both cases the ninth race looked like one of the more wide-open, competitive races on a card whose other events were much more manageable. Serious players probably looked at them similarly and thought, "This is a good race to use a lot of horses and hope for something silly to happen." So the winners did not have as much of an impact on the payoff as their odds indicated. The key to playing the pick six profitably is not necessarily to come up with improbable longshots, but to use horses that other bettors don't — such as the 3-to-1 shot who upsets an odds-on favorite.

After I have done my preliminary handicapping of a pick six, I look at the selections of newspaper handicappers to get a sense of the way the public is likely to bet. If I love a horse and consider him a single, but he's going to be an even-money favorite and everybody else's single, there is no edge in the pick six. If I love a horse who may be 5 to 2 but who is in a seemingly wide-open race where the public will be using many contenders, that constitutes a valuable edge. And the best situation of all, of course, arises when the public will be singling a favorite who is very vulnerable. Disliking a 3-to-5 shot may be as good a basis for a pick six play as finding a horse who looks like a certain winner.

When one horse does appear to be an overwhelming, unbeatable favorite, a pick six player should ask himself: If something unforeseen happens to this favorite, who wins the race? If the rest of a field is evenly matched, it is too costly to play a backup ticket which uses, say, six other horses in an attempt to beat the favorite. But when there is clearly a second-best horse in the field, it may be relatively economical to take a shot for an upset that will eliminate most bettors from the pick six.

In the 1988 Breeders' Cup at Churchill Downs, the standout of the day was Easy Goer in the Juvenile. He was the most brilliant American 2-year-old of the decade, and he had just won the Champagne Stakes at Belmont Park with a runaway victory over Is It True, earning a figure of 116. Even though the track at Churchill Downs was muddy, and Easy Goer had never raced in the mud, no handicapper in his right mind would take a bold stand against this champion. Nevertheless, it was feasible to play the pick six to take a chance that he might lose. These were the last four figures for the main contenders in the field:

Easy Goer	116	110	113	102
Is It True	108	101	110	97
Music Merci	69	100	94	73
Double Quick	84	93	62	76
Into Bucks	81	93	78	40
Leading Prospect	71	80	57	44
Mountain Ghost	62	91	79	89
Tagel	(raced in Europe)			

If Easy Goer for some reason did not run his race, then the colt he had trounced in New York, Is It True, was a standout over the rest of the field. With only this one other horse to consider, it was economical to fashion a pick six ticket that allowed for a possible upset. When Easy Goer didn't handle the mud and the 9-to-1 Is

It True beat him, a pick six otherwise dominated by favorites returned more than $15,000.

This Breeders' Cup race underscored the principle that handicapping a race for the pick six is unlike handicapping a race normally. In order to be successful, a gambler usually needs to be opinionated and bold. I will frequently declare, "This horse can't lose!" or "Throw this favorite out!" A handicapper who can't muster this kind of confidence is never going to make a giant score. There are times I may play a $500 exacta, one way, and stubbornly refuse to reverse it because I have an ironclad conviction. If I had been betting an exacta in the Breeders' Cup Juvenile, I might have played a cold Easy Goer–Is It True combination. But hard-headed confidence is a fatal flaw for a pick six player, for it is rarely a good idea to view a horse as unbeatable or to take a strong stand against a particular horse. When Crist and I would compare notes on a pick six, I would frequently say that I had singled such-and-such a horse or played on the assumption that a certain thing would happen and I would ask, "What was your approach?" But it was the wrong question entirely. Crist tried to avoid having what could be characterized as a single approach, and that kind of flexibility is the secret of playing the pick six.

THE PICK THREE

The pick three was introduced in 1986 in California, where it is called the daily triple, and it became instantly popular there — partly because of the inherent virtues of the wager, and partly because horseplayers at Santa Anita, Hollywood Park, and Del Mar were starved for action. The paternalistic managements of the western tracks have long objected to trifectas, and they meted out exactas in small quantities in order to protect their customers from the temptations of these riskier wagers. Because of the pick three's success in the West, tracks around the country started to offer it, but they found their customers much less enthusiastic. At Gulfstream Park, which offers exactas and trifectas on every race and two pick threes a day, there might be $100,000 in every exacta and trifecta pool but only $45,000 in a pick three pool. Fans at most tracks outside the West have shown similar preferences, partly because they have a longer familiarity with exactas and trifectas, but also because they see them as better wagers. And there is a good reason for this preference.

When a horseplayer handicaps a racing card, he may consider himself fortunate to locate one solid betting opportunity; it is a rare day, indeed, when he will find several. If he has a strong opinion on one race, it makes more sense to bet an exacta or a trifecta rather than to play that race in a combination with other races where he has no insights. That is why exactas have eclipsed daily doubles in popularity, and that is why most horseplayers — when they are given a choice — prefer trifectas to pick threes.

Therefore, I believe that a sound rule governing pick threes is this: A handicapper must have good insights or solid convictions about two of the three races in order to bet at all. If I love a 5-to-2 shot in a pick three event but have no opinions in the other two races, I see little sense in playing many contenders in the other races and praying for longshots to win. Too many bad things can happen to wreck the bet. I would rather play that 5-to-2 shot in exactas or trifectas or as a single in a pick six.

What constitutes a good insight or solid conviction in a pick three race? Pretty much the same factors as in the pick six. Because small-scale bettors will typically single at least one horse on a pick three ticket, a handicapper should identify the horse or horses most likely to be singled and judge whether they are especially vulnerable. Barry Meadow is a serious student of the pick three, and in *Money Secrets at the Racetrack* he summed up his approach: "Without an edge, there is no point in playing the pick three. If you like the same horses as everyone else, to the same degree, skip the pick three, just as you'd pass a 4-to-5 shot if you think his odds are too low, even if he's the most likely winner. . . . But several situations yield potential pick three profits — and if you restrict your action to these circumstances, you can do well:

"1. The public is certain to overbet a horse you hate.
"2. The public is certain to underbet a horse you like.

"3. At least one and preferably two of the races are wide open, which will eliminate small bettors who can afford to use only the top one or two choices."

This is sound counsel. When a bettor has determined that a pick three might offer decent value, he may then construct a play in the manner of a pick six, with main-ticket and backup horses in each race. In the pick six, however, a bettor is almost always playing to have one winning ticket. In the pick three, he can afford to bet more combinations and to vary the size of the wagers. Let us say that our pick three looks like this:

Race	Main Ticket	Backup
1	2-5	6
2	3	1-4-10
3	1-9	2-3-6

Our main ticket has only four combinations. Our three backup tickets will have 2, 12, and 6 combinations respectively — a total of 20. These should not be playing in equal strength. A horseplayer should approach the pick three, and virtually all wagers, with this philosophy: I am betting because I have a strong opinion, and if that opinion is right I want to make a big score. If I am reasonably accurate in my handicapping of the same race, but not perfect, I want to make a small profit or at least protect myself. If I am wrong, I shall suffer the consequences. Therefore, in the above pick three, a reasonable play might be to put $20 on the four main ticket combinations and $5 on each of the eighteen backup combinations.

Given the greater manageability of pick three investments, a bettor might also want to play a minimum $2 or $3 ticket that includes every backup horse with every other backup horse. In the pick six it is too expensive, and usually superfluous, to try to get two remote longshots on the same ticket, but in the pick three it can be cheap enough to shoot for an occasional bonanza in this fashion.

THE TRIFECTA

The trifecta has become the most popular wager in American racing, despite the best efforts of the industry to make it unattractive. Almost all states impose an onerous level of takeout on the trifecta. Many tracks offer only one or two trifectas a day, on the cheapest, least handicappable races. Yet horseplayers love to bet them, anyway. At Aqueduct and Belmont, the ninth-race trifecta is typically offered on a sorry field of maiden New York–breds, but even so, the handle on that trifecta will be larger than any exacta pool, larger than the pick six pool, and two or three times the size of any win pool. When I am named the czar of American racing, I shall decree that trifecta wagering be offered on every race, because it is absurd to deny the public the opportunity to bet as it wants. I shall also decree that takeout be reduced to the level of other wagers.

The public's fondness for trifectas is well founded. When a bettor holds a strong opinion on a race, he is apt to have insights about the whole race, not just one horse. If he dislikes an even-money favorite and is correct, why not try to capitalize fully on that opinion and throw the favorite out of a trifecta, shooting for a huge payoff? If a race looks as if it might be characterized by a destructive pace that kills all the speed, why not try to turn that insight into a crusher score by playing a trifecta with closers running 1-2-3?

Despite the proved popularity of trifectas and the great opportunities for profit they offer, there is a scarcity of literature on strategy for this wager. The reason, in part, is that so many handicapping books are written by Californians, who haven't had much exposure to trifectas; many others are written by wimps whose idea of ecstasy is collecting a $2.80 show payoff that they deem to be an overlay. However, my experiences in Australia convinced me that trifecta strategy is a subject worthy of thought and study, because astute bettors like Mr. D. found their best opportunities in the trifecta pools — for reasons that surely apply in the United States, too.

While a horse's odds may accurately reflect his chances of winning, trifecta pools are not nearly so efficient. Certain combinations are considerably overbet in relationship to their probability of winning, and other combinations are greatly underbet. Mr. D. had designed a computer program that achieved close to break-even results by playing the combinations that were mathematically most favorable and avoiding the unfavorable ones — and this was before he had exercised any handicapping judgment. After he had applied his own opinions, trifectas were the basis of his professional success. Regardless of the strength of his handicapping convictions, though, Mr. D. would always steer clear of the combinations that did not promise to offer value. His top choices in a race might be, in order, 7, 9 and 1, but when his computer spit out 100 trifectas for him to bet, there might be only a token wager on the 7-9-1 combination — or none at all.

What constitutes a trifecta that offers good value or poor value? A combination of three favorites will usually yield an undervalued payoff. A combination of three extreme longshots will usually return much less than its probabilities suggest it should. But the central fact in all trifecta betting is this: Large numbers of bettors play this wager by boxing horses — by taking all the combinations of certain numbers. (A three-horse box of 1, 7, and 9 would be six combinations: 1-7-9, 1-9-7, 7-1-9, 7-9-1, 9-1-7, 9-7-1.) Some tracks give small-scale players an incentive to play this way by permitting $1 wagers on a trifecta box but not on straight combinations. Boxing horses is not inherently a bad bet — such as betting a longshot to show, for example — but by its very nature it involves placing an equal amount of money on each combination, even though those combinations may not have remotely similar chances of winning.

If, for example, a horseplayer boxes three horses who are 6 to 5, 4 to 1, and 20 to 1, a trifecta combination with the 6-to-5 shot winning has a vastly greater chance of winning than the one with the 20-to-1 shot on top. And there will be enough similar wagers in the pool that if these horses do finish 1-2-3, with the 20-to-1 shot winning, the payoff will be disappointingly small. Indeed, some customers may be grumbling that larceny was afoot, that sinister forces must have loved the 20-to-1 shot because the trifecta paid such a short price. Conversely, if the 6-to-5, 4-to-1, and 20-to-1 shots finish in that order, the trifecta is apt to pay a price that will seem surprisingly high, considering that the two obvious horses ran 1-2.

In general, trifectas are a good bet when a favorite wins with anything but the most obvious other contenders second and third. They are a good bet when a favorite runs out of the money. They are an inferior bet when a solid favorite finishes second or third. Handicappers should be aware of the situations that will yield more or less value and tailor their bets accordingly.

If I dislike a favorite, I may play many trifecta combinations in the hope that he will be out of the money. If I like a horse at a decent price but believe that a solid favorite is likely to be in the money, I will look for betting options other than the trifecta. But trifectas are most useful for enhancing the value of a short-priced horse. If a horse with a standout speed figure is the favorite, I will always prefer to play him on top in a trifecta unless I think there is a great likelihood that the second and third choices are going to dominate the rest of the field. Sometimes I will "key" the horse — using him in the top position with my other contenders second and third. The total of combinations in such a play is calculated by multiplying the number of other contenders times that number minus one. If I am keying No. 1 over 6, 7, 8, and 9, there are four other horses, and the number of combinations is 4 × 3, or 12, as follows:

1-6-7 1-7-6 1-8-6 1-9-6
1-6-8 1-7-8 1-8-7 1-9-7
1-6-9 1-7-9 1-8-9 1-9-8

However, an even better way to play trifectas is to put a solid horse on top, with the stronger contenders used in the second and third spots and marginal contenders in the third position only. Some outsiders may not figure to do better than to sneak into third place, but if they do, they can generate sensational trifecta payoffs.

To calculate the cost of such a ticket with a single horse on top, multiply the number of horses in the second position by the number of horses in the third position minus one. If No. 1 is being used in the top position, with 6, 7, and 8 in the second spot and 6, 7, 8, 9, 10, 11 in the third spot, there are 3 × (6-1) or 15 combinations:

1-6-7	1-7-6	1-8-6
1-6-8	1-7-8	1-8-7
1-6-9	1-7-9	1-8-9
1-6-10	1-7-10	1-8-10
1-6-11	1-7-11	1-8-11

I have spent enough time fidgeting in lines at mutuel windows to understand that a surprising number of horseplayers — even sophisticated ones — don't know how to ask for such a ticket. Many limit their bets to the ones they can express easily. The magic words in making multiple wagers are "part wheel" and "with" — which correspond to buttons on American Totalizator machines and which mutuel clerks everywhere recognize. A part wheel is a wager involving two or more components, and "with" separates those components. The above bet is properly called: "Trifecta part wheel: 1 with 6-7-8 with 6-7-8-9-10-11."

Of course, there are many sound ways to bet the trifecta besides using a single horse on top. When a play involves many combinations, I will structure it so that I have my largest investment on my primary horses and smaller wagers on the marginal ones, as in the pick three. Nevertheless, this is an area in which I feel that I — like the rest of America's horseplayers — have only skimmed the surface. I have never approached racetrack betting by looking for purely mathematical methods — I leave this task to others — but trifecta-betting strategy would appear to be one of the most promising unexplored frontiers in the game.

THE TWIN TRIFECTA

The twin trifecta (or double triple) might appear to be about as difficult as the pick six. A bettor has to select the first three finishers in two different races, and the mathematical probability of hitting these six numbers is about the same as picking six winners. But the twin trifecta is, in fact, much more elusive than the pick six, and its greater degree of difficulty demands a wholly different betting philosophy.

Pick six bettors have the luxury of trying to handicap winners, and it is often relatively easy to separate contenders from noncontenders. But a bettor playing the twin trifecta must deal with noncontenders who still may find a way to stagger home in third place — as they often do. (That is why I like to play normal trifectas with tickets including outsiders in the third position.) Moreover, the races that make up a twin trifecta will almost always be full fields of cheap horses. There are no 4-to-5 shots who can be singled to ease a bettor's task, which is one reason the twin trifecta came into existence. After California's initial success with the pick six, many smaller tracks offered pick sixes of their own, with disappointing results. Because their betting pools are smaller, they need more time for jackpots to grow and start attracting serious wagers. But racing secretaries cannot card pick sixes that foil bettors day after day. It takes only one card with a few small fields and a couple of odds-on favorites to make the pick six an easy target for decent handicappers; then the jackpot will be back to zero again. But with the twin trifecta, a racing secretary has to put on only two difficult races a day — such as maiden races with twelve-horse fields — and he can keep a jackpot building for weeks.

Pick six bettors who confront a troublesome race can always choose to spend a bit more money and add a horse or two to their ticket. But in a twin trifecta, every horse can increase the cost of the ticket exponentially. If the unit of the wager is $2, boxing three horses in each of the twin trifecta races costs $72. Boxing four horses in each costs $1,152. Boxing five in each costs $7,200. Bettors do not casually decide to throw another horse into their ticket.

Because of this degree of difficulty, a bettor should pass the twin trifecta if there are too many unknown quantities in the races, such as first-time starters or horses who have been laid off. It is too expensive to include these horses in a twin trifecta investment and too dangerous to leave them out. A handicapper must have solid opinions that enable him to narrow the contenders sharply in at least one of the two fields — and preferably in both.

The twin trifecta is very different from the pick six, or virtually any other wager, for that matter, in that a bettor doesn't need to concern himself too much with finding horses that the public will overlook. I might pass a pick six because it looks as if it will be dominated by favorites, but I would relish the opportunity to play an "obvious" twin trifecta. Unless favorites run 1-2-3 in both races, bettors who hit a twin trifecta rarely find the payoff to be an anticlimax. Because value is not an important consideration, there is nothing wrong with boxing horses or using a solid favorite in the third position, as there would be in a normal trifecta wager. The name of the game is to come up with a winning ticket.

For a twin trifecta race to be bettable, it should have some or all of the following features:

A key horse. If a handicapper can identify one solid horse and key him on top (or both first and second) with the other contenders, the twin trifecta becomes much more manageable. Using several contenders in equal strength is too expensive.

Absolute eliminations. Because it takes only one implausible third-place finisher to spoil a twin trifecta play, a handicapper needs to identify numerous horses who cannot possibly finish in the top three. For this reason, bettors should not necessarily be intimidated by bad maiden races; many horses in them may be so hopeless that they can be thrown out completely. (The toughest fields are often those for rock-bottom claimers who have won only one or two races in their careers. Because all of these cheap horses have shown enough life to have won a race at some time, it may be hard to find eliminations.)

Smaller-than-normal fields. When the twin trifecta jackpot is growing, an attractive opportunity may arise when a track cards races with less than full fields. Even one or two late scratches can change the mathematics of the wager profoundly. With a pair of twelve-horse fields, there are 1.74 million possible outcomes to the twin trifecta. Reduce each field to eleven horses, and there are 980,100 possible results.

In the twin trifecta, a bettor does not make all of his wagers at once. He plays the first half and, if he wins, exchanges each winning combination for one combination on the second half and also collects a consolation payoff in the process. (If, for example, he holds six winning combinations, he can exchange them and box three horses.) But before making his initial wager, he should have his entire plan of attack mapped out meticulously and should know exactly how many combinations he wants to have if he gets alive.

I play the twin trifecta in much the same way that Steve Crist attacks the pick six, with multiple combinations. I will say: If I am dead right about the first half, I want to give myself maximum opportunities in the second half. If I am reasonably accurate in the first half, I'll give myself a reasonable chance in the second half. If I am barely right in the first half, I would like to be alive just enough to win if my opinion is perfect in the second half. My analysis and strategy for a twin trifecta might look like this:

FIRST RACE	SECOND RACE
Analysis:	**Analysis:**
Numbers 2, 4, and 6 are the solid contenders; 8 and 10 are marginal.	No. 1 is a solid horse with 3, 5, 7 the contenders and 9 a possibility.
First Combination:	**Exchange:**
Box 2,4,6 to be alive with 24 tickets. (Cost: $288)	Key 1 over 3, 5, 7, 9 (12 combinations)
	Key 1 in second place with 3, 5, 7, 9 (12 combinations)

(continued on page 196)

Second Combination:	Exchange:
Part wheel	**Key 1 over 3, 5, 7, 9**
2, 4, 6 with	(12 combinations)
2, 4, 6 with	
8, 10	
to be alive with 12 tickets.	
(Cost: $288)	

Third Combination:	Exchange:
Part wheel	**Key 1 over 3, 5, 7**
2, 4, 6 with	(6 combinations)
8, 10 with	
2, 4, 6, 8, 10	
to be alive with 6 tickets.	
(Cost: $216)	

In such a play I have given myself a range of opportunities. If I am dead right about the first race, with my top three horses running 1-2-3, I can give myself a maximum chance to win. If my key horse in the second race merely finishes first or second with any of the four other contenders, I will win the twin trifecta. But if I am barely right about the first race, with one of my marginal horses, 8 and 10, finishing second, I'll still have an outside chance to win the jackpot if my analysis of the second race is nearly perfect.

THE PSYCHOLOGY OF EXOTIC BETTING

When I went to California for the first time, lured by the pick six, I felt I could handle what I knew would be the most difficult part of the wager: mental stress. I had already learned, from years of painful and costly experience, that the worst mistake any gambler can make is to let tough losses unhinge him. I had just finished writing *The Winning Horseplayer,* and this was one of my central points: When a typical bettor misses winning thousands of dollars because of a photo finish, a disqualification, or bad racing luck, he will proceed to lose thousands of dollars more because he abandons all self-control. I declared that if I lose a $10,000 photo finish, I will go to the bar, belt down a shot of Jack Daniel's, and return to the track the next day with the trauma banished from my mind.

During most of my time at Santa Anita, I wasn't picking enough decent horses to get involved in photo finishes. But one day, after making a $540 investment in the pick six, I learned what this new game was all about. I had singled horses in the first two legs of the pick six — one a speed-figure standout, the other a first-time starter whom Jeff Siegel had assured me could not lose. When they paid $7.80 and $5.80 respectively, I was in business, with several contenders in each of the remaining races. I won with a 5-to-2 shot, with a 4-to-1 shot, and then with a 9-to-1 shot who upset an odds-on favorite. The final leg of the pick six had not looked particularly interesting when I first handicapped it, but it had suddenly become the most important race of my life. There were three evenly matched contenders in the field of six, and I had all three on my ticket. I had a chance to win the entire Santa Anita pick six pool. My horses vied for the lead, and when they turned for home abreast of one another, running 1-2-3, I felt the way Sir Edmund Hillary must have felt when he got within a furlong of the summit of Mount Everest. Only one other horse, a longshot named Flint Hills, was in contention, sitting on the rail, but he had no room to run, with a wall of horses in front of him. His jockey could only sit and pray that a hole opened while I prayed that the wall would remain intact. A sixteenth of a mile from the wire, as the innermost of my speed horses began to tire and drift out, the hole opened, and Flint Hills shot through — beating me out of a $121,471 payoff.

"Welcome to the pick six, Andy," said one of the hardened press box regulars who knows that such heartbreak is an inescapable part of the game. I did, too, in theory — but I had not quite been prepared for this, and one shot of Jack Daniel's could not obliterate the thought of what might have been. The downside of a wager that can change your life is the wager that could have changed your life but didn't — and the accompanying awareness that such an opportunity may not arise for months, for years, or ever again. The advent of the exotic-wagering era has introduced to the sport unprecedented potential for pain and suffering. In addition to the excruciating defeats, a handicapper who concentrates on the exotics will necessarily endure longer droughts and losing streaks than a more conservative player. He will rarely have the confidence-building satisfaction that comes from a long succession of winning days. Because of all of the psychological pitfalls, a bettor needs to proceed cautiously if he intends to emphasize wagers like the pick six or the twin trifecta.

A bettor cannot become totally preoccupied by these high-risk forms of gambling. He must play them as part of an overall strategy that includes slightly more conservative wagers — just as a smart investor may have some of his money in treasury bonds while he is speculating in foreign currencies. While I rarely bet to win and never bet to place or show, exactas still constitute a substantial portion of my action. And I will play trifectas and pick threes with enough marginal combinations and savers that they don't necessarily constitute an all-or-nothing gamble. Even when I am betting seriously on a pick six, I will play my key horse or horses in other wagers. If I am singling a 5-to-2 shot in the pick six, I will probably bet him in the exacta, too. Many horseplayers who get involved in pick sixes commit the sin of changing the way they would ordinarily bet, looking to hedge and cover themselves if they have selected one or two winners. That is absurd; once a handicapper has made his pick six investment, he should play the rest of the card as he normally would.

Anyone who pursues pick sixes and twin trifectas ought to do so selectively. The most important decision a bettor may make is whether he wants to play at all — just as a poker player's most important move may be to fold immediately rather than get involved in a hand with inferior cards. If a handicapper has no strong opinion, he should not feel compelled to play just because a large carryover pool exists, or because he himself has contributed to that pool. Better opportunities will come soon enough. Nor should he compromise by making a scaled-down investment because he doesn't have a strong enough conviction. While it is reasonable for a horseplayer to make a smaller-than-usual win, exacta, or trifecta bet because his confidence in a particular race is not high, pick sixes and twin trifectas are not ordinarily won with halfway measures. They are unavoidably expensive wagers, and if a bettor is going to play them at all he ought to play aggressively. Steve Crist argues, "The worst pick six bet is one larger than $8 and less than $64. Anyone is entitled to a lark of up to $8. A play of $64 on a very easy card is the minimum requirement for a fighting chance. Everything in between is too much to squander and too little to maneuver with." Crist advises that a player who puts in $32 a day would be better advised to bet $192 once a week or $768 once a month and make a serious attempt to hit the wager. Either that, or join forces with other bettors to form a syndicate that can make regular serious plays. Exotic wagering will defeat both those who are too timid and those who are reckless. A bettor needs to pick his spots judiciously and then, when he commits himself, bet as aggressively as possible.

But no matter how prudently a bettor plays the exotics, he will never avoid the psychological stress involved. He will necessarily endure long waits for the one or two big scores that he hopes will make his year a success. Years ago I would monitor my performance as a horseplayer day by day, hoping to put together winning streaks that lasted several days in a row. As I have become more oriented to the exotics, I have forced myself to take a much longer view, and I am prepared to wait through many unproductive months in the expectation that one bonanza will make my overall results satisfactory. A bettor who needs more frequent gratification should adopt a more conservative strategy.

Anyone who chooses to play exotic wagers frequently must accept, too, the fact that he is going to suffer some horribly painful defeats. The $121,471 photo finish that I lost at Santa Anita was not a rare, unforeseeable bit of bad luck. It was, in a sense, almost inevitable, for it is unusual to find any six consecutive race results that are foreordained because the winning horse was so much the best. Races are routinely determined by luck, by tactics, by the bob of a head in a photo finish. Anybody who can't accept this part of the game had better find a new hobby or, at the very least, ought to avoid the potentially high-paying wagers where such defeats may jeopardize his mental health. Of course, it is human nature to remember vividly the bad luck responsible for a setback; we think of our triumphs as being fully deserved instead of remembering the good luck that may have made them possible. A horseplayer may cope better with the stressful nature of exotic wagering if he recognizes and savors the times when he has indeed won a large payoff because of a photo finish, a disqualification, or an act of God. I will always cherish the memory of the pick six that made me a winner at the 1988 Saratoga meeting.

I had been virtually resigned to a break-even month as I made a small pick six investment on the next-to-last day of the meeting. I received a perfect ride from Eddie Maple (an event that almost falls into the act-of-God category by itself) to hit a winner paying $37.80. Four other short-priced horses put me on the brink of collecting the pick six, and I didn't see how I could miss the final race, the John A. Morris Handicap. The stakes had drawn a weak group of five fillies and mares. Clabber Girl had standout speed figures, and Grecian Flight was the only front-runner; the others were overmatched. I had both contenders on my ticket.

I couldn't have imagined the way the race would develop. Angel Cordero Jr., the rider of Clabber Girl, was smart enough to realize that Grecian Flight was the only speed in the field, and so he gunned his filly out of the gate and engaged in a head-and-head duel for the lead. The pace was suicidal, and Clabber Girl and Grecian Flight both collapsed from their exertions, finishing last and next to last, a result that would have blown me out of the pick six — had it not been for the act of God that saved me.

As post time for the Morris approached, the skies over Saratoga darkened eerily. Lightning cracked in the distance, and the ensuing thunderclaps rattled the old grandstand. Suddenly a storm blew in with a ferocity more appropriate to the tropics than upstate New York. Electricity flickered off and on. The racing strip was turned into a quagmire. The storm passed after about twenty minutes, but the track was in such bad shape — and was covered with so many tree branches — that the New York Racing Association had no choice but to cancel the balance of the program. Wagers on the John A. Morris Handicap were refunded, and the pick six was turned into a pick five. When electricity was restored to the track's computer, the results were calculated, and the pick five paid $4,731. With tickets on both Clabber Girl and Grecian Flight, I had two winners — a return of $9,462. The John A. Morris Handicap was rescheduled for the next day and run as a betless exhibition race. When Clabber Girl and Grecian Flight finished last and next to last, the $9,462 was safely in my pocket, and I was congratulating myself for the brilliant handicapping that had given me another triumphant season at Saratoga. I would prefer to dwell on such memories rather than the traumas produced by exotic wagering.

EIGHT

A Week in Las Vegas

When I walked into the Mirage Hotel's Race and Sports Book to begin a week of all-out gambling and gazed at the giant television screens and electronic displays on the wall, I wondered if I had died and gone to a horseplayer's heaven. I had been in Las Vegas many times before, but now, in December 1992, there had been an explosion of racing action. The Mirage was simulcasting the entire cards from Aqueduct, Calder, Laurel, Philadelphia Park, the Fair Grounds, Hawthorne, Turfway Park, the Meadowlands, Hollywood Park, Bay Meadows, Freehold, and Garden State. Even if I showed some restraint and ignored the latter two harness tracks, I would have the chance to bet more than ninety races a day.

This was a revolutionary change for Las Vegas, for the nation's racing industry, and for horseplayers. Handicapping has always been an intensive activity; bettors try to learn every nuance of their home track and might pore over a single racing card for hours. I had always thought it would be irresponsible to bet seriously unless I had seen the trip of every horse in his previous start, knew the day-by-day biases of a racetrack, knew the tendencies of the principal trainers who operate there. Obviously, this was impossible for anybody betting ten tracks a day. But might not there be virtue in an extensive — as opposed to intensive — approach to horse betting? I had spent the entire fall gambling in the traditional fashion at Laurel; I had gone to the track every day and taken exhaustive trip notes on every horse. I was doing everything right except for one thing: I was losing money. Like so many tracks, Laurel was plagued by a shortage of horses, and the quality of its programs had declined. Unbettable cheap races, maiden races, and small fields proliferated, yet I was betting them anyway. Perhaps I could fare better in Las Vegas, where I could scan ninety possibilities a day and be much more selective about the races I would play.

Horseplayers across the country were getting similar opportunities, as many tracks overcame the technological and legal barriers that stood in the way of interstate simulcasting. But nobody offers simulcasting with the scope, the style, and the excitement of Las Vegas. Although it is popularly associated with the image of gaudy high-rollers at the craps table, Las Vegas has always had an intriguing subculture of horseplayers, too. The city is a magnet for just about anybody who has ever been thrown out of an American racetrack for an illegal act. Its horse parlors teem with rumors of larceny and intrigue; instead of the soulless combat between handicappers and parimutuel machines, Las Vegas has traditionally been a battleground between wise guys and wary bookmakers.

As recently as the early 1980s, the Vegas race books were bookie joints in the old-fashioned sense. The prototype was a joint on the Strip called the Rose Bowl, where the decor consisted of garish candy-striped wallpaper and photographs of old-time jockeys, and where high-tech electronics were noticeably absent. Entries were displayed on sheets of cardboard hung on the walls. Results and payoffs were posted with Magic Markers. There was no television; the call of the races that came over the public address system was a re-creation emanating from an office in downtown Las Vegas. Yet the atmosphere in the Rose Bowl always seemed electric, and even if the regulars couldn't see the races, they could fill in the gaps with their imagination.

I was in the Rose Bowl one day when the announcer was calling,

It's Pitman going to the lead! A customer who had bet this 40-to-1 shot started yelling, "Come on, Gonzales!" exhorting a jockey hundreds of miles away to win a race that had already taken place. *It's Pitman leading by two as they turn for home.* "I told everybody about this horse!" the customer screamed. "Everybody!" *And as they come to the wire, it's . . . an inquiry!* Because this was all a re-creation, the bettor had to wait only a matter of seconds to learn that his longshot had been disqualified. "How could they take him down?" he asked indignantly. "He never touched anybody!"

When simulcasting became a reality, the big hotels like Caesars Palace and the Hilton tried to outdo each other by constructing glitzy race books, where customers sat at desks with their own reading lights and watched the coast-to-coast action on giant screens. It was mesmerizing; a horseplayer could bet a three-horse parlay on the first race at Hollywood, the feature race at Belmont, and a race at Arlington and watch them simultaneously, larger than life.

But the essential nature of the betting warfare in Las Vegas hadn't changed. If a trainer had a first-time starter ready to win, if a sharpie was attempting to orchestrate a fixed race, or if a smart handicapper had unearthed his best betting situation of the year, they would all aspire to bet in Las Vegas, where they could get their money down without depressing their odds. The smart ones would try to use well-known Las Vegas gamblers as conduits for their money; if a high roller had just lost $100,000 at the Caesars Palace craps tables and now wanted to recoup by betting $5,000 on a longshot, the casino might be reluctant to turn him down. That was just the way Nevada race books lost huge sums on a succession of suspicious races in northern California, leading one bookmaker to declare, "I'd rather book professional wrestling than a race from Golden Gate Fields."

There were Las Vegas regulars, too, who were formidable opponents for any bookmaker. Oddsmaker Roxy Roxborough told me about one of them, the legendary Mr. C.: "He's one of the most clued-in guys in town, and he's made an art of sweet-talking bookmakers. He'll come to a race book manager and say, 'I'll give you nine or ten plays a day — $2,000 to win and $500 exactas and quinellas.' If you're a dyed-in-the-wool bookmaker, you know you can get beaten by an occasional smart horse, but you don't think anybody can beat you playing nine or ten races a day. Well, Mr. C. is a great handicapper who will win or lose 2 percent on his own opinions. But he also has private clockers working for him and he gets great information, and one of those $2,000 bets might be on a 20-to-1 first-time starter who can't lose. One day he had three big plays — a $9 winner that he handicapped, plus a $37 horse and a $40 horse he got from his clockers. He beat one joint for $100,000 in a day."

The whole city hummed with rumors of hot horses, or what the locals universally describe as steam horses or steamers. This was the local preoccupation — even though there might be twenty red herrings for every genuine hot horse that a wise guy like Mr. C. was betting. "If a stranger walks in here and wants to bet $1,000 on a horse," said a race book manager at the Stardust, "the word will have traveled all the way up and down the Strip by the time he gets out the front door. People in this town don't handicap; most of them don't know how to read the *Racing Form*. All they're looking for is the steam."

The bookmakers had one defense against the steamers; they were under no obligation to take anybody's bets. For the unwary visitor who may have heard so much about the high-rolling action in Las Vegas, the reluctance of the race books to accept wagers often came as a shock. If a customer wanted to bet even a medium-size exacta or parlay or was trying to bet a horse who had been designated a steamer, the ticket seller's computer screen would flash the words, GET APPROVAL. The seller would shout, "Key!" and a supervisor would have to key in a code to authorize the bet.

On one visit to Las Vegas I was wandering through the race book at the Sands Hotel, where conspicuous signs told customers how liberal its betting policies were — 300-to-1 limits on exactas and quinellas, for example. I glanced up at the television screen and saw that the horses were approaching the gate for a race at

Philadelphia Park and hastily consulted my speed figures. I went to the window and asked for a $30 exacta of a 7-to-2 shot over a 6-to-5 shot.

"Key!" The supervisor came to the window, contemplated my intended bet, and gravely informed me that it was too large. "We'll let you have $2 each way," he said. Thanks a lot. And this was by no means unusual. Mighty Caesars Palace turned me down when I wanted to bet $10 on a daily double at Flagler Dog Track. But there was no predictability to the policies at any of the race books. They were inconsistent, irrational, and infuriating.

By 1992, most of the leading bookmakers in Nevada had concluded that they didn't want to be bookmakers at all. Now that interstate betting was feasible, they could hook up their betting terminals to the racetracks' own parimutuel systems. They still booked bets on parlays and the popular "house quinellas" — the return is calculated by multiplying the payoff on the winner times half of the place price on the second horse — but for the most part they were happy to serve as the middleman between their customers and the track. If someone wanted to bet $1,000 on an exacta at Golden Gate Fields, the race book would happily take it, risk free, and collect a percentage for transmitting it to the track.

At the time the conversion to parimutuel wagering was gathering momentum, one new bookmaker appeared in Las Vegas determined to buck the trend. The Sport of Kings was going to to be a plush establishment devoted to horse betting. It would offer English-style fixed-odds betting on many races as well as realistic future-book prices, and it would take virtually unlimited action. Greg Peters, the entrepreneur who conceived the Sport of Kings, proclaimed that he had no fear of the Vegas wise guys. "In fifty years I've never met anybody who was a winner," he declared publicly. "Bookmakers used to pay runners 25 percent and they still drove Cadillacs and had enough money left over to buy their clients gifts. An open bookmaking place like this should make a fortune."

The Sport of Kings was the talk of the town for months before it opened. Could its bold approach succeed? The Las Vegas cognoscenti scoffed. Roxborough said, "Don't you think that if the best strategy for a bookmaker was to take all of the bets, somebody might have stumbled onto that strategy before now?"

When the Sport of Kings opened, it did indeed book wagers fearlessly. One plunger asked to bet a $40,000 quinella on the two favorites in the Alcibiades Stakes at Keeneland; the house took the action and collected when Eliza and True Affair finished 1-3. But the Las Vegas insiders quickly proved to be correct; the Sport of Kings got killed. Wise guys stung the establishment for a reported $48,000 on a 5-to-2 steamer at Philadelphia Park. Good handicappers crushed logical short-priced favorites in New York; one customer bet $1,000 on a cold pick three that paid $70. When oddsmaker Bruce Karp put up fixed odds on races in southern California, most of his prices were very astute — and elicited no action. But when he put up 30 to 1 on June's Reward in a race at Santa Anita where the horse wound up going off at 4 to 1, at least one alert bettor made the Sport of Kings pay dearly for the lapse in judgment.

The Sport of Kings reportedly lost $1 million in its first month of existence — though much of the deficit stemmed from ill-judged bookmaking of football as well as horse races. The establishment that had looked with such condescension on the timidity of other race books was forced to join them in the conversion to parimutuel betting. If there had been any doubt before the Sport of Kings' experiment, the future of horse betting in Las Vegas had been decided — and it was parimutuel.

This was, in most respects, a welcome change. While serious handicappers were losing the chance to make large wagers without affecting the track odds, they now could shoot for large payoffs on trifectas, pick threes, pick sixes, pick nines — which Las Vegas establishments had been understandably reluctant to book. Moreover, the whole ambience of the race books was altered. In the past, they had properly viewed their customers as dangerous adversaries; they rarely rolled out the red carpet for big bettors — as the hotels' casino operations do — because those bettors might be astute enough to cost the house money. Now they loved handicappers.

•   •   •

I had gone to Las Vegas for a final one-week gambling binge before chaining myself to my word processor to write this book. This week would be one of total immersion in the speed figures that were my subject. I mapped out a basic approach to studying ninety races a day — the handicapping version of the Evelyn Wood Speed-Reading System.

I would immediately identify the horse with the best figure in his most recent race and determine whether he might have a clear edge over his rivals. Was he a double or a triple figure? Or, perhaps, were there two or three horses in the field who had a significant edge over all the rest?

I would scan the past performances and make a superficial assessment of the likely pace of the race. Was there possibly a sole front-runner who could get the lead easily? Or were there several tearaway speed horses who would ensure a hot pace and set up the race for a come-from-behind runner?

I would try to watch races at each track attentively enough to judge if any strong bias existed. This isn't always easy when several races may be run simultaneously, and I knew I wouldn't be able to detect many subtleties. But if a bias was so strong that it was dictating the results of race after race, I wanted to be able to capitalize. If a race seemed to offer possibilities from the standpoint of speed figures, pace, or bias, I would study it more deeply. But if it didn't appear to be easily analyzable, I wouldn't bother with it further.

I also alerted a few friends at major tracks that they could expect a morning phone call for a consultation. I am fortunate enough to include among my friends some of the best all-round handicappers in the game: Paul Cornman in New York, Jeff Siegel in southern California, and Steve Davidowitz in northern California. There is a popular notion that professional gamblers are closed-mouth loners, but most of the pros I know love to talk about a day's races — especially with somebody who has a different perspective. In my youth, my ego got in the way of such discussions — as it does for many horseplayers. I wanted to be right, I wanted to be the World's Greatest Handicapper, and if a friend expressed a contrary opinion, my inclination was to challenge it rather than to weigh its validity. Now I don't care about ego and I don't care about trying to prove that I'm smarter than the other guy; if a friend successfully demolishes my opinion on a race and persuades me that he is right, I'll shamelessly bet his horse as if the insights were my own. On the final day of my previous trip to Las Vegas, I had phoned Siegel, who had told me that he liked six horses on the card, four of them showing no form: two first-time starters and two whose recent workouts suggested that they were going to come to life. Siegel's selections went six for six. When I left town with a healthy profit that was largely the result of his brainpower, I was happy to hail him as the World's Greatest Handicapper.

I started my daily handicapping routine at 6:00 A.M., plowing through the three regional editions of the *Daily Racing Form* and making my calls before I took my seat in the Mirage's race book in time for the first Eastern races at 9:30. On the first day I found one race at Laurel which seemed likely to start my venture on a winning note. Mt. Airy Knight and Striking Point had earned recent speed figures that gave them an edge over their rivals in this seven-horse field. Both possessed a respectable finishing kick, while the other five horses were all one-dimensional speedsters. I had brought a $7,000 bankroll to Las Vegas, and I invested $1,000 of it in exactas and trifectas based on the likelihood that a five-horse battle for the early lead would set up the race for my two closers.

But nothing of the sort happened. One of the supposed front-runners stood in the gate and broke twenty lengths behind the field. Another broke down. The jockey on another chose not to try for the early lead. So the speedster Silas Green was able to take command of the race after setting a moderate pace. My two horses rallied to finish second and third but never threatened the leader.

If I had been at Laurel, this would have been a disappointing end to the day, but I was in Las Vegas, and I had at least another fifty races with which to recoup. Instead, I proceeded to dig myself deeper into a hole. I tried to capitalize on an obvious dead-rail bias at Hawthorne, but all of the jockeys in Chicago were aware of it, too, and they tried to take their horses 15-wide, 20-wide if necessary; the races were so freakish that there was no way to predict who would go widest. My expert consultants were as cold as I was. At the end of the nighttime Meadowlands card, I had bet twenty races, cashed one paltry ticket, and was losing $2,800. The next day I picked a few more winners and had a near-miss in Hollywood Park's pick six, but wound up with another losing day; I had blown half of my original bankroll.

Every confirmed gambler will confront such discouraging situations throughout his life, and the way he deals with them will determine his success or failure in the long run. Even if a losing streak extends from days into weeks, a bettor must try to keep his thought processes from being disrupted. Of course, he shouldn't get overly aggressive and try recklessly to recoup. He should pass marginal races, become more selective, and wait for solid betting opportunities. On the third day of my stay in Vegas, I found a few situations that were ideal to rescue me; one in particular was a classic illustration of the power of speed figures:

11 | **1 MILE 70 YDS** CALDER START FINISH

1 MILE 70 YARDS. **(1.42) CLAIMING. Purse $7,000. 3-year-olds and upward. Weights 3-year-olds, 120 lbs. Older, 122 lbs. Non-winners of three races at a mile or over since Septembe 25, allowed 2 lbs. Two such races since October 7, 4 l;bs. Such a race sicne October 28, 6 lbs Claiming Price $11,000; for each $1,000 to $9,000, 2 lbs. (Races where entered for $8,000 or less no considered.)**

LASIX—Alpine Secret, Justin Russ, Glory for Lucy, Viking King, World of Magic, The Money Advisor, Time for Class, Gula

Klucko — Dk. b. or br. g. 4, by Koluctoo Bay—Winzit, by Three Bagger
$9,000 Br.—Bozzo Jerry (Fla) — **112**
Own.—High End Racing Stable Inc — Tr.—Canet Julian (9 2 0 3 .22)

Lifetime		1992	21	3	3	5	$17,€
51 7 7 9		1991	21	4	4	3	$17,4
$36,101		Turf	1	0	0	0	$1
		Wet	4	1	0	1	$3,8

27Nov92-10Crc	fst	6f	:22^{1}	:46^{2}	1:12	3↑Clm 7500	68	7	5	6^{4}	5$^{4\frac{1}{4}}$	3^{1}	1^{1}	Toribio A R	b 114	*.90	91-15 Klucko114^{1}BluCod114^{4}ContrryContr114	Angled in drvg
18Nov92- 5Crc	sly	1	:47^{4}	1:14^{1}	1:41	3↑Clm 10000	61	5	8	7^{13}	5$^{5\frac{1}{2}}$	4$^{7\frac{1}{2}}$	3$^{8\frac{1}{4}}$	Caldwell D A^{7}	b 107	3.20	82-16 GloryforLucy112$^{4\frac{1}{2}}$ChrsHrdn112$^{3\frac{3}{4}}$Klcko107	Broke in air
11Nov92-10Crc	gd	7f	:23	:46	1:25	3↑Clm 6500	76	5	2	1$^{1\frac{1}{2}}$	1^{2}	1^{2}	2no	Olivero C A^{5}	b 114	*2.10	90-14 RechNewHigh114^{no}Klucko114$^{3\frac{1}{2}}$CertinCircls107	Gamely
6Nov92- 6Crc	gd	7f	:23^{1}	:46^{3}	1:25	3↑Clm 8500	68	6	1	3$^{2\frac{1}{2}}$	2$^{2\frac{1}{2}}$	2$^{3\frac{1}{2}}$	2$^{4\frac{1}{2}}$	Rivera M A	b 116	7.10	85-17 AmericnDrmr115$^{4\frac{1}{2}}$Klucko116^{1}DshingViking112	Gamely
20Oct92- 4Crc	fst	6f	:22^{3}	:46^{2}	1:12^{3}	3↑Clm 6500	63	10	3	5$^{3\frac{1}{4}}$	4^{3}	3$^{1\frac{1}{2}}$	1^{2}	Rivera M A	b 116	3.10	88-15 Klucko116^{2} BlueCode116^{hd}Manolo'sMemory118	Driving
19Sep92- 2Crc	fst	6½f	:22	:45^{2}	1:18^{3}	3↑Clm 8000	65	5	4	4^{6}	7$^{7\frac{1}{2}}$	7^{8}	7^{6}	Toribio A R	b 112	11.10	86-11 Ensignio112^{2}OnMorWork116$^{\frac{1}{2}}$Mr.Prosprity112	Stopped
12Sep92- 4Crc	fst	7f	:23	:46^{1}	1:25	3↑Clm 6500	71	1	6	5$^{2\frac{1}{4}}$	3^{3}	4^{8}	3$^{6\frac{1}{2}}$	Toribio A R	b 120	*2.00	83-14 Viking King120^{5} Foxy Reality120$^{1\frac{1}{2}}$Klucko120	Late rally
4Sep92- 4Crc	gd	7f	:22^{2}	:45^{4}	1:25^{3}	3↑Clm 6500	76	6	3	4^{2}	2^{1}	1^{1}	1^{3}	Toribio A R	b 116	*1.80	87-21 Klucko116^{3} Blue Code116^{1} Valid Prospect116	Driving
29Aug92- 1Crc	fst	1^{70}	:48^{2}	1:12^{1}	1:43	3↑Clm 8000	78	8	4	4^{3}	3^{4}	3^{6}	3$^{12\frac{1}{2}}$	Toribio A R	b 112	18.20	85-05 DbbsnDbbs109^{3}NctrnlFPs114$^{9\frac{1}{2}}$Klc112	Lacked response
1Aug92- 8Crc	fm	1$\frac{1}{16}$ Ⓣ	:46^{3}	1:10	1:41	3↑Alw 16600	70	4	6	6^{6}	6$^{8\frac{1}{2}}$	6^{9}	7$^{8\frac{1}{2}}$	Morales C E	b 116	53.20	86-08 SilverConquest111^{no}Zmego116$^{1\frac{1}{2}}$TlktivKing116	Faltered

LATEST WORKOUTS Oct 13 Crc 4f fst :49^{2} B

Beau's Class — B. c. 3(May), by Beaudelaire—Lawdy Day, by Bosun
$11,000 Br.—Johnson Sam T Jr (Fla) — **114**
Own.—Schemer Esther & S — Tr.—Rose Harold J (21 2 2 2 .10)

Lifetime		1992	17	1	2	1	$1[illegible]
21 1 2 1		1991	4	M	0	0	$[illegible]
$19,848		Turf	8	0	0	0	$2,[illegible]
		Wet	2	0	0	0	$1,4

20Nov92- 2Crc	sly	6f	:21^{4}	:45^{3}	1:11^{3}	Clm 12500	65	5	5	4$^{3\frac{1}{2}}$	5$^{2\frac{1}{4}}$	4^{3}	4$^{6\frac{1}{4}}$	Gonzalez M A	b 116	6.80	87-12 ProgrssNts118$^{1\frac{1}{4}}$Jblr'sPwr114$^{1\frac{1}{2}}$TrGrnPw114	Weakened
13Nov92- 2Crc	fst	7f	:23^{2}	:47	1:26^{3}	Clm 10000	60	2	2	6$^{3\frac{1}{4}}$	4$^{3\frac{1}{2}}$	2$^{1\frac{1}{2}}$	3^{1}	Gonzalez M A	b 116	4.40	81-14 Dr. Regent107^{no} Ⓓ Peaceful Babe112^{1} Beau's Class116	
13Nov92-Crowded backstretch, forced out late; Placed second through disqualification																		
5Aug92- 5Crc	fst	7f	:22^{4}	:46^{1}	1:25^{4}	Clm 12500	66	7	2	7$^{7\frac{1}{2}}$	7$^{6\frac{1}{2}}$	5$^{5\frac{1}{4}}$	4^{4}	De'Oliveira WG	b 116	4.40	82-15 Jeblar'sPower116^{no}TotalDevotion112$^{2\frac{1}{2}}$RebelDoctor116	
5Aug92-Eight wide, late rally in distress, did not return to unsaddling area																		
23Jly92- 7Crc	fst	1$\frac{1}{16}$	:47^{3}	1:12^{4}	1:48	Clm 14000	76	10	10	10^{21}	9^{14}	5$^{6\frac{3}{4}}$	2^{1}	De'Oliveira WG	b 116	25.00	86-13 ManRullah111^{1}Beau'sClass116^{4}Watul112	Rallied 6-wide
11Jly92- 6Crc	fm	*1⅛ Ⓣ			1:48^{1}	Clm 25000	47	7	2	2^{1}	3$^{3\frac{1}{2}}$	5^{12}	7^{20}	Rodriguez P A	b 116	10.10	61-19 ColdNovl120$^{\frac{1}{2}}$RomnEmissry116$^{3\frac{1}{2}}$SpkMn111	4 wd faded
21Jun92- 8Crc	fst	1^{70}	:46^{4}	1:12^{3}	1:43^{4}	3↑Alw 15000	49	7	7	7$^{8\frac{3}{4}}$	8^{13}	11^{19}	11$^{26\frac{3}{4}}$	Lee M A	b 110	7.90	67-06 ChnnelThirteen110$^{8\frac{1}{2}}$Dnzig'sRwrd113^{3}YnkAx117	Outrun
13Jun92- 6Crc	sf	*1⅛ Ⓣ			1:51^{1}	Clm 25000	66	4	7	7$^{5\frac{1}{4}}$	6$^{7\frac{1}{2}}$	5$^{9\frac{1}{2}}$	5^{7}	Nunez E O	b 112	14.40	59-34 SndThSpndr112^{1}ThrOvr111^{1}NorthrnDsign116	No threat
6Jun92- 8Crc	fst	1$\frac{1}{16}$	:47^{4}	1:13^{2}	1:48	3↑Alw 16600	62	5	8	9^{10}	6^{8}	6^{9}	4$^{11\frac{1}{2}}$	Nunez E O	b 111	16.30	75-13 Brdonthwr114$^{8\frac{1}{2}}$SttlBrz120^{2}ⒹBllGtor118	Checked ealry
6Jun92-Placed third through disqualification																		

LATEST WORKOUTS Nov 8 Crc 6f sly 1:16^{1} B

Alpine Secret

B. g. 5, by Private Account—Cassaway, by Cormorant
$11,000 Br.—Beler Constantine P (Ky)
Own.—Petelain Stables
Tr.—Bracken James E (16 2 2 3 .13)
116

Lifetime							
49 4 3 6	1992	11	0	1	0		$6,055
$94,521	1991	14	2	1	2		$31,085
	Turf	5	0	0	0		$150
	Wet	9	1	0	2		$15,720

8Nov92- 1Crc	sly	1 1/16	:494	1:143	1:472	3↑ Clm 16000	56	2	6	66	612	615	613½	Lee M A	Lb	116	10.90	76–09	SprinklesExpress1161BobThHt1124½Psportu111	Outrun	7
21Oct92-10Crc	fst	170	:482	1:134	1:44	3↑ Clm 20000	67	2	6	711	713	613	613	Saumell L	Lb	116	43.80	80–18	ProdtoRson1144HppyIntntons116hdBshrm112	No factor	7
11Sep92- 4Med	fst	170	:453	1:102	1:404	3↑ Clm 16000	62	1	9	815	815	711	612½	Garcia A A	L	115	32.40	81–07	BndthBuck117½TBonTddy115noMkADcision115	No rally	9
1Sep92- 2Mth	fst	1 1/16	:482	1:131	1:451	3↑ Clm 16000	64	2	8	814	812	812	816	Ferrer J C	Lb	115	8.40	67–23	Twice The Star1172HopeUs115noCallisto117	No menace	8
19Aug92- 7Mth	gd	1	:472	1:123	1:381	3↑ Clm 16000	80	7	8	815	87¾	78	67¼	Ferrer J C	L	115	12.40	74–28	TcThStr115hdBndthBc1176¼HlnSccss117	Wide into lane	8
15Aug92- 3Mth	sly	170	:473	1:123	1:431	3↑ Clm 28000	68	3	6	79¾	711	712	710	Ferrer J C		112	12.80	70–19	SurtinlySecret1131Nybrdi115½ClenndBold113	No threat	7
25Jly92- 7Mth	gd	1 1/16 Ⓣ	:463	1:104	1:424	3↑ Clm 32000	73	8	8	820	816	712	512¾	Wilson R	L	115	23.80	77–10	Spyglass1157¼ Royal Rue1154BlindPursuit115	Late gain	8
18Jly92- 3Mth	fst	1 1/16	:473	1:12	1:433	3↑ Clm 40000	81	6	5	58	55	44	46½	Ferrer J C	L	112	6.40	84–12	LineScore1112Accssion110¾RinbowQurtz113	No str bid	6
7Jly92- 6Mth	fst	170	:462	1:114	1:434	3↑ Clm 40000	78	7	7	717	69¾	55	22	Ferrer J C	L	115	11.10	75–17	GiniMcCown1152AlpinScrt115½Accssion111	Closed well	7
20Jun92- 8Mth	my	1 1/16	:46	1:103	1:43	3↑ Alw 26000	64	1	8	820	818	817	819¾	Olea R E	L	115	25.90	74–13	RootBoy1191½Fiftysevnvtt1174¼Brukbooki115	No factor	8

20Jun92-Originally scheduled on turf

LATEST WORKOUTS Nov 17 Crc 5f fst 1:033 B · Nov 5 Crc 4f fst :501 B · Oct 29 Crc 5f fst 1:022 B · Oct 16 Crc 3f fst :373 B

Justin Russ

Dk. b. or br. c. 3(May), by Court Trial—Sister Belle, by Bravest Roman
$11,000 Br.—Newchance Farm (Fla)
Own.—Tortora Toni
Tr.—Tortora Emanuel (38 5 9 7 .13)
1095

Lifetime							
26 2 4 1	1992	10	1	2	0		$18,280
$37,690	1991	16	1	2	1		$19,410
	Turf	2	0	0	0		$350
	Wet	5	0	0	0		$3,680

19Nov92- 7Crc	my	1 1/16	:482	1:134	1:473	3↑ Clm 15000	69	4	4	65½	75½	55	47¾	HomistrRBJr5	Lb	113	10.90	81–18	StrSprm1161½KoolHch1162ThMnyAdvsr114	Lcke It resp	7
7Nov92- 7Crc	fst	170	:492	1:141	1:434	3↑ Clm 35000	61	5	4	54½	58	512	518	Diaz M R5	Lb	113	10.60	76–13	ContinntlMorn1113SovrignShild1113½SirOtto114	Outrun	5
24Oct92- 9Crc	fst	1 1/16	:472	1:131	1:473	3↑ Alw 17600	81	6	3	56¼	41½	1½	11½	Diaz M R5	Lb	107	3.90	89–10	JustnRuss1071½Momroo11510IslndJzz115	Driving inside	9
10Oct92- 7Crc	fst	1 1/16	:473	1:124	1:46	3↑ Clm 20000	82	2	4	410	69	410	46	Diaz M R5	Lb	108	24.20	91–03	DbbsnDbbs111½ThMnAdsr1125StrSpr116	Late rlly 8-wd	7
30Sep92- 8Crc	fst	1 1/16	:472	1:131	1:47	Clm 12500	68	5	4	48½	26	23½	24	Olivero C A5	Lb	111	10.50	88–14	Dr. Cooley1154 JustinRuss1111CountryTown112	Gamely	8
19Sep92-12Crc	fst	1⅛	:474	1:124	1:53	3↑ Clm 25000	63	5	3	36	411	414	417	Olivero C A5	Lb	107	6.90	81–04	PrtThree1115½OhMyJoeyPie1162½OneEydJck116	Faded	7
19Sep92-Originally scheduled on turf																					
3Sep92-10Crc	sly	1 1/16	:484	1:141	1:472	3↑ Clm 20000	26	2	1	3nk	77½	714	738	Bracho J A5	Lb	109	8.60	52–16	StrSuprem1123RchNwHigh1123KoolHooch116	Stopped	8
29Feb92- 5GP	fst	1 1/16	:48	1:13	1:451	Clm 40000	78	7	3	32½	2½	11½	21	Penna D	Lb	116	9.80	85–16	Favorable Tab1161 Justin Russ1162½ Johnny Bush116		9
29Feb92-Brushed 1st turn,lugged in inside 3/16																					
1Feb92- 8GP	fm	1⅛ Ⓣ	:464	1:111	1:492 +	Alw 18000	51	9	9	78¾	119½	1118	1218¼	Thibeau R J Jr	Lb	112	97.00	— —	DshForDtty1141½InMyFtstps115½DtchPlns112	Wide trip	12

LATEST WORKOUTS Dec 3 Crc 4f fst :511 B · Nov 28 Crc 4f fst :492 B · Nov 1 Crc 4f fst :511 B · Oct 19 Crc 4f fst :502 B

Glory for Lucy

Ro. c. 4, by On to Glory—No No Lucy, by T V Colony
$9,000 Br.—Goolsby Nancy (Fla)
Own.—Ballou Francis W
Tr.—Hurtak Daniel C (31 3 2 4 .10)
114

Lifetime							
30 9 2 1	1992	15	5	2	0		$28,805
$58,005	1991	8	1	0	1		$14,730
	Turf	1	0	0	0		$170
	Wet	2	1	0	0		$4,290

18Nov92- 5Crc	sly	1	:474	1:141	1:41	3↑ Clm 10000	76	1	5	56¼	2hd	14	14½	Toribio A R	L	112	2.00	90–16	Glory for Lucy1124½ChrisHardin1123¾Klucko107	Driving	8
7Nov92-11Crc	fst	1 1/16	:483	1:134	1:481	3↑ Clm c-6500	74	1	3	34	32½	1½	12	Toribio A R	L	119	*2.20	86–13	GloryforLucy1192Sinareg1071WorldofMagic114	Driving	12
7Nov92-Claimed from Rising Sun Stable, Mongeon Kathy P Trainer																					
25Oct92- 2Crc	fst	1⅛	:483	1:133	1:531	3↑ Clm 6500	88	1	4	32	23	11½	14	Toribio A R	L	116	1.70	97–12	GloryforLucy1164LordRaj1162½WorldofMgic116	Driving	7
16Oct92-10Crc	fst	1 1/16	:48	1:14	1:481	3↑ Clm 6500	67	1	4	58½	33½	22½	21	Toribio A R	L	116	3.00	85–17	MyIRequst1161GloryforLucy1161KurtisTwo113	Gamely	9
7Oct92- 5Crc	fst	1	:471	1:122	1:401	3↑ Clm 7500	71	3	6	617	615	68½	45	Portillo D A7	L	107	7.70	89–12	BluOvrYou1124FoxyRlty113noWorldofMgc112	Late rally	7
18Sep92-10Crc	fst	7f	:222	:462	1:263	3↑ Clm 6500	56	5	6	108	88¾	56½	54¾	Portillo D A7	L	109	6.00	77–16	BlOvrY1201½Mgn'sMcgvr111nkVldPrspct116	No menace	10
6Aug92- 4Crc	fst	7f	:223	:454	1:263	3↑ Clm 6500	54	6	4	129	109¾	814	67½	Alferez J O	L	116	4.00	74–20	What Is Hip1161½BlueOverYou1163½Duma116	No threat	12
19Jly92- 2Crc	fst	7f	:223	:46	1:244	3↑ Clm 8500	54	6	8	88¼	67	58½	512½	Bracho J A5	L	111	2.20	78–09	DrDomno1166Wschs1143½CortMtch112	10 wide, no kick	9
28Jun92- 6Crc	fst	7f	:224	:461	1:251	3↑ Clm 8000	78	1	7	67½	66¼	43½	22	Bracho J A5	L	111	6.70	87–09	DearDomino1142GloryforLucy111noSeneglise109	Rallied	11
26Apr92- 7Crc	fst	7f	:223	:454	1:252	3↑ Alw 16200	81	2	6	711	67½	32	11½	HomeisterRBJr10	L	109	18.90	93–07	GlrfrLc1091½IrshSr1195½FrtntWsh110	Bmpd stumbld, dr	9

Viking King

B. h. 5, by Far North—Prove Us Royal, by Prove It
$10,000 Br.—Conrad Marian L (Ky)
Own.—Raffa Joseph W
Tr.—Root Richard R (15 1 0 2 .07)
116

Lifetime							
38 8 4 6	1992	13	4	2	0		$20,310
$93,920	1991	7	1	0	2		$18,627
	Turf	16	3	3	3		$51,452
	Wet	3	0	0	0		$2,381

Entered 5Dec92- 1 CRC

26Nov92- 2Crc	fst	1 1/16	:48	1:131	1:463	3↑ Clm 32500	60	2	1	1½	1hd	68¼	715¾	Vasquez J	L	114	12.80	78–08	ThsTmTony111½HppyIntntns1164SvrgnShld107	Stopped	8
7Nov92- 6Crc	fst	1⅛	:492	1:143	1:56	3↑ Clm 20000	67	3	1	13	11	14	11	Vasquez J	L	114	1.90	83–13	VikingKing1141ClassicGuy114hdFortunteJet114	Driving	6
7Nov92-Originally scheduled on turf																					
23Oct92- 8Crc	fm	*1⅛ Ⓣ			1:481	3↑ Clm 20000	84	2	1	11½	12½	12	2nk	Vasquez J	L	114	9.00	81–19	Onbfrtlv116nkVkngKng114½ChrgrsEx112	Y'ld grudgingly	8
16Oct92- 2Crc	fst	7f	:222	:454	1:254	3↑ Clm 8500	69	2	5	13½	12½	15	2½	Suckie M C	L	116	3.40	85–15	AmricnDrmr111½VkngKng1164Jbotnsky116	Just missed	8
26Sep92-11Crc	fst	1	:473	1:133	1:414	3↑ Clm c-6500	46	3	1	1hd	3½	813	1016	Vasquez J		118	*1.30	70–12	DshngVkng1165PrctclJst116½MjrWhrlwnd116	Gave way	11
26Sep92-Claimed from Tucker Paula J, Vivian David A Trainer																					
12Sep92- 4Crc	fst	7f	:23	:461	1:25	3↑ Clm 6500	85	6	1	11½	12½	15	15	Vasquez J		120	3.40	90–14	VikingKing1205FoxyRelity1201½Klucko120	Convincingly	8
9Aug92- 2Crc	fst	1	:472	1:122	1:404	3↑ Clm 6500	69	6	1	12	15	15	11½	Vasquez J		116	3.10	91–10	VikingKing1161½MyIRequest107nkFoxyRlity116	Driving	9
30Jly92- 2Crc	fst	6f	:222	:461	1:123	3↑ Clm 6500	56	10	1	3nk	1½	21½	55¼	Vasquez J		116	4.00	83–12	SltBst1111½BlOvrY116nkTyrntBss116	Broke outward st	12
19Jly92- 2Crc	fst	7f	:223	:46	1:244	3↑ Clm 8500	53	4	2	1hd	2hd	24	613	Vasquez J		116Δ	9.90	78–09	DearDomino1166Wsichus1143½CourtMtch112	No threat	9

19Jly92-Dead heat

LATEST WORKOUTS Nov 5 Crc 3f fst :363 H · Oct 11 Crc 5f fst 1:02 B

World of Magic B. h. 5, by Wardlaw—Magic Saber, by Saber Thrust

$9,000 Br.—Bakerman Robert (Fla)

Own.—Bakerman Robert Tr.—White William P (29 5 4 7 .17) **1075**

Lifetime 67 10 6 9 $43,617 | 1992 22 2 2 6 $14,820 | 1991 23 5 4 1 $17,515 | Turf 6 0 0 0 $505 | Wet 4 1 0 1 $2,660

15Nov92-10Crc	fst	1 1/16	:482	1:141	1:473	3↑Clm 7500	59	3	1	11	2½	34½	612¾	Lee M A	Lb	114	2.40	76-11 CurtiBirdi109¾FiddlDiddl1095½ScondStrit114	Gave way 8
7Nov92-11Crc	fst	1 1/16	:483	1:134	1:481	3↑Clm 6500	69	4	1	11	12½	2½	33	Lee M A	Lb	114	2.50	83-13 GloryforLucy1192Sinrg1071WorldofMgic114	Weakened 12
25Oct92- 2Crc	fst	1⅛	:483	1:133	1:531	3↑Clm 6500	78	3	1	12	13	21½	36½	Lee M A	Lb	116	*1.00	90-12 GloryforLcy1164LordRj1162½WrldfMgc116	Drftd out str 7
7Oct92- 5Crc	fst	1	:471	1:122	1:401	3↑Clm 7500	73	7	2	21½	1½	31	34	Lee M A	Lb	112	*.90	90-12 BluOvrYo1124FoxyRlty113noWorldofMgc112	Weakened 7
27Sep92- 8Crc	fst	1⅛	:473	1:13	1:561	3↑Alw 15000	71	6	2	11	11½	2hd	45½	Lee M A	Lb	116	8.90	76-12 ClassicGuy1132½Momaroo116hdOcenProspect107	Faded 9
16Sep92-10Crc	fst	170	:472	1:124	1:443	3↑Clm 6500	80	5	1	12½	14	15	11	Lee M A	Lb	116	*1.50	90-06 WorldofMgic1161MyIRequest120½CurtiBirdi111	Driving 11
29Aug92-12Crc	fst	1⅛	:484	1:14	1:53	3↑Clm 6500	80	10	1	12	12½	2½	27	Lee M A	Lb	116	3.10	91-05 ThMnAdvsr1187WrldfMgc1164Cln-Ar116	Best of others 10
19Aug92- 2Crc	fst	1 1/16	:463	1:121	1:471	3↑Clm 6500	67	5	1	13½	15	21½	38½	Bracho J A5	Lb	115	*2.20	82-18 Momroo1167½L'Arb1161WorldofMgc115	4-wd weakened 8
8Aug92- 1Crc	fst	1 1/16	:472	1:123	1:463	3↑Clm 8500	62	6	4	3nk	2hd	55	512	Bracho J A5	Lb	111	4.90	82-07 ExplsvBrv1161ThMnyAdvsr1134½Mmr114	6-wide, faded 8
1Aug92- 8Crc	fm	1 1/16 Ⓣ	:463	1:10	1:41	3↑Alw 16600	71	10	4	31½	2½	57	58	Olivero C A5	Lb	111	72.70	87-08 SilverConquest111noZmego1161½TalktiveKing116	Faded 11

LATEST WORKOUTS Nov 30 Crc 4f fst :50 B

The Money Advisor B. c. 4, by Bates Motel—Mindy K, by GAllant Romeo

$11,000 Br.—Weber Lucille M (SC)

Own.—Miron Julie Tr.—Plesa Edward Jr (30 8 5 4 .27) **1135**

Lifetime 44 14 7 5 $105,980 | 1992 22 10 5 1 $60,375 | 1991 22 4 2 4 $45,605 | Turf 3 0 0 0 $405 | Wet 7 1 2 3 $12,775

19Nov92- 7Crc	my	1 1/16	:482	1:134	1:473	3↑Clm 14000	76	6	6	53	33	33½	33½	Hosang G J	Lb	114	2.20	85-18 StrSprm1161½KoolHch1162ThMnyAdvsr114	Slow st., wd 7
30Oct92-10GP	fst	1 1/16	:471	1:114	1:433	3↑Clm c-10500	81	4	2	26	33½	44½	1nk	Hosang G J	Lb	116	*1.10	94-03 TMAdsr116nkEplsBr120nkSprlsEprss120	Fully extended 8
30Oct92-Claimed from Black D & P & C Stables, Ziadie Ralph Trainer																			
10Oct92- 7Crc	fst	1 1/16	:473	1:124	1:46	3↑Clm 18000	91	5	3	310	24	24	2½	Hosang G J	Lb	112	1.80	96-03 Dbbsn'Dbbs111½ThMnAdsr1125StrSprm116	Rlld, 5-wide 7
3Oct92-11Crc	fst	1 1/16	:482	1:133	1:461	3↑Clm 13000	93	7	4	34	32½	13	16½	Hosang G J	Lb	114	*1.00	96-09 ThMnAdsr1146½Shf'sFrstDnc1088Dr.Ctn113	Ridden out 7
23Sep92-10Crc	sly	170	:471	1:123	1:44	3↑Clm 14000	76	7	8	89¼	79¼	67¼	24½	Lee M A	Lb	112	*1.60	88-15 DbbsnDbbs1094½ThMAdsr112nkPsprt116	Rallied 10 wide 9
7Sep92-12Crc	fst	1 1/16	:472	1:131	1:454	3↑Clm 10500	94	4	4	411	3nk	12½	16	Lee M A	Lb	112	*2.20	98-07 ThMnAdsr1126ShfsFrstDnc116nkEplsBr112	Drvg 6-wide 8
29Aug92-12Crc	fst	1⅛	:484	1:14	1:53	3↑Clm 6500	91	8	5	33	22½	1½	17	Hosang G J	Lb	118	*.90	98-05 ThMnyAdvsr1187WrldfMgc1164Cln-Ar116	Convincingly 10
8Aug92- 1Crc	fst	1 1/16	:472	1:123	1:463	3↑Clm 8000	80	4	6	56¼	56	31½	21	Hosang G J	Lb	113	*1.20	93-07 ExplosvBrv1161ThMonyAdvsr1134½Mmr114	Rlld 7-wide 8
1Aug92-12Crc	fst	1 1/16	:482	1:131	1:464	3↑Clm 6500	89	11	5	2½	13½	15	18	Hosang G J	Lb	116	2.40	93-11 ThMonyAdvisor1168FiftyTwoJo1206Kskovsh116	Driving 11
22Jly92-10Crc	fst	1⅛	:48	1:123	1:533	3↑Clm 6500	72	3	6	711	813	612	210	Hosang G J	Lb	118	2.20	85-11 FiftyTwoJo11610ThMonyAdvisor118nkL'Arbi116	Rallied 11

Time For Class B. c. 4, by Classic Trial—Timeless Reason, by Timeless Moment

$11,000 Br.—Hatcher Mr-Mrs H M (Fla)

Own.—Winbound Farms Tr.—Gullo Gary P (19 8 1 3 .42) **1115**

Lifetime 30 4 5 1 $68,900 | 1992 11 2 0 0 $18,680 | 1991 19 2 5 1 $50,220 | Turf 19 2 4 0 $48,540

26Nov92-11Crc	fst	1⅛	:474	1:14	1:532	3↑Clm 7500	82	3	2	25	2½	11	11	Gonzalez M A	Lb	114	4.80	96-08 TimeForClss1141MyIRequest1145LordRj114	Stiff drive 10
15Nov92- 8Crc	gd	*1½ Ⓣ			2:351	3↑Clm 25000	73	1	5	721	55½	58	613¼	Lee M A	Lb	112	6.70	61-31 Brngr1163BrcWhtKn1163½SrOtto111	Lckd late respons 9
30Oct92- 4GP	fm	*1 Ⓣ			1:361	3↑Alw 26000	73	1	8	89½	107¾	84¾	96¾	Krone J A	Lb	115	10.30	91 — ContofNn1151ColdNovl112nkTlktvKng115	Showed little 12
21Oct92- 9Crc	fm	*1 1/16 Ⓣ			1:441	3↑Alw 16000	83	2	6	54	54	44½	42½	Lee M A	Lb	115	5.70	88-09 Kvn'sDvl1152½FftyOks110noHstShrtstp115	Lt rlly, 5-wd 8
15Aug92- 8Crc	fm	*1⅛ Ⓣ			1:45	3↑Alw 17700	78	10	8	915	84¾	711	78½	Lee M A	Lb	122	12.80	88-02 SpanishBit114nkSideBr115hdFiftyOks111	Bmpd, no thrt 10
17Jly92- 9Crc	fm	*1 1/16 Ⓣ			1:443	3↑Alw 16600	86	8	8	74¾	52¾	3½	11½	Thibeau R J Jr	Lb	116	7.60	89-14 TmFrClss1161½AnmlsLvU.1161BrnSprc112	Driving 9 wd 8
4Jly92- 6Crc	fm	1 1/16 Ⓣ	:47	1:11	1:423	Alw 16600	80	10	5	54¼	31½	4¾	41¼	Thibeau R J Jr	Lb	116	35.80	86-13 StdlyDRght1151Sky111nkAnmlsLvU.116	Lckd rsp, 5 wde 10
20Jun92- 8Crc	fm	*1⅛ Ⓣ			1:494	3↑Alw 16600	69	5	7	74	74	78	79	Thibeau R J Jr	Lb	117	7.20	64-27 ColdNovl1081½StudlyDoRght1132AnmlsLuvU.117	Evenly 9
30May92- 8Crc	fm	*1⅛ Ⓣ			1:463	3↑Alw 17700	79	3	2	33½	64¾	57½	46½	Thibeau R J Jr	Lb	119	45.40	82-11 Onebeforetwelv1191FiftyOks1143½Incrdibl119	Late rally 9
19Jan92- 2Aqu	fst	1 1/16 ⊡	:483	1:142	1:48	Clm 25000	52	7	7	813	712	714	720¼	Chavez J F	b	117	35.30	48-29 DrssdShppr1172¼AllSlr117hdAdncngEnsgn117	No factor 8

LATEST WORKOUTS Oct 7 Crc 6f fst 1:162 B

Gulah Dk. b. or br. g. 5, by Pass Catcher—Tallahassee, by Iron Ruler

$10,000 Br.—Dotter Robert L (Fla)

Own.—Dotter Robert L Tr.—Dotter Robert L (1 0 0 0 .00) **1095**

Lifetime 24 3 4 1 $32,195 | 1992 1 0 0 0 $60 | 1991 3 0 0 0 | Wet 2 0 1 0 $1,710

21Nov92- 4Crc	gd	7f	:22	:453	1:244	3↑Clm 8500	25	8	2	41¾	89½	1025	1025¾	Vasquez J		116	34.40	65-08 J'sBB1091RchNHgh1141¼Kll'mAll-Ar112	Stopped badly 10
23Sep91- 8FE	sly	6f	:231	:473	1:132	3↑Alw 6500	24	3	8	75	811	918	922½	Giblin S M	b	118	67.25	60-19 LopdArgnt1132RnnngDsr1242½NoOpnn118	Showed little 10
4Sep91- 5WO	fst	6½f	:222	:454	1:174	3↑Clm 16000	31	7	3	32	1112	1125	1123½	Hemsley D L	b	118	118.30	62-20 Snp'nBrk1131Trvso1182¾ScrmngCncl116	Dropped back 11
25Aug91- 2WO	fst	6f	:224	:461	1:114	3↑Clm 20000	36	3	1	76¾	714	722	719	Villeneuve F A	b	118	41.95	67-14 Alpine Bank1181½ CrossKeys1131½Treviso118	No factor 7
24Nov90- 8Pha	fst	6f	:22	:451	1:104	3↑Alw 11500	50	2	7	713	714	715	723	Bravo J	b	113	8.60	67-22 SilentnReady11610FgerDncer1163VideoMgic113	Outrun 7
30Oct90- 5Pha	fst	6½f	:211	:44	1:164	Clm 25000	49	4	7	715	713	617	617¾	Velez J G	b	116	5.80	75-10 DesertWest1144Celin'sRbu1194½VidoMgic116	No factor 7
8Sep90- 8Crc	fst	1 1/16	:493	1:134	1:471	3↑Clm 32500	73	2	5	52¼	65¾	713	710	Rydowski S R	b	111	6.80	76-20 ProdtoRsn1123Dr.DnEys1121SIB.Shrp113	Showed little 8
26Aug90- 7Crc	fst	7f	:221	:452	1:252	3↑Clm 25000	82	4	2	29	25	2hd	1¾	Rydowski S R	b	111	8.00	88-14 Gulah111¾DiamondBank1162¼SlutetheMoon112	Driving 6
15Aug90- 8Crc	fst	6f	:22	:454	1:123	Clm 25000	78	2	4	65½	54	41¼	21½	Rydowski S R	b	118	*1.50	85-18 So Dashing1161½ Gulah1182¼HunchPlay111	Second best 7
5Aug90- 8Crc	fst	6f	:222	:454	1:114	3↑Clm 30000	75	1	7	89¼	810	88½	76¼	Rydowski S R	b	116	10.10	85-14 Al'sExcellor1091¾Jabotinsky1201½NobleWind112	Outrun 8

Time for Class had earned a better figure in his last start than any of his rivals. His 82 translated to a 3½-length edge over Glory for Lucy and The Money Advisor, both of whom had just earned 76s. However, both of those colts had earned much higher figures in recent outings. Glory for Lucy had run an 88 three races earlier. The Money Advisor had recorded figures of 91 and 93 in October.

Was Time for Class's top figure a legitimate one that he was likely to repeat today? Were Glory for Lucy and The Money Advisor likely to reproduce their peak performances? These are the sorts of questions that usually leave a handicapper mired in uncertainty. But in the eleventh race at Calder, I thought I had all the right answers.

Even a superficial look at Time for Class's last running line suggested that he had earned his figure honestly. He had chased a rival who had opened a five-length lead while setting a fast pace, a half mile in 47⅘ seconds. Chasing and running down a loose speedster is never an easy task, but Time for Class had done it and scored a one-length victory. In that race, he had taken a sharp drop to the $7,500 claiming level, a descent that was understandable because he hadn't finished in the money since July. But now trainer Gary Gullo was signaling his renewed confidence in the 4-year-old by stepping him up in class. He could have entered the colt in this race for a $9,000 price tag and received a four-pound weight concession, but instead he was trying to protect Time for Class from being claimed by entering him for $11,000. (And Gullo, who was 8 for 19 at the Calder meeting, is clearly a man who knows what he is doing.) Many horseplayers dream of having a pipeline to inside information from a stable, but the way a trainer moves a claimer up or down in class will often speak eloquently about his intentions and his view of the animal.

While Gullo evidently felt good about his horse in this race, the same could not be said about the trainers of the other contenders. Glory for Lucy had scored three runaway victories in a row, most recently for a $10,000 claiming price. But trainer Daniel Hurtak, who could have entered the horse for $11,000 here, instead put him into the race for $9,000 — a bargain basement price tag that was advertising, "Claim me!" Glory for Lucy undoubtedly had some physical problems; this negative-looking drop in class didn't necessarily mean that he was going to drop dead on the track, but it certainly suggested that he was not ready to improve on his last figure or duplicate his best previous performance.

The Money Advisor had been taking drops in class that looked even more ominous. Here was a paragon of consistency, a money machine who had won ten races in 1992 alone. Yet after running well for $13,000 and $18,000 and earning figures in the 90s, which suggested he could step up in class sharply, The Money Advisor was dropped to $10,500. He, too, might as well have carried a sign that said, "Claim me!" Eddie Plesa did claim him, and did get a good race out of his new acquisition for $14,000. But now Plesa was dropping the horse to $11,000. As with Glory for Lucy, these negative indications made it seem unlikely that The Money Advisor was ready to improve on his last figure or two.

Time for Class was the one to beat. I overcame my usual aversion to win betting and wagered $200 on him.

ELEVENTH RACE
Calder
DECEMBER 6, 1992

1 MILE 70 YARDS. (1.42) CLAIMING. Purse $7,000. 3–year–olds and upward. Weights, 3–year–olds, 120 lbs. Older, 122 lbs. Non–winners of three races at a mile or over since September 25, allowed 2 lbs. Two such races since October 7, 4 l;bs. Such a race sicne October 28, 6 lbs. Claiming Price $11,000; for each $1,000 to $9,000, 2 lbs. (Races where entered for $8,000 or less not considered.)

Value of race $7,000; value to winner $4,200; second $1,260; third $770; fourth $350; balance of starters $70 each. Mutuel pool $75,451. Perfecta Pool $68,046 Trifecta Pool $100,678

Last Raced	Horse	M/Eqt.A.Wt	PP	St	1/4	1/2	3/4	Str	Fin	Jockey	Cl'g Pr	Odds $1
26Nov92 11Crc1	Time For Class	Lb	4 111	9	7	6¹	6²½	2½	1⁵	12¾	Portillo D A⁵	11000	9.20
19Nov92 7Crc3	The Money Advisor	Lb	4 113	8	1	8⁴	8³	6hd	3¹	2¾	HomstrRBJr⁵	11000	1.40
18Nov92 5Crc1	Glory for Lucy	L	4 114	5	9	9⁷	9⁷	8⁵	2hd	3³	Nunez E O	9000	4.60
8Nov92 1Crc6	Alpine Secret	Lb	5 116	3	8	10	10	9⁸	6⁵	4¹½	Lee M A	11000	27.50
19Nov92 7Crc4	Justin Russ	Lb	3 109	4	10	7hd	7½	7¹½	5²½	5¹	Diaz M R⁵	11000	8.80
27Nov92 10Crc1	Klucko	b	4 112	1	6	4¹	3¹	3¹½	4¹½	6⁵	Toribio A R	9000	9.80
20Nov92 2Crc4	Beau's Class	b	3 114	2	5	5³½	5½	5½	7⁴	7⁸	Gonzalez MA	11000	8.50
26Nov92 2Crc7	Viking King	L	5 116	6	2	2⁴	1hd	1¹	8⁷	8⁸	Vasquez J	10000	7.20
15Nov92 10Crc6	World of Magic	Lb	5 109	7	4	1¹	2⁶	4¹½	9¹⁴	9	Bracho J A⁵	9000	12.40
21Nov92 4Crc10	Gulah	L	5 114	10	3	3¹	4½	10	10	—	Guidry M†	10000	77.20

Gulah, Eased.

OFF AT 5:12 Start good. Won driving. Time, :22⁴, :46³, 1:13³, 1:39⁴, 1:44¹ Track fast.

$2 Mutuel Prices:

9–TIME FOR CLASS	20.40	7.40	4.00
8–THE MONEY ADVISOR		3.00	2.40
5–GLORY FOR LUCY			2.80

$2 PERFECTA 9–8 PAID $68.20 $2 TRIFECTA 9–8–5 PAID $234.60

B. c, by Classic Trial—Timeless Reason, by Timeless Moment. Trainer Gullo Gary P. Bred by Hatcher Mr–Mrs H M (Fla).

TIME FOR CLASS bumped with KLUCKO while moving along the rail at the far turn, eased out between horses after steadying behind VIKING KING, quickly drew off and was kept to pressure. THE MONEY ADVISOR, wide throughout, finished well. GLORY FOR LUCY split horses leaving the far turn and rallied mildly. ALPINE SECRET made up ground too late. JUSTIN RUSS failed to seriously menace. KLUCKO bumped with time for class at the far turn, made a run between horses approaching the stretch and tired. BEAU'S CLASS tired. VIKING KING tired badly from his early efforts. WORLD OF MAGIC, prominent to the far turn, drifted out while tiring badly. GULAH gave way suddenly after going a half and was eased.

Owners— 1, Winbound Farms; 2, Miron Julie; 3, Ballou Francis W; 4, Petelain Stables; 5, Tortora Toni; 6, High End Racing Stable Inc; 7, Schemer Esther & S; 8, Raffa Joseph W; 9, Bakerman Robert; 10, Dotter Robert L.

Trainers— 1, Gullo Gary P; 2, Plesa Edward Jr; 3, Hurtak Daniel C; 4, Bracken James E; 5, Tortora Emanuel; 6, Canet Julian; 7, Rose Harold J; 8, Root Richard R; 9, White William P; 10, Dotter Robert L.

† Apprentice allowance waived: Gulah 5 pounds. Overweight: World of Magic 2 pounds.

Klucko was claimed by Petro M P; trainer, Ritvo Kathy.

Time for Class scored in a runaway over the two favorites, as each of them virtually duplicated the figure he had earned in his previous start. But what made this a classic situation was the price: The superior horse in the field paid $20.40 to win. It was a classic in the same sense that the movie *Casablanca* is: They don't make em like that anymore.

In the years before speed handicapping became fashionable, lucrative winners like Time for Class were commonplace. The betting public shunned horses who were stepping up in class sharply, even if they were in excellent form. But now I never expect to see obvious horses like Time for Class paying big prices to win, and I was so unprepared for this opportunity that I was guilty of underbetting the Calder race — a rare sin for me. The chances for making a profit on solid figure horses almost always come from multiple wagers — as they did in two races at Laurel on the same day.

The third race at Laurel was a nondescript claiming event for rock-bottom fillies and mares, and from a speed-handicapping standpoint it was a no-brainer. Easy Best had a 63 in her last start. I've Got Jessica's last four numbers were 56, 66, 52, and 65. Only one other horse in the field had earned a figure as high as 49 in the last two months — and that was a plodder who had earned a decent number in a route race and was now entered inappropriately in a sprint. The race required no imagination, but when Easy Best and I've Got Jessica ran 1-2, nearly seven lengths ahead of the rest of the field, I collected a respectable $26.80 exacta. An even better opportunity lay ahead.

7

1 1/16 MILES. **(1.414) CLAIMING. Purse $13,500. 3-year-olds and upward. Weights: 3-year-olds, 119 lbs.; Older, 122 lbs. Non-winners of two races at one mile or over since November 10, allowed 3 lbs. One such race, 5 lbs. Claiming price $18,500; for each $1,000 to $16,500, 1 lb. (Races where entered for $15,000 or less not considered.)**

LASIX—Muddy Rudder, Lick, Best Lord, Sycamore Slew, Lightning Strikes, Thundrbforthestorm, Dess's Cherokee, Bisher.

Muddy Rudder

B. g. 7, by Double Zeus—Steamboat Annie, by Potomac
$18,500 Br.—Barnesville Thoroughbred Farm (Md)
Own.—Stonefield Andrew J
Tr.—Devereux Joseph A (31 7 2 3 .23)
115

Lifetime						
71 10 20 15	1992	12	2	3	1	$26,250
$255,770	1991	20	1	6	4	$79,190
	Turf	16	0	5	4	$55,425
	Wet	6	1	2	1	$24,235

26Nov92- 6Lrl gd 1 1/16 :493 1:143 1:462 3↑Clm 14500 74 2 1 11 1hd 1hd 1hd Hutton G W Lb 117 4.90 81-18 MuddyRudder117hdSycmoreSlw1171BstLord119 Driving 6
6Nov92- 2Lrl fst 1 1/16 :482 1:131 1:451 3↑Clm 8500 72 7 1 11½ 12 12½ 13½ Hutton G W Lb 117 *3.10 87-10 MddyRddr1173½Ronok'sImg1173¼LnImprssn117 Driving 8
24Oct92- 3Lrl fm 1 1/16 Ⓣ:472 1:112 1:41 3↑Clm 11500 67 3 9 101010 11 915 914½ Hutton G W Lb 117 9.30 82-03 DixieDncer1175½RighteousMn1181¾BestLord117 Outrun 10
13Oct92- 6Lrl fst 1 1/16 :48 1:124 1:442 3↑Clm 18500 67 4 4 2½ 1hd 32½ 56¾ Hutton G W Lb 117 5.60 84-08 SptmbrStr117noHvYTstfd1173½DctrIchbd112 Weakened 7
4Oct92- 9Pim fst 1 1/16 :49 1:134 1:454 3↑Clm 20000 70 7 2 1hd 2hd 21 41½ Luzzi M J Lb 117 *1.20 73-23 WolfTon1151BrothrRobrts113½DctrIchbd117 Weakened 7
5Sep92-11Mth fm 1 1/16 Ⓣ:47 1:104 1:424 3↑Clm 25000 70 8 7 73¾ 84 86¼ 78½ Luzzi M J Lb 115 7.50 81-19 Anglus1151¼ThirdndMorris113nkWildrThnEvr118 No bid 10
7Aug92-10Lrl fst 1 1/16 :48 1:13 1:443 3↑Clm 25000 82 1 3 44 42½ 33 26¼ Prado E S Lb 117 *1.80 84-17 LttlBldJhn1176¼MddyRddr1171¾PrttyAmsng117 Rallied 8
26Jly92- 4Lrl fst 1⅛ :474 1:122 1:51 3↑Clm 35000 87 1 1 2hd 1hd 1hd 21 Prado E S Lb 117 *.70 84-28 ArcticOcen1151MuddyRudder11711¼LerndJk117 Gamely 3
26Jly92-Originally scheduled on turf
12Jly92- 8Lrl fst 1 1/16 :481 1:124 1:434 3↑Clm 35000 87 3 2 2hd 1hd 21 23½ Prado E S Lb 117 7.90 90-13 Dess'sCherokee1123½MuddyRudder117nkLnc117 Gamely 6
4Jly92- 8Lrl fst 6½f :223 :452 1:154 3↑Clm 35000 69 2 7 65 56¾ 67¼ 58 Guerra W A Lb 117 25.30 90-08 Dss'sChrok1121Jwlr'sChoic117¾ColonlHill117 No factor 8
LATEST WORKOUTS Nov 21 Lrl 5f fst 1:011 H

Lick

Ch. g. 5, by Thirty Eight Paces—Slick and Slippery, by Full Out
$18,500 Br.—Leatherbury & Wayson (Md)
Own.—Feifarek Kenneth J
Tr.—Posey D Scott (17 3 4 2 .18)
117

Lifetime						
57 11 12 3	1992	16	4	3	0	$45,035
$155,415	1991	18	2	5	1	$36,620
	Turf	3	0	1	0	$2,875
	Wet	4	1	1	0	$12,800

27Nov92- 8Lrl fst 1 1/16 :471 1:12 1:433 3↑Clm 18500 80 5 3 33 44½ 45 44¼ Rocco J Lb 117 1.80 91-15 DctrIchbd119nkSptbrStr1173HYTstfd117 Rated, no rlly 6
6Nov92- 9Lrl fst 1 1/16 :473 1:122 1:434 3↑Clm 18500 85 7 1 13 12 11½ 2¾ Rocco J Lb 117 3.10 93-10 Arctic Ocean119¾ Lick1172¾ Doctor Ichabod119 Gamely 8
27Oct92- 6Lrl fst 1 1/16 :47 1:113 1:432 3↑Clm 18500 87 1 1 12 1hd 1½ 2½ Rocco J L 117 *1.10 95-17 Doctor Ichabod117½ Lick117nk Wild John117 Gamely 7
26Sep92- 2Pim gd 1⅛ :464 1:11 1:501 3↑Hcp 16000s 72 1 2 3½ 32½ 59½ 511½ Rocco J Lb 117 6.80 73-18 Asserche118½AmeriVly1126HveYouTstifid115 Gave way 9
23Aug92- 6Lrl fst 1 1/16 :463 1:114 1:434 3↑Clm 16000 88 2 2 25 1½ 14 14½ Rocco J Lb 117 *1.80 94-14 Lick1174½ Johnny Use To1104½ Cap White115 Driving 6
19Jly92- 8Lrl fm 1⅛ Ⓣ:483 1:124 1:49 3↑Clm 16000 75 2 4 42½ 45 58 56¾ Rocco J Lb 119 2.90 79-14 Confrontation1151¼ BailDenied1174WolfeTone117 Rank 6
7Jly92- 4Lrl fst 1 1/16 :48 1:123 1:434 3↑Clm 16000 81 2 1 1½ 12½ 14 16½ Rocco J Lb 117 *2.10 94-07 Lick1176½ Alice's Beau115no Johnny Use To112 Driving 7
26Jun92- 3Pim fm 1 1/16 Ⓣ:482 1:14 1:461 3↑Clm 16000 76 9 1 13 12½ 11½ 63 Johnston M T Lb 118 3.50 67-26 MntnMdnss118hdCmnlthClb118noAssrch118 Weakened 9
5Jun92- 8Pim sly 1⅛ :48 1:124 1:531 Clm 20000 77 1 2 22 22 22 21½ Johnston M T Lb 114 4.80 68-32 HaveYouTestified1141½Lick1146PrinceDeklb112 Gamely 5
5Jun92-Originally scheduled on turf
16May92- 8Pim gd 1 3/16 :47 1:113 1:58 3↑Hcp 12000s 70 9 5 44½ 66½ 68 79¾ Johnston M T Lb 116 12.30 63-18 Bishr112½OncOvrKnightly112¾WorkingLt113 Weakened 10
LATEST WORKOUTS Nov 25 Bow 3f fst :38 B Oct 18 Bow 5f fst 1:02 B

Sycamore Slew

Dk. b. or br. g. 4, by Seattle Slew—Melody Tree, by High Tribute
$18,500 Br.—SB Syndicate (Ky)
Own.—Bassford Elaine L
Tr.—Leatherbury King T (125 26 20 20 .21)
117

Lifetime						
27 4 4 0	1992	16	2	2	0	$30,070
$74,259	1991	9	2	~~1~~	0	$36,239
	Turf	10	1	0	0	$11,100
	Wet	1	1	0	0	$17,979

26Nov92- 6Lrl gd 1 1/16 :493 1:143 1:462 3↑Clm c-14500 74 4 2 21 2hd 2hd 2hd Pino M G L 117 4.10 81-18 MuddyRudder117hdSycmoreSlw1171BstLord119 Gamely 6
26Nov92-Claimed from Seven Valleys Farm, Potts Dennis L Trainer
7Nov92- 4Lrl fst 1⅛ :48 1:13 1:502 3↑Clm 11500 89 2 1 1½ 12 1½ 2nk Pino M G L 117 4.00 88-18 FdrlLgu112nkSycmorSlw11718MorningMood117 Gamely 6
25Oct92-12Lrl fm 1 1/16 Ⓣ:47 1:113 1:421 3↑Clm 25000 55 3 8 108½ 1111 1110 1012½ Ladner C J III L 117 16.70 78-06 SpectculrMitch115½LernedJke117hdNvyPilot110 Outrun 12
10Oct92- 6Lrl fst 1 1/16 :481 1:13 1:441 3↑Alw 22600 79 7 7 712 58½ 56 610 Fenwick C C III L 117 25.10 82-08 BaronMthew117¾Mjesty'sTurn1133AmeriVly113 Outrun 8
22Sep92- 9Pim fm 1 1/16 Ⓣ:471 1:122 1:451 3↑Clm 16000 79 8 7 717 65½ 31 11¼ Pino M G L 117 6.50 75-24 SycmrSl1171¼SpctclrMtch117½Cnfrnttn115 Wide, drvng 9
14Jly92- 4Lrl fm 1⅛ Ⓣ:48 1:113 1:473 3↑Alw 22000 78 5 6 66 66½ 67¾ 510 Fenwick C C III 117 14.70 83-08 CrtivAct1171¾Logrtmo-Ch1174¾I'mALIDvl117 No factor 6
22Jun92- 3Bel gd 1 Ⓣ:48 1:122 1:363 Clm 35000 77 6 9 95¾ 103½ 84¼ 66¼ Davis R G 117 10.00 73-20 SovereignJustic1172Princ'sCov1171¾PrivtFlg117 Outrun 10
18Jun92- 1Bel fm 1 Ⓣ:45 1:094 1:35 Clm 35000 65 1 11 1113 104¾ 87½ 812 Madrid A Jr 117 6.20 75-11 Gills1171½ I'm So Bubbly117¾Dr.Bartolo117 Stead 1/4 pl 12
28May92- 2Bel fm 1 1/16 Ⓣ:464 1:11 1:412 Clm 50000 85 7 9 97½ 84¼ 63½ 54¾ Madrid A Jr 117 26.90 84-16 A.M.Swngr113nkIndnWrrr1171½Crtc'sCrnr117 No factor 9
18May92- 3Bel gd 1¼ Ⓣ:503 1:403 2:05 Clm 50000 84 1 8 87½ 84¾ 64¼ 43¾ Smith M E 117 10.80 61-26 HghlndDvtn117¾TsPrspct117hdAClltRs117 Belated rally 9

Lightning Strikes

Ch. g. 4, by Huckster—Anna's Queen, by Xoda
$18,500 Br.—Murphy Annabel & W F (Fla)
Own.—Schickedanz Bruno
Tr.—Wright Michael W (6 0 1 1 .00)
117

Lifetime						
35 7 3 3	1992	13	3	0	1	$40,989
$114,193	1991	16	2	1	1	$48,015
	Turf	8	1	1	0	$28,302
	Wet	4	1	1	1	$18,036

27Nov92- 8Lrl fst 1 1/16 :471 1:12 1:433 3↑Clm 18500 77 1 4 45 54¾ 55¼ 56 Hutton G W Lb 117 6.50 89-15 DoctorIchbd119nkSptmbrStr1173HvYTstfd117 Checked 6
4Nov92- 4Grd sl 1¼ :482 1:39 2:06 3↑Clm 19000 78 2 8 79 66¼ 57½ 54¾ Bahen S R Lb 119 8.00 82-24 StgActr1161¼CrwndMny1182½HghPrnr116 Saved ground 8
11Oct92- 8WO fst 1 1/16 :473 1:121 1:452 3↑Clm 32000 70 9 5 64 86¾ 79 710¼ Attard L Lb 118 8.45 77-20 BndthRd115¾Mrrbnt1151¼NrthrStr121 Never dangerous 9
27Sep92- 3WO fst 1 1/16 :49 1:13 1:46 3↑Clm c-25000 71 2 2 21½ 33½ 613 610¾ Lauzon J M Lb 118 2.90 73-19 T.DoblU.1186BrvAnthony116hdBndthRd119 Not keep up 7
27Sep92-Claimed from Fraser Paul, Charalambous John Trainer
17Sep92- 2WO fst 1 3/16 :481 1:124 1:593 3↑Clm c-20000 77 6 4 42½ 1hd 12 1½ Lauzon J M Lb 124 *1.45 90-17 LghtnngStrs124½BrvAnthn1161CrndMn116 Bore out str. 6
17Sep92-Claimed from Schickedanz Bruno, Wright Michael W Trainer
26Aug92- 6WO gd 1 1/16 :474 1:123 1:454 3↑Clm 20000 88 5 4 42 3½ 2hd 12¼ Lauzon J M Lb 121 3.80 85-23 LghtnngStrks1212¼BndthRd1243½LcFrbs117 Ridden out 7
13Aug92-10WO gd 1 1/16 :48 1:132 1:452 3↑Clm 24000 78 6 3 22½ 31½ 34 36½ Lauzon J M Lb 122 *2.05 80-13 BndthRd1161BrrBsh1185½LghtnngStrks122 Lacked rally 9
18Jly92- 3WO fst 1 1/16 :473 1:124 1:452 3↑Clm 24000 82 5 3 31½ 2hd 1hd 11¼ Lauzon J M Lb 116 4.90 87-13 LghtnngStrks1161¼WllwBrz1181DnGrsnt116 Ridden out 10
21Jun92- 8WO fm 1 1/16 Ⓣ:454 1:113 1:433 3↑Hcp 20000s 72 6 7 65½ 53 57¾ 55½ Lauzon J M Lb 114 *2.35e 70-24 Sword Dance116¾ CleverRuse117½Falk115 Showed little 12
LATEST WORKOUTS ●Nov 16 Lrl 5f fst 1:014 H Oct 30 WO tr.t 5f fst 1:043 B ●Oct 21 WO tr.t 5f sly 1:023 H Oct 6 WO 5f fst 1:01 B

Thundrbforthestorm Dk. b. or br. c. 4, by Five Star Flight—Rabida, by Rollicking
$18,500 Br.—Thomas Elizabeth F (Va)
Own.—Thomas Mrs Elizabeth F Tr.—Tagg Barclay (54 7 6 7 .13) 117
Lifetime 24 5 1 1 $86,585 | 1992 4 0 0 0 $1,730 | 1991 13 4 1 1 $73,050 | Turf 3 0 0 0 $2,100 | Wet 6 1 1 0 $34,980

17Nov92- 6Lrl fst 1 1/16 :491 1:132 1:441 3+ Clm 18500 80 3 2 2½ 2½ 3nk 4¾ Fenwick C C III L 117 10.30 88-16 DctrIchbd1193PrttyAmsng117½HvYTstfd117 Weakened 9
13Oct92- 9Lrl fst 7f :232 :462 1:233 3+ Clm 35000 67 8 9 915 914 912 78¾ Fenwick C C III L 117 58.40 80-14 Ebonizer115¾ Little Casino1192½ ColonelHill117 Outrun 9
22Aug92- 8Mth fst 1 :472 1:114 1:37 3+ Alw 27000 75 5 7 64¼ 77½ 78½ 715 Marquez C H Jr L 115 13.90 72-16 SmrtTime1152TimlyWrning1196½Pulvrizing115 No rally 7
16Aug92- 9Mth sly 6f :212 :442 1:101 3+ Sneakbox 70 5 5 821 821 817 710½ Marquez C H Jr L 113 19.60 79-14 FrndlyLovr119nkDontclsyrys115nkArbrcrst117 No threat 8
20Sep91- 9Med fst 1⅛ :46 1:093 1:462 Pegasus H 75 5 7 710 817 822 824½ Marquez C H Jr L 111 74.70 78-07 Scan1191¾ Sea Cadet1194 Sultry Song114 No factor 8
20Sep91-Grade I
2Sep91-10Pha fst 1⅛ :471 1:11 1:50 Pa Derby 78 2 10 107¾118¾10131014 Marquez C H Jr L 117 48.90 74-18 ValleyCrossing1191½GalaSpinwy122noRiflery117 Outrun 11
2Sep91-Grade II
24Aug91- 9Mth yl 1 1/16 Ⓣ:481 1:123 1:434 Choice H 80 8 9 96 86¾ 57¼ 615½ Marquez C H Jr L 117 14.50 70-18 StrofCozzen1156½TinCnAli1114AuggisHr113 Lacked bid 11
24Aug91-Grade III
27Jly91- 8Mth my 1 1/16 :461 1:11 1:44 Restoration 96 6 6 67¾ 43½ 2hd 11½ Marquez C H Jr L 117 13.50 89-17 Thndrbforthstrm1171½StrfCzzn1193¾TnCnAl113 Driving 8
27Jly91-Originally scheduled on turf
4Jly91-10Mth fm 1 1/16 Ⓣ:461 1:10 1:412 + Lamplghtr H 83 7 10 106 95¼ 88¾ 711¾ Gryder A T L 114 24.70 82-14 Futurist1152 Lech1152¾ Auggies Here108 Outrun 11
4Jly91-Grade III
16Jun91- 8Mth fm 1 1/16 Ⓣ:464 1:101 1:413 + J Msorley 85 8 7 75¼ 86¾ 62¼ 42½ Marquez C H Jr L 113 24.40 90-06 Mr.Peregrine113¾BrickWall119½WildDncer113 Late gain 10
LATEST WORKOUTS Nov 28 Lrl 4f fst :483 Hg Nov 14 Lrl 7f fst 1:27 H Oct 9 Lrl 4f gd :50 B

Dess's Cherokee B. h. 5, by Cherokee Fellow—Tennat, by Tentam
$18,500 Br.—Kinsman Stud Farm (Fla)
Own.—Greene Fred A Jr Tr.—Mitchell H Steward (41 7 5 6 .17) 117
Lifetime 51 9 13 9 $169,150 | 1992 19 4 2 3 $54,450 | 1991 7 1 3 1 $28,750 | Wet 3 0 1 0 $4,290

28Nov92- 6Lrl fst 7f :241 :474 1:234 3+ Clm 25000 77 8 4 77½ 87¼ 66½ 53½ Prado E S Lb 117 *2.50 84-18 Kelli'sSecrt117¾ArcticOcn1171¼MjsticGm117 No threat 8
14Nov92- 6Lrl fst 6f :22 :444 1:091 Clm 30000 84 4 6 58 612 69½ 66 Hamilton S D Lb 115 8.30 89-17 Stalker1171¾ Little Casino119hd Colonel Hill117 Outrun 7
13Oct92- 9Lrl fst 7f :232 :462 1:233 3+ Clm 35000 79 4 7 78¾ 78¾ 56½ 53¼ Hamilton S D5 Lb 112 7.30 86-14 Ebonizer115¾LittleCasino1192½ColonelHill117 No threat 9
1Oct92- 8Pim fst 1 1/16 :474 1:114 1:442 3+ Alw 22300 68 2 7 716 717 715 612¼ Seefeldt A J Lb 117 3.50 70-29 Alexis's David1133 T. V.Supper117½BlueBuck117 Outrun 7
19Sep92- 8Pim fst 1 1/16 :481 1:13 1:44 3+ Alw 25000 76 1 3 34 68½ 510 69¼ Hamilton S D5 Lb 112 *2.10 75-22 Pulverizing112½ Lost Dutchman1171¼ Coringa112 Faded 6
4Aug92- 8Lrl fst 6½f :223 :461 1:164 3+ Aiw 20580 93 1 1 58¼ 54½ 43 41¼ Hamilton S D5 Lb 114 *1.70 92-20 Encstc122½Apprtontofollw114¾FrtntLnc122 Belated bid 5
12Jly92- 8Lrl fst 1 1/16 :481 1:124 1:434 3+ Clm 35000 93 5 3 42½ 33 11 13½ Hamilton S D5 Lb 112 2.70 94-13 Dess'sCherokee1123½MuddyRudder117nkLnc117 Driving 6
4Jly92- 8Lrl fst 6½f :223 :452 1:154 3+ Clm 35000 88 4 8 75½ 77¼ 52¼ 11 Hamilton S D5 Lb 112 5.70 98-08 Dess'sCherok1121Jwlr'sChoic117¾ColonlHill117 Driving 8
2Jun92- 4Pim fst 6f :224 :451 1:102 Clm 35000 89 1 5 615 616 59½ 51¾ Seefeldt A J Lb 114 4.80 91-13 Big Jewel114hd AmeriRun114hdEagleMill114 Stride late 6
23May92- 6Pim fst 6f :231 :463 1:11 Clm 35000 87 4 6 612 57 45½ 2¾ Hamilton S D7 Lb 107 3.10 89-14 DirectApproch114¾Dess'sCherokee107¾ElHero114 Wide 6
LATEST WORKOUTS Nov 7 Bow 4f fst :531 B Nov 3 Bow 3f sly :38 B Oct 26 Bow 3f fst :391 B Oct 17 Bow 3f fst :394 B

Bisher B. g. 4, by Spring Double—Destry Again, by Search for Gold
$18,500 Br.—Sporting Life Stable (Md)
Own.—Alecci John V Tr.—Patty Karen A (44 11 7 4 .25) 119
Lifetime 33 6 9 5 $100,690 | 1992 18 4 5 3 $64,480 | 1991 15 2 4 2 $36,210 | Turf 3 0 0 0 $300

13Nov92- 6Lrl fst 1⅛ :472 1:113 1:50 3+ Alw 20300 86 5 5 66 66 21½ 1½ Prado E S Lb 117 *1.40 90-16 Bisher117½ Turpial1146¾ Ojinsky117 Very wide 7
13Nov92-Originally scheduled on turf
17Oct92- 4Lrl fst 7f :234 :47 1:24 3+ Million H 81 3 6 610 611 510 47¼ Pincay L Jr Lb 117 *1.60 80-18 Snw'sDynsty1123¾Crny'sKd1121¾OhSyJs109 Sluggish st 6
26Sep92- 4Pim gd 1 1/16 :464 1:114 1:433 3+ Alw 6500s 91 7 10 89¾ 32½ 22 2nk Desormeaux KJ Lb 117 *1.10 86-18 ScrThrtyEght117nkBshr11711½Aldn'sCrwn117 Very wide 10
11Sep92- 9Pim fst 1 1/16 :464 1:114 1:44 3+ Alw 21500 80 9 10 919 813 59½ 35 Turner T G Lb 117 11.90 79-27 Baron Mathew1173¾ Prayer Rug1171¼ Bisher117 Rallied 11
18Jly92- 7Lrl fm 1½ Ⓣ:523 2:082 2:313 3+ Md Mil Mar H 59 7 4 32½ 916 919 922 Prado E S Lb 115 6.70 70-09 NoFmr117nkWorkngLt1142½HvYTstfd116 Dropped back 9
10Jly92- 9Lrl fm 1⅛ Ⓣ:48 1:122 1:484 3+ Alw 21500 69 2 3 43½ 76¼11161112¼ Prado E S Lb 119 8.90 75-10 AlpnChoc1191¼MstrMcGrth117noHstyRqst117 Fell back 11
20Jun92- 9Pim fst 1 1/16 :472 1:113 1:44 3+ Alw 19000 85 4 5 57 55½ 23 22 Prado E S Lb 123 2.10 82-20 Perfect Star1182 Bisher1232¼ Blue Buck118 Wide 7
11Jun92- 8Pim fm 1 1/16 Ⓣ:47 1:112 1:43 3+ Alw 19000 91 8 6 68 66½ 55½ 72¾ Prado E S Lb 123 12.80 83-17 UpinFront118¾SlwofBills118½MrylndMoon112 No factor 11
31May92-10Pim gd 1 1/16 :47 1:111 1:44 3+ Alw 18000 89 3 4 46½ 35½ 2hd 13 Prado E S Lb 124 2.60 84-10 Bisher1243 Driver o' Gold1074½ Bay Capp109 Driving 6
16May92- 8Pim gd 1 3/16 :47 1:113 1:58 3+ Hcp 12000s 84 8 7 77 56 1½ 1½ Prado E S Lb 112 8.50 72-18 Bshr112½OncOvrKnghtly112¾WrkngLt113 Wide, driving 10

Bisher's most recent figure, an 86, was clearly better than anybody else's, but several horses in the field — Lick, Sycamore Slew, and Dess's Cherokee — had earned numbers in the mid to upper 80s in their next to last starts. If I hadn't been following these horses on a day-to-day basis when I was at Laurel, I might have dismissed this race as being too wide open, too tough. But I knew enough about the horses to recognize which figures were legitimate and which weren't, and I concluded that this was the outstanding play on the Mirage's menu that day.

Sycamore Slew had earned an 89 in his next-to-last start under circumstances he would surely never again see in his life. The field consisted of six plodders, and he fell into an uncontested two-length lead by default. Under slightly more normal circumstances in his next start, he had earned a figure of 74, which better reflected his true ability. Dess's Cherokee did show an 84 in his next-to-last race, but he had had an ideal pace situation in that race. The leaders had battled the first half mile in 44⅘ seconds, which should have helped the stretch-runner, yet he still couldn't pass a horse in the stretch. I doubted that he would even duplicate the 77 of his last start; most of the wins in his career had come in sprints, and now he was going a distance where he had generally been less effective.

From the standpoint of figures, Bisher and Lick were the best. Bisher's last six figures in route races on the dirt were 86, 91, 80, 85, 89, and 84. He was as consistent and reliable as they come. Lick's last three numbers were 80, 85, and 87. But what about that weak last race?

Lick was a habitual front-runner whose best performances almost always came when he was on or near the lead, but the *Racing Form*'s comment on his last race was, "Rated, no rally." This was a polite euphemism for "What was the pinhead jockey doing with the horse?" but that wouldn't have fit in the allotted space. Lick had appeared likely to take the lead in that six-horse field, but his rider, Joe Rocco, chose not to send him to the front. How would he run today?

At first glance, there appeared to be plenty of speed in this field — Muddy Rudder, Sycamore Slew, and Thundrbforthestorm had all been racing on or near the lead in their last starts. But they weren't really fast. Muddy Rudder and Sycamore Slew had been running 1-2 in their last start after covering the quarter mile in 25 seconds and the half mile in :49⅗. Thundrbforthestorm had dueled for the lead in 49⅕ seconds. By contrast, Lick routinely ran his first half mile in :47-and-change. He was going to control this race and do it with ease. His best figures were virtually even with Bisher's, anyway, and today he would have everything in his favor. Bisher was the type of one-dimensional stretch-runner who usually needed a fast pace in front of him to do his best, and he wouldn't get it today. This looked like a cold Lick-Bisher exacta.

SEVENTH RACE
Laurel
DECEMBER 6, 1992

1 $\frac{1}{16}$ MILES. (1.414) CLAIMING. Purse $13,500. 3-year-olds and upward. Weights: 3-year-olds, 119 lbs.; Older, 122 lbs. Non-winners of two races at one mile or over since November 10, allowed 3 lbs. One such race, 5 lbs. Claiming price $18,500; for each $1,000 to $16,500, 1 lb. (Races where entered for $15,000 or less not considered.)

Value of race $13,700; value to winner $7,695; second $2,835; third $1,485; fourth $810; fifth $405; sixth $270; seventh $200.
Mutuel pool $45,196. Exacta Pool $70,875. Triple Pool $51,360.

Last Raced	Horse	M/Eqt.A.Wt	PP	St	¼	½	¾	Str	Fin	Jockey	Cl'g Pr	Odds $1
27Nov92 8Lrl4	Lick	Lb 5 117	2	1	1²	1³	1³	1²	1³	Rocco J	18500	3.20
13Nov92 6Lrl1	Bisher	Lb 4 119	7	7	7	7	7	5³	2²	Prado E S	18500	1.90
26Nov92 6Lrl1	Muddy Rudder	Lb 7 115	1	3	4³	2½	21½	2¹	3½	Hutton G W	18500	11.20
28Nov92 6Lrl5	Dess's Cherokee	Lb 5 117	6	2	5²	6³	3hd	3¹	4¾	Johnston MT	18500	4.10
17Nov92 6Lrl4	Thundrbforthestorm	Lb 4 117	5	6	62¼	5hd	5hd	4½	5⁵	FnwickCCIII	18500	6.10
26Nov92 6Lrl2	Sycamore Slew	L 4 117	3	4	31½	3½	41½	62¼	62¼	Reynolds L C	18500	6.60
27Nov92 8Lrl5	Lightning Strikes	Lb 4 117	4	5	2hd	4²	6³	7	7	Douglas F G	18500	10.70

OFF AT 2:48. Start good. Won driving. Time, :24², :48 , 1:12⁴, 1:39 , 1:45³ Track fast.

$2 Mutuel Prices:

2-LICK	8.40	4.00	2.80
7-BISHER		3.20	2.40
1-MUDDY RUDDER			3.00

$2 EXACTA 2-7 PAID $20.60. $3 TRIPLE 2-7-1 PAID $110.40.

Ch. g, by Thirty Eight Paces—Slick and Slippery, by Full Out. Trainer Posey D Scott. Bred by Leatherbury & Wayson (Md).

LICK set the pace near the rail and dug in to turn back BISHER. The latter closed gamely between horses. MUDDY RUDDER faded. DESS'S CHEROKEE saved ground and hung. THUNDRBFORTHESTORM was no threat. SYCAMORE SLEW weakened. LIGHTNING STRIKES, wide, gave way.

Owners— 1, Feifarek Kenneth J; 2, Alecci John V; 3, Stonefield Andrew J; 4, Greene Fred A Jr; 5, Thomas Mrs Elizabeth F; 6, Bassford Elaine L; 7, Schickedanz Bruno.

Trainers— 1, Posey D Scott; 2, Patty Karen A; 3, Devereux Joseph A; 4, Mitchell H Steward; 5, Tagg Barclay; 6, Leatherbury King T; 7, Wright Michael W.

Lick was claimed by Miller Michael J; trainer, Regan Scott T.

Scratched—Best Lord (26Nov92 6Lrl3).

The $20.60 payoff on this exacta helped me move into the black by the end of my third day in Las Vegas. As I contemplated the day's events, I experienced a revelation of sorts. Handicappers have traditionally approached horse races by looking for potential winners who are standouts. I have always started my analysis of the speed figures in a race by identifying the single horse who has an edge over the rest c the field. Yet it is a memorable event for any handicapper to come up with a genuine standout who pays a long price. There are too many sharp bettors with toŏ much information at America's tracks to let solid horses pay huge overlay prices. Certainly, we may cash bets on horses with good dope in wide-open races, but I have to search my memory for the times in recent years when I have proclaimed, "This horse can't lose!" and have collected a $20 mutuel. I wouldn't expect to find a horse like Time for Class for weeks or months, and I believe the handicapping books that recommend a quest for sizable win payoffs on solid horses may be sending their readers on a mission impossible. The readers then feel inadequate when they don't collect the generous win prices that are supposedly the object of the game.

By contrast, though, I had collected, in the space of a few hours,

$20 payoffs on both the Easy Best–I've Got Jessica and the Lick-Bisher exactas, and they were both standouts. In fact, wagers like these sometimes seem so easy and obvious that horseplayers shrug off the achievement of picking them. Tell a fellow handicapper that you doped out a $20 winner and he'll shower you with praise; brag that you collected a $20 exacta and he'll probably shrug and say, "Anybody could have picked that." Indeed, these modestly priced exactas often represent the most probable outcome of a race. If the crowd sees a race as a virtual two-horse affair, with the favorites at odds of 2 to 1 and 5 to 2, the exacta combining those two horses will almost always pay in the $20–$25 range. Given the relative ease of cashing bets like this, might it not make sense for handicappers to seek out situations where two horses have a huge edge over the rest of the field instead of the traditional spots where one horse has a big edge?

This idea was germinating in my mind as I started to handicap Tuesday's races, and as I did, one opportunity leaped off the pages of the *Daily Racing Form.* This one, too, was at Laurel, but unlike the Lick-Bisher exacta it didn't require any special knowledge of the horses. It was a speed handicapper's equivalent of a fastball down the middle of the plate.

9 START 7 FURLONGS LAUREL FINISH

7 FURLONGS. **(1.212) MAIDEN SPECIAL WEIGHT. Purse $15,500. Fillies and Mares, 3-4-and-5-year-olds. Weight, 3-year-olds, 120 lbs. Older, 122 lbs.**

Coupled—Tin Oaks and How Lovely.
LASIX—Thirty Eight Kimbo, Tin Oaks, Brook House, Strawberry Cocoon.

Thirty Eight Kimbo — **Ro. f. 3(May), by Thirty Eight Paces—Aladamy, by Dewan** — Lifetime 13 0 5 2 $14,160 — 1992 13 M 5 2 $14,160 — 1991 0 M 0 0
Br.—Cowne Lloyd R & Penny S (Va)
Own.—Souder Donald E — **Tr.—Souder Donald E (26 1 4 2 .04)** — **120**

27Nov92-11Lrl fst 6f :221 :452 1:102 3+ⒻMd Sp Wt **63** 9 6 64¼ 55 36½ 38½ Hutton G W Lb 120 4.90 80-19 DptMss1206¾AtmnRsh1201¾ThrtEghtKmb120 No threat 10
15Nov92- 2Lrl fst 1 1/16 :474 1:132 1:463 3+ⒻMd 20000 **66** 5 2 2hd 1hd 1hd 2no Hamilton S D Lb 117 5.10 80-20 I'mVvd119noThrtyEghtKmbo1177½Adothony119 Gamely 9
29Oct92- 1Lrl fst 6f :23 :464 1:12 3+ⒻMd 14500 **59** 2 1 21½ 33 32 2¾ Hutton G W Lb 119 5.20 80-15 IdlPris119¾ThrtyEghtKmbo119½AutumnRush117 Rallied 7
22Oct92-10Lrl fst 6f :222 :462 1:122 3+ⒻMd Sp Wt **37** 4 10 1010 1012 910 98½ Johnston M T Lb 119 18.50 70-20 BBlm1193¼StrwbrryCocoon119hdHowLvly122 No factor 14
15Oct92- 3Lrl fst 6½f :223 :464 1:192 3+ⒻMd c-11500 **29** 5 6 52¾ 53 43½ 49½ Hutton G W Lb 119 *1.40 70-19 Judr'sMnt1196APrvtMttr119½PlmpChckd119 No threat 9
15Oct92-Claimed from Miller Jane D, Miller Jane D Trainer
5Sep92- 6Del fst 6f :224 :464 1:12 ⒻMd Sp Wt **59** 1 5 2hd 2hd 2hd 2no Douglas F G Lb 122 *1.90 87-12 CryptcRnnr122noThrtyEghtKmb1224Mrs.Crr122 Gamely 7
20Aug92- 5Lrl fst 6f :223 :472 1:123 3+ⒻMd 16000 **47** 1 4 21 1hd 22½ 27 Hutton G W Lb 117 5.90 71-17 Aln'sTrn1177ThrtyEghtKmbo1173PckUp117 Held place 10
20Aug92-Disqualified from purse money
9Aug92- 2Lrl fst 6f :224 :473 1:144 3+ⒻMd 16000 **32** 2 4 34 35 45 31¾ Douglas F G Lb 117 *3.30 65-21 MsclMsq115nkBornPrfct1171½ThrtyEghtKmb117 Closed 10
25Jun92- 2Pim fst 1 1/16 :48 1:123 1:453 3+ⒻMd 35000 **25** 8 7 77¼ 912 918 923 Douglas F G Lb 113 9.40 53-25 Vaulted1141¼ImperialMonrch1181¾ChicBrod112 Outrun 9
12Jun92- 7Del fst 1 1/16 :481 1:14 1:472 3+ⒻMd Sp Wt **51** 3 2 2hd 1hd 21 22 Jones S R Lb 112 *1.00 73-19 CrockRck1122ThrtyEghtKmb1126¾GrlBrwn112 2nd best 7

Biras Creek — **Ch. f. 3(Jan), by Graustark—As Hot As, by Shecky Greene** — Lifetime 2 0 0 1 — 1992 2 M 0 1 — 1991 0 M 0 0
Br.—Folsom Robert S (Tex)
Own.—Rosenborg Suzanne — **Tr.—Price Harry W Jr (—)** — **120**

Entered 7Dec92- 4 PHA
17Nov92- 1Pha fst 1 1/16 :493 1:154 1:511 3+ⒻMd 8000 — 5 7 813 926 — — Black A S b 118 4.90 — — Tortola11514OutlawSquaw1201¾Lbnc118 Sqzd st, eased 9
7Nov92- 2Mtp gd *1 1:43 3+ⒻSpec'l Wt — 3 3 42½ 34 311 318 Moran A3 137 —— — — FoolishDancer14710GildedMiss1458BirsCreek137 Evenly 4
LATEST WORKOUTS ●Nov 30 Del 4f fst :472 Bg Oct 30 Fai tr.t 5f fst 1:05 B

Dixie Data

B. f. 4, by Dixieland Band—Deo Data, by Tom Rolfe
Br.—Beedham Phil & Dick Richard (KY)
Own.—Sharp Bayard — Tr.—Peoples Charles (7 0 1 1 .00) — **122**

Lifetime 11 0 4 2 $17,543 | 1992 11 M 4 2 $17,543 | 1991 0 M 0 0 | Turf 1 0 0 0 | Wet 2 0 1 0 $3,100

14Nov92- 7Lrl fst 6f :22 :45^4 1:12^2 3↑Ⓕ Md Sp Wt 47 8 2 10^{15} 10^{15} 6^{10} 3^4 Rocco J 122 6.00 75–17 Tears In Time120^4 BrookHouse120^{hd}DixieData122 Wide 10
17Sep92-10Pim fst 6f :23^2 :47^1 1:13^1 3↑Ⓕ Md Sp Wt 51 5 9 10^{18} 9^{14} 9^{11} 5^{3¾} Agnello A 122b 8.80 75–17 Sh'sSoMsty118^{nk}ChcltDlt118^{2½}OpnMrrg118 Bore out st. 10
17Sep92-Dead heat
25Jly92- 1Lrl my 7f :23^4 :48^2 1:27^2 3↑Ⓕ Md Sp Wt 52 4 6 7^{8¾} 7^{7¾} 3^{6½} 2^{2½} Reynolds L C 122 3.00 68–22 Runaway Sally115^{2½} Dixie Data122^{no} I'm Vivid110 Wide 7
14Jly92- 5Lrl fst 6f :22^3 :46^1 1:12^1 3↑Ⓕ Md Sp Wt 56 6 11 12^{9½} 9^{12} 6^8 3^4 Pino M G 122 16.90 76–15 Rougegait115^{hd} Fort Bound115^4 Dixie Data122 Wide 13
28Jun92- 6Pim fm 1$\frac{1}{16}$ Ⓣ:47^3 1:13^2 1:45^4 3↑Ⓕ Md Sp Wt 46 8 2 2^2 2^{½} 5^{3½} 8^{12} Castillo F^5 118 12.40 60–15 CinnamonItch112^{¾}Acar'sBby107^{1}StillBusy107 Fell back 11
6Jun92- 7Pim fst 6f :23^1 :46^3 1:12^4 3↑Ⓕ Md Sp Wt 55 6 5 5^{1½} 7^{10} 5^{7½} 4^7 Hamilton S D^7 115 4.60 74–14 SouthrnSultn113^{4½}Rouggt113^{1½}RunwySlly113 No threat 8
26May92- 3Pim sly 6f :23 :46^3 1:12^3 3↑Ⓕ Md Sp Wt 44 6 3 4^4 5^{7½} 4^{10} 5^{12½} Guerra W A 122 6.20 70–20 NtonlAccont114^{8½}Rprmnd113^{1}IGlooCnOo107 Weakened 8
3May92- 7Pim fst 6f :23^1 :47^2 1:13^2 Ⓕ Md Sp Wt 51 5 2 5^3 4^2 2^3 2^{¾} Prado E S 122 12.80 77–17 Dior'sAngel112^{¾}DixieDat122^{no}NtionlAccount114 Closed 11
31Mar92- 9Pim fst 6f :23^1 :47 1:12^2 3↑Ⓕ Md Sp Wt 49 9 2 4^{2½} 3^3 2^{3½} 5^{8½} Prado E S 122 5.10 74–19 CrftyNEgr114^{3½}Kmonn112^{3½}ImprlMnrch122 Weakened 10
1Mar92- 3Lrl fst 6f :23^1 :47^4 1:14^1 Ⓕ Md Sp Wt 56 2 5 2^2 2^3 2^{3½} 2^{7½} Prado E S 122 *1.30 62–30 SpicyMythology122^{7½}DixieDt122^{4½}PlsntFbl122 2nd best 8

Tin Oaks

B. f. 3(Feb), by Deputy Minister—Squan Song, by Exceller
Br.—Skara Glen Stable (Ky)
Own.—Cohen I — Tr.—Gaudet Dean (24 2 0 3 .08) — **120**

Lifetime 3 0 0 0 $1,530 | 1992 3 M 0 0 $1,530 | 1991 0 M 0 0

27Nov92-11Lrl fst 6f :22^1 :45^2 1:10^2 3↑Ⓕ Md Sp Wt 35 1 1 7^{9¾} 8^{9¼} 9^{14} 8^{19¾} Fenwick C C III L 120 8.60e 69–19 DputyMss120^{6¾}AtmnRsh120^{1¾}ThrtyEghtKmbo120 Wide 10
14Nov92- 7Lrl fst 6f :22 :45^4 1:12^2 3↑Ⓕ Md Sp Wt 4 6 1 3^{4½} 3^{6½} 8^{14} 9^{21¼} Fenwick C C III Lb 120 *1.30e 58–17 TersInTim120^{4}BrookHous120^{hd}DixiDt122 Dropped back 10
22Oct92-10Lrl fst 6f :22^2 :46^2 1:12^2 3↑Ⓕ Md Sp Wt 44 8 11 9^{9¾} 8^9 8^{9¾} 4^{5¾} Fenwick C C III L 119 *1.80e 73–20 BBlm119^{3½}StrwbrryCocn119^{hd}HwLvly122 Passed faders 14
LATEST WORKOUTS Nov 7 Lrl 5f fst 1:01 Hg ●Oct 17 Lrl 4f fst :48 H Oct 10 Lrl 5f gd 1:02^3 Bg

Dream Awhile

Dk. b. or br. f. 3(Apr), by Capote—Dreamworld, by Alydar
Br.—Calumet Farm & Lukas D W (Ky)
Own.—Riggs Mrs Augustus IV — Tr.—Lukas D Wayne (—) — **120**

Lifetime 6 0 0 2 $7,918 | 1992 1 M 0 1 $2,470 | 1991 5 M 0 1 $5,448 | Wet 1 0 0 1 $2,880

3Nov92- 6CD fst 6f :21^3 :45^4 1:12 3↑Ⓕ Md Sp Wt 62 3 3 4^{nk} 4^3 3^{3½} 3^{5¾} Allen K K LB 119 22.10 80–14 OWckd114^{¾}MdmBrzng119^{5}DrmAhl119 No late response 12
10Nov91- 3CD fst 6f :22^2 :47^1 1:12^3 Ⓕ Md Sp Wt 61 5 6 4^{1½} 5^{3½} 4^{5½} 4^{6½} Sellers S J LB 119 9.00 77–19 DawnLaunch119^{3}GloryWon119^{½}CozyColony114 No rally 12
9Oct91- 3Kee fst 1$\frac{1}{16}$:49^4 1:14^3 1:46^4 Ⓕ Md Sp Wt 25 7 4 3^{2½} 7^{12} 7^{20} 6^{23} Day P B 121 2.20 47–27 FloresPeak121^{6}DonnaSaysSo116^{2½}RiverOrchid121 Tired 8
7Aug91- 3Sar fst 7f :22^4 :45^2 1:24 Ⓕ Md Sp Wt 14 5 7 8^{10} 8^{15} 8^{15} 8^{29½} Smith M E 117 *.70e 55–09 Vivno117^{8}PnnntFvr117^{10}BournToMony117 Broke in air 8
19Jly91- 4Bel fst 6f :22^2 :46^1 1:11^3 Ⓕ Md Sp Wt 54 5 4 3^1 3^{nk} 4^{3½} 4^{8¾} Bailey J D 117 *.70e 73–15 Mattie North117^2 Secretly117^{6¾} Lizeality117 Tired 7
20Jun91- 4Bel my 5f :21^2 :44^3 :57^3 Ⓕ Md Sp Wt 52 6 7 6^8 6^{7½} 4^{6½} 3^{6½} Bailey J D 117 3.30 93–06 IFellForIt117^{3}FutureQustion117^{3½}DrmAwhil117 Greenly 7
LATEST WORKOUTS Nov 28 Bow 4f fst :49^3 B Nov 21 Bow 3f fst :36^4 H Oct 31 CD 4f fst :50 Bg Oct 27 Bow 4f fst :50^2 B

Argenteous

Dk. b. or br. f. 3(Mar), by Cox's Ridge—Argentario, by Believe It
Br.—Cox Edward A Jr (Ky)
Own.—Christiana Stables — Tr.—Clark Henry S (17 5 0 2 .29) — **120**

Lifetime 4 0 0 0 $1,240 | 1992 2 M 0 0 $1,240 | 1991 2 M 0 0

27Nov92-11Lrl fst 6f :22^1 :45^2 1:10^2 3↑Ⓕ Md Sp Wt 43 3 9 8^{10} 9^{11} 7^{11} 6^{16½} McCarron G 120 8.10 72–19 DptyMss120^{6¾}AtmnRsh120^{1¾}ThrtyEghtKmb120 Outrun 10
14Nov92- 7Lrl fst 6f :22 :45^4 1:12^2 3↑Ⓕ Md Sp Wt 43 7 3 8^{11} 7^{10} 5^9 4^{5¾} McCarron G 120 10.80 73–17 Tears In Time120^4 BrookHouse120^{hd}DixieData122 Wide 10
18Nov91- 3Aqu fst 1 :46^2 1:12^1 1:39 Ⓕ Md Sp Wt 48 7 6 6^{3½} 5^4 6^8 6^{10} Lidberg D W b 117 5.30e 57–27 WyfthWrld117^{2}RylChrtr117^{4¾}Slpththnmy117 No factor 8
7Nov91- 6Aqu fst 7f :23^2 :47^2 1:25^2 Ⓕ Md Sp Wt 40 5 5 9^6 11^{11} 10^{11} 7^{15} Lidberg D W b 117 28.90 60–19 AplchSnst117^{3½}ⒹSlvpln117^{1½}WyofthWorld117 No threat 11
LATEST WORKOUTS Nov 21 Pim 5f fst 1:01^2 H ●Nov 13 Pim 3f fst :35^2 B ●Nov 7 Pim 5f fst 1:01 H Oct 31 Pim 5f sly 1:04 B

Prettyfineandmine

Ch. f. 4, by Horatius—Surgency, by Surge Ahead
Br.—Shane Margaret M (Del)
Own.—Eltringham-Shane Stable — Tr.—Shane M Terry (2 0 1 0 .00) — **122**

Lifetime 2 0 1 0 $3,830 | 1992 2 M 1 0 $3,830 | 1991 0 M 0 0 | Wet 1 0 1 0 $3,255

9Oct92- 2Lrl my 7f :23^1 :47^3 1:26^2 3↑Ⓕ Md Sp Wt 49 4 4 5^{9½} 5^{12} 3^{7½} 2^{9¾} Chavez S N 122 25.10 65–22 ChocltDlit119^{9¾}Prttyfinndmin122^{nk}OpnMrrig119 Rallied 8
24Sep92- 2Pim fst 6f :23^2 :47^1 1:14 3↑Ⓕ Md 25000 42 5 5 7^{12} 7^{15} 7^{13} 4^{5¾} Chavez S N 122 11.20 69–21 ShckysFrl118^{2½}Bl'sMt118^{1½}ExbrntAnswr118 Stride late 9
LATEST WORKOUTS Nov 29 Pim 6f fst 1:18 B Nov 17 Pim 3f fst :38^3 B Nov 4 Pim 6f fst 1:17^3 B Oct 24 Pim 5f fst 1:04 B

Brook House

B. f. 3(May), by Dancing Count—Queen Ana, by An Act
Br.—Steele James B Jr (Md)
Own.—Steele James B — Tr.—McCormick Harold F (6 0 1 1 .00) — **120**

Lifetime 3 0 1 0 $4,260 | 1992 3 M 1 0 $4,260 | 1991 0 M 0 0

27Nov92-11Lrl fst 6f :22^1 :45^2 1:10^2 3↑Ⓕ Md Sp Wt 51 5 10 9^{11} 7^9 5^9 5^{13½} Reynolds L C Lb 120 10.00 75–19 DptMss120^{6¾}AtmnRsh120^{1¾}ThrtEghtKmb120 Stumbled 10
14Nov92- 7Lrl fst 6f :22 :45^4 1:12^2 3↑Ⓕ Md Sp Wt 47 5 9 6^9 4^7 3^5 2^4 Reynolds L C Lb 120 8.70 75–17 TearsInTime120^{4}BrookHouse120^{hd}DixieData122 Rallied 10
29Oct92- 1Lrl fst 6f :23 :46^4 1:12 3↑Ⓕ Md 14500 50 7 7 6^6 4^{4½} 4^{3½} 4^{4½} Reynolds L C b 119 19.90 76–15 IdlPrs119^{¾}ThrtyEghtKmb119^{½}AtmnRsh117 Sluggish st. 7
LATEST WORKOUTS Oct 21 CT 4f fst :50^2 Hg Oct 17 CT 4f fst :50^1 Hg Oct 14 CT 3f fst :39^2 B

Strawberry Cocoon

Ro. f. 3(Apr), by Spectacular Bid—Moth, by Drone
Br.—Claiborne Farm & Hermitage Farm (Ky)
Own.—Jones Don — Tr.—O'Brien Maura C (6 0 1 0 .00) — **120**

Lifetime 6 0 2 0 $7,020 | 1992 5 M 2 0 $6,300 | 1991 1 M 0 0 $720 | Wet 1 0 0 0 $345

16Nov92- 5Pha fst 7f :22^3 :46^3 1:27^4 3↑Ⓕ Md Sp Wt 33 1 7 5^{5½} 2^{2½} 1^{hd} 2^{8½} Delgado A L 119 *.60 59–25 Adlph'sAccnt119^{8½}StrbrrCcn119^{4½}Ac'sGrl122 No match 11
22Oct92-10Lrl fst 6f :22^2 :46^2 1:12^2 3↑Ⓕ Md Sp Wt 50 3 7 7^{5½} 5^7 4^{4½} 2^{3½} Delgado A L 119 41.50 76–20 BBlum119^{3½}StrwbrryCocoon119^{hd}HowLovly122 Rallied 14
9Oct92- 1Lrl my 6f :23^2 :47^3 1:12^4 3↑Ⓕ Md 25000 51 1 6 7^5 8^{10} 6^9 5^{5½} Barthlow C T^{10} L 109 34.00 71–22 SyIt'sGold119^{3½}BeeBlum119^{no}IGlooCnOo114 Very wide 8
28Mar92- 7Pim fst 6f :23^1 :47^3 1:13^3 3↑Ⓕ Md 25000 18 4 7 5^{5½} 8^{8¾} 9^{11} 8^{16} Peterson T L L 112 5.10 61–26 PrsistntCook113^{5½}OopsIAm114^{hd}PrttyPcs112 No factor 11
10Mar92- 4Lrl fst 6f :22^4 :46^3 1:12^4 Ⓕ Md Sp Wt 40 7 3 5^{2½} 6^8 6^{10} 5^{9½} Peterson T L 120 9.20 67–18 MardelaSprings120^{1½}Jadeeda120^{4½}CrftyNEger120 Wide 8
21Aug91- 3Pha fst 5½f :22^3 :46^3 1:06 Ⓕ Md Sp Wt 22 4 6 7^{14} 7^{12} 6^{11} 4^{11½} Matz N^5 114 *.80 72–16 Sunny'sSdkck119^{2½}StrdyAffr119^{2½}TnsyTm119 Off slow 7
LATEST WORKOUTS Dec 3 Bow 4f fst :51^2 B

How Lovely

Gr. f. 4, by Dr Carter—Victoria Beauty, by Bold Native
Br.—Ocala Stud Farms Inc (Fla)
Own.—Cohen I — Tr.—Gaudet Dean (24 2 0 3 .08) — **122**

Lifetime 5 0 1 1 $6,820 | 1992 4 M 0 1 $3,410 | 1991 1 M 1 0 $3,410 | Wet 1 0 0 0 $465

27Nov92-11Lrl fst 6f :22^1 :45^2 1:10^2 3↑Ⓕ Md Sp Wt 53 10 8 10^{12} 10^{11} 6^{11} 4^{12½} Ladner C J III b 122 8.60e 76–19 DptMss120^{6¾}AtmnRsh120^{1¾}ThrtEghtKmb120 No factor 10
14Nov92- 7Lrl fst 6f :22 :45^4 1:12^2 3↑Ⓕ Md Sp Wt 40 2 6 7^9 6^{9½} 4^9 6^{6¾} Ladner C J III b 122 *1.30e 72–17 TersInTim120^{4}BrookHous120^{hd}DixiDt122 Stumbled st. 10
22Oct92-10Lrl fst 6f :22^2 :46^2 1:12^2 3↑Ⓕ Md Sp Wt 50 13 9 8^{7¾} 7^9 6^{7½} 3^{3½} Ladner C J III b 122 *1.80e 76–20 BBlum119^{3½}StrwbrryCocoon119^{hd}HowLovly122 Rallied 14
9Oct92- 2Lrl my 7f :23^1 :47^3 1:26^2 3↑Ⓕ Md Sp Wt 35 2 1 2^2 2^{1½} 4^{7½} 5^{16½} Ladner C J III b 122 3.20 58–22 ChocltDlt119^{9¾}Prttyfnndmn122^{nk}OpnMrrg119 Gave way 8
11Jly91- 6Lrl fst 6½f :22^3 :46^2 1:18^4 3↑Ⓕ Md Sp Wt 74 3 6 4^{1¾} 3^2 2^{3½} 2^{2½} Vasquez J b 115 *.80e 80–16 SmrtAppel122^{2½}HowLovely115^{5½}GrittleCkes115 Rallied 9

With just a superficial look at this maiden race, it was obvious that Thirty Eight Kimbo and Dream Awhile dominated the field. Thirty Eight Kimbo had run figures of 63, 66, and 59 in her last three starts; Dream Awhile's only recent race was a 62. Nobody else in the field had recently run better than a 53 in her last start. Moreover, an analysis of the pace of the race suggested that the top two horses were even better than the numbers indicated.

Thirty Eight Kimbo had faced several of these same rivals on November 27; she had pressed an unusually fast pace for maiden fillies, a half mile in 45⅖ seconds, and that pace should have benefited the stretch-runners in the field. Yet Thirty Eight Kimbo had held on reasonably well and finished four lengths in front of Brook House, How Lovely, Tin Oaks, and Argenteous. This same bunch of plodders had raced against one another on November 14, and even with an optimal pace in front of them — a half mile in :45⅘ — nobody closed effectively. Thirty Eight Kimbo was the only one of the locals who had any tactical speed.

Into the midst of the Maryland fillies had come an invader from Kentucky, Dream Awhile; trained there by Wayne Lukas, she was now in the hands of Ben Perkins Jr., one of the top horsemen in Maryland. Dream Awhile had speed, too; she had battled for the lead at Churchill Downs in 21⅗ seconds (though fractions at that track are often deceptively fast). Nevertheless, that race had been a good one; the second-, fourth-, and fifth-place finishers in that field had come back to win their subsequent starts.

Thirty Eight Kimbo and Dream Awhile were not only the two best horses, but the only two horses with any early speed in a group of plodders. They weren't one-dimensional front-runners, though, so there didn't seem much chance that they would hook up in a destructive duel. I figured that Dream Awhile would take the lead with Thirty Eight Kimbo chasing her, and they would parade around the track in that order. This situation looked so solid that if I bet anything less than $1,000 on the combination, I would deserve to be banished from Las Vegas on grounds of sheer wimpishness. A pair of $500 exactas might depress the prices in the Laurel parimutuel pool, however, so this looked like an ideal spot to bet a quinella booked by the house. With the aid of a friend, I made the rounds of local establishments, betting $100 here and $100 there. Then, as the race itself approached, I couldn't resist swinging for a home run. Brook House looked like the best of the plodders to me; she had encountered considerable trouble at the start of her last race and still finished creditably. So, in addition to my $1,000 quinella, I took my shot for glory with a pair of $250 trifectas, using Brook House in the third spot.

NINTH RACE

Laurel

DECEMBER 8, 1992

7 FURLONGS. (1.21²) MAIDEN SPECIAL WEIGHT. Purse $15,500. Fillies and Mares, 3-4-and-5-year-olds. Weight, 3-year-olds, 120 lbs. Older, 122 lbs.

Value of race $16,700; value to winner $8,835; second $3,255; third $1,705; fourth $930; fifth $465; sixth $310; balance of starters $300 each. Mutuel pool $32,690. Exacta Pool $48,762 Triple Pool $59,423

Last Raced	Horse	M/Eqt.A.Wt	PP	St	¼	½	Str	Fin	Jockey	Odds $1
27Nov92 11Lrl3	Thirty Eight Kimbo	b 3 120	1	1	1½	1¹	1⁴	1¾	Hutton G W	3.40
3Nov92 6CD3	Dream Awhile	3 120	5	5	3¹	4¹½	2²	2⁵	Turner T G	1.40
27Nov92 11Lrl6	Argenteous	3 120	6	7	7³	7⁵	5½	3¹	McCarron G	47.80
27Nov92 11Lrl5	Brook House	Lb 3 120	8	9	6²	5¹	4hd	4nk	Reynolds L C	10.00
14Nov92 7Lrl3	Dixie Data	4 122	3	10	10	9³	7³	5¹	Agnello A	4.90
27Nov92 11Lrl4	How Lovely	b 4 122	10	3	4¹½	3hd	3hd	6¾	Prado E S	a-10.20
16Nov92 5Pha2	Strawberry Cocoon	L 3 120	9	6	5hd	6½	6³	7¹¾	Delgado A	6.20
9Oct92 2Lrl2	Prettyfineandmine	4 122	7	4	8²	8hd	8³	8¹³	Chavez S N	16.60
27Nov92 11Lrl8	Tin Oaks	L 3 120	4	2	2hd	2hd	9¹⁰	9¹⁰	Ladner C J III	a-10.20
17Nov92 1Pha	Biras Creek	b 3 120	2	8	9¹½ 10	10	10	Juarez C	92.80

a-Coupled: How Lovely and Tin Oaks.

OFF AT 4:14 Start good, Won driving. Time, :23⁴, :48 , 1:14¹, 1:27¹ Track fast.

$2 Mutuel Prices:

2-THIRTY EIGHT KIMBO	8.80	4.60	3.80
5-DREAM AWHILE		3.60	3.60
6-ARGENTEOUS			12.20

$2 EXACTA 2-5 PAID $31.20 $3 TRIPLE 2-5-6 PAID $1,032.90

Ro. f, (May), by Thirty Eight Paces—Aladamy, by Dewan. Trainer Souder Donald E. Bred by Cowne Lloyd R & Penny S (Va).

THIRTY EIGHT KIMBO set the pace along the rail and held off DREAM AWHILE. The latter raced between horses on the turn and closed willingly. ARGENTEOUS, very wide, rallied mildly. BROOK HOUSE steadied behind horses on the turn, swung wide and failed to menace. DIXIE DATA was no factor. HOW LOVELY wide, weakened. STRAWBERRY COCOON weakened. TIN OAKS fell back.

Owners— 1, Souder Donald E; 2, Riggs Mrs Augustus IV; 3, Christiana Stables; 4, Steele James B Jr; 5, Sharp Bayard; 6, Cohen I; 7, Jones Don; 8, Eltringham-Shane Stable; 9, Cohen I; 10, Rosenborg Suzanne.

Trainers— 1, Souder Donald E; 2, Perkins Ben W Jr; 3, Clark Henry S; 4, McCormick Harold F; 5, Peoples Charles; 6, Gaudet Dean; 7, O'Brien Maura C; 8, Shane M Terry; 9, Gaudet Dean; 10, Price Harry W Jr.

The only surprise in this race was the fact that Thirty Eight Kimbo showed the superior early speed and took the lead along the rail, with Dream Awhile chasing her. The leader set a moderate pace, and the two speed horses dominated the race, finishing five lengths ahead of the rest of the field. When the television camera panned to the rear of the pack, it appeared that Brook House was going to complete the trifecta; at the finish, though, the longshot Argenteous had caught her for third place — costing me a five-digit return. But the quinella had paid a generous price: The winner's payoff times half of the second finisher's place price returned $15.80, and I collected $7,900 for my $1,000 wager. I was virtually assured of a profitable week.

As I bet so many races in such a short period of time, compressing the usual experience of a horseplayer, I was reminded that handicapping is a cyclical game. There are times and places when any way of playing the horses — speed handicapping included — will be highly effective. At other times and places the same approach may seem an exercise in futility. I hadn't cashed a ticket yet on a race at Aqueduct. New York racing during the winter has long been dominated — in the view of suspicious bettors, at least — by so-called juice trainers, the men who give New York a reputation of being the nation's worst hotbed of illegal drug use. This view does not derive from the paranoia of losers; the best handicappers are the ones most keenly aware that horses' performances are not conforming to the laws of nature. When I spoke to Paul Cornman each morning, the word "juice" peppered his analysis of every race, and worries about it clearly undermined his own confidence. I like such-and-such a horse, he would say, but I'll probably get beat by the juice. And he was usually right.

Betting at Hawthorne, too, had been fruitless. The track bias continued to be so powerful that when top-figure horses won, it was a happy accident because they had managed to go wider than anybody else. But speed figures had been extremely effective at Laurel and Hollywood Park. I have always preferred betting at Hollywood to the other southern California tracks, perhaps because its 1⅛-mile circumference makes the races there a bit less speed-oriented and more comprehensible to an Easterner. There was no bias at Hollywood, and logical horses were winning regularly. I had one of my better scores of the week when I played a daily triple by singling a 9-to-2 figure standout and using the top two figure horses in the other two races — and collected a whopping $570 payoff. Because Hollywood's races were so productive, I was devoting more time to handicapping the cards there, and I found an opportunity in a maiden field that I otherwise might have glossed over.

6 1 1/16 MILES HOLLYWOOD FINISH START

1 1/16 MILES. **(1.40) MAIDEN CLAIMING. Purse $17,000. 2-year-olds. Weight 119 lbs. Claiming price $32,000; if for $28,000 allowed 2 lbs.**

LASIX—Hitumwhenyacan, Tamakun, Flying At the Wire, Duke Rumelius, Tasso's Boy, Stall Mate, Circus Bucks, My Liberty, Brig Time, Loville Slew.

Hitumwhenyacan Dk. b. or br. c. 2(Apr), by Time to Explode—Doon's Doll, by Matsadoon
Lifetime 2 0 0 0 $1,500 — 1992 2 M 0 0 $1,500
DELAHOUSSAYE E (117 23 28 13 .20) $32,000 Br.—Drakos Christopher (Ky) 119
Own.—Drakos Christopher Tr.—Smith Michael R (8 0 0 1 .00)
4Nov92- 3SA fst 6f :213 :45 1:10 Md 62500 55 8 1 74¾ 65 66½ 613¾ Delahoussaye E LBb 118 4.00 72-18 CnnotBIgnord1184½StllMt1156Phroh'sHrt118 Wide trip 8
9Oct92- 4SA fst 6f :213 :442 1:10 Md 50000 72 10 7 86½ 73½ 54½ 46 Atkinson P LB 118 20.30 80-14 Shrl'sMmoon1183½Blgr'sLd118hdPhrh'sHrt118 Wide trip 12
LATEST WORKOUTS Dec 4 SA 5f fst :591 H Nov 29 SA 7f fst 1:264 H Nov 24 SA 6f fst 1:143 H Nov 16 SA 6f fst 1:142 H

Tamakun Dk. b. or br. c. 2(Apr), by Johnlee n' Harold—Where's Kasey, by Cabildo
Lifetime 2 0 0 0 $700 — 1992 2 M 0 0 $700
CASTANON A L (33 3 0 1 .09) $32,000 Br.—Garcia Henry (Cal) 119
Own.—Garcia Enrique G Tr.—Perez Dagoberto (7 2 0 1 .29)
4Dec92- 3Hol fst 6f :22 :452 1:091 SMd Sp Wt 37 2 6 715 712 715 619½ Castanon A L LB 118 92.40 74-09 KngdomFnd1185½I'mRnd1181EldrdPt118 Steadied start 7
21Nov92- 1Hol fst 6f :222 :453 1:103 SMd Sp Wt 43 2 5 55 57 58 513 Pincay L Jr LB 118 10.60 74-11 Trumphl'sBonty1185PlsrRod118½PtrDbln118 No mishap 7
LATEST WORKOUTS Nov 29 Hol 7f fst 1:294 H Nov 14 Hol 6f fst 1:141 H Nov 6 Hol 6f fst 1:16 Hg Oct 31 Hol 5f gd 1:011 H

Frozen River B. c. 2(Apr), by Eskimo—River Gal, by Bold Skipper
Lifetime 4 0 0 1 $4,950 — 1992 4 M 0 1 $4,950
DESORMEAUX K J (97 26 17 12 .27) $32,000 Br.—Franks John (Fla) 119
Own.—WaranchRebecca&Ronald&Slly Tr.—Van Berg Jack C (56 5 4 7 .09)
5Sep92- 6Dmr fst 1 :454 1:111 1:374 Md Sp Wt 48 6 5 57 57½ 48½ 515 Stevens G L B 117 12.00 63-18 Corby117½Goldigger'sDrm1178BigWy117 Bumped break 8
8Aug92- 6Dmr fst 6f :221 :452 1:093 Md Sp Wt 59 8 2 41 32½ 36½ 610 Solis A B 117 12.30 81-09 Crfty1174Corby1175CozzyBtMdsl117 Wide backstretch 8
26Jly92- 3Hol fst 5½f :22 :45 1:042 Md Sp Wt 45 6 1 44½ 45½ 46½ 311 McCarron C J B 117 16.70 80-11 WheelerOil117hdBossSoss11711FroznRivr117 No mishap 7
21May92- 3Hol fst 4½f :221 :46 :522 Md Sp Wt 40 5 7 88¼ 86½ 67 Solis A B 117 10.10 89-11 Brrett'sBullet117hdFltWizrd117½Altzrr117 Greenly, wide 10
LATEST WORKOUTS Dec 3 Hol 7f fst 1:281 H Nov 23 Hol 7f fst 1:274 H Nov 15 Hol 7f fst 1:28 H Nov 8 Hol 5f fst 1:02 H

Flying At The Wire Dk. b. or br. c. 2(Mar), by Flying Victor—Veiled Beauty, by Petrone
Lifetime 2 0 1 0 $3,800 — 1992 2 M 1 0 $3,800
MCCARRON C J (75 11 8 8 .14) $32,000 Br.—Carruth A Brent & Terri (Cal) 119
Own.—Blush of Fame Farm Tr.—Heap Blake (6 1 0 0 .17)
11Nov92- 2Hol fst 6½f :212 :441 1:173 SMd 32000 46 10 7 78¾ 59 55¼ 54¾ Stevens G L 119 3.10 79-09 JsssRrds1191SdIslnd119noPrPrfrr117 Wide backstretch 12
16Oct92- 2SA fst 6f :213 :451 1:112 SMd 32000 58 8 11 98¾ 86¾ 43½ 21 Stevens G L B 118 5.30 78-12 IHsPs1181FlnAtthWr1181½FllMH118 Wide,stumbledlate 12
LATEST WORKOUTS Dec 5 Hol 4f fst :503 H Nov 28 Hol 6f fst 1:162 H Nov 6 Hol 4f fst :504 H Nov 1 Hol 6f fst 1:173 H

Habitrack Dk. b. or br. g. 2(Feb), by My Habitony—Knight Traker, by Knights Choice
Lifetime 1 0 0 0 — 1992 1 M 0 0
VALENZUELA P A (92 16 16 20 .17) $32,000 Br.—Antonacci & Sierra Stable (Cal) 119
Own.—Sierra Stable Tr.—Ellis Ronald W (7 1 2 1 .14)
9Nov92- 6SA fst 6½f :213 :45 1:164 SMd Sp Wt 58 11 5 75½ 64½ 79½ 614¼ Gryder A T B 118 55.70 72-17 Prfthnnts1185GlngCrn118¾KndmFnd118 6-wide stretch 12
LATEST WORKOUTS Dec 1 SA 4f fst :48 H Nov 25 SA 6f fst 1:15 H Nov 4 SA 3f fst :363 Hg Oct 23 SA 6f fst 1:142 H

Speedy Con Dk. b. or br. c. 2(Feb), by Fast Account—Con's Sister, by Summer Time Guy
Lifetime 0 0 0 0 — 1992 0 M 0 0
ARIAS J C (14 0 0 1 .00) $32,000 Br.—Hawn W R (Cal) 119
Own.—Hawn W R Tr.—MacDonald Mark (10 1 1 1 .10)
LATEST WORKOUTS ●Dec 2 SA 1 fst 1:433 H Nov 26 SA 7f fst 1:332 H Nov 19 SA 6f fst 1:163 H Nov 9 SA 5f fst 1:031 H

Enter The Mill B. g. 2(Feb), by The Miller—Enter In, by Key to the Kingdom
Lifetime 1 0 0 0 — 1992 1 M 0 0
LINARES M G (12 0 0 0 .00) $28,000 Br.—Thompson Lewis E Jr (Cal) 117
Own.—Thompson Lewis E Jr Tr.—Neumann Julie (7 0 1 0 .00)
14Nov92- 6Hol fst 1 1/16 :471 1:12 1:442 Md 28000 24 7 12 108½ 811 819 932½ Linares M G Bb 116 146.40 47-21 Tager1185 Mr. Chairman1183 Loville Slew118 Outrun 12
LATEST WORKOUTS Dec 2 SA 5f fst 1:033 H Nov 25 SA 5f fst 1:043 H Nov 8 SA 6f fst 1:162 Hg Oct 15 SA 5f fst 1:022 H

Tasso's Boy

Dk. b. or br. g. 2(May), by Tasso—Ready Set, by Northern Jove

NAKATANI C S (94 18 9 12 .19)
Own.—Hirmez Zuhair

Br.—Malmuth Marvin (Cal)
Tr.—Luby Donn (12 2 2 0 .17)

$32,000

119

Lifetime	1992	7 M 1 1	$7,800
7 0 1 1			
$7,800			

14Nov92- 6Hol fst 1¹⁄₁₆	:47¹ 1:12 1:44²	Md 32000	48 10 6 3¹ 5³¹⁄₄ 6¹¹ 6¹⁸¹⁄₂	Delahoussaye E	LBb 118	*2.60	61–21 Tager118⁵ Mr. Chairman118³ LovilleSlew118	Wide early 12
23Oct92- 9SA fst 1	:47 1:11⁴ 1:38²	Md 32000	35 2 6 5⁵ 6⁶¹⁄₂ 6⁹ 6¹⁴¹⁄₄	Delahoussaye E LBb	117	*1.70	60–21 ThBrklyMn117³¹Mr.Dlphn115⁴ᵏSyslтTc117	Lacked rally 10
11Sep92- 4Dmr fst 1	:47 1:12³ 1:39	Md 32000	54 7 10 85³⁄₄ 42¹⁄₂ 3¹ 2³⁄₄	Delahoussaye E LBb	118	3.40	71–23 Super Snazzie118² Tasso's Boy118² ⒹMr. Dolphin116	10
11Sep92-Poor start, wide early, lugged in lane								
27Aug92- 4Dmr fst 1	:46⁴ 1:12² 1:38³	Md 35000	53 2 4 32¹⁄₂ 31¹⁄₄ 3³ 38¹⁄₂	Flores D R	LBb 115	9.90	66–24 Kalembo117²¹SaysItTwice117⁶Tsso'sBoy115	Weakened 9
14Aug92- 6Dmr fst 6f	:22 :45¹ 1:12	⑤Md 32000	53 8 7 75¹⁄₂ 64³⁄₄ 53³⁄₄ 64³⁄₄	Solis A	LBb 117	13.90	74–15 TopOfThMoon117²LgclGn117ⁿᵏVdAlrt117	Jostled, wide 11
20Jly92- 6Hol fst 6f	:22 :45² 1:10⁴	Md 40000	52 5 7 86 6¹¹ 41⁰ 49¹⁄₂	Flores D R	LBb 117	48.30	76–15 AlbrtBddr117¹³QtBCc117⁷JsssRrds115	Wide backstretch 9
29Jun92- 4Hol fst 5¹⁄₂f	:22¹ :46¹ 1:04³	⑤Md 35000	39 10 9 101⁸10¹³ 811 7¹²¹⁄₄	Alvarado F J	LB 115	86.30	78–09 JstSd117⁴¹QtByChnc117ⁿᵏRttrEvrD117	Off slowly, wide 10

LATEST WORKOUTS   Dec 2 SA 6f fst 1:15² H   Nov 23 SA 5f fst 1:02 H   ●Nov 9 SA 6f fst 1:12⁴ H   Nov 3 SA 5f gd 1:02³ H

Stall Mate

B. c. 2(May), by Stalwart—On Your Own Time, by Sharpen Up

PEDROZA M A (109 10 5 18 .09)
Own.—Clear Valley Stables

Br.—Oxley John C (Ky)
Tr.—Shulman Sanford (42 5 2 8 .12)

$32,000

119

Lifetime	1992	6 M 1 1	$12,925
6 0 1 1			
$12,925			

27Nov92- 4Hol fst 1¹⁄₁₆	:47¹ 1:12³ 1:45¹	Md 32000	50 7 6 42¹⁄₂ 63¹ 48 5¹0¹⁄₄	Valenzuela P A	LBb 119	2.30	64–22 Mr.Chirmn1197¹DukeRumlius117¹BrigTim119	Wide trip 10
18Nov92- 4Hol fst 6f	:22¹ :45 1:09³	Md 32000	64 1 4 4² 42¹⁄₂ 45 49	McCarron C J	LBb 118	3.40	83–09 Dr.Berend118⁴¹Mr.TimMan118ⁿᵈRzz'nJzz118	No mishap 11
4Nov92- 3SA fst 6f	:21³ :45 1:10	Md 55000	78 1 7 86¹ 75¹⁄₄ 24 24¹⁄₂	Desormeaux K J	LBb 115	11.60	81–18 CnnotBIgnrd118⁴¹StllMt115⁶Phrh'sHrt118	Best of rest 8
12Oct92- 6SA fst 6f	:21⁴ :45² 1:10⁴	Md c–32000	58 10 2 3ⁿᵏ 2ⁿᵈ 34¹⁄₄ 34¹⁄₂	Stevens G L	LBb 118	*1.10	78–14 TomatoCper118²Rzz'nJzz118²¹StllMte118	Bumped start 11
12Oct92-Claimed from DeGroot & Dutch Masters III, Baffert Bob Trainer									
16Aug92- 6Dmr fst 6f	:22 :45² 1:10⁴	Md Sp Wt	51 1 4 4² 41¹⁄₂ 35¹⁄₄ 41⁰¹⁄₂	McCarron C J	Bb 117	1.90	74–13 SncJons117¹⁰OurConductor117¹⁄₂Mr.Expo117	No mishap 7
29Jly92- 6Dmr fst 5¹⁄₂f	:21² :45 1:03⁴	Md Sp Wt	62 10 2 2¹ 2¹⁄₂ 22¹⁄₂ 46¹⁄₄	Delahoussaye E	Bb 117	1.90	85–07 DevilDimond117⁶DrToDul117¹SuddnHush117	Weakened 10

LATEST WORKOUTS   Dec 6 SA 3f fst :37² H   Nov 1 SA 3f my :37² H   Oct 25 SA 5f my 1:03³ H   Oct 19 SA 4f fst :48¹ H

Circus Bucks

B. g. 2(Apr), by Badger Land—I'll Be Around, by Isgala

STEVENS G L (95 12 13 16 .13)
Own.—SlonAndrew–MryLouise&MikH

Br.—Iselin James H (Ky)
Tr.—Hess R B Jr (38 6 7 6 .16)

$32,000

119

Lifetime	1992	2 M 0 0	$1,275
2 0 0 0			
$1,275			

14Nov92- 6Hol fst 1¹⁄₁₆	:47¹ 1:12 1:44²	Md 28000	63 6 9 75¹ 64³ 58 49¹⁄₂	Stevens G L	LBb 116	5.70	70–21 Tger118⁵Mr.Chirmn118³LovllSlw118	Improved position 12
12Oct92- 6SA fst 6f	:21⁴ :45² 1:10⁴	Md 32000	33 8 11 119¹111³111110¹⁴	Desormeaux K J	LBb 118	5.70	68–14 TomtoCpr118²Rzz'nJzz118²¹StllMt118	Off slowly, wide 12

LATEST WORKOUTS   Dec 1 Hol 4f fst :49² H   Nov 25 Hol 4f fst :50² H   Nov 11 Hol 4f fst :49⁴ H

Something Nice

Dk. b. or br. g. 2(Mar), by Haughty But Nice—Somethinglorious, by Something-fabulous

PINCAY L JR (104 12 16 11 .12)
Own.—Munoz Gilbert

Br.—Matos Tony (Cal)
Tr.—Garcia Oscar (4 0 0 0 .00)

$32,000

119

Lifetime	1992	2 M 0 1	$3,825
2 0 0 1			
$3,825			

27Nov92- 4Hol fst 1¹⁄₁₆	:47¹ 1:12³ 1:45¹	Md 32000	52 2 10 10¹³ 99² 79 49¹⁄₄	Solis A	B 119	6.00	66–22 Mr.Chrmn1197¹DukRumls117¹BrgTm119	Wide into lane 10
29Oct92- 2SA fst 6f	:22 :46 1:12	Md 32000	53 10 7 10⁶ 86¹⁄₂ 76 32¹⁄₂	Solis A	B 118	5.70	73–18 ⒹIntntTAssnt118⁴HpOfGld118²SthnNc118	Wide, rallied 10

LATEST WORKOUTS   Nov 19 SA 4f fst :49 H   Nov 12 SA 5f fst 1:01¹ Hg   Nov 7 SA 4f fst :49² H   Oct 23 SA tr.t 5f fst 1:01¹ H

Loville Slew

Dk. b. or br. g. 2(Apr), by Tsunami Slew—Quickner, by To the Quick

VALENZUELA P A (92 16 16 20 .17)
Own.—Cox or Guiltian JrorHarabedian

Br.—Gravel Hill Enterprise Inc (Ky)
Tr.—Dominguez Caesar F (27 4 3 2 .15)

$32,000

119

Lifetime	1992	11 M 1 4	$18,775
11 0 1 4			
$18,775			

27Nov92- 4Hol fst 1¹⁄₁₆	:47¹ 1:12³ 1:45¹	Md 32000	36 6 4 52³ 86³ 812 819	Stevens G L	LBb 119	11.40	56–22 Mr.Chirmn1197¹DukeRumlius117¹BrigTim119	Wide trip 10
14Nov92- 6Hol fst 1¹⁄₁₆	:47¹ 1:12 1:44²	Md 32000	65 4 5 6⁴ 3³ 3⁵ 38	Nakatani C S	LBb 118	6.20	71–21 Tger118⁵Mr.Chirmn118³LovilleSlew118	Not enough late 12
29Oct92- 4SA fst 6f	:21⁴ :45² 1:10²	Md 32000	59 4 4 4² 31¹⁄₂ 3³ 48¹⁄₂	Flores D R	LBb 118	4.80	75–18 Mrmoe118⁵FigueroDrive118²¹CrimeTyme118	Weakened 8
29Aug92- 6Dmr fst 5¹⁄₂f	:22¹ :45⁴ 1:05¹	Md 32000	52 8 2 62¹⁄₂ 41³⁄₄ 42¹⁄₂	Nakatani C S	LB 118	*2.70	81–12 Buckmeistr118⁴InvitdWinnr118ᵏVidoAlrt118	Wide trip 8
19Aug92- 6Dmr fst 6f	:22² :46 1:11	Md 50000	36 1 6 63¹⁄₂ 10⁷ 10⁹¹10¹³¹⁄₂	Delahoussaye E	LB 117	14.90	71–12 OfEgles117¹¹StylishKnight117³¹IrishHeven117	Faltered 10
6Aug92- 6Dmr fst 6f	:22² :45² 1:10³	Md 50000	62 2 3 4⁴ 34¹ 33¹⁄₂ 36	Desormeaux K J	LB 117	2.60	80–12 FrTw117⁴⁴StylshKnght117¹⁄₂LvllSlw117	Not enough late 8
23Jly92- 3Hol fst 6f	:22¹ :45⁴ 1:10³	Md 50000	61 2 5 31¹⁄₂ 31¹⁄₂ 33 26	Nakatani C S	LB 117	3.90	81–10 BtngPlsr117⁶LlISI117ⁿᵈStlshKnght117	Lugged out drive 6
2Jly92- 4Hol fst 5¹⁄₂f	:22² :44⁴ 1:04	Md 55000	59 5 5 43¹ 34¹⁄₂ 35¹ 36¹⁄₄	Nakatani C S	LB 114	4.90	86–12 ImpriRdg117¹⁄₄GdPrsnttn117⁵LlISl114	Broke awkwardly 8
11Jun92- 4Hol fst 6f	:22 :46 :58³	Md 32000	57 3 6 87 77 53¹⁄₄ 32¹	Nakatani C S	LB 117	5.30	86–13 Weyburn117¹⁄₄Dle'sBest117³⁄₄LovillSlw117	4-wide stretch 9
29May92- 4Hol fst 4¹⁄₂f	:22¹ :46¹ :52³	Md 62500	36 1 7 77¹⁄₂ 6⁵ 66³⁄₄	Flores D R	Bb 117	9.00	88–10 GryGoGo117¹⁄₄FlghtOfHonr114³⁄₄GdPrsnttn117	No threat 9

LATEST WORKOUTS   Oct 16 SA 6f fst 1:14³ H

The 1¹⁄₁₆-mile races at Hollywood Park are a bastard distance on a 1¹⁄₈-mile track. The starting gate is so close to the first turn that horses breaking from outside posts have no chance to get into a decent tactical position and save ground. Other tracks of Hollywood's size (such as Laurel) restrict 1¹⁄₁₆-mile races to ten horses because those outside horses are at such a disadvantage. Hollywood, however, permits fields of twelve at the distance, and the outside horses are doomed. At the entire fall meeting, not a single horse would win a route race from post 10, 11, or 12.

Circus Bucks, the horse with the best figure in his most recent start, was a virtual throw-out because he was starting from post position 10. Habitrack, who had the second-best number in his last start, was the type of horse I have always found irresistible. He looked terrible, or at least he would to anybody without speed figures; he had finished sixth, 14½ lengths behind the winner, in the only start of his career. But he had made his debut in an exceptionally strong 2-year-old maiden race — the winner had earned a figure of 91 — and the validity of that number had already been confirmed. A few days earlier, the third-place finisher in the field, Kingdom Found, had come back to win by 5½ lengths, running a huge figure of his own. Moreover, Habitrack's dope suggested that trainer Ron Ellis might have conceived of that race as a prep for today. Habitrack was dropping into a maiden-claiming race, stretching out from a sprint to a route, and getting a switch to jockey Pat Valenzuela.

When I phoned Jeff Siegel for my morning consultation, he concurred that Habitrack had interesting form. He said that the top-figure horse, Circus Bucks, had been visually unimpressive in his last start; he had no kick in the stretch. Stall Mate, who had run some decent figures in sprints, didn't look as if he wanted to go a distance, either. But there was one horse that Siegel particularly liked: Hitumwhenyacan. "He ran a terrific race with a big figure the first time out," Siegel said, "and I liked him in his last start. I don't know what happened to him — he just didn't run. But since that race he's come back and trained extremely well." Those works — seven furlongs in 1:26⅘, five furlongs in :59⅕ — suggested that Hitumwhenyacan was being pointed for a distance race and that he was sharp.

I still preferred Habitrack and, hoping to make him a vehicle for a big score, singled him in a pick six investment. But now, imbued with my new philosophy of looking for two horses who figured to dominate a field, I bet a substantial Habitrack-Hitumwhenyacan quinella.

SIXTH RACE Hollywood

DECEMBER 10, 1992

$1\frac{1}{16}$ MILES. (1.40) MAIDEN CLAIMING. Purse $17,000. 2-year-olds. Weight 119 lbs. Claiming price $32,000; if for $28,000 allowed 2 lbs.

Value of race $17,000; value to winner $9,350; second $3,400; third $2,550; fourth $1,275; fifth $425. Mutuel pool $205,943. Exacta pool $150,680. Trifecta pool $235,947.

Last Raced	Horse	M/Eqt.	A.Wt	PP	St	¼	½	¾	Str	Fin	Jockey	Cl'g Pr	Odds $1
9Nov92 ^{6}SA^{6}	Habitrack	LB	2 119	5	3	$3^{\frac12}$	2^{hd}	$2^{1\frac12}$	$1^{\frac12}$	1^{2}	ValenzuelPA	32000	7.40
14Nov92 ^{6}Hol^{6}	Tasso's Boy	LBb	2 119	8	10	10^{hd}	$9^{1\frac12}$	$5^{1\frac12}$	3^{2}	$2^{1\frac14}$	Nakatani C S	32000	18.30
4Nov92 ^{3}SA^{6}	Hitumwhenyacan	LBb	2 119	1	2	$1^{1\frac12}$	1^{1}	$1^{\frac12}$	$2^{1\frac12}$	$3^{2\frac14}$	DelhoussyeE	32000	2.90
5Sep92 ^{6}Dmr^{5}	Frozen River	B	2 119	3	5	$5^{\frac12}$	$7^{1\frac12}$	$3^{\frac12}$	4^{2}	4^{1}	DesormuxKJ	32000	2.60
14Nov92 ^{6}Hol^{4}	Circus Bucks	LBb	2 119	10	6	6^{2}	5^{hd}	4^{1}	$5^{1\frac12}$	5^{1}	Stevens G L	32000	5.80
27Nov92 ^{4}Hol^{4}	Something Nice	Bb	2 119	11	8	9^{4}	8^{2}	$6^{1\frac12}$	$6^{2\frac12}$	$6^{3\frac12}$	Alvarado F T	32000	14.50
11Nov92 ^{2}Hol^{5}	Flying At The Wire	LB	2 119	4	7	8^{hd}	$6^{\frac12}$	$7^{2\frac12}$	7^{5}	7^{8}	McCarron CJ	32000	5.50
14Nov92 ^{6}Hol^{9}	Enter The Mill	Bb	2 117	7	9	$11^{1\frac12}$	10^{hd}	$9^{\frac12}$	8^{4}	$8^{4\frac12}$	Linares M G	28000	324.80
27Nov92 ^{4}Hol^{5}	Stall Mate	LBb	2 119	9	4	$4^{1\frac12}$	4^{2}	8^{1}	9^{3}	$9^{3\frac12}$	Pedroza M A	32000	12.30
27Nov92 ^{4}Hol^{8}	Loville Slew	LBb	2 119	12	1	2^{1}	3^{hd}	$10^{\frac12}$	10^{1}	$10^{1\frac12}$	Flores D R	32000	34.30
	Speedy Con	Bb	2 119	6	12	12	$11^{\frac12}$	11^{2}	$11^{1\frac12}$	$11^{\frac12}$	Arias J C	32000	90.10
4Dec92 ^{3}Hol^{6}	Tamakun	LBb	2 119	2	11	7^{hd}	12	12	12	12	Castanon AL	32000	124.80

OFF AT 3:06. Start good. Won driving. Time, :22^{4}, :46^{3}, 1:12^{1}, 1:38^{4}, 1:45^{3} Track fast.

$2 Mutuel Prices:				
	5–HABITRACK	16.80	8.80	6.40
	8–TASSO'S BOY		14.20	8.60
	1–HITUMWHENYACAN			4.60

$2 EXACTA 5–8 PAID $213.00. $2 TRIFECTA 5–8–1 PAID $1,208.60.

Dk. b. or br. g, (Feb), by My Habitony—Knight Traker, by Knights Choice. Trainer Ellis Ronald W. Bred by Antonacci & Sierra Stable (Cal).

HABITRACK, within close attendance of the early pace, responded when called upon in the drive and proved best. TASSO'S BOY, devoid of early speed, saved ground along the inner rail on the far turn while on the move, looked dangerous early in the drive but did not have the needed additional late punch. HITUMWHENYACAN made the early pace and weakened a bit in the drive. FROZEN RIVER, outrun early but not far back, advanced to get within close range of the lead on the far turn but then weakened in the drive. CIRCUS BUCKS, taken up sharply going into the clubhouse turn to avoid heels, raced wide down the backstretch while in contention, came into the stretch four wide and lacked the necessary response in the drive. SOMETHING NICE, wide down the backstretch after being five wide into the clubhouse turn, was five wide into the stretch. FLYING AT THE WIRE, outrun early, moved up a bit before going a half but did not have the needed kick in the last quarter. STALL MATE also close up early, faltered badly. LOVILLE SLEW, close up early when hustled and four wide just before going into the clubhouse turn, came in entering the clubhouse turn, raced wide down the backstretch and also faltered badly. SPEEDY CON, wide down the backstretch, was five wide into the stretch. TAMAKUN was six wide into the stretch.

Owners— 1, Sierra Stable; 2, Hirmez Zuhair; 3, Drakos Christopher; 4, WaranchRebecca&Ronald&Sally; 5, Sloan Andrew-Mary Louise & Mike H; 6, Munoz Gilbert; 7, Blush of Fame Farm; 8, Thompson Lewis E Jr; 9, Clear Valley Stables; 10, Cox or Guiltian Jr or Harabedian; 11, Hawn W R; 12, Garcia Enrique G.

Trainers— 1, Ellis Ronald W; 2, Luby Donn; 3, Smith Michael R; 4, Van Berg Jack C; 5, Hess R B Jr; 6, Garcia Oscar; 7, Heap Blake; 8, Neumann Julie; 9, Shulman Sanford; 10, Dominguez Caesar F; 11, MacDonald Mark; 12, Perez Dagoberto.

Scratched—Duke Rumelius (27Nov92 ^{4}Hol^{2}); My Liberty (27Nov92 ^{4}Hol^{7}); Brig Time (27Nov92 ^{4}·

Habitrack won, paying $16.80 — and I lost my entire bet, in a bad ending to a bad final day in Las Vegas. I missed the pick six and missed the quinella when Hitumwhenyacan finished third, beaten out of second place by a rival who had benefited from a perfect rail trip. This is the type of situation that makes many horseplayers decry the evil temptations of gimmick wagers and vow that they will start betting horses to win. I try to accept such losses as an inevitable consequence of the way I choose to play the game. Those who live by the gimmick will sometimes die by the gimmick. I will undoubtedly continue to blow many bets on horses like Habitrack, with the hope that the big scores when I connect will more than compensate for the near-misses.

My frustration in this case was eased, too, by the fact that this had been a successful trip overall. With my starting bankroll of $7,000, I had bet a total of $21,000 and wound up with a net profit of $4,850. Speed figures had been the foundation of every winning bet, and their effectiveness during this week gave me a hint of their potential for the future. As simulcasting increases and its technology takes new forms — such as betting at home via cable TV — I can envision scanning hundreds of races every day, nationally and internationally, searching for the best figure horses. What a brave new world it could be!

ACKNOWLEDGMENTS

The *Daily Racing Form*'s inclusion of my speed figures in its past performances made this book possible. Publisher Jack Farnsworth, marketing director Katherine Wilkins and her assistant Mandy Minger have given me valuable support. Scott Finley and programmers Joshua Glickman and Li Yu were responsible for the computer research project which radically changed some of my longest-held ideas about the application of speed figures.

The figures are the product of a group effort, and their accuracy is due to the diligence of Randy Moss, Dick Jerardi, Joe Cardello, Paul Matties, Dennis Harp, and my partner, Mark Hopkins. Over the years Mark has been responsible for solving many technical and computer-related problems which have mystified me.

The *Washington Post,* and its sports editor George Solomon, have indulged and supported my itinerant gambling life, and many of the experiences chronicled in this book grew out of *Post* assignments and have been adapted from my columns in the *Post*. George deserves credit for not laughing me out of the office when I told him that I wanted to write my horse-racing column from Sydney, Australia, for a few months.

For assistance on this manuscript I am indebted to my editor, John Sterling, and also to the ultimate arbiter of English usage and syntax: Pauline Beyer, my mother.

APPENDIX

ONE-TURN SPEED RATINGS

5 FUR.		5½ FUR.		6 FUR.		6½ FUR.		7 FUR.		1 MILE	
:56	131	1:02	133	1:08	135	1:15	124	1:21	127	1:34	124
−1	127	−1	130	−1	132	−1	121	−1	125	−1	122
−2	124	−2	126	−2	129	−2	119	−2	122	−2	120
−3	120	−3	123	−3	126	−3	116	−3	120	−3	117
−4	117	−4	120	−4	123	−4	113	−4	118	−4	115
:57	113	1:03	117	1:09	120	1:16	111	1:22	115	1:35	113
−1	110	−1	114	−1	118	−1	108	−1	113	−1	111
−2	106	−2	110	−2	115	−2	106	−2	110	−2	109
−3	103	−3	107	−3	112	−3	103	−3	108	−3	107
−4	99	−4	104	−4	109	−4	100	−4	105	−4	105
:58	96	1:04	101	1:10	106	1:17	98	1:23	103	1:36	103
−1	92	−1	98	−1	103	−1	95	−1	101	−1	101
−2	89	−2	95	−2	100	−2	92	−2	98	−2	99
−3	85	−3	92	−3	98	−3	90	−3	96	−3	97
−4	82	−4	89	−4	95	−4	87	−4	93	−4	95
:59	79	1:05	86	1:11	92	1:18	85	1:24	91	1:37	92
−1	75	−1	83	−1	89	−1	82	−1	89	−1	90
−2	72	−2	79	−2	86	−2	80	−2	86	−2	88
−3	68	−3	76	−3	83	−3	77	−3	84	−3	86
−4	65	−4	73	−4	81	−4	74	−4	81	−4	84
1:00	62	1:06	70	1:12	78	1:19	72	1:25	79	1:38	82
−1	58	−1	67	−1	75	−1	69	−1	77	−1	80
−2	55	−2	64	−2	72	−2	67	−2	74	−2	78
−3	52	−3	61	−3	70	−3	64	−3	72	−3	76
−4	49	−4	58	−4	67	−4	62	−4	70	−4	74
1:01	45	1:07	55	1:13	64	1:20	59	1:26	67	1:39	72
−1	42	−1	52	−1	61	−1	57	−1	65	−1	70
−2	39	−2	49	−2	59	−2	54	−2	63	−2	68
−3	35	−3	46	−3	56	−3	52	−3	60	−3	66
−4	32	−4	43	−4	53	−4	49	−4	58	−4	64
1:02	29	1:08	40	1:14	51	1:21	47	1:27	56	1:40	62
−1	26	−1	38	−1	48	−1	44	−1	54	−1	60
−2	23	−2	35	−2	45	−2	42	−2	51	−2	58
−3	19	−3	32	−3	42	−3	39	−3	49	−3	56
−4	16	−4	29	−4	40	−4	37	−4	47	−4	54
1:03	13	1:09	26	1:15	37	1:22	35	1:28	44	1:41	52
				−1	34	−1	32	−1	42	−1	50
				−2	32	−2	30	−2	40	−2	48
				−3	29	−3	27	−3	38	−3	46
				−4	26	−4	25	−4	35	−4	44
				1:16	24	1:23	22	1:29	33	1:42	42

TWO-TURN SPEED RATINGS

1 MILE		1-70		1¹⁄₁₆		1¹⁄₈		1¹⁄₄	
1:34	133	1:38	134	1:40	137	1:47	132	2:00	133
−1	131	−1	132	−1	135	−1	130	−1	131
−2	129	−2	130	−2	133	−2	128	−2	130
−3	126	−3	128	−3	131	−3	126	−3	128
−4	124	−4	126	−4	129	−4	124	−4	126
1:35	122	1:39	124	1:41	127	1:48	122	2:01	125
−1	120	−1	122	−1	125	−1	120	−1	123
−2	118	−2	120	−2	123	−2	119	−2	122
−3	116	−3	118	−3	121	−3	117	−3	120
−4	114	−4	116	−4	119	−4	115	−4	118
1:36	112	1:40	114	1:42	117	1:49	113	2:02	117
−1	110	−1	112	−1	115	−1	111	−1	115
−2	108	−2	110	−2	113	−2	108	−2	113
−3	106	−3	108	−3	111	−3	106	−3	112
−4	103	−4	106	−4	109	−4	105	−4	110
1:37	101	1:41	104	1:43	107	1:50	104	2:03	108
−1	99	−1	102	−1	106	−1	102	−1	107
−2	97	−2	100	−2	104	−2	100	−2	105
−3	95	−3	98	−3	102	−3	99	−3	104
−4	93	−4	96	−4	100	−4	97	−4	102
1:38	91	1:42	94	1:44	98	1:51	95	2:04	100
−1	89	−1	92	−1	96	−1	93	−1	99
−2	87	−2	90	−2	94	−2	90	−2	97
−3	85	−3	88	−3	92	−3	88	−3	96
−4	83	−4	86	−4	90	−4	87	−4	94
1:39	81	1:43	84	1:45	88	1:52	86	2:05	92
−1	79	−1	82	−1	86	−1	84	−1	91
−2	77	−2	80	−2	84	−2	82	−2	89
−3	75	−3	78	−3	83	−3	81	−3	88
−4	73	−4	76	−4	81	−4	79	−4	86
1:40	71	1:44	74	1:46	79	1:53	77	2:06	84
−1	69	−1	73	−1	77	−1	75	−1	83
−2	67	−2	71	−2	75	−2	74	−2	81
−3	65	−3	69	−3	73	−3	72	−3	80
−4	63	−4	67	−4	71	−4	70	−4	78
1:41	61	1:45	65	1:47	69	1:54	68	2:07	76
−1	59	−1	63	−1	68	−1	67	−1	75
−2	57	−2	61	−2	66	−2	65	−2	73
−3	55	−3	59	−3	64	−3	63	−3	72
−4	53	−4	57	−4	62	−4	61	−4	70
1:42	51	1:46	55	1:48	60	1:55	60	2:08	69
−1	49	−1	54	−1	58	−1	58	−1	67
−2	47	−2	52	−2	56	−2	56	−2	66
−3	45	−3	50	−3	55	−3	54	−3	64
−4	43	−4	48	−4	53	−4	53	−4	62
1:43	41	1:47	46	1:49	51	1:56	51	2:09	61
−1	39	−1	44	−1	49	−1	49	−1	59
−2	38	−2	42	−2	47	−2	47	−2	58
−3	36	−3	40	−3	45	−3	46	−3	56
−4	34	−4	39	−4	44	−4	44	−4	55
1:44	32	1:48	37	1:50	42	1:57	42	2:10	53

BEATEN LENGTHS ADJUSTMENTS

Margin	5F	5½F	6F	6½F	7F	Mile	1-70	1 1/16	1 1/8	1 1/4
neck	1	1	1	1	1	0	0	0	0	0
½	1	1	1	1	1	1	1	1	1	1
¾	2	2	2	2	2	1	1	1	1	1
1	3	3	2	2	2	2	2	2	2	1
1¼	4	4	3	3	3	2	2	2	2	2
1½	4	4	4	3	3	3	3	3	2	2
1¾	5	5	4	4	4	3	3	3	3	3
2	6	6	5	5	4	4	3	3	3	3
2¼	7	6	6	5	5	4	4	4	4	3
2½	7	7	6	6	5	4	4	4	4	4
2¾	8	7	7	6	6	5	5	5	5	4
3	9	8	7	7	6	5	5	5	5	4
3¼	9	9	8	7	7	6	5	5	5	5
3½	10	10	9	8	7	6	6	6	6	5
3¾	11	10	9	9	8	7	6	6	6	5
4	12	11	10	9	8	7	7	7	6	5
4¼	12	12	10	10	9	8	7	7	7	6
4½	13	12	11	10	9	8	8	8	7	7
4¾	14	13	11	11	10	9	8	8	8	7
5	15	14	12	11	11	9	9	8	8	7
5½	17	15	13	13	12	10	10	9	9	8
6	18	17	15	14	13	11	10	10	9	9
6½	20	18	16	15	14	12	11	11	10	9
7	21	19	17	16	15	13	12	12	11	10
7½	23	21	18	17	16	14	13	13	12	11
8	24	22	20	18	17	14	14	13	13	11
8½	26	23	21	19	18	15	15	14	13	12
9	27	24	22	20	19	16	16	15	14	13
9½	29	26	24	22	20	17	17	16	15	14
10	30	28	25	23	21	18	17	17	16	14
11	33	30	28	25	24	20	19	18	18	16
12	36	33	30	27	26	22	21	20	19	17
13	39	36	33	30	28	24	22	22	21	19
14	42	39	35	32	30	25	24	24	23	20
15	45	41	38	34	32	27	26	26	25	21

PAR FIGURES

These are the average winning figures — or pars — for various classes at certain major racetracks. They have been updated for this new edition of *Beyer on Speed*. They are pars for older male horses and are not applicable to races limited to 2- or 3-year-olds. The claiming pars apply only to unrestricted races — not to ones limited to state-breds or horses who meet certain eligibility conditions, such as "nonwinners of a race in the last six months." MSW denotes maiden special weight races. Allowance categories represent the most common conditions for those races — N1X refers to events for nonwinners of one race other than maiden or claiming. **The pars for races limited to fillies and mares will typically be eight points lower than those for males.** No pars are listed for classes where the data was either insufficient or too erratic to derive a meaningful average.

TRACK	4000	5000	6000-7400	7500-9000	10000-14000	15000-20000	21000-34000	35000-49000	50000-75000	MSW	N1X	N2X	N3X
AP		76	77	78	81	84	88	90		82	86	92	96
AQU				80	86	88	91			79	90	93	98
BEL } SAR }					81	86	89	93		90	95	99	102
BM } GG }	74	76	77	79	82	85	89			81	87	90	
CBY	69	71			73	74				66	76	78	87
CD		71		75	77	83	87	92	93	86	94	97	
CRC		72	74	76	77	78	82			79	85	89	93
CT	71		74	77	79	82	89			61	77	79	
DED	71	73		76	80	83				66	79	82	86
DEL		75	77	80	82	85		91		78	85	90	97
DMR } HOL } SA }				81	83	87	91	94	97	93	99	101	103
ELP	69	72		74	77	82				79	88	91	
EMD		69		73	75	76	80			71			
FG		74		80	81	83	88	91	93	86	89	92	97
FL	63		70	71	72					51	63	70	72
FPX		74	76	77	82	86							
GP			72	75	79	84	87		94	80	89	93	97
HAW			75	78	79	84				77	83	88	92
HOO	70	72		74	79	81				68	81	83	
HOU		74		77	79	85	87	89			79	85	90
KEE				77	82	86	92			87	89	96	104
LAD		74		79	81	86	90			72	81	86	90
LRL } PIM }		68		78	79	81	83			72	81	88	90
LS	71	74		77	81	85	88	91		76	84	88	92
MED		73		75	77	81	85	89		75	83	88	89
MNR		73		75	76	78	86			73	76	80	82
MTH		68		69	74	79	85	90		78	88	92	94
OP		75	76	77	80	83	88	91	93	83	86	92	97
PHA		74	76	77	81	83	87			71	80	86	92
RET		73		79	81	83				67	84	87	
RP		73		76	78	79				65	78	80	86
SUF		70	74	75	76	83				62	74	80	83
SUN		74	75	76	78	83	85			69	80	82	
TAM			73	75	77	78				69	77	81	82
TDN		71		73	75					55	72	74	
TP		68		75	78	82	86	89		74	82	88	
TUP	71	72	74	77	78	80					80	82	
WO				74	75	80	82	89	90	76	86	91	95

BIBLIOGRAPHY

Brohamer, Tom. *Modern Pace Handicapping*. New York: William Morrow, 1991.

Carroll, Charles. *Handicapping Speed*. New York: Lyons & Burford, 1991.

Hambleton, Tom, et al. *Pace Makes the Race: An Introduction to the Sartin Metholodogy*. New York: O. Henry House Publishers, 1991.

Meadow, Barry. *Money Secrets at the Racetrack*. Anaheim, Calif.: TR Publishing, 1988.

Quinn, James. *Figure Handicapping*. New York: William Morrow, 1992.

Quirin, William. *Thoroughbred Handicapping: State of the Art*. New York: William Morrow, 1984.

—— *Winning at the Races*. New York: William Morrow, 1979.